Science and Religion around the World

Science and Religion around the World

EDITED BY
John Hedley Brooke and
Ronald L. Numbers

UNIVERSITY PRESS

2011

OXFORD
UNIVERSITY PRESS

Oxford University Press, Inc., publishes works that further
Oxford University's objective of excellence
in research, scholarship, and education.

Oxford New York
Auckland Cape Town Dar es Salaam Hong Kong Karachi
Kuala Lumpur Madrid Melbourne Mexico City Nairobi
New Delhi Shanghai Taipei Toronto

With offices in
Argentina Austria Brazil Chile Czech Republic France Greece
Guatemala Hungary Italy Japan Poland Portugal Singapore
South Korea Switzerland Thailand Turkey Ukraine Vietnam

Published by Oxford University Press, Inc.
198 Madison Avenue, New York, NY 10016

www.oup.com

Oxford is a registered trademark of Oxford University Press

Library of Congress Cataloging-in-Publication Data
Science and religion around the world /
edited by John Hedley Brooke and Ronald L. Numbers.
    p. cm.
Includes bibliographical references (p.) and index.
ISBN 978-0-19-532819-6 (hardback) — ISBN 978-0-19-532820-2 (pbk.)
1. Religion and science. I. Brooke, John Hedley. II. Numbers, Ronald L.
BL240.3.S3485   2011
201'.65—dc22   2010015392

9 8 7 6 5 4 3 2 1

Printed in the United States of America
on acid-free paper

Dedicated to the memory of our friend and colleague Margaret (Maggie) J. Osler (1942–2010), with gratitude for her spirited advice on this project, for her enduring scholarship on the relations between natural philosophy and theology in seventeenth-century Europe, and for her much-valued contributions to the history of science profession.

Acknowledgments

The origin of this volume dates back to discussions among the historians attending the inaugural meeting of the International Society for Science and Religion, held in Granada, Spain, in August 2002. Several conversations with Peter Harrison proved especially helpful. After deciding to pursue this collaborative project, we were most fortunate in receiving the encouragement of the John Templeton Foundation, especially from Charles L. Harper Jr., and Paul K. Wason. With the foundation's generous financial assistance we were able to bring the contributing authors together in the spring of 2007 for a working conference at Green College, University of British Columbia, where our friend and collaborator Keith Benson wined and dined us. While there we benefited greatly from the critical commentary of UBC professors John Beatty, Robert Brain, Dennis Danielson, Joy Dixon, Richard Menkis, and Leo K. Shin, as well as from the participation of Marwa Elshakry, Margaret Osler, and Steve Paulson. Subsequent to the conference we received valuable input from C. Mackenzie Brown, Richard M. Jaffe, Tofigh Heidarzadeh, and Deepak Kumar. We are indebted to Cynthia Read, our editor at Oxford University Press, for first seeing merit in this project and then for waiting patiently while we completed this manuscript; to Kathryn J. Schmit and Mary Sutherland for carefully copyediting the manuscript; and to Joellyn Ausanka for shepherding the book through production.

Contents

Contributors

John Hedley Brooke held the Andreas Idreos Chair of Science and Religion and the directorship of the Ian Ramsey Centre at Oxford University from 1999 to 2006. He is an emeritus Fellow of Harris Manchester College Oxford and honorary professor of the history of science at Lancaster University. In 2007 he was appointed Distinguished Fellow at the Institute of Advanced Study, University of Durham. He is currently president of the International Society for Science and Religion. His books include *Science and Religion: Some Historical Perspectives* (Cambridge University Press, 1991) and (with Geoffrey Cantor) *Reconstructing Nature: The Engagement of Science and Religion* (T and T Clark, 1998), originally given as the Gifford Lectures.

Geoffrey Cantor is professor emeritus of the history of science at the University of Leeds and honorary senior research fellow at University College, London. His publications on issues of science and religion include *Michael Faraday: Sandemanian and Scientist* (Macmillan, 1991) and *Quakers, Jews, and Science* (Oxford University Press, 2005). He co-authored *Reconstructing Nature: The Engagement of Science and Religion* (T and T Clark, 1998) with John Hedley Brooke and co-edited *Jewish Tradition and the Challenge of Darwinism* (University of Chicago Press, 2006) with Marc Swetlitz. His most recent book is *Religion and the Great Exhibition of 1851* (Oxford University Press, 2011).

Mark Csikszentmihalyi, formerly of the University of Wisconsin–Madison, is professor of East Asian languages and culture at the University of California, Berkeley. His research focuses on the interface between ethics and natural philosophy in early China. His publications include *Religious and Philosophical Aspects of the Laozi* (State University of New York Press, 1999), edited with Philip J. Ivanhoe, *Material Virtue: Ethics and the Body in Early China* (Brill, 2004), and *Readings in Han Chinese Thought*

(Hackett, 2006). At present he is translating a set of Song dynasty essays on the Zhuangzi by Li Yuanzhuo. He also edits the *Journal of Chinese Religions* and serves an associate editor of the *Journal of the American Academy of Religion*.

Ahmad S. Dallal, formerly chair of the Arabic and Islamic Studies Department at Georgetown University, became provost of the American University of Beirut in 2009. After earning a doctorate in Islamic studies at Columbia University in 1990, he taught at Smith College, Yale University, and Stanford University before going to Georgetown. The author of *An Islamic Response to Greek Astronomy: Kitab Ta'dil Hay'at al-Aflak of Sadr al-Shari'a* (Brill, 1995), he has recently published *Islam, Science, and the Challenge of History* (Yale University Press, 2010), originally presented as part of the Terry Lecture Series at Yale. He is currently finishing a book-length comparative study of eighteenth-century Islamic reform titled *Islam Without Europe: Traditions of Reform in Eighteenth-Century Islamic Thought*.

Noah Efron teaches in the Program in Science, Technology and Society at Bar-Ilan University. A past president of the Israeli Society for History and Philosophy of Science, he currently serves as a member of the executive committee of the International Society for Science and Religion. Efron has been a member of the Institute for Advanced Study in Princeton, a fellow at the Dibner Institute for History of Science and Technology at MIT, and a fellow at Harvard University. He is the author, most recently, of *Judaism and Science: A Historical Introduction* (Greenwood, 2006). He lives with his wife, daughter, son, bunny, and dog in Tel Aviv, where he is a member of the city council.

Steven Feierman, professor of history and sociology of science and professor of history at the University of Pennsylvania, holds a Ph.D. in history from Northwestern University and a D.Phil. in social anthropology from Oxford University. An expert on the history and ethnography of medicine, religion, politics, and science in Africa, he has spent many years doing research in Africa. Among his books are *Peasant Intellectuals: Anthropology and History in Tanzania* (University of Wisconsin Press, 1990) and *The Shambaa Kingdom* (University of Wisconsin Press, 1974). He has won fellowships from the Guggenheim Foundation, the Institute for Advanced Study at Princeton, the Center for Advanced Study in the Behavioral Sciences at Stanford, the Wissenschaftskolleg zu Berlin, the National Endowment for the Humanities, the Fulbright Program, and the National Science Foundation.

Peter Harrison is Andreas Idreos Professor of Science and Religion at the University of Oxford, where he is also a fellow of Harris Manchester College and director of the Ian Ramsey Centre. His several books include *The Bible, Protestantism, and the Rise of Natural Science* (Cambridge University Press, 1998), *The Fall of Man and the Foundations of Science* (Cambridge University Press, 2007), and *Wrestling with Nature: From Omens to Science* (University of Chicago Press, 2011), edited with Ronald L. Numbers and Michael H. Shank.

Ekmeleddin İhsanoğlu has served since 2005 as secretary general of the Organization of the Islamic Conference, headquartered in Jeddah, Saudi Arabia. From 1980 to 2004 he was director general of the OIC Research Centre for Islamic History, Art, and Culture (IRCICA). In 1984 he founded the first department of the history of science in Turkey, at the University of Istanbul, which he chaired until 2000. A former president of the International Union of History and Philosophy of Science, he has won the UNESCO Avicenna Medal (2004) and the Alexandre Koyré Medal of the International Academy of History of Science in (2008). In addition to editing and contributing to the projected fifteen-volume *History of Ottoman Scientific Literature* (IRCICA, 1997–), the two-volume *History of the Ottoman State and Civilization* (IRCICA, 2000), and *Culture and Learning in Islam* (UNESCO, 2003), he is author of *Science, Technology, and Learning in the Ottoman Empire* (Ashgate, 2003), *Turks in Egypt and Their Cultural Heritage* (IRCICA, 2006); and *History of the Ottoman University—Darülfünun* (IRCICA, in press).

John M. Janzen is professor of anthropology at the University of Kansas. He researches and writes on the socio-cultural dimensions of African health and healing and on theoretical issues in medical anthropology. He has studied healing traditions in Africa, their characteristics and interactions, the construction of healing narratives and institutions, postwar trauma healing, and restorative social arrangements. From 1998 until 2006 he directed the Kansas African Studies Center and spearheaded the Center's project on Identity, Voice, and Community: New African Immigrants. In 2008–2009 he served as guest curator of the exhibition African Healing Journeys at the Museum of Archeology and Anthropology of the University of Pennsylvania.

Bernard Lightman is professor of humanities at York University, Toronto, Canada, where he directs a new research institute in science and technology studies and edits the journal *Isis*. His books include *The Origins of Agnosticism* (Johns Hopkins University Press, 1987), *Victorian Science in Context* (University of Chicago Press, 1997), *Victorian Popularizers of Science* (University of

Chicago Press, 2007), and *Evolutionary Naturalism in Victorian Britain* (Ashgate, 2009). He was the general editor of the four-volume *Dictionary of Nineteenth-Century British Scientists* (University of Chicago Press, 2004) and currently edits a monograph series titled *Science and Culture in the Nineteenth-Century*, published by Pickering and Chatto.

David C. Lindberg is Hilldale Professor Emeritus of the History of Science at the University of Wisconsin–Madison. A past president of the History of Science Society and a recipient of its Sarton Medal, he has written numerous books, including the widely translated *The Beginnings of Western Science* (University of Chicago Press, 1992), which won the 1994 Watson Davis Prize of the History of Science Society. With Ronald L. Numbers he has edited *God and Nature: Historical Essays on the Encounter between Christianity and Science* (University of California Press, 1986), *When Science and Christianity Meet* (University of Chicago Press, 2003), and the eight-volume *Cambridge History of Science* (2003–).

David Livingstone is professor of geography and intellectual history at the Queen's University of Belfast. He is the author of a number of books, including *Putting Science in its Place: Geographies of Scientific Knowledge* (University of Chicago Press, 2003) and *Adam's Ancestors: Race, Religion, and the Politics of Human Origins* (Johns Hopkins University Press, 2009). He is currently completing a study of the geographies of Darwinism under the title *Dealing with Darwin* and is beginning a new project on the history of environmental determinism to be called *The Empire of Climate*. A fellow of the British Academy, he was awarded an Order of the British Empire (OBE) for services to geography and history.

Donald S. Lopez Jr. is the Arthur E. Link Distinguished University Professor of Buddhist and Tibetan Studies in the Department of Asian Languages and Cultures at the University of Michigan. He is the author or editor of a number of books, including *Buddhism and Science: A Guide for the Perplexed* (University of Chicago Press, 2008); *Buddhist Scriptures* (Penguin, 2004); *Prisoners of Shangri-La: Tibetan Buddhism and the West* (University of Chicago Press, 1998); *Elaborations on Emptiness: Uses of the Heart Sūtra* (Princeton University Press, 1996); and *Curators of the Buddha: The Study of Buddhism under Colonialism* (University of Chicago Press, 1995). He was elected to the American Academy of Arts and Sciences in 2000.

Ronald L. Numbers is Hilldale Professor of the History of Science and Medicine at the University of Wisconsin-Madison. He has written or edited more than two dozen books, including, most recently, *When Science and*

Christianity Meet (University of Chicago Press, 2003), coedited with David Lindberg; *The Creationists: From Scientific Creationism to Intelligent Design*, new ed. (Harvard University Press, 2006); *Science and Christianity in Pulpit and Pew* (Oxford University Press, 2007); *Galileo Goes to Jail and Other Myths about Science and Religion* (Harvard University Press, 2009); and *Biology and Ideology: From Descartes to Dawkins* (University of Chicago Press, 2010), coedited with Denis R. Alexander. He is a past president the History of Science Society, the American Society of Church History, and the International Union of History and Philosophy of Science. In 2008 the History of Science Society awarded him the Sarton Medal for lifetime scholarly achievement.

B. V. Subbarayappa is an honorary professor at the National Institute of Advanced Studies in Bangalore. He has served as executive secretary of the Indian National Science Academy in New Delhi, as coordinator of the National Commission for the History of Science in India, and as director of the Discovery of India Project, at the Nehru Centre in Bombay. A full member of the International Academy of History of Science and a charter member of the International Society for Science and Religion, he served from 1997 through 2001 as president of the International Union of History and Philosophy of Science/Division of History of Science. In 1999 the University of Bologna awarded him an honorary doctorate.

Science and Religion around the World

Introduction: Contextualizing Science and Religion

John Hedley Brooke and Ronald L. Numbers

The past quarter-century has seen an explosion of interest in the history of science and religion. But all too often the scholars writing it have focused their attention almost exclusively on the Christian experience, while sometimes mentioning Jews and Muslims in passing. At a time when religious ignorance and misunderstanding have lethal consequences, such provincialism must be avoided. Thus in this pioneering effort we go beyond the Abrahamic traditions to examine the way nature has been understood and manipulated in regions as diverse as ancient China, India, and sub-Saharan Africa. We do not, however, slight Judaism, Christianity, and Islam and the literature devoted to the place of science in those cultural traditions. For these monotheistic religions a division into ancient and modern periods, in separate chapters, has been adopted for convenience, though we recognize the arbitrariness of any attempt to fix a sharp divide marking the distinction—even in Europe, where the seventeenth century witnessed a remarkable expansion in the quality and scope of scientific activity. In contemporary societies, it is often taken for granted that science goes hand in hand with secularity and undermines religious authority in the process. For this reason we are including a chapter in which historical connections between science and *un*belief are explored.

Because the claim of universalism is associated with Western science, it is often assumed that, when exported, scientific knowledge simply diffused unchanged into other regions, which have either been receptive or not, as the case may be. But what really happens when the science of one culture encounters that of another or becomes enmeshed in a different set of values? The issue here is not whether laws of nature corroborated within one scientific culture might fail if applied elsewhere. It would be ridiculous to suggest that the laws of aerodynamics that apply when a plane flies over

Texas might be inapplicable over China or Tibet! What may differ, however, are perceptions of meaning and significance when claims for scientific knowledge are assessed from within contrasting worldviews. When different cultures collide, imported foreign science has sometimes been a means to impress, as when Jesuit missionaries brought their astronomical knowledge to China in the sixteenth and early seventeenth centuries. Missionary contact could also be a catalyst for new scientific initiatives through dialogue between representatives of indigenous and imported knowledge systems. The wide range of possibilities makes it particularly desirable to look at science and religion not parochially but around the world.

The innocent word "and" in that conjunction of *science* with *religion* conceals multiple possibilities that will be fully revealed only through the examination of diverse locations and traditions. When speaking of science *and* religion, are we speaking of addition, of overlap, of fusion, of confusion, of separation, of complementarity, or of conflict? Historically, according to time and place, the relationship has been constructed in all of these ways, which is why the sound bites we so often hear should be resisted. Different religions have maintained different practices and priorities in their prescriptions for the religious life. Within each there have been divisions of opinion concerning the most appropriate attitude to take toward secular knowledge. Issues of concern in one religious tradition may be of little notice in others. There appears, for example, to have been no equivalent within Islam to the trial of Galileo in Rome when the implications of a sun-centered astronomy were assessed.

While a reverence toward sacred texts has been a feature of many religious cultures, the principles governing exegesis have varied widely, sometimes in response to new scientific knowledge. Within Christianity there was frequent recourse to a principle of biblical "accommodation." The argument was that the language of Scripture had been accommodated to human limitations and was intended to be accessible to all. It could not therefore be presumed to convey technical scientific information, such as whether the earth was stationary at the center of the universe or in orbit around the sun. The authority of Scripture would then be judged to lie in the moral sphere and in what the Bible teaches about a spiritual relationship between God and humankind. Galileo used this argument to defend himself, and it was common among the Protestant astronomers of the seventeenth century. But this is very different from the line taken by those ultraconservative Christians today who have insisted on a young earth on the basis of a literal reading of the six "days" of creation recorded in the book of Genesis—an interpretation, incidentally, rejected by Augustine, Origen, and other fathers of the Christian Church. Within contemporary Islam a different argument has been gaining popular support despite the concerns expressed by serious

Muslim scientists. This is the argument that the supernatural origins and authority of the Holy Qur'an can be demonstrated by its otherwise inexplicable anticipation of the details of modern science. Within contemporary Judaism one approach to the authority of the Hebrew Bible holds that modern evolutionary theory has actually substantiated the authority of the ancient text. Questions concerning the origin and design of the universe have not been as pressing for all religious constituencies as they have recently become for the anti-Darwinian lobby in North America and, increasingly, the rest of the world.

The study of religious diversity helps us to correct stereotypes. Whether a religion is mono- or polytheistic may have implications for how the natural world is classified and understood. The quest for a unified knowledge of a universe in which the same laws were supposed to hold everywhere was a prominent feature of Isaac Newton's science. The very concept of a "law" of nature arguably had, as one of its roots, the monotheistic belief in a deity who had ordained the laws that govern the universe—a phrase still used by Charles Darwin in nineteenth-century Britain. But other religions exist in which the question of whether God exists is of little import. This would be true of most forms of Buddhism, where what really matters is a highly disciplined practice of meditation designed to liberate the spirit from a preoccupation with the self and the suffering attendant on that preoccupation. Whereas the idea of a stable self, which may even look forward to its continuation in a life after death, has been a prominent motif in the history of Christianity, it is the transient, even illusory, character of the self that tends to be stressed by Buddhists. This has led to claims for a special relationship between Buddhism and the cultivation of the neurosciences, one aspect of which has been the study, through brain imaging, of the short- and longer-term effects of meditation on the brain. Such contrasts between the major world religions suggest that there is much to be learned from a historical perspective on how their ever-changing relations with the sciences have been constructed and understood.

There are deeper reasons why a historical approach is not a luxury but a necessity. The very words "science" and "religion" have meant different things in different times and places. Within many cultures the question "What constitutes a religion?" could hardly have been formulated in times past. In the Christian world, for example, other societies were interpreted through the lens of one's own tradition, which was usually held to provide the only route to salvation. Those outside the fold could be dismissed as pagans or heretics, as when Christian theologians sometimes asked whether Muslims personified a mixture of Judaism and idolatry or some other combination that denied the divinity of Christ. Eventually, however, the cumulative effect of European encounters with other cultures contributed to a different perception, in which the word "religion" came to stand for a particular set of beliefs that differentiated one civilization from another. The shift was deeply significant because it eventually had to be conceded, however tacitly, that Christianity was one religion among many, which included Judaism and Islam. The designation of Buddhism or "Boudhism" as a religion distinct from paganism did not occur until the early 1820s, when European scholars undertook the quest for the historical Buddha and his teachings. "Hindooism" appeared in 1829, "Taouism" in 1839, and "Confusianism" in 1862. Many attempts have been made to specify a set of characteristics that all "religions" share; but this has proved an elusive goal. Some of the pressure to identify possible commonalities, such as belief in the supernatural, has undoubtedly come from secular critics of religion seeking a target that would simplify their destructive mission.

If the word "religion" has its own history, the same is true of the word "science." For much of its history science simply denoted an organized body of knowledge. In this sense, theology could claim to be a science; in medieval Christendom, it was the queen of the sciences because of the dignity of its subject matter. As late as the second half of the nineteenth century, theology was still being referred to as a science, albeit a suspect one, by Darwin's disciple Thomas Henry Huxley. A stronger meaning of that word (*scientia* in Latin) also enjoyed currency in the period commonly known as the "scientific revolution." In sixteenth- and seventeenth-century Europe the word commonly referred to knowledge that was demonstrably true. This actually created a problem for those we customarily think of as the pioneers of experimental methods in science because they found it difficult to claim that their conclusions were more than *probably* true, since experimental data were often compatible with more than one theoretical interpretation. The older term "natural philosophy," which is often said to come closest to modern meanings of science, referred, as the name implies, to a branch of philosophy, and it had a broader reference than the specialized sciences we think of today. For Newton and many of his contemporaries, the compass of science included discussion of God's relation to nature and even attempts to infer the attributes of the deity from the appearance of design in the workings of nature. It would be strange today to hear physicists claiming, as Newton effectively did, that it is in the nature of their subject to consider how God interacts with the world.

An additional problem with the word "science" is that, although it is often used in the singular (on the supposition that there is a unique scientific method), it should really be pluralized to reflect the fact that different scientific disciplines exist with their own distinctive methods. How the sciences have been classified in different cultures and allocated their place in a hierarchy of disciplines is an absorbing question. One of the reasons

Copernican astronomy proved contentious in some parts of Europe was that it could be interpreted as an attempt to raise the status of mathematical astronomy from a science that dealt only in the prediction of planetary motions to one describing the real structure of a solar system. Once we have acknowledged these differences, deeper insight can be gained by examining the diversity of relations between "sciences and religions" than by generalizing "science and religion." We hope this book will make it easier and more attractive to do so.

In their chapter on the contours of science, religion, and medicine in sub-Saharan Africa, Steven Feierman and John Janzen show that an examination of societies other than our own can be even more challenging (see chap. 10). They ask whether current Western assumptions built into the use of the words "science" and "religion" really map onto the beliefs held by peoples in other parts of the world, particularly on matters of illness and health. A deeply embedded distinction between "illnesses of God" and illnesses brought by other (human or spirit) agents may take us by surprise: an "illness of God" is one that just happens, without any moral cause, whereas illnesses ascribed to human agency are seen as resulting from violations of a moral order within a local community. Traditionally, the medical practitioner needed to "intervene simultaneously and in intertwined (perhaps integrally melded) ways with both sick bodies and moral relations, with herbs and with spirits, with symptoms and with personal quarrels." Treatment would be "inseparable from a set of actions that, in Europe or North America, would be some combination of three elements: treatment in an internist's office, family therapy, and religious ritual." In pre-colonial African societies, Feierman and Janzen explain, the efficacy of technical processes, such as the smelting of iron, was believed to depend on the moral context in which they were performed. In agricultural rituals there was also a seamless integration of technical, moral, social, and symbolic acts. In the treatment of disease, consecrated objects were accorded potency in part because of their links to ancestors who had first created them. Attempts to analyze the accompanying practices through the categories of either "science" or "religious belief" simply fail to do justice to elaborate holistic understandings of the relations between natural and moral order.

This distinction is far from a purely academic matter. During the colonial period, missionaries brought their preconceptions of where lay the boundaries between science and religion, and their imposition of post-Enlightenment categories was an overwhelming threat to the prevailing knowledge system. Traditional practices were disparaged by the missionaries as heathen and superstitious, and the locus of illness was placed firmly in the mechanical failure of individual bodies. This dislocation of the individual from the community was also reflected in the missionaries' assumption that if human acts were to blame, it was the sins of the individual rather than dysfunctions in communal relations that were responsible. In their discussion of post-colonial African cosmologies, Feierman and Janzen sample some of the attempts being made to reconcile the biomedical knowledge and cosmopolitan professionalism of today with the legacy of this ancestral holistic cosmology. Their sympathetic survey leads to an arresting conclusion: "It would appear that the moral and humanistic envelope of knowledge that integrates science and religion may well be a genuine contribution of African tradition to the world community."

The problem of mapping modern Western distinctions onto other systems of modeling nature is not confined to the African example. In studies of ancient civilizations there can be a degree of artificiality in defining science and religion, and the relationship between them. As Mark Csikszentmihalyi observes in chapter 7, the set of disciplines that we associate today with the sciences was so deeply embedded in the ritual and religious life of the Chinese that it was not seen as an independent entity until interaction with the West introduced the terms "science" and "religion" in the nineteenth century via recently coined Japanese translations. This does not mean, however, that it is impossible to recognize skills, activities, and achievements that invite the description "scientific." In pre-Imperial China, metallurgical skills made possible the casting of massive bronze bells, sets of which were designed to achieve a complete Eastern musical scale. The completeness of the scale signified the moral integrity and political power of the patrons for whom they made. The discovery of such bells in ancient tombs has been interpreted as evidence of belief in an afterlife, while their design and manufacture presupposed a remarkable grasp of acoustics.

In presenting a cross-section of Chinese scientific activity over many centuries, Csikszentmihalyi identifies three characteristic approaches to the understanding of nature. An interest in "natural sets" was matched, in the long period from the third century BCE to the sixteenth century, by a deep fascination with "natural cycles" of various kinds. A third preoccupation was with "natural patterns," as in Chinese astronomy, a science that proved capable of hybridization with the science brought by Muslim scholars and the Jesuit missionaries who arrived in the late sixteenth and early seventeenth centuries. It was in the practice of medicine that the importance of natural cycles and correspondences can be seen most easily: five bodily organs (liver, heart, spleen, lungs, and kidneys) were correlated with various sets of fives—for example, the five tastes (sour, bitter, sweet, spicy, and salty) of remedial nutrients and the five materials of wood, fire, earth, metal, and water. The cyclicity of the four seasons was also incorporated into an integrated medical scheme preserved and transmitted by a professional class of physicians.

Of particular interest is Csikszentmihalyi's assertion that Confucianism, Daoism, and Buddhism influenced the development of the natural sciences in different ways. Insofar as Confucianism served as a kind of state ideology during the Imperial period, it could act as an obstruction to the reform of traditional methods of inquiry. Buddhists entering China from India and Tibet brought the belief that illness had its source in the disfunctioning of the mind, for which techniques of meditation provided both moral and medical therapy. Where Daoism enjoyed a degree of institutional independence in what is now Sichuan province, it arguably created the most propitious conditions for the development of Chinese science. This was a context in which a Daoist quest for immortality found expression in alchemical research, the practice of chemical experimentation leading eventually to the discovery of gunpowder.

New forms of science emerged in China in the sixteenth and seventeenth centuries, particularly through the integration of indigenous with Western knowledge brought by the Christian missionaries. Some Jesuits served in official positions, such as the directorship of the Astronomical Bureau, where Johann von Bell worked on a calendar system that was adopted in 1644 by Emperor Shunzhi. But there were also tensions, not only on religious grounds but also because of complaints from some Chinese that Western astronomers were giving insufficient attention to traditional methods of linking events in nature with human affairs. Nevertheless, a combination of Chinese with Western scientific approaches was possible because of a firmly held belief that studying patterns of events in the heavens, and thereby making accurate predictions of celestial motions, was an effective way of understanding events on earth. The perception that foreign forms of science may be associated with different and unattractive value systems has, however, been a recurring phenomenon.

Csikszentmihalyi begins his essay with reference to reform movements in twentieth-century China, where "anticipation of the economic and technological advantages of scientific development was tempered by a sense that science was not unconnected to religions and values, and that foreign cultural or ideological values had to be resisted." In the interplay between different cultures it is clear that the natural sciences have featured as markers of what is distinctive in each culture but also as a means of mediation between them.

This dual role features prominently in B. V. Subbarayappa's discussion of science in India (chap. 8), where an indigenous astronomy had originally been developed to assist the performance of religious practices—in fixing, for example, the most auspicious dates and times for sacrificial rites. The study of star patterns was subsequently enriched by the planetary astronomy of the Greeks, principally that of Ptolemy, which was later to provide a paradigm of mathematical astronomy in Europe. The manner in which the sciences could fill a mediating role is illustrated by the adoption of Hindu numerals by Muslim mathematicians, a two-way transmission of medical systems between India and Muslim lands, and a conspicuous interaction between Hindu and Muslim astronomers. With the much later advent of British colonial rule (1757–1947), influential Indian thinkers recognized that the imported science had a rigor that had been lacking in traditional modes of thought. At the same time, European scholars were interested in recovering the indigenous traditions in astronomy, mathematics, and medicine. Despite the existence of conservative reform movements in India, which reaffirmed the authority of the sacred Vedic texts, and despite some antagonism to Christianity that found expression under British rule, Subbarayappa sees little obstruction to the assimilation of Western scientific progress in India. The old and the new could coexist: traditional almanacs continued to be produced even while serious astronomical research was conducted at the Madras Observatory. Even the potential threat to religious values posed by Charles Darwin's theory of evolution rarely materialized in India because what mattered in prevalent forms of the religious life was the cultivation of an inner spiritual evolution, a goal largely untouched by Darwin's case for the material derivation of species from their progenitors.

On Subbarayappa's interpretation, the peaceful coexistence of traditional religious practices with new forms of science has been a particular feature of Indian culture, at least among intellectuals. It was possible in antiquity to study eclipses methodically even while they were regarded by many Hindus as terrible portents. From the eighteenth century onward, the scientific and technical education offered by the colleges that were established under colonial rule seemingly had little impact on traditional forms of worship. Even among contemporary Indian scientists Subbarayappa detects a willingness to regard literacy in the sciences and spiritual awareness as complementary rather than oppositional. For some who have pondered the relationship between the scientific and religious quests, there has been an underlying consonance in the search for an ultimate unity in a Supreme Being and in the organization of the natural order. The experimental investigations of the physicist J. C. Bose, in the early years of the twentieth century, provide an example. Respected for his work on electromagnetic waves, Bose also studied the comparable responses of plants and animals to identical stimuli, seeking to detect what Subbarayappa describes as "the Hindu idea of unity in his investigations of nature." A grounding of the unity of nature and the universality of its laws in the existence of a single transcendent mind has also featured prominently in Jewish, Christian, and Muslim conceptions of natural philosophy.

A story of the coexistence of science with religion in India is not, however, the whole story. When Jawaharlal Nehru became India's first prime minister, following independence from Britain, he was convinced that investing in science and technology was the avenue to greater material prosperity, which India badly needed. While acknowledging that religious values and standards had served humanity well by providing guidance for human conduct, he was deeply critical of the belief that human affairs were ordained by a supernatural agency. This was a belief that, in his view, took the place of reasoned thought and inquiry and was therefore incompatible with a critical scientific mentality. It was science, and science alone, that could "solve the problems of hunger and poverty, of insanitation and illiteracy, of superstition and deadening custom and tradition." This has been a powerful modern image—of science as the great liberator from superstition—and yet, as Subbarayappa notes in conclusion, the expansion of science in India has taken place during a period that has also seen a remarkable expansion in religious allegiances and practices.

One of the most pervasive Asian religions, Buddhism, had its origins in India, the Buddha sharing with other Indian teachers the belief that beings are reborn in various states throughout the universe. As Donald Lopez observes in chapter 9, there have been many claims, from the nineteenth century to the present, that Buddhism is more compatible than any other religion with the presuppositions of modern science. One form of the argument is that, with its disavowal of a creator and its commitment to a naturalistic nexus of cause and effect, Buddhism places fewer obstacles in the path of scientific enquiry than do the theistic traditions, in which the question of divine intervention has been an issue. The emphasis placed on meditation as a means of disciplining the mind in the search for mental bliss has led to claims that contributions to the science of psychology were inscribed within Buddhist philosophy and even, by some, that Buddhism constitutes a science of the mind. Lopez shows not only that Buddhism has existed in many forms but also that nineteenth-century attempts by Western scholars to reconstruct the original Buddha and his teachings led to portrayals that would have been unrecognizable to Asian practitioners. Nevertheless, for those in the West disenchanted with a traditional monotheism, Buddhism, as a religion whose founder was neither a god nor a prophet of God, could be particularly appealing. The image of the Buddha as a great reformer, critical of Brahmin priestcraft and the caste system it controlled, was augmented with the claim that the religion he founded was the one most suited to serious dialogue with science. Through colonial contact this Western Buddha was "exported back to Asia and sold to Asian Buddhists, who sent him into battle against the Christians." When Christian missionaries denounced Buddhist beliefs and practices as superstitious, the claim that, on the contrary, Buddhism was more in tune than Christianity with the spirit of science made for a forceful riposte. A similar pattern was replicated when a "New Buddhism" was promoted in Japan in the early years of the twentieth century. Its defenders were even prepared to claim that the Buddha had anticipated modern scientific discoveries and that the denial of a continuous self perfectly chimed with psychology's rejection of the soul.

Lopez's analysis touches on a point of general importance for the discussion of science and religion. The authority that professional science enjoyed by the end of the nineteenth century meant that a variety of religious traditions would claim a special relationship with it. As Lopez puts it, "once declared to be a science, Buddhism—condemned as a primitive superstition both by European missionaries and by Asian modernists—jumped from the bottom of the evolutionary scale to the top." In a revealing conclusion, he argues that in each of its periods of conjunction with science a different form of Buddhism was invoked. Not only that, but in those same conjunctions "science" has meant many different things, including a rational methodology, a range of established theories, a set of instrumental techniques, and the manipulation of matter. Compatibility theses gain their plausibility, he suggests, only when there is a narrowing of scope and ambition in defining both science and the religion.

Ahmad Dallal takes up the question of compatibility in his essay on early Islamic contributions to the sciences in chapter 5. Dallal engages two misconceptions that have distorted an evaluation of the achievements of Muslim scientists in the period from the ninth to the eleventh centuries and beyond. The first, for which Western historians were in part responsible, is that Arabic culture merely preserved the legacy of the Greek philosophers without adding anything new. The second is that, even if there were innovations in the study of nature, the sciences in the Islamic world never achieved independence from a theocracy that eventually stifled it. From Dallal's survey of Arabo-Islamic originality, particularly in astronomy, mathematics, optics, and medicine, the shortcomings of the first view become readily apparent. As for reports of an early decline in the quality of Arabic science, Dallal considers these to have been exaggerated. Furthermore, while the physical sciences were valued for practical religious reasons, their cognitive content had its own integrity. The Qur'an encouraged an appreciation of the marvels in a creation that God could have chosen to make much less accommodating to humankind. But this did not require any bending of scientific knowledge to fit specific Qur'anic texts. In sharp contrast to the efforts made by some Muslims today to celebrate the scientific content of the Qur'an, Dallal cites, among others, the example of al-Biruni, who insisted that the sacred book did not pronounce on questions of natural science. This partitioning of authority was a way of achieving compatibility without threatening the cognitive autonomy of the science.

Chapter 6 extends this discussion to the relations between Islam and science in the modern period. Ekmeleddin İhsanoğlu reviews the scientific contributions of Muslim cartographers, geographers, and astronomers in the Ottoman Empire. Their achievements were such that visitors would sometimes compare the scientific knowledge available in Istanbul favorably with that of Western Europe. Confidence in their own scientific traditions meant that Muslim scholars were at first largely indifferent to what might be learned from European astronomers; but, as İhsanoğlu shows, the selective translation, transfer, and assimilation of European science from the seventeenth century on provided new stimulus without leading to any serious questioning of Islamic faith and values. One common explanation for the lack of conflict was articulated by a Hungarian convert to Islam, Ibrahim Müteferrika. While insisting that it was a requirement of his religion to believe that the universe is the work of an exalted creator, he observed that once that was accepted, it was of little religious moment how the components of the universe were ordered and arranged. According to İhsanoğlu, it was not until the mid-nineteenth century that Muslim scholars felt the need for a more assertive program of harmonization between specific scientific theories, the Qur'anic verses, and the traditions of the prophet. This was the period when, in Britain and North America, attempts to harmonize the Bible with the latest geology were in fashion and the challenge of Darwin's theory of evolution lay just around the corner. İhsanoğlu discusses the impact of Darwin's science on Muslim sensibilities, noting, however, that Muslims first experienced the disruptive Western philosophy in French sources, such as the materialism of Baron d'Holbach and the evolutionary biology of Jean-Baptiste Lamarck.

Under what circumstances do questions about the relations between science and religion become increasingly urgent? Important considerations for İhsanoğlu are the political aspects of a divergence of attitude between graduates of the new and older educational institutions, the emergence of a small intellectual elite bent on attacking religion, the threat from new forms of Western science, and high-profile public events, such as Ernest Renan's provocative statement at the Sorbonne in 1883 that Islam had inhibited Muslim success in the world of science. Twentieth-century attempts to reaffirm a special accord between modern science and Islam are seen by İhsanoğlu as an expression of religious revival and social solidarity in the Muslim world.

One of the troubling Western texts that influenced Muslim thinkers in the late nineteenth century was John W. Draper's *The Conflict between Religion and Science* (1874). Although Draper's aggressive attack was launched against the dogmatism of the Roman Catholic Church—indeed, the book praised Islam for its relative freedom—at least one Muslim author, Ahmed Midhat, worried that young Muslims might think that Draper's critique applied to their religious tradition. Draper tried to limit his target to Catholicism, saying, for example, that he had no quarrel with the Protestant Churches. But there is no doubt that his book, along with Andrew Dickson White's *History of the Warfare of Science with Theology in Christendom* (1896), did much to promote a conflict model in discussions of science and religion in general. But is a more nuanced view of the relations between science and the Christian traditions possible?

In their discussion of the period from the advent of Christianity to the end of the seventeenth century (chap. 3), Peter Harrison and David C. Lindberg argue that a richer view is indeed possible. Theirs is not a simple story because it has to include both opposition to and encouragement of the natural sciences. In Augustine, perhaps the most influential of the church fathers, they detect a "deep ambivalence" toward a science of nature, with Augustine declining to give it a high priority yet acknowledging its value when subservient to Christian theology. A complication, as in the case of Islam, was the retrieval of Aristotelian philosophy, with its naturalism, its assertion of an eternal world, and its denial of an immortal soul. Harrison and Lindberg refer to the ways in which this challenge was met by medieval Christian scholars, notably Thomas Aquinas, who was aware of differences among Muslim philosophers concerning whether an eternal world could also be a created world. They describe how the revival during the Renaissance of other classical philosophies of nature, combined with the challenge to the centralized authority of the Catholic Church associated with the Protestant Reformation, created new opportunities for synthesis that were both attractive to Christian philosophers and propitious for the sciences. Their examples include the integration of atomism with a theology in which God was directly involved in the motion of otherwise passive matter; the articulation of a concept of "laws" of nature that presupposed divine legislation in nature; and the fusion of a Pythagorean with a Christian philosophy of creation, in which, as in the thinking of both Johannes Kepler and Isaac Newton, God was a formidable mathematician. The Catholic Church's assertion of authority in its condemnation of Galileo has to be seen in the context of Reformation and Counter-Reformation politics; and, as Harrison and Lindberg point out, this tragic episode should not obscure the fact that astronomy had enjoyed special patronage from the Church, especially in connection with the determination of Easter. The Roman Church was far from repressive of all scientific activity, and members of the Jesuit order made substantial contributions to the physical sciences. Commenting on Protestant understandings of biblical authority, Harrison and Lindberg confound modern expectations by suggesting that literal readings of Scripture did sometimes go hand in hand with scientific innovation. With particular reference to Francis Bacon and his plea for empiricism, their chapter ends with the possibility of arguing that the study of God's creation was not a marginal activity but a religious duty.

Extending the discussion of Christianity and science into the modern period, in chapter 4 John Hedley Brooke notes the presence of many different attitudes toward the sciences. He shows how opinions have been divided, from the early eighteenth century to the present, on the question whether a Christian theology of nature requires belief in divine intervention in the workings of nature. He also explores central Christian teachings, such as the doctrines of creation and of the fallen state of humankind, that have been interpreted and reinterpreted in ways both conducive and obstructive to scientific endeavor. He adds that popular understandings of the significance for religious belief of new forms of science have often differed markedly from judgments made by intellectual elites. This has been particularly noticeable in debates over Darwin's theory of evolution. In his discussion of earlier threats to the faith, Brooke observes that these can easily be exaggerated given that ways of re-establishing harmony were usually available. A particularly important resource, in this respect, was the cultivation of a natural theology in which the existence and attributes of the creator were inferred from an expanding knowledge of the natural world. Opinions differed again on the weight to be attached to arguments that were presented independently of revelation; but, from the late seventeenth century until well into the nineteenth, arguments for design forged a strong link between Christian theology and the sciences.

An ironic pattern, however, emerges from Brooke's account. If, during the seventeenth century, Christianity had provided valuable intellectual resources for the encouragement of scientific activity, by the end of the eighteenth century the sciences of celestial dynamics and chemistry, as well as the earth and life sciences, were beginning to provide a new range of resources for attacks on the religion that had helped to nurture them. Such attacks, as in eighteenth-century France, were largely motivated by repugnance toward the intolerance shown by different branches of the Christian Church toward each other and to dissenters, not primarily because of religious opposition to the natural sciences. In Britain a correlation between religious dissent and enthusiasm for the sciences is illustrated by the Unitarian minister Joseph Priestley, who believed that science and his purified Christianity were fighting on the same side against popular superstitions. Other examples of Christian involvement in the sciences are given for both the eighteenth and nineteenth centuries, when receptivity toward new scientific theories could still be influenced by religious predispositions. Brooke gives particular consideration to Darwin's theory of evolution by natural selection and the reasons it has been so divisive within Christendom. As he points out, certain features of Darwin's theory proved attractive to Christian thinkers. These included an ultimate unity in the common ancestry of all human races and the recognition that, however abhorrent the extent of pain and suffering in the world, the woes of humankind could be seen as part of an indisputably creative process. For much of the twentieth century, pressures increased for the separation of scientific and religious discourse in the West, a process that could hardly become complete as long as the despisers of religion continued to appeal to scientific progress in their assaults on the supernatural. In response to science-based critiques of faith, some Christian apologists have claimed that twentieth-century developments in quantum theory, chaos theory, and in the understanding of a finely tuned universe have created new spaces for the discussion of divine activity in the world. The picture that Brooke paints of Christianity's engagement with the sciences is complex and multifaceted, precluding the imposition of simplistic models whether of peace or conflict.

An endemic diversity in religious attitudes to the study of nature is also a prominent theme in Noah Efron's discussion of early Judaism in chapter 1. Contrary to those who have appealed to a distinctive and enduring Jewish mentality to account for the conspicuous achievements of Jewish scientists in the twentieth century, Efron stresses that both the Hebrew Bible and the cumulative rabbinic tradition enshrined in the Talmud were used in ever-changing geographical and historical contexts to justify radically different, even inconsistent, perceptions of the value of science. Comparing the Israelites with other ancient cultures, Efron nevertheless detects two characteristic features: an initial indifference to the study of astronomical patterns, which other cultures used to regulate their calendars, and, more positively, an interest in anatomical and taxonomic studies relating to dietary taboos and the determination of which foods were kosher. The philosopher Georg Wilhelm Friedrich Hegel famously claimed another contrast between ancient Jewish and pagan conceptions of nature when he argued that the Bible desacralized or de-deified the natural world, effectively denuding nature of power and rendering it subservient to human ends. From Efron's broader perspective, Hegel was privileging one among many possible and competing readings of the Hebrew Bible, whose greatest legacy was a plurality in the manner in which nature could be construed—as both matter and as sacrament, as both passive and active, as given to humans to mold to their desires and as beyond human interference.

The Talmud, like the Bible, was used to justify many different and conflicting views. Ambivalence toward medicine and astrology, for example, was one consequence: "For some, astrology was a true science. For others, it was false. For still others, it was false for Jews but true for everyone else."

Though speaking with many voices, the Talmud nevertheless provided a warrant for Jews to seek wisdom about nature from pagans, Muslims, and Christians. This was of crucial importance during the medieval period, when Jewish scholars, particularly in Spain, played a unique role in mediating between Muslim and Christian cultures. As Efron puts it, "most of the great Jewish natural philosophers of medieval times were not so much the product of a Muslim ambiance or a Christian ambiance as they were a product of moving from one to the other and often back again."

Outstanding among Jewish thinkers was the twelfth-century physician-rabbi Moses Maimonides, who valued natural philosophy for its manifestation of God's power in the world, at the same time insisting on its autonomy as a field of inquiry. Despite detractors, his attainment of this balance provided inspiration for many successors. As within Christianity and Islam, anxious voices worried that if the natural sciences were granted autonomy they would tend toward the exclusion of spiritual priorities. Those who restricted their study to traditional themes, however, were less able to benefit from the intermingling of the different religions. If the cultural mix helped to spur an interest in the study of nature, the natural sciences in return held the promise of establishing a form of knowledge that could be shared and appreciated independently of religious allegiance. In this connection, Efron stresses the ecumenism of the sixteenth-century Jewish writer David Gans, who devoted himself to making natural philosophy available and intelligible to a broad Hebrew-reading audience. In facilitating a dialogue between Christian and Jewish intellectuals that became possible at the University of Padua, natural philosophy and mathematics were particularly propitious.

Efron concludes his survey with a discussion of Baruch Spinoza, generally regarded as the most creative and influential Jewish philosopher of the early-modern period. Spinoza's critique of a supernatural theism elicited many contemptuous reactions. Efron suggests that it is a mistake to seek specifically Jewish roots for Spinoza's controversial pantheism. He was primarily a European intellectual, deeply indebted to the French philosopher René Descartes and other non-Jewish authors. Indeed, Spinoza may have been "the first Jew for whom science was not just a vehicle to bridge between Jews and other believers, but a vehicle by which to discredit the worldview that took religious identity to be fundamental and binding." On this reading, "Spinoza may have been the first Jew for whom science was a constitutive part of a philosophy that called for Jews, Christians, Muslims, and atheists to be considered, first and foremost, as citizens."

In countries where Jews constituted an immigrant minority, the degree to which they were marginalized or allowed to enjoy a fuller citizenry depended on attitudes and values in their host cultures. Instead of ascribing Jewish propensities for involvement in the sciences to the critical, disputational character of a traditional Talmudic education, as some have done, Geoffrey Cantor gives greater weight in the modern period to the impulse to escape from marginality through success in secular activities, such as a life in science. In chapter 2 Cantor emphasizes the diversity of views in the Jewish traditions he examines, illustrating the contrasting reactions of Jewish thinkers to the Enlightenment, to Darwin's theory of evolution, and to the new opportunities that arose for them, especially in North America, from the middle years of the twentieth century.

A respect for the sciences and for the power of reason, characteristic of Enlightenment philosophy, was shared by groups of reforming Jews, particularly in eighteenth-century Germany, where a movement that became known as *Haskalah* challenged rabbinical domination and the communal insularity that was judged to flow from it. This movement, personified in the leadership of Moses Mendelssohn, gradually gathered momentum, eventually spreading to other parts of Europe by the early years of the nineteenth century. It may not have produced many figures actively engaged in scientific research; but Cantor sees its significance in its evocation and transmission of science as a symbol of modernism: exciting developments in philosophy and the sciences were presented to Jewish audiences in influential Hebrew-language texts.

Turning to Jewish responses to evolutionary theory, Cantor identifies two correspondents of Darwin, Raphael Meldola and Naphtali Levy, who in different ways gave Darwin encouragement—Meldola by his staunch defense of natural selection, Levy by his assurance that it was possible to give an exegesis of biblical texts such as Genesis 2:7 ("the LORD God formed man from the dust of the ground") in accordance with belief in a long process of evolution from inorganic matter to the emergence of humankind. Paradoxically, some of the rabbis who were most receptive to Darwin's theory were those who expressed a particular affinity with the mystical thought of the Jewish Kabbalah. Cantor cites the example of Abraham Isaac HaKohen Kook, who became the first Ashkenazi Chief Rabbi of Israel. For Kook, biological evolution was simply absorbed within a comprehensive evolutionary cosmology, in which the unity of a progressing creation was given special emphasis. By contrast, there were rabbis who in their conservatism showed indifference or opposition to the historical sciences. Outside ultra-orthodoxy, however, their influence was set to diminish. The statistical data that Cantor provides for current attitudes toward evolution in the United States suggest that American Jews are less opposed than the American population as a whole. While Jewish biologists of the eminence of Richard Lewontin and Stephen Jay Gould have been avowed secularists, Cantor notes their resistance to schemes of sociobiology that might encourage social and especially anti-Semitic prejudice.

During the twentieth century, particularly in the United States, a career in the sciences provided opportunities for Jews to achieve greater social equality: "through science a Jew could move outside the ghetto to become a member of the 'Republic of Learning.'" Cantor identifies impediments to this process from a prevailing Protestant Christian culture, but these were less marked in the field of scientific endeavor than in other avenues of study and employment. A turning point came during the interwar period, when Jewish scientists of distinction immigrated to America to escape fascist persecution in Europe and when second-generation American Jews seized their opportunity through an education in science and technology. Eventually Jews would play a disproportionately large role in American science: of American Nobel laureates in the sciences, one-third have been Jewish.

To illustrate the diversity of views among Jewish representatives of a science-based secularity, Cantor compares the attitudes toward religion of three distinguished Jews: Sigmund Freud, Albert Einstein, and Steven Weinberg. Convinced of the irrationality of religious beliefs, Freud pursued his science in ways that were nonetheless affected by religious perceptions and ideals deeply ingrained in him. He considered that his Jewish background had not only freed him from conventional prejudices but had also given him the emotional strength to propound his radical views on the primacy of the sex drive. Although Einstein rejected the idea of a personal God, he put the case for a "cosmic religion" in which it was still possible to believe that the universe was infused with an immanent intelligence. In this way, Einstein distanced himself from atheistic interpretations of scientific knowledge. Exhibiting a different sensibility, Weinberg has been a spokesman for those contemporary scientists who either despise religion or for whom it holds no interest.

In his discussion Cantor draws a striking contrast between Jewish and Christian engagement with the sciences. He is unable to detect in Jewish discourse a significant tradition of natural theology, which in Christian cultures enlisted scientific knowledge to establish the existence and attributes of the deity. In Christian contexts, the need to affirm the rationality of faith was in part a response to atheistic philosophies of nature and to the rationalism of the Enlightenment. If, as Newton believed, knowledge of the solar system entailed belief in a divine mathematician, this was a powerful resource for Christian apologists seeking evidence of design in the universe. But there was a catch. In his will the seventeenth-century English chemist Robert Boyle made provision for public lectures designed to prove the correctness of the Christian religion. But it was said of the Boyle lecturers that nobody had doubted the existence of God until they undertook to prove it! This dialectical relation between belief and unbelief is important because the form that atheism takes usually depends on the form of theism it seeks to subvert. It is for this reason that historians of Christianity, Catholic and Protestant alike, have seen in the excessive claims of natural theology one of the sources of modern atheism. Extravagant claims that scientific knowledge provided proof of God's wisdom and power were apt to invite refutation.

The forging of a link between science and unbelief was, however, a far from straightforward process; it took place at different times in different national contexts. This is the theme of Bernard Lightman's essay (chap. 11), in which he stresses that it would take more than just a new scientific theory to make unbelief socially acceptable. Radical philosophers in eighteenth-century France attempted to forge a link among science, freedom of thought, and the repudiation of an authoritative Church intolerant of dissent. There were even attempts by figures such as Denis Diderot and Baron d'Holbach to cast Newton's science in a nontheistic mold: it was argued that if matter were granted only its own powers, rather than having the benefit of acting under the direction of a transcendent deity, "nature" could be granted full autonomy. But, as Lightman indicates, the association of Newtonianism with theism, even in so anticlerical a figure as Voltaire, formed a serious obstruction to radical unbelief. Voltaire welcomed Newton's science as an antidote to atheism, to materialism, and to Spinoza's philosophical monism.

For a more influential fusion of science with unbelief it is necessary to turn to Britain during the nineteenth century, where Darwin's account of human evolution could far more easily be appropriated to challenge traditional religious beliefs. The form that unbelief took within the inner circle of Darwinians, including Darwin himself, must not, however, be identified with the kind of self-assured atheism preached by prominent Darwinians today. It was possible for Thomas Henry Huxley and Herbert Spencer to build unbelief into the foundations of their evolutionary cosmology; but the word coined by Huxley to describe this unbelief was "agnosticism." Huxley did not claim that science disproved the existence of God. He even rejected the notion that science and religion had to be in conflict. He was, nevertheless, adamant that Darwin's theory was incompatible with the creation narratives in Genesis. The effect, reinforced by the attempts of anthropologists to explain the origins of religion naturalistically, was to challenge all who believed they had privileged access to knowledge of God. The scientific naturalism that Huxley promoted was one in which scientists could ignore, even as a possibility, the idea of supernatural interference with the order of nature. In the influential philosophy of Spencer there was a welding together of science, agnosticism, naturalism, and an unshakable belief in social progress.

By the end of the nineteenth century, the industrialized societies of Britain, Europe, and the United States provided conditions where agnosticism and its association with science could gain ground. Receptivity to a science-based unbelief varied, however, from place to place. When the Bolsheviks were in power in Russia, atheism was the official state doctrine—in sharp contrast, in twentieth-century United States, the establishment of a public space for unbelief took longer than in Europe. Why was this? The absence of an established church in America appears to be part of the answer, as the separation of church and state allowed religious affiliation to be a voluntary involvement with church communities offering social support in an otherwise highly individualistic society. Conversely, for many Americans, irreligion continued to be stained by its association with communism.

Lightman's stress on the importance of geographic and political parameters in shaping attitudes to science, to unbelief, and to the construction of relations between them reinforces the central message of this book. Science-religion dialogues have taken many forms. They have been conducted very differently in different times and places. There is no unique solution to the problem of how best to describe the place of the sciences in, or their bearings on, the world's religions. As David N. Livingstone observes in his concluding reflections:

> In places where science and religion are fused into an indivisible entity, or indeed where speaking of "science and religion" at all is a misconception, the conversation will differ markedly from contexts where epistemic apartheid operates to keep science and religion in isolation from each other. Where the aim is to harmonize the claims of faith with the findings of science, a different dynamic will be in operation, one that sharply contrasts with situations where religious dogma imperiously stifles scientific inquiry or where scientific enterprises ride roughshod over spiritual sensibilities.

Our hope is that readers will gain from this book a heightened sense of the value of plural perspectives and of the importance of location for the construction and perception of science/religion relations. In his conclusion (chap. 12) Livingstone draws attention to the many examples of cross-cultural synthesis to be found in the various chapters and the many ways in which both science and religion have featured as resources in the shaping of cultural politics. There are certainly differences that require further exploration—contrasts, for example, between popular and elite responses to scientific innovation and between different elites within the same religious tradition. But the differences detailed here are sufficient to show, in Livingstone's words, that they are differences that make a difference.

1

Early Judaism

Noah Efron

Great Jewish scientists of the twentieth century—Jacques Loeb, Albert Einstein, Richard Feynman, and so forth—were frequently mystified and sometimes miffed to hear themselves described as only the latest in a legacy of Jewish scientists stretching back thousands of years.[1] This way of looking at things enjoys enduring popularity, especially among proud Jews, but it oversimplifies a complicated state of affairs. There has been no single, enduring Jewish attitude toward nature and its study. In each age and locale, a mix of theological, social, and practical concerns determined how large a role natural knowledge would take in Jewish intellectual life and how creative and original the contributions of Jews would be. Jews have been at times apathetic about what they sometimes called "natural wisdom," at times opposed to its study, and at times its vanguard. This is no surprise. When looked at over the span of millennia, Judaism has very few constants. Jews have lived around the globe, spoken dozens of languages and dialects, made their living and organized their communities in countless ways, eaten different foods, worn different clothes, worshipped differently. Little can be said to be true of all these people in all these places at all these times. As a result, the roots of the extravagant successes of Jews in twentieth-century sciences cannot be explained by the attitudes or efforts of Jews of earlier epochs. The social, spiritual, and intellectual lives of earlier periods differed greatly from those of recent times and, as I hope to show in this essay, so too did their attitudes toward unraveling the secrets of nature.

ANCIENT HEBREWS AND NATURAL WISDOM

The Hebrew Bible records little about the nature of the cosmos. What appears is partial, enigmatic, and inconsistent. The account in Genesis 1: 6–18 is familiar—it begins "And God said: 'Let there be a firmament (*raqi'a*) in the midst of the waters, and let it divide the waters from the waters'"[2] and carries on from there—but just what this "firmament" is remains uncertain, as does the shape and structure of the universe it defines. In Judges 5:20, the stars are alive, battling for Israel on their celestial paths. In Isaiah 38:8–9, God causes the shadows on a sundial to move backward, as a divine omen. In an astonishing passage in Joshua (10:12–13) that would be cited time and again by generations of Jews and Christians pondering astronomy, the sun and moon stop in their paths: "Then spoke Joshua to the LORD . . . 'Sun, stand thou still upon Gibeon; and thou, Moon, in the valley of Aijalon.' And the sun stood still, and the moon stayed." In this passage, nature is lawful, but only to a point.

The ancient Hebrew cosmos, it seems, was unfixed. The Bible's heavens are nowhere formalized or modeled or described in numbers, in the way the heavens were, say, in the detailed astronomical tables Babylonian priests recorded on cuneiforms. Although the Hebrew calendar was eventually formalized in the fourth century, until that time each new month was declared only after two witnesses testified to seeing the new moon. In contrast to other great ancient cultures, Israelites were reticent to rely on the regularity of the heavens and *calculate* their calendar in advance. Further, the heavens—their shape, structure, and workings—were of only marginal interest among Israelites. Describing the patterns of the cosmos absorbed other ancient cultures and led them to remarkable feats of induction; but this was of scant interest in the Bible.

The earth, however, was a different story. Ancient Israelites sought to divine the pattern behind the animals and plants they came across. What happens on earth, what is immediate and knowable, was *portentous* to ancient Israelites. Understanding earthly ontology—the categories by which nature is organized—mattered more to them than understanding the heavens. Deuteronomy 22:9–11 spits out injunction after odd injunction: "Thou shalt not sow thy vineyard with two kinds of seed . . . Thou shalt not plow with an ox and an ass together . . . Thou shalt not wear a mingled stuff, wool and linen together." Mixing things that do not *naturally* go together is prohibited. At the bottom of all of these odd taboos is a wish to preserve the purity of natural kinds.[3]

The importance to ancient Hebrews of properly categorizing plants and animals, of aggregating and dividing them, is evident in the rules of *kashrut*—of what is prescribed to eat and what is proscribed. With these rules, all the animals on earth were organized and categorized. Mammals with cloven hoofs were distinguished from those without, ruminants were set aside, fish with fins distinguished from sea creatures without fins, and so forth. It was crucial to categorize animals according to such features (spurring rabbis for generations to study animal anatomy), because the taxonomy carried spiritual weight. Ancient Hebrews saw nature as ordered, and they saw the *order* of nature as in some way sanctified.

Just how much the Israelites could and should control nature, however, was a matter of ambivalence. This ambivalence showed in the Bible's uneasy pronouncements about medicine, astrology, and magic, three disciplines that involved manipulating nature, sometimes waylaying its course, sometimes controlling it to serve human ends. These three disciplines are generally portrayed in the Bible as effective but frequently as also dangerous and illicit, for they grant humans power that ought to rest in God's hands. The prophet Isaiah warns in mocking tones against "enchantments," "sorceries," "astrologers," "stargazers," and "prognosticators"; all these will prove themselves worthless (Isa. 47:11–14). Deuteronomy catalogues the magical technologies Israelites are commanded to ignore: divination, enchantment, sorcery, charming, necromancy, and more (Deut. 18:10–14).

These prohibitions were not always honored. Astrology found purchase in ancient Hebrew culture, as evidence from late antiquity shows. Josephus describes Jews misguidedly following astrologers into revolt against the Romans, with tragic results.[4] Ancient parchments recovered from Qumran have recently been identified as a "zodiacal physiognomy," predicting the physical and spiritual characteristics of newborns from the arrangements of the stars at time of birth.[5] Ancient Hebrews understood that the powers of nature could be exploited by those who understood nature's laws. In this way, they were not unlike neighboring Mediterranean cultures.

In other ways, though, ancient Hebrews differed from their neighbors. Scholars have long argued that ancient Hebrews introduced a new, influential attitude toward nature. Georg Wilhelm Friedrich Hegel observed that the Israelite religion altered the very nature of nature itself: "Nature [in the Old Testament] is now degraded to the condition of something powerless, . . . it is made a means."[6] As Hegel saw it, nature in the Hebrew Bible had become "undeified." Many scholars since Hegel have developed this theme, finding that the Bible *desacralized* nature, stripping it of the inherent and independent force that pagan cultures had attributed to it.[7]

Going further, some scholars have concluded that in desacralizing nature, the Bible gave warrant for people to *exploit* nature, which was now conceived as inert matter, and that this warrant eventually led to the rise of science.[8] Others disagree, finding their Bible chockablock with totems, taboos, myths, and magical conceptions of nature animated by sprites and spirits.[9] Scholars of both sorts recognize that this is not an *either-or* proposition, that the Israelites rejected some pagan attitudes toward nature and embraced others. Judaism is perhaps best seen as a third way, as something different in kind from both paganism and Greek rationalism. The order of nature, as it comes across in the Bible, is sometimes fixed and sometimes fluid. Manipulating and controlling nature is sometimes admired and sometimes detested. The ambiguities concerning nature and its manipulation are so profound, so tightly bound into the woof and warp of particular passages, that they seem part of a point of view. It is not just that the Bible packages together conflicting views under the same covers. It also privileges views that conflict with one another. In the end, this might be its greatest legacy. It was this feature of the Bible's treatment of nature that left it fertile ground for all sorts of later opinions about nature. Jews through the generations justified a great variety of opinions about nature, natural philosophy, and science by reference to the Bible. This later diversity is usually attributed to the supple flexibility of Jewish traditions of interpretation, which allowed sacred texts to be read in a great many different ways. This is true enough, but it is not the whole story. The Bible could also be used, in later generations, to justify many different attitudes toward nature—as mere matter and as sacrament, as passive and as active, as given to humans to mold to their desires and as beyond human meddling—because these many different attitudes were there to begin with. Insofar as nature is concerned, the Bible was evocative, powerful, and opinionated, yet it remained an open book.

THE SAGES OF THE TALMUD AND NATURAL WISDOM

Jewish tradition has it that the Bible is written Torah and the Talmud is oral Torah. Together they are the most important of Jewish books, and by almost any practical measure the Talmud is the more important of the two. The Talmud is what some historians have called a *constitutive* text; it helped to *constitute* Judaism, partly determining the nature of Jewish life for the more than fifteen centuries since it was completed.

The Talmud was not composed in a single time or place; it gathers texts produced over hundreds of years and across thousands of miles. Many are commentaries on earlier texts, and there are commentaries on commentaries. The Mishnah, which was redacted into its final form in about 200 BCE by Rabbi Yehudah ha-Nasi, is a codex of business, civil, family, and religious law incorporating an oral tradition that had developed over the prior four centuries. Along with other contemporary records of legal discourse, which became known as the *Tosefta*, the Mishnah became the heart of academy curricula from Tiberias to Babylon—a focus of study, discussion, and disputation between the leading rabbis of generation after generation. Reports of these discussions and disputes, along with the original Mishnah passages they concerned, were gathered into two collections: the Palestinian Talmud and the Babylonian Talmud, which were redacted in roughly 425 and 500, respectively.

The Palestinian Talmud and the Babylonian Talmud give extraordinary glimpses of the cultures that produced them. Although on the surface they seem to be simple protocols of rabbinic discussions about how best to interpret passages of the Mishnah and to draw from these proper legal conclusions, they also include a great amount of discussion that has nothing to do with law. The Talmud is filled with information, customs, ideas, and attitudes assimilated from Babylonian, Greek, Roman, Assyrian, Egyptian, and other cultures. It displays complicated reactions to these influences, at times anxious, at times accepting, at times registering a mixture of feelings of cultural superiority and of cultural inferiority that is hard to distill down to its constituent parts. All these attitudes find expression in the portrayal of nature in the Talmud.

One canonical Talmudic consideration of the size and structure of the universe, for instance, compares Jewish views with those of the "sages of the nations" and reaches the nonplussed conclusion that "their view is preferable to ours" because it fits better with observation and reason (BT Pesahim, 94b). This remarkable passage suggests that about matters of nature, Talmudic sages considered observation and reason as (sometimes, at least) more reliable sources of authority than text and tradition. Further, the robust intellectual chauvinism that characterizes many of the ethical deliberations in the Talmud was (sometimes, at least) absent from deliberation about nature. The admission that the "sages of the nations" were right and the "sages of Israel" were wrong is offered with startling ease. On reflection, this ease may indicate that understanding nature was simply not important to the rabbis. Further proof of this is the fact that, in many places in the Talmud (and then for centuries after the Talmud), a synonym for philosophy of nature was "Greek wisdom." Other synonyms were "external wisdom," "foreign wisdom," and "the wisdom of the nations." Together, these names suggest that natural philosophy was considered to be a matter peripheral to Jewish concerns.

Still, indifference is not the only attitude toward philosophy of nature (and philosophy in general) on display in the Talmud. Rabban Gamaliel boasted that "there were a thousand pupils in my father's house; five hundred studied Torah and five hundred studied Greek wisdom." But in the same passage, one also finds: "Cursed be a man who rears pigs and cursed be a man who teaches his son Greek wisdom!" (BT Sotah, 49b). In a single paragraph, "Greek wisdom" spurs enthusiasm and scorn.

However they regarded natural wisdoms, the rabbis of the Talmud were eager to employ them, when the need arose. Many discussions in the Talmud settled on mathematics when it served some practical end, though once the subject arose these discussions often digressed, devoting more attention to the numbers than was strictly required. Astronomy earned vigorous inquiry, perhaps because of its relevance to determining precisely when religious feasts and the Sabbath began. Even after the calendar was formalized by Hillel II in the middle of the fourth century (so Hai Gaon [d. 1038] is reputed to have reported), rabbis continued to determine the start of each month afresh by relying on witnesses who observed the new moon with their own eyes. The rabbis remained generally suspicious of formulas, hesitating to count them as a source of knowledge.

Similar ambivalence about how best to learn about nature is evident in discussions of animals and plants. Most reports of animals and plants combine observation, experience, the opinions of experts, and folk wisdom. But the rabbis of the Talmud were more exacting in their deliberations on animals when a matter of ritual practice was at stake. They were careful, for instance, in their anatomies of various worms, ants, hornets, eels, etc., as they enumerated the qualities indicating these animals are not kosher.

Still, when it came to manipulating nature for human ends, the rabbis were conflicted about when and how it should be done. The Talmud reports bans on magic, not because magic does not work but because in certain circumstances it *does* work. The same rabbis who rejected magic and sorcery were expected to master it, especially when it might cure illness (BT Menachot, 65a): "Used as a remedy, [magic] is not forbidden" (BT Shabbat, 67b). Indeed, the rabbis were enthusiastic about medicine, even though it was often linked with magic as a technology for intervening in nature.

The Talmud contains a great number of incidental references to illness and cure, disease and medicine.[10] One finds information about human anatomy and physiology, about gynecology and obstetrics, about a great number of sicknesses and their treatment, about the advisability of various diets, about the effects of aging, about hygiene, mental illness, materia medica, and much more. Because medical matters were usually a digression in the Talmud, they appear unsystematically, and they are unsystematic when they appear. The medicine in the Talmud displays obvious Egyptian, Mesopotamian, Greek, and Roman influences, but these are difficult to identify with precision.

Still, the rabbis were not without ambivalence about medicine. On the one hand, they recognized the importance of physicians, surgeons (who, among other things, performed circumcisions), and bloodletters. But physicians and surgeons were treated with suspicion, perhaps because their craft was similar to that of the sorcerer. The Mishnah observed that "the best of physicians are destined to go to hell" (BT Kiddushin, 4:14).

Astrology was also a vexed issue for the rabbis in the Talmud, who disagreed about whether it worked for Jews and (if it worked or if it didn't) whether it ought to be used. Some rabbis were enthusiastic about the powers that astronomy conferred. Samuel, the great headmaster of the Nehardea

Talmudic academy, boasted, "I am as familiar with the paths of heaven as with the streets of Nehardea" (BT Berachot, 58b), and he formulated agricultural and medical advice based on this expertise (BT Eruvin, 56a). Other Talmudic rabbis rejected the idea that the stars affect health, fate, and character, at least not those of Jews.[11] Even these rabbis did not typically see astrology as nonsense (though some rabbis of a later period did). They saw it as a sort of wisdom, with a sort of validity. But they did not assume that nature's "laws" necessarily apply to Jews in all circumstances. This was because, in the view of these rabbis, God himself (and not the nature he created) controlled the fate of Jews. Once again, the rabbis of the Talmud present conflicting views side by side. For some, astrology was a true science. For others, it was false. For still others, it was false for Jews but true for everyone else.

In this way, astrology is like all other natural wisdom in the Talmud—for, as we have seen, there is no single Talmudic view of nature, natural philosophy, natural history, medicine, magic, and so forth. The Talmud refracts the views of a great number of people, living in many different places, over the course of centuries, pondering a bewildering catalog of topics. It reflects influences from within the varied Jewish traditions upon which it draws, as well as the varied ancient Mediterranean cultures near which it was composed. The Talmud speaks in many voices.

This multiplication of voices is both a norm in the Talmud and a foundational approach to exegesis. About anything beyond matters of ritual and law, opinions expressed in the Talmud are typically counterbalanced by conflicting opinions. ("These *and* these are the words of the living God," as one much-cited midrash concludes about a pair of logically compatible alternatives, capturing a basic principle of Talmudic reasoning.)[12] One finds in the Talmud interest in nature and indifference, and one finds, in the fragments of natural philosophy of the Talmud, approaches that are naturalistic, magical, mythological, and theistic.

This fact had enduring repercussions. The plentitude of the Talmud lets it serve as a source, or prooftext, for every manner of attitude toward nature and its study for almost a millennium and a half after its composition. Those who wished to study nature found in the Talmud sources for demonstrating that they were standing on the shoulders of rabbinic giants. Those who wished to dismiss the study of nature found support for their distaste. And those whose attitudes toward nature stood somewhere between enthusiasm and rejection found in the Talmud ample backing for their own views.

In this way, the Talmud, like the Bible before it, served as a source for *all* of these attitudes toward nature and *none* of them. The Talmud canonized a plural attitude of Jews towards science that would pertain for as long as the Talmud's influence on Jewish intellectual life remained strong. It also canonized the notion that nature is a realm about which Jews do not have unique insight. The parochialism that one finds rarely turned up in matters of natural knowledge and craft. For later generations eager to understand and harness nature, the Talmud provided support for their enthusiasm and warrant to seek wisdom from the scholars of the pagans, Muslims, and Christians.

JEWS AND NATURAL PHILOSOPHY IN THE MIDDLE AGES

Over the centuries that followed the completion of the Babylonian Talmud and Jerusalem Talmud, Jewish settlement spread, often far from the Middle East. The fortunes of Jews in Persia and Palestine waned and waxed. In the late fifth century, Persian synagogues and Torah schools were ordered shut, and rabbinic courts were stripped of their authority. The Jewish rebellion that ensued was efficiently dispatched. Conditions then improved, and by the end of the sixth century the famous Babylonian academies of Sura and Pumbeditha resumed as seats of Jewish learning and law. Their leaders (who were called *Geonim*) saw that the academies functioned, served as judges, and issued legal opinions, often in answer to legal queries submitted from far-flung communities. These leaders and their academies provided a center and a central authority, in a rough way, for a quickly spreading Jewish diaspora. In the ninth century, the great academies began to decline. The *Geonim* took to living in Baghdad (the academies had been relocated there), and their authority waned too. Jews were by then spread through much of the Middle East, North Africa, and Europe. Jewish culture ceased to have a center, or even two or three dominant centers, as it had in the past. Jews in lands that came under the sway of Islam developed a character that differed from that of Jews in Byzantium, which differed from that in the Western Roman Empire. They developed different customs and traditions and different attitudes toward many things, including natural philosophy.

It was in Muslim lands that natural philosophy received the most careful and creative attention from the seventh to the twelfth centuries, and it was in Muslim lands that it found its most enthusiastic reception among Jews during those years. This had much to do with the spread of Islamic civilization over vast territories in which other cultures had laid deep roots. By virtue of geography alone, Islam became "the meeting point for Greek, Egyptian, Indian and Persian traditions of thought, as well as the technology of China."[13] This was an asset of incalculable value. It allowed the practical know-how of each culture to diffuse throughout Islamic civilization and bridged with a single scholarly tongue—Arabic—vast geographical and cultural divides, linking people and traditions that otherwise might not find common language.

Amid all this diversity, Jews found a place in Arabic mathematics, natural philosophy, and medicine. That they would do so is no surprise. The Jews of Islamic lands congregated early in the cities in which translation and research were carried out. They were a literate community. Jews adopted Arabic not only as a language of the street but also as their scholarly language.

For all these reasons, Jews embraced Arabic natural philosophy and medicine beginning in the ninth century. Isaac ben Solomon Israeli (or Ishaz b. Sulayman al-Isra'ili, as he is known in Arabic literature, ca. 855–955) was said by contemporaries to be a master of all seven sciences: grammar, logic, rhetoric, arithmetic, geometry, music, and astronomy. Sa'adya ben Yosef al-Fayyūmī (882–942), a younger contemporary and occasional correspondent of Israeli, was born in Upper Egypt, lived for a time in Aleppo, and settled in Baghdad, where he became a leader of the Jewish community, a *Gaon*, and a writer of enormous influence. Many of Sa'adya Gaon's essays include piquant facts and detailed discussions of natural philosophy and endeavor to demonstrate that rational inquiry and Torah are not at odds. This message fit well in the cosmopolitan ambience of tenth-century Baghdad.

But if it was in the Middle East that Jews first found a place in Islamic civilization (and that Islamic civilization first found a place in Judaism), it was in Spain that this acculturation reached its most brilliant expression. Jews had lived on the Iberian peninsula under Roman and then Visigoth rule, under the latter suffering forced conversions to Christianity and persecution. When Tarik b. Zayid overtook Spain for Islam in 711, those Jews who remained practiced their religion in secret. The arrival of Muslims changed all that, and the conquerors were greeted as saviors. As Islamic culture took root under the rule of the Ummayad caliphs, Jews thrived; by the tenth century, Spain was home to the most energetic Jewish community in the world, which enjoyed what came to be known as the "Golden Age." By the start of the eleventh century, however, the Ummayad dynasty began to decline. As the end of the century approached, beginning in 1086, armies of the zealous Berber Almoravid dynasty successfully invaded the Iberian peninsula, and in 1145 they were followed by the armies of the Almohad dynasty. Conditions for Jews deteriorated. Many Jews crossed over to Christian lands in northern Spain and beyond. As Jews were traveling north, Christian troupes were moving south, beginning what came to be known as the *reconquista*, or Christian reconquest of Spain.[14]

These upheavals affected the intellectual culture of Jews in many ways. Beginning at the end of the eleventh century, Arabic ceased to be the sole language in which the Jews of Spain (or, for that matter, of North Africa and the Middle East) wrote about scholarly matters such as astronomy, astrology, and mathematics. Hebrew was pressed into service, and over several generations a rich technical vocabulary was devised in Hebrew where none had existed earlier, initiating the process that one historian has called the "secularization of the Hebrew tongue."[15] Writing natural philosophy in Hebrew was at once a contraction of Jewish intellectual horizons and an expansion. Jews writing Hebrew astronomy were no longer doing so in the broader milieu of Arabic science (though they still drew on Arabic sources, to be sure); in this sense, their audience was narrower than it had been. At the same time, Jews writing Hebrew astronomy were now writing for Jewish audiences in Europe beyond the sway of Islamic culture. In this sense, their audience was broader. The fitful switch from Arabic to Hebrew reflects the fact that fewer Jewish intellectuals were fully at home with a philosophical vernacular, not Arabic and not Latin. Language would, from this point on, remain a barrier—never completely insurmountable, but a barrier nonetheless—between Jewish and non-Jewish intellectuals until the start of modern times.

The gradual evolution of Hebrew-language natural philosophy corresponded with another change. The political instability in Spain led Jews to travel, some southward, to North Africa and the Middle East, but most northward, into Christian Europe. Most of the great Jewish natural philosophers of medieval times were not so much the product of a Muslim ambiance or a Christian ambiance as they were a product of moving from one to the other and often back again. Even those Jews who stayed in one place often found at home a mixture of Muslim and Christian influences. Jews played a unique role in mediating between these cultures (often literally translating from one to the next).

All of these trends—the gradual adoption of Hebrew as a language of natural philosophy and the increasingly Judaeocentric attitude that went with it, the growing tendency of Jews to pass between Muslim and Christian spheres of influence, and their place in bridging and translating between these two great civilizations—are evident in the work of the outstanding Jewish natural philosophers of the period.

Abraham Bar Hiyya (d. ca. 1145) is a good example. Bar Hiyya lived most of his life in Barcelona, a Christian city of considerable Muslim culture. His writing focused on astronomy, astrology, mathematics, philosophy, and the Jewish calendar, about which he wrote stand-alone books and which he also combined into an encyclopedia of sorts. Bar Hiyya also collaborated with a Christian intellectual named Plato of Tivoli on the translation of numerous Arabic natural philosophy texts into Latin. One of these texts was Bar Hiyya's own treatise on geometry, which contained the first European exposition of algebra and the first solution of the quadratic equation. Decades later, Leonardo Fibonacci discussed the work at length in his *Practica geometriae.*

A younger contemporary of Bar Hiyya, Abraham ibn Ezra (1089–1167), wrote at least twenty-three treatises, including books on number theory, on astronomical instruments, and on astrology. But Ibn Ezra's commitment to natural philosophy was best expressed in his grand commentaries on almost all of the books of the Bible. Commenting on a verse in Exodus,[16] for example, Ibn Ezra wrote that in order to understand such passages fully, one must master metallurgy, natural history (both flora and fauna), anatomy, physiology, astronomy, and astrology.

Although Ibn Ezra's commentaries enjoyed enduring popularity, some contemporaries criticized his enthusiasm for natural philosophy. One was Judah Halevi (ca. 1075–1141). Halevi was a poet of exquisite talent, but his most enduring work was an odd book called *Kitāb al-Radd wa-l-Dalīl fi al-Dīn al-Dhalīl* (The book of refutation and proof concerning the despised faith) or, more commonly, the *Kuzari*. The book conveys an imagined conversation between a Khazar king and an Aristotelian philosopher, a Muslim, a Christian, and a Jew, all of whom the king has invited to discuss their worldviews. The *Kuzari* reads like a rebuttal, aiming to discredit "the appeal to astrology for the rational explanation of phenomena" so common among Spanish Jews of the age, especially Ibn Ezra. In a poem, Halevi expressed his worry more broadly: "Let not Greek wisdom tempt you, for it bears flowers only and no fruit."[17]

No one was more keen to discredit astrology than Moses ben Maimon (1135–1204), who was also known in Latin as Maimonides and among Jews by his Hebrew acronym, Rambam, "This wisdom, which is called the decree of the stars," Maimonides wrote in reply to a query from French rabbis, "is not wisdom at all, but mere foolery. . . . Those who wrote treatises on it . . . were the Chasdeans, the Chaldeans, the Canaanites and the Egyptians, but the wise Greeks . . . scorned, mocked and condemned these four nations . . . compiling proofs rejecting their notions completely."[18]

Maimonides grew up in Cordoba, leaving the city with his family after the Almohad conquest of Spain began. After a time, in about 1160, he settled in Fez, Morocco. Five years later he moved to Egypt, where he lived out the rest of his life, briefly in Alexandria and then permanently near Cairo. There he became court physician and a rabbi of tremendous international reputation. He wrote a treatise on logic and a good number of medical treatises, but the greatest part of his work was of a more religious character. He wrote many letters and *responsa* (replies to legal queries), carrying on correspondence with Jews throughout Islam and beyond. He wrote a massive compendium of Jewish law called the *Mishneh Torah* (Second to the Torah). And he wrote his magnum opus, a philosophical and religious masterpiece called *Moreh Nevuhim* (The Guide for the Perplexed). Save his letters and the *Mishneh Torah*, Maimonides composed all his essays in Arabic.

Maimonides' biggest impact on Jewish natural philosophy was on the way some Jews understood the place and role of natural philosophy (and of philosophy in general).[19] On the one hand, Maimonides propounded a limited sort of natural theology, in which nature—God's handiwork—bears testimony to God's power. At the same time, he insisted that humans were incapable of achieving positive knowledge of God's essence. This led him to what has been labeled his "negative theology," the notion that only negative attributes of God—what God is *not*—can be known with certainty. At the same time, Maimonides believed, it was possible for scholars to come to know God's activity. "It is in studying natural science and metaphysics," one historian wrote of Maimonides' view, "that man achieves the only knowledge of God granted him."[20]

While ascribing this religious purpose to natural philosophy, Maimonides at the same time insisted that natural philosophy was autonomous and that a true understanding of the structure of the cosmos was attainable through reason, if at all. For Maimonides, both theology and natural philosophy were realms in which humans had only limited capacities to *know* with certainty. This was part of why Maimonides thought there was no *real* conflict between knowledge attained by revelation and that attained through reason. When there seemed to be a conflict, it owed to our imperfect grasp either on God or on God's work, or both.

The combination that we find in Maimonides' writing—according natural philosophy a role in the apprehension of God's works while insisting that it retain its autonomy as a field of inquiry—was a powerful one. It ensured that Maimonides would be an inspiration and a prooftext for Jewish scholars writing about natural philosophy for generations to follow. It may also have fanned the flames of controversies that arose over Maimonides' views and his books. Several times, in several places, rabbis tried to prevent Jews from reading Maimonides' works. The earliest clash was primarily one over the authority of the exilarchs, or appointed Jewish religious leaders, and questioned the validity of relying on Maimonides' code of laws instead of the word of rabbinic leaders. The second controversy, which took place in Spain and Provence at roughly the start of the thirteenth century, expanded to include the question of whether Greek wisdom had any place in Jewish scholarship. R. Moshe ben Naḥman (1194–1270), or Naḥmanides as he came to be known in Latin, described contemporary Maimonides enthusiasts witheringly: "they have filled their belly with the foolishness of the Greeks . . . They did not enter profoundly into the ways of our Torah; the ways of alien children suffice for them."[21] Conflicts over the probity of reading Maimonides continued until Dominicans burned Maimonides' books in 1232, and the stunned anti-Maimonides camp among Jews quelled their objections.

The attitude of Naḥmanides (Ramban in the Hebrew acronym) toward Maimonides' books is telling. When the second controversy over these books broke out in Montpellier in 1232, Naḥmanides sought middle ground. He condemned Jewish "philosophizers" who were more committed to philosophy than to Torah. At the same time, he asked the French rabbis to rescind their *herem* (excommunication), arguing that it was anyway unnecessary in their quarters, needed if anywhere only in the south, in Provence and Spain, where philosophy was inappropriately esteemed.

Naḥmanides' own attitudes toward natural philosophy were subtle. He was critical of these disciplines (he argued, for instance, that Maimonides' *Guide* had been written for students who had been led astray by Aristotle and Galen), but he was not dismissive. The problem with natural philosophy and medicine, as Naḥmanides saw them, was not so much what they included as what they ignored by focusing on matter and excluding spiritual matters. They thus produce a picture of the cosmos that is not so much wrong as partial. Problems arise when the natural philosopher or the doctor does not realize that their disciplines provide only incomplete insight. This view—that natural philosophy is valid as far as it goes, but that it is rather less valuable than the study of Torah—is one that recurs from epoch to epoch.

When Naḥmanides wrote to the Montpellier rabbis about Maimonides, he described an important change in the demography of Jews in Europe, and one that affected Hebrew natural philosophy. Provence, a region in the southeast of France, had become by Naḥmanides' time a center of unique and influential Jewish scholarship. When Spain was invaded by the Almohads, waves of Spanish Jews escaped to Provence, and what had been a center of Ashkenazi rabbinic culture absorbed a great number of Sephardi scholars who brought with them very different sensibilities and very different libraries. This meeting of cultures produced extraordinary results. It set in place the fractured intellectual backdrop against which the controversies over Maimonides found their most fraught expression. But it also produced a bright flash of interest among Jewish scholars in philosophy and natural philosophy, and led to the creation of a remarkable library of Hebrew natural philosophy.

A good portion of the new library owes to the work of a single family named ibn Tibbon. Judah ibn Tibbon (ca. 1120–90) has been called the "father of the translators." He translated Bahya ibn Pakudah's *Duties of the Hearts* from Arabic to Hebrew, as well as books by Ibn Gavirol and books of Hebrew grammar. Judah's son, Samuel ibn Tibbon (1150–1230), and grandson, Moses ibn Tibbon (d. ca. 1285), translated into Hebrew books of metaphysics, logic, mathematics, astronomy, physics, and medicine from originals in Arabic and Latin. Other translators too produced collections of breadth and ambition. By the fourteenth century, the scholars of Provence had generated an enviable Hebrew library of Greek and Islamic classics, including Aristotle, Euclid, Hippocrates, Menelaus of Alexandria, Galen, Ptolemy, Porphyry, Avicenna (Ibn Sina), Averroës (Ibn Rushd), al-Farabi, al-Kindi, Thabit ibn Qurra, al-Razi, and many others, as well as original Hebrew essays and commentaries.

For a certain sort of Provençal intellectual, these books were an essential part of a scholarly library. Dozens of manuscript copies of, say, Ibn Rushd's epitomes of Aristotle's *Physics* or his *On the Heavens* (to pick representative examples) survive from this time; these are likely a small fraction of the original numbers. The same is true for scores of other books.[22] In time, these books found their way into schools. Some critics objected to these subjects, but most who did complained not that they are inherently bad but because they came to dominate the interests of those who embraced them, leaving little time or taste for Talmud.[23] Of course, this complaint itself is testimony to how popular these subjects seem to have been, at least among some Provençal Jews.

Perhaps the greatest Jewish natural philosopher of medieval times was a Provençal Jew named Levi ben Gershom (1288–1344), or Gersonides (and Ralbag in the Hebrew acronym). Gersonides lived for most of his life in Orange, in the south of France. When he was only twenty-nine years old, he began writing his magnum opus, a massive work in six books titled *Milhamot ha-Shem* (Wars of the Lord). He also wrote a book on logic, one on mathematics, one on geometry, and commentaries of Ibn Rushd's glosses on Aristotle. But it was Gersonides' astronomy, above all else, that earned him a reputation beyond Hebrew-readers. He relayed that he drew up astronomical charts "at the request of many great and noble Christians." Philippe de Vitry, who later became the bishop of Meaux, consulted Gersonides about a mathematical question that arose in his work. In 1342, Gersonides dedicated a Latin work on trigonometry to Pope Clement VI. He drew horoscopes or astrological charts at the behest of at least two popes.[24] Gersonides is a good example of how Jewish natural philosophers became integrated, in a small but significant way, into the broader fabric of European natural philosophy. Consulting with bishops, dedicating books to popes, and casting horoscopes for them; all these things betoken a sort of intellectual intertwining that other Jewish intellectuals, working on more narrowly religious themes, never experienced.

The success of Jews like Gersonides as natural philosophers meant less than it at first seems, and more. Natural philosophy was available only to a small, elite minority of Jews. Although it sometimes brought Jews together with Christian and Muslim scholars, it did not promise somehow to improve the station of Jews in general in Christian society. Its practitioners did not expect it to. Natural learning was a rarified interest, shared by small numbers of scholars (small numbers of Jews and small numbers of Christians and Muslims as well). Its social impact was limited.

But, at the same time, it had symbolic impact that affected how Jews viewed natural learning itself. Some Jews came to see natural learning as linked to other nations and other religions. It continued to be referred to as "external," "Greek," or "foreign" wisdom. It was the sole area, in medieval times, in which books written by others—by pagans, Muslims, and Christians—were eagerly translated into Hebrew and scrutinzed by Jews. It was a matter about which Hebrew texts were sought by non-Jewish scholars. It had not escaped Jews that the meeting of different cultures seemed to spur interest in natural knowledge, just as in its limited way the pursuit of natural knowledge seemed to spur the meeting of cultures.

This point becomes clearer still when the fate of Jewish natural philosophy on the Iberian Peninsula and in southern France is compared with its fate elsewhere in Europe. In Italy, where they were exposed to the cultural ambience of Spain, Jews displayed interest in natural learning. Shabbtai Donnolo (913–ca. 982) was a physician in southern Italy who wrote books on medicine, pharmacy, and astrology that reflected varied influences, but particularly Greek and Latin ones.[25] Jews who lived well to the north of Donnolo were far less likely to be similarly conversant, because natural philosophy and medicine were less popular in the Byzantine west than they were the south and east, and because the Jews of these lands were less enthusiastic about translating and absorbing foreign books. Copied manuscripts of natural philosophy (and certainly medical) texts survive from this time, but they are far fewer, less elaborate, and less original than those produced to the south and the east. Scholars have argued that there was a spike of interest among central European (especially Prague) Jews in philosophy and natural learning beginning in the late fourteenth century. But this interest was modest when compared with that displayed for generations by the Jews of Spain and southern France, and even of Italy.

Of course, the association of natural philosophy with a Republic of Letters that included Muslims and Jews nurtured enduring Jewish ambivalence toward natural knowledge. The greatest objection to natural philosophy, among those few who objected at all, seems to have been not that it was inherently bad or wrong but that it was *unseemly*. For one thing, it was feared that natural learning, taken seriously, would crowd out traditional Jewish disciplines of study. The concern was for *bittul Torah*, "nullifying the Torah" through misdirection of attention to something of inferior value. Also, natural philosophy was often seen as alien, foreign. Some Jews found this troubling. If God did not choose to reveal the secrets of natural philosophy with his Torah at Sinai, how significant could it be? Jews enthusiastic about natural learning began to insist that, in fact, God *did* reveal these secrets to Jews. They advanced the view, which became commonplace in Hebrew works of natural philosophy (especially astronomy), that these disciplines had first been mastered by Jews, who were shorn of this knowledge when they were exiled from the Holy Land, but not before they taught it, in imperfect form, to the Chaldeans, Egyptians, and, indirectly, the Greeks.

Although opposition to natural learning was seldom vigorous among medieval Jews, original and innovative study was also rare. There were few Jews like Gersonides who made observations or advanced novel theories. For most Jews, celestial measurement and geometric proof had relatively little to do with the sort of traditional Jewish scholarship that mattered to them most. In the end, there was little religious motivation to pursue it.

Still, in certain circumstances, medieval Jews took to these topics with creativity and vigor. Some of the reasons for this are clear. Medicine had obvious practical appeal, as well as intellectual. When exposed to them, Jews (like others of other backgrounds and beliefs) were drawn to the inherent fascinations of nature and number. And, for some at least, the promise of pursuing knowledge that is *human* knowledge, that invites them to collaborate in a grand community of Christian, Muslim, and pagan scholars, had its own magnetic attraction.

JEWS AND EARLY-MODERN NATURAL PHILOSOPHY

Jews attuned to natural philosophy in the early-modern period frequently lamented that the tradition of their medieval forebears had diminished: Hebrew natural philosophy texts were rarely copied and scholars remained innocent of the subject. There were many reasons why this was so. The fifteenth and sixteenth centuries saw great upheavals for the established Jewish communities of Europe, Africa, and Asia. The watershed year 1492, for example, began with the completion of the *reconquista* and the expulsion of Jews from Spain. This expulsion was unprecedented in the numbers it affected, but it was not unique. Jews had earlier been expelled from most of western Europe: from England in 1290 and from parts of France in 1306 and 1394. By 1492 small-scale expulsions, city-by-city or region-by-region, were common in central Europe as well. The net effect was to jar and jolt the Jewish communities of central Europe. By the middle of the sixteenth century, each Ashkenazi Jewish community had become a patchwork of smaller communities, many from other cities in Germany, Bohemia, Moravia, or Poland, some of descendants of Spanish and Portuguese Jews, some Italians as well as itinerants from northern Africa and Palestine.

Great expulsions and migrations meant that Jewish cultures were shuffled and reshuffled, with unsettling effects. Upheavals disturbed local traditions of study and at the same time introduced all manners of "new" literature—including philosophy and natural philosophy—that had earlier had little purchase in Ashkenazi culture.[26] The mass conversions of Jews to Christianity and piecemeal return of New Christians (or *Conversos*, as they are sometimes known) to Judaism facilitated a sort of cultural osmosis, as not just people converted and reverted but ideas and customs as well. The economics of print technology meant that books were produced in greater numbers, crossing more borders and traveling farther, before settling on the desk of a scholar or, in ever-increasing numbers, an avid householder. Events like the discovery of the New World and the publication of a book, Copernicus's *De Revolutionibus*, implying that the ancients were wrong to place the earth at the center of their model of the heavens, opened to renewed scrutiny received wisdom about the universe. New seaborne contacts with exotic places had similar effects. The Reformation and Counter-Reformation saw a fracturing of Christianity, a seismic shift that failed to reach an easy equilibrium. The order of the world seemed less fixed than it had before, for Europe's Jews and Christians alike and for the relations *between* Europe's Jews and Christians. Overall, these relations were marked by a level of mutual alienation greater than that of medieval Europe. But, especially for all that concerned nature and natural philosophy, they also took on a new and complicated uncertainty.

There were Jews at this time who embraced natural philosophy, in part because they saw it as a sort of ecumenical wisdom that had traction for Jews and Christians alike. One Jew who took this approach was David Gans (1541–1613). Gans—who met and admired the towering astronomers of his day, Tycho Brahe and Johannes Kepler—spent much of his life describing, teaching, and promoting liberal disciplines among Jews. He wrote introductions to astronomy, mathematics, geometry, geography, and history. He wrote primers for schoolchildren and surveys for householders. Everything Gans wrote served his overriding ambition to make liberal disciplines, and especially natural philosophy, available and intelligible to a broad, unscholarly, Hebrew-reading audience. This ambition was unprecedented in scope and would remain unmatched for two centuries.

Gans was not, however, alone in his enthusiasm for natural philosophy and other liberal arts. A small group of Jewish devotees of natural philosophy found an unexpected foothold at the court of Holy Roman Emperor Rudolf II, which hosted Jewish alchemists, metallurgists, doctors, and engineers. In this, Rudolf's court was unusual but not unique. Natural philosophy and, especially, medicine were also esteemed elsewhere, nowhere more than in Italy. By the sixteenth century, the University of Padua was recognized as the site of the best medical school in Europe, and its student body was perhaps the continent's most diverse. Students came from England and from all over the Continent, with great numbers coming from German lands. Protestants sought to study there, and the College of Physicians and Philosophers did not hesitate to accept them. The same was true for Jews. They too came from everywhere Jews lived in Europe, bringing with them different languages and customs. The welcome they found in Padua was mixed—and often harsh. According to the written rules of the university, they were not supposed to be there at all. Few were awarded the degree of *doctorates in artibus et medicine*, settling instead for the less-esteemed degree of *magister*. They were taxed and tuitioned at rates higher than their Christian classmates and, as some of them later complained, subject to taunts and ridicule.[27]

Padua was a forge for a particular sort of early-modern Jewish intellectual. Its graduates were an eccentric cast, and an influential one. Joseph Solomon Delmedigo (1591–1655) was fifteen when he began medical studies in Padua. There he encountered Galileo, in the final years of his tenure at the university and just as he embarked on his first research with his newly crafted telescope.[28] Astronomy would remain a passion throughout Delmedigo's life, as would the other mathematical disciplines. After completing his studies, Delmedigo began a life of wandering. He traveled to Cairo, then Constantinople, through Vilnius, Lublin, and Krakow. Later he found his way to Hamburg and then to Amsterdam. Through his travels, he met princes and noblemen (whom he served as physician), top-flight Christian scholars like Johan Buxtorf the younger (1599–1664), Jewish scholars like Menasse ben Israel (1604–57), and *converso* scholars like Benedict de Castro (1597–1684). In time, he wrote his popular *Sefer Elim*, a book with an enthusiastic description of Copernican astronomy, admiring notice of Kepler (whom he judged "the greatest mathematician of our time"), praise of logarithms, mention of Galileo's telescope, and the first description in print of the liquid-in-glass thermometer.[29] Delmedigo never abandoned the passion for natural philosophy and mathematics that he absorbed as a student in Padua.

The author of the most enduring early-modern Hebrew book of natural philosophy and medicine was Tobias Cohen (1652–1729). As a young man, Cohen left the Poland of his youth for medical studies in Frankfurt. There, he faced unremitting hostility. Finally, he left Frankfurt and matriculated in Padua, but his fury over this experience in Frankfurt never faded. After graduation from Padua in 1683, he traveled to Turkey, where he worked as a court physician in Constantinople and Adrianople. There he wrote a compendium called *Ma'aseh Tuviah* (The Work of Tobias), a book intended to cover the total of heaven and earth. In it, he dismissed Copernicus as "the first born Son of the devil," miffed that Copernicus's heliocentric astronomy was inconsistent with the position put forth in the Talmud.[30] But Cohen was not a head-in-the-sand fundamentalist who rejected new information as a matter of custom and principle. He was enthusiastic about "the new medicine that resides in the bosom of the physicians of our day," including Paracelsian iatrochemistry, which he endorsed. He included chapters on medical wonders issuing from the New World, such as coffee, sassafras, and sarsaparilla. In the end, he produced a handbook that would help Jews demonstrate to Christians that they were not innocent of natural wisdom and that neither was their intellectual legacy, the Jewish tradition. Tobias Cohen may have believed that natural knowledge could improve the station of adept Jews because of his own experience. Medicine and natural philosophy had opened doors for Cohen himself, transforming an orphan boy from *Mideleuropa* into a courtier in Constantinople.

The careers of Jews like Cohen, Delmedigo, and many others who studied medicine at Padua demonstrate that among Jews seeking discourse with Christian intellectuals of the day, natural philosophy, mathematics, and similar disciplines were among the subjects most likely to support such dialogue. There were several reasons for this. One was the belief, shared by early-modern Jews and Christians, that these subjects were first revealed by God to the Jews of the Bible and that their living descendants might be in a position to aid in recovering that *prisca sapientia*, or "ancient wisdom." Still another was the persuasion, steeled by the religious battles following the Reformation, that natural philosophy might, by its nature, be a subject about which agreement might be reached even by people who would never see eye to eye about God and Jesus.

Many graduates of Italian medical schools shared a vaguely universal natural theology, a sense that nature was worthy of study because in nature were traces of God's handiwork. Jacob ben Isaac Zahalon (1630–93) composed a "physicians' prayer" that went, "I pray . . . that I may discover the secrets of Thy wonderful deeds and that I may know the peculiar curative powers which Thou has placed in herbs and minerals . . . and that through them I shall tell of Thy might." David Nieto (1654–1728) wrote that "there is not a single creature, even among the least of them, that does not show in some form of its constitution the impress of God." Jacob Ḥamiz (d. ca. 1676) insisted that "one must understand natural things in order to know what is beyond nature." And Delmedigo himself wrote that "contemplating every one of [God's] creatures leads man to recognize his exalted Creator."[31] These views have the unusual virtue of being theological in nature, but they are still views about which Jews and Christians might agree. Natural theology was the only theology Jews and Christians could share (save, perhaps, bits of Kabbalah or Cabbala). In an epoch in which theology remained the "queen of the sciences," it is perhaps no surprise that natural philosophy—which might serve as a foundation of belief, but not of polemic—remained the subject most earnestly shared by Jews and Christians.

Jewish physicians assumed odd roles in early-modern Europe. They were citizens of both the Jewish communities in which they lived and the scholarly community with whom they studied and corresponded and, in a way, they were citizens of neither. While they often held positions of some influence among Jews, they were subject to suspicions and found themselves moving from place to place with great frequency. And while they often wrote in Latin and vernacular languages, corresponded warmly with Christian colleagues, and found that their services were sought by kings, they were at the same time aware that their scholarship and their probity were subject to suspicion because they were Jews. Jewish doctors seemed to have entrée to the learned and the leaders of both Jewish and Christian societies, and yet to be fully at home in neither. They seemed to live both in the center and at the margins of two societies at once.

Indeed, the question of whether Jewish and Christian societies ought properly remain asunder was one that came to be asked with greater frequently in the centuries that followed, and it was frequently linked, through a complicated chain of reasoning, with inquiry into natural philosophy. The celebrated career of Baruch Spinoza (1632–77) provides an illustration. Spinoza was of *converso* heritage, though he was raised a Jew from the start and received his education in a Jewish religious school in Amsterdam. He left these Jewish studies at seventeen, and at about this time began studying Latin, natural philosophy, and philosophy. Before he reached age thirty, Spinoza distributed among friends an outline of the ideas he would further develop throughout his life. In it he stated that "God is, in relation to his effects or creatures, no other than an immanent cause," by which he meant that God comprises everything found in nature and has no existence outside these things or outside of nature. This point of view, which identifies God with nature and rules out from the start the notion of a Transcendent God who controls the world according to God's fleeting and changeable will, was criticized by contemporaries who recognized that for Spinoza "God exists, but only philosophically."

Spinoza's impact on his own tumultuous times and, for that matter, on modern thought has been almost incalculably large. As one historian put it, "Spinoza imparted order, cohesion, and formal logic to what in effect was a fundamentally new view of man, God, and the universe rooted in philosophy, nurtured by scientific thought, and capable of producing a revolutionary ideology." It was for this reason that "Spinoza . . . emerged as the supreme philosophical bogeyman of Early Enlightenment Europe."[32] And Spinoza was known for natural philosophy just as he was known for political philosophy. Already in the summer of 1661, before Spinoza had published a word, he received word from Henry Oldenburg, who wished to meet the Jewish heretic who had not yet turned thirty. Oldenburg was touring the Netherlands before accepting a post as secretary of the Royal Society in London when he met Spinoza and spent some hours in his company, discussing philosophy.[33] Two years later, Oldenburg wrote Spinoza hoping to broker a collaboration between the Dutch philosopher and Robert Boyle, arguably the greatest natural philosopher of the age: "unite your abilities in striving to advance a genuine and firmly based philosophy. . . . May I urge you especially, by the acuteness of your mathematical mind, to continue to establish basic principles, just as I ceaselessly try to coax my noble friend Boyle to confirm and illustrate them by experiments and observations frequently and accurately made."[34]

Oldenburg saw in Spinoza an original and important mathematician and natural philosopher. Descartes, whose philosophy was the original spur of much of Spinoza's work, had famously insisted on a break between material reality, which operated by mechanistic laws of cause and effect, and a spiritual reality that could not be described mechanistically. Spinoza collapsed these two realities into a single one and insisted that this encompassing reality must be explained it its entirety by the laws of nature. He wrote that "nothing, then, can happen in Nature to contravene her own universal laws, nor anything that is not in agreement with these laws or that does not follow from them." This was a view more radical in its implications than anything advocated by the most renowned natural philosophers of Spinoza's day, such as Boyle or Newton.[35]

There is no doubt that Spinoza was, by a very wide margin, the most creative and influential *Jewish* natural philosopher (and political philosopher and ethical philosopher—in short, the most creative and influential Jewish *philosopher*) of the early-modern period. Scholars have tried for years, and they are still trying, to trace the "Jewish roots" of Spinoza's views, but without great success. For one thing, there is not that much evidence that his Jewish background left too much of an impression on Spinoza. More to the point, Spinoza's books and letters reveal more immediate influences—men like Descartes—who were not Jews. Spinoza was a Jew, of course, but even more than this, he was a European intellectual. This is also how he was seen by most of the Europeans that he, in turn, so impressed and scandalized.

This simple fact matters. It is no coincidence that natural philosophy and mathematics and geometry are crucial elements of the philosophy that rendered it both untenable and unnecessary for Spinoza to remain a member of the Jewish community. David Hume concluded that Spinoza's "doctrine of the simplicity of the universe, and the unity of that substance" was powerfully corrosive of any notion of godly oversight, be it a Jewish God or a

Christian one. Spinoza's philosophy (like Descartes before him) challenged long-accepted views of what counts as legitimate sources of knowledge, replacing tradition with what Spinoza took to be the methods of science.[36] Spinoza's effort to find a geometry of theology, ethics, and politics was powerfully corrosive of existing structures of authority (and it is no surprise that Spinoza's books were banned in the Netherlands in 1674 and suppressed less systematically before this).[37] In taking the rational individual as its basic element, Spinoza's philosophy goes a long way toward eliminating by caveat the notion that there are innate differences between races and peoples.

And if this is true, then Spinoza was perhaps the first Jew for whom science was not just a vehicle to bridge between Jews and other believers, but a vehicle by which to discredit the worldview that took religious identity to be fundamental and binding. Spinoza may have been the first Jew for whom science was a constitutive part of a philosophy that called for Jews, Christians, Muslims, and atheists to be considered, first and foremost, as citizens.

He was certainly not the last. While Spinoza's radical conclusions were spurned by all but a few Jews in the seventeenth and eighteenth centuries, in time more Jews began see science as a foundation for their worldview and ceased to see their religion as the alpha and omega of their identity.[38] In the centuries since Spinoza, as the next essay shows, Jews continued to find science intertwined in complex patterns with their own identities and their notions of how they fit into the world beyond the ghetto walls.

NOTES

1. See, for example, Cyrus Adler, "Albert Einstein—The Flowering of Many Centuries of Jewish Endeavor," in *Lectures, Selected Papers, Addresses* (Philadelphia: Privately printed, 1933), 346.

2. All Bible translations are from the 1917 *Jewish Publication Society Bible*, edited by Max Margolis. This translation consciously followed the KJV, although there are small changes throughout.

3. Mary Douglas, *Purity and Danger: An Analysis of Concepts of Pollution and Taboo* (London: Routledge and Keegan Paul, 1966).

4. Flavius Josephus, *Wars of the Jews, or History of the Destruction of Jerusalem,* 6:288.

5. Francis Schmidt, "Ancient Jewish Astrology: An Attempt to Interpret 4QCRYP-TIC (4Q186)," in *Biblical Perspectives: Early Use and Interpretation of the Bible in Light of the Dead Sea Scrolls*, ed. Michael E. Stone and Esther Chazon, 189–205 (Leiden: Brill, 1998).

6. Georg W. F. Hegel, *Lectures on the Philosophy of Religion* (New York: Humanities Press, 1962), 2:128.

7. See, for instance, H. Wheeler Robinson, "The Hebrew Conception of Nature," in *Inspiration and Revelation in the Old Testament* (Oxford: Clarendon Press, 1946), 1–16; Mircea Eliade, *The Sacred and the Profane* (New York: Harper and Brothers,

1959); and Theodore Hiebert, *The Yahwist's Landscape: Nature and Religion in Early Israel* (New York: Oxford University Press, 1996), 16. Similar claims have featured in Protestant accounts of the links between the Bible and the rise of science. For example, the Dutch Calvinist historian Reijer Hooykaas argued that a biblical worldview tended to promote the "de-deification" of nature. See *Religion and the Rise of Modern Science* (Edinburgh: Scottish Academic Press, 1972).

8. The most influential examples are: Harvey Gallagher Cox, *The Secular City: Secularization and Urbanization in Theological Perspective* (New York: Macmillan, 1965), and Lynn White, "On the Historical Roots of our Ecological Crisis," *Science*, March 10, 1967, 1203–7.

9. Howard Eilberg-Schwartz, *The Savage in Judaism: An Anthropology of Israelite Religion and Ancient Judaism* (Bloomington: Indiana University Press, 1990).

10. See the more than 2,000 relevant passages cited in the massive concordance assembled by Julius Preuss in the first years of the twentieth century: *Biblisch-talmudische Medizin: Beiträge zur Geschichte der Heilkunde und der Kultur überhaupt* (Berlin: S. Karger, 1911). An English translation with emendations by Fred Rosner is available: Julius Preuss, *Biblical and Talmudic Medicine* (Northvale, N.J.: Jason Aronson, 1996).

11. For instance, BT Shabbat, 156a: "Rabbi Johanan maintained: Israel is immune from planetary influence . . . Rab too holds that Israel is immune from planetary influence . . . From R. Akiba too [we learn that] Israel is free from planetary influence."

12. About this, see Menachem Fisch, *Rational Rabbis: Science and Talmudic Culture* (Bloomington: University of Indiana Press, 1997).

13. David C. Lindberg, ed., *Science in the Middle Ages* (Chicago: University of Chicago Press, 1978), 13.

14. L. P. Harvey, "In Granada under the Catholic Monarchs: A Call from a Doctor and Another from a *Curandera*," in *The Age of the Catholic Monarchs, 1474–1516: Literary Studies in Memory of Keith Whinnom* (Liverpool: Liverpool University Press, 1989), 71–75.

15. Shlomo Sela, "Abraham Ibn Ezra's Special Strategy in the Creation of a Hebrew Scientific Terminology," *Micrologus: Nature, Sciences and Medieval Societies* 9 (2001).

16. Exodus 20:2: "I am the LORD thy God, who brought thee out of the land of Egypt, out of the house of bondage; Thou shalt have no other gods before Me."

17. Y. Tzvi Langermann, "Some Astrological Themes in the Thought of Abraham ibn Ezra" in *Rabbi Abraham ibn Ezra: Studies in the Writings of a Twelfth-Century Jewish Polymath*, ed. I. Twersky and J. Harris, 71 (Cambridge, Mass.: Harvard University Press, 1993).

18. Maimonides, "Letter on Astrology," in *A Maimonides Reader*, ed. Isadore Twersky, 463–73 (New York: Behrman House, 1972).

19. This point is made vigorously by Norbert Samuelson in "Judaism and Science," in *The Oxford Handbook of Religion and Science*, ed. Philip Clayton, 41–44 (Oxford: Oxford University Press, 2006).

20. Shlomo Pines, "Maimonides" in *Dictionary of Scientific Biography* (New York: Scribner, 1970).

21. Naḥmanides' letter was reprinted in *Monatsschrift für die Geschichte und Wissenschaft des Judentums* 9 (1860): 184–95.

Early Judaism

43

22. Gad Freudenthal, "Science in the Medieval Jewish Culture of Southern France," *History of Science* 33 (1995): 28–29.

23. Gad Freudenthal, "Holiness and Defilement: The Ambivalent Perception of Philosophy by its Opponents in the Early Fourteenth Century," *Micrologus: Nature, Sciences and Medieval Societies* 9 (2001): 176–77.

24. Gad Freudenthal, "Levi ben Gershom (Gersonides), 1288–1344," in *The Routledge History of Islamic Philosophy* (London: Routledge, 1996), 739–54.

25. D. B. Ruderman, *Jewish Thought and Scientific Discovery in Early Modern Europe* (New Haven, Conn.: Yale University Press, 1995), 23.

26. Elhanan Reiner, "The Attitude of Ashkenazi Society to the New Science in the Sixteenth Century," *Science in Context* 10.4 (1997): 589–603.

27. Isaac Barzilay, *Yoseph Shlomo Delmedigo, Yashar of Candia: His Life, Works and Times* (Leiden: Brill, 1974), 35.

28. Barzilay, *Yoseph Shlomo Delmedigo*, 161.

29. Jacob Adler, "J. S. Delmedigo and the Liquid-in-Glass Thermometer,"*Annals of Science* 54.3 (1997): 293–99.

30. Tobias Cohen, *Ma'aseh Tuviyah* (Venice, [1707] 1974), 44b.

31. Quoted from Ruderman, "The Impact of Science on Jewish Culture and Society in Venice (with Special Reference to Jewish Graduates of Padua's Medical Schools)," in *Essential Papers on Jewish Culture in Renaissance and Baroque Italy*, ed. D. B. Ruderman, 536–37 (New York, New York University Press, 1992).

32. Jonathan Israel, *Radical Enlightenment: Philosophy and the Making of Modernity, 1650–1750* (Oxford: Oxford University Press, 2001), 159–60.

33. Ibid. 161.

34. Ibid., 242.

35. Ibid., 242–57.

36. "The method of interpreting Scripture," Spinoza wrote in his *Tractatus Theologico-Politicus*, "is no different from the method of interpreting nature" (Spinoza, 1991, 141). The same was true, as he saw it, of the method for establishing just government. "[The] laws and rules according to which all things are and are changed from form to form, are everywhere and always the same," Spinoza wrote in his *Ethics*, "so that there must also be one and the same method of understanding the nature of all things whatsoever, that is to say, by the universal laws and rules of nature . . . I shall therefore pursue the same method in considering the nature and strength of the affects and the power of the mind of them, which I pursued in our previous discussion of God and the mind, and I shall consider human actions and appetites just as if I were considering lines, planes or bodies" (Spinoza, 2000, preface).

37. Jonathan Israel, "The Banning of Spinoza's Works in the Dutch Republic (1670–1678)," in *Disguised and Overt Spinozism around 1700*, ed. Wiep van Bunge and W. N. A. Klever (Leiden: Brill, 1996).

38. Adam Sutcliffe, "Quarreling over Spinoza: Moses Mendelssohn and the Fashioning of Jewish Philosophical Heroism," in *Renewing the Past, Reconfiguring Jewish Culture: From al-Andalus to the Haskalah*, ed. Ross Bran and Adam Sutcliffe, 167–88 (Philadelphia: University of Pennsylvania Press, 2004).

2

Modern Judaism

Geoffrey Cantor

Although the present chapter can discuss only a few of the many contexts in which Jews have engaged science in the period since the Scientific Revolution, there are some general considerations that need to be addressed at the outset. The first is that, outside the modern state of Israel, Jews have constituted a social minority and often a very small proportion of the population of any country. Thus the situation of Jews has been greatly affected by the relations between the Jewish community and the host culture, and the histories of Jewish communities have been intimately bound up with the social histories of other countries, cultures, and religions. In turn, Jewish participation in science and attitudes toward science must be located on a broader canvas that places the Jewish community within a larger social framework. Often, too, science has formed a crucial aspect of modernism, and Jewish engagements with science need to be understood as part of a wider debate over how Jews should participate in the modern world.

Second, it would be incorrect to portray Jews as adopting a single position on science—or almost any other subject—since within any Jewish community (let alone *between* Jewish communities) there exist various groups and movements adopting different positions on religious, social, and political issues. Viewed historically there are two main traditions: Sephardi (who are descended from the medieval communities in Spain and Portugal) and Ashkenazi (descendants of communities from Germany, Russia, and Central and Eastern Europe). A broad spectrum of opinion exists within the Ashkenazim. At one end stand the Haredi (ultra-Orthodox) groups who unwaveringly adhere to the Torah and firmly maintain the oral tradition through study of the Talmud and other rabbinical works. By contrast, Modern Orthodoxy, which developed in the late nineteenth century, maintains a firm commitment to Jewish law and tradition but also seeks to synthesize aspects of the modern world, often including science. Moreover, the impact of the Enlightenment in the eighteenth century and of emancipation and the higher biblical criticism in the nineteenth resulted in the emergence of various progressive movements, which to a greater or lesser degree allow more freedom in interpreting traditional texts and also emphasize engagement with the modern world. Taking the Reform movement as central in this process, the Conservative (or Masorti) movement has adopted a more traditionalist approach, while the Liberal and Reconstructionist movements place even less emphasis on tradition. Many Jews do not join any of these movements, and there are also a large number who lead totally secular lifestyles. To add a further complexity, some contemporary Jews would describe themselves as atheists—perhaps aligning themselves socially and culturally with the Jewish community but rejecting any belief in God and eschewing religious practices. Given this considerable diversity of positions, there is no single Jewish perspective on science.[1] Nevertheless, there are recurrent themes, some of which will be encountered in this chapter.

I address three historically important foci for understanding Jewish involvement with science since the early eighteenth century: first, the ways in which traditional Jewish societies engaged the Enlightenment; second, Jewish responses to Darwin's theory of evolution in the late nineteenth and twentieth centuries; and third, the role of Jews in the scientific community—principally the American scientific community—during the past half-century. In the final section we will reflect more broadly on Jewish attitudes to modern science.

HASKALAH

Following the successes in philosophy and in the sciences associated with such seventeenth-century writers as Descartes, Newton, and Locke, progressive thinkers of the eighteenth century argued that the light of reason should be used to illuminate all areas, including politics, society, and religion. Traditional dogmas would be subjected to critical examination and rejected if found wanting. A rational, empiricist approach would, it was argued, lead to true knowledge and an improved quality of life. Particularly in the major intellectual centers of Europe, the sciences flourished as flagships of the Enlightenment: scientific societies proliferated, science books were published in large numbers, and crowds flocked to lectures on scientific subjects. New areas of research abounded, such as electricity, taxonomy, and the study of society. More important than any specific innovation, however, was the ethos of optimism that the Enlightenment engendered and the belief that it opened an era of improvement and progress.

However, throughout the eighteenth century the majority of Jews across much of Europe lived in traditional communities, in which authority was exercised by rabbis. Education was centered on the study of Torah (the five books of Moses) and Talmud (a compilation of rabbinical arguments dating from early in the Christian Era), but secular subjects received scant attention. The lives of these Jews were circumscribed not only by their commitment to traditional rituals and practices but also by the restrictions imposed by the local civic and ecclesiastical authorities, who often viewed Jews as inferior, kept them in ghettos, prevented them from entering many occupations and from participating in civic life, and barred their access to schools and universities. Yet there was some assimilation, especially in the larger and more affluent European cities, such as Berlin, where small numbers of wealthy Jews tried to emulate the lifestyles of their Christian neighbors. Our concern here is less with these merchants and bankers who established themselves within civic society than with the small but growing number of Jews, especially in Germany, who engaged the new and exciting intellectual currents of the Enlightenment. A strong and increasingly visible movement for Jewish enlightenment—*Haskalah*, its proponents being *maskilim* (those who possess understanding)—emerged by about 1780, its most eminent exponent being Moses Mendelssohn (1729–86). Even from fairly early in the century, a small number of Jews embraced the new and controversial patterns of thought.

These early *maskilim* sought to address what they perceived to be the intellectual inferiority of the Jews, which they attributed to the community's insularity and rabbinical domination. Becoming aware of the new and exciting currents of European thought, they grasped the possibilities offered by modern learning and strove to effect a major change in Jewish society by forging a specifically Jewish version of the Enlightenment. They argued that Jews had to break the bonds of insularity, enter society as citizens, and engage modern ways of thought by opening their minds to secular studies, especially the study of philosophy and the sciences. Adopting the beacon of rationality, many *maskilim* were highly critical of mystical systems, such as Kabbalah, and also of religious enthusiasts, such as the self-proclaimed messiah Sabbatai Zevi (1626–76) and his followers. Similarly they generally viewed Yiddish as an unsophisticated language of the common people and instead considered that Hebrew was the proper idiom to be adopted by Jews in philosophical discourse. Although not all *maskilim* were totally opposed to traditional Judaism, many of them endeavored to create within the Jewish community a new, vibrant, and innovative intellectual elite that would challenge and ultimately replace the power of the rabbis and lead the Jewish community into the modern world, with its exciting social and intellectual possibilities but also, some recognized, its attendant dangers.[2]

The extensive writings of the *maskilim* ranged over philosophy, ethics, linguistics, medicine, and the sciences. Despite sharing a general proscience attitude, only a minority wrote specifically on scientific topics. One example is the medically trained Aaron Gumpertz (1723–70), who wrote *Ma'amar Hamada* (Treatise on science, 1765), in which he not only displayed his familiarity with recent developments in science but insisted that the study of science posed no threat to Jewish faith.[3] The career and writings of another *maskil*, Mordechai Gumpel Schnaber (1741–97), otherwise known as George Levison, deserve further discussion, as they illustrate the difficulty of straddling the worlds of traditional Judaism and Enlightenment philosophy. Born into a rabbinical family in Berlin and having been trained by an eminent Talmudist, Schnaber moved to London around 1770 in order to study medicine at the acclaimed medical school founded by the brothers John and William Hunter. He subsequently became a physician at the General Medical Asylum in London, was patronized by the Swedish king, who invited him to Stockholm in order to set up a hospital and a medical school, and spent the latter part of his life as a physician in Hamburg. He also published two English-language books on medical topics. Thus he moved far outside the traditional Jewish community and pursued a fairly high-profile career in the world of medicine and secular learning.

At the same time, Schnaber contributed to the *Haskalah* by publishing works in Hebrew specifically for a Jewish readership. His earliest publication was *Ma'amar haTorah vehaḥokhmah* (A dissertation on the law and science, 1771), which contained a distillation of scientific knowledge, including a discussion of Newton's laws of motion. Yet Schnaber also provided his readers with a justification for studying secular science and accepting its compatibility with Jewish learning: "There is nothing in wisdom [i.e., secular knowledge] which will disobey [= contradict] the Torah." In making this claim Schnaber was not original, but he represented himself as reviving the tradition of Maimonides, who was portrayed as having integrated medieval Jewish and secular learning. Critical of the rabbis of his own day for having turned their backs on science, Schnaber sought to rejuvenate Jewish tradition by inculcating it with recent advances in scientific knowledge. These views also provided him with a legitimation of his own career, which spanned the religious and the secular. Yet in the mid-1770s a controversy erupted between Schnaber and the main Ashkenazi synagogue in London. One of his detractors charged him with publicly proclaiming that the "Torah is not from Heaven, and that there is no reward and punishment, and denying the resurrection of the dead." He was also charged with abandoning kosher food and failing to perform the duty of putting on phylacteries. While we should not explain his dissension from the community by his enthusiasm for modern science, his emphasis on rationalistic modes of thought apparently encouraged him to question various aspects of Jewish tradition.[4]

In the later 1770s *Haskalah* became consolidated around the figure of Mendelssohn in Berlin, who was the movement's main publicist and was recognized as the preeminent Jewish philosopher of his generation by non-Jewish contemporaries, including Immanuel Kant. Another focus was provided by the Society of Friends of the Hebrew Language, founded in Königsberg in 1782, which attracted mainly students and tutors who were eager to spread Enlightenment values through the Jewish community. While the active members of the movement were drawn mainly from the rising bourgeoisie and supplemented by young men from more orthodox backgrounds who were attracted to the exciting ideals of *Haskalah*, support was provided by wealthy and often fairly assimilated Jews in Prussia, Copenhagen, and Poland. The *maskilim* founded a Hebrew-language periodical, *Hame'asef* (The gatherer), which was published somewhat irregularly from 1783 until 1811 and was dedicated to advancing science, knowledge, and rational thought. It included articles on various scientific subjects, including Newtonian mechanics. The *maskilim* also possessed their own publishing house in Berlin, which produced many works—including a science textbook, *Reshit Limudim* (Elements of knowledge, 1788) by Baruch Lindau, which was "the most famous, up-to-date book on the Hebrew bookshelf at the end of the eighteenth century."[5]

The initial *Haskalah* movement in Germany peaked during the final two decades of the eighteenth century. Although it gained support from some rabbis, arguments frequently flared with those rabbis who feared that *Haskalah* would erode traditional Jewish observance and that they would lose influence over their congregations. Thus one writer rejected the new curriculum proposed by a *maskil* by arguing that such a move would render the Torah "of secondary significance, while that of lesser importance, namely the study of the sciences, would be rendered of greater significance, and that, Heaven forbid, the Torah would be forgotten by the Jews."[6] For their part, many *maskilim* viewed the rabbis as men whose power was vested in keeping Jews separate from the rest of society and in maintaining their congregations in ignorance of important and exciting developments in philosophy and the sciences.

By the early decades of the nineteenth century the *Haskalah* movement was no longer confined principally to Germany, its traditional stronghold. Modernist ideas were increasingly influencing other Jewish communities, especially in Poland and Russia. As with the earlier heyday of the movement, some of these later *maskilim* sought some synthesis with traditional Judaism, but in many cases there was outright opposition and hostility between tradition and innovation. During this later period, however, *Haskalah* became an increasingly populist movement and one that had a significant impact on the controversial issue of education. Thus while attacking the rabbis for feeding their students with (what they claimed was) useless Talmudic learning, later *maskilim* founded a number of schools for Jewish children, including girls, who were taught modern subjects, often including elementary mathematics and science.

Although in the long term *Haskalah* exerted a significant influence on many Jewish communities, we should not accept at face value the self-image projected by many *maskilim* who saw a simple choice between traditional Judaism on the one hand and enlightenment on the other. As Ira Robinson has argued, the Kabbalistic tradition derived from the writings of the sixteenth-century Jewish mystic Isaac Luria could also absorb aspects of modern science, since it could be used to unify the spiritual realm with the physical world created by God. For example, in the often reprinted *Sefer haberit* (Book of the covenant), first published in 1797, Pinhas Elijah Hurwitz sought to present Orthodox Jews with a manual of scientific knowledge. Although many aspects of science were discussed in this work, it is important to appreciate that Hurwitz presented the recent scientific discoveries of the gentiles as inferior to the Kabbalah and argued that while Jews should familiarize themselves with certain aspects of science, if they overemphasized science they would lose sight of the transcendent ethical truths contained in Kabbalah and forsake their religious duties. He argued that since all truths are contained in Kabbalah modern scientists were merely rediscovering the truth embedded in traditional Jewish teachings. Moreover, if Kabbalah and science failed to agree, Hurwitz considered modern knowledge to be in the wrong. Thus modern science was not to be valued for its own sake (the prominent view among *maskilim*) but was to be treated as a handmaiden to Torah.[7] As we shall see, this strategy was later adopted by some Orthodox Jews in addressing the theory of evolution.

A small number of Jews of the period—often physicians—produced creative research in science and medicine. Schnaber, for example, wrote an innovative work on how to cure sore throat (using horseradish and mustard), while his English contemporary Emanuel Mendes da Costa published several contributions to the study of fossils and shells.[8] However, we misrepresent the significance of the sciences to eighteenth- and early-nineteenth-century Jewish history if we focus exclusively on these few innovators. Of greater importance was the impetus of *Haskalah*, and particularly the publication of a number of Hebrew-language texts, in introducing many Jews to modern developments in philosophy and the sciences. Moreover, in their writings the advocates of *Haskalah* repeatedly evoked science as a symbol of modernism and speculated on the potential future achievements if Jews committed themselves to the new world of learning.

JEWS AND EVOLUTION

The response of religious communities to the challenges posed by the theory of evolution provides useful historical insights not only into their attitudes toward science but also into their belief systems and authority structures. While an extensive literature exists on Christian responses to evolution and the staunch opposition to evolution by many fundamentalist groups is a recurrent story in the contemporary media, little has been written on Jewish attitudes to Darwin's theory. Did it pose a similar threat to Jews? Although Jewish responses have covered a fairly wide range, there are some significant differences between Jewish and Western Christian attitudes to evolution. Before identifying some specifically Jewish approaches to the topic, we shall look briefly at two of Darwin's Jewish correspondents.

In the last decade of his life Darwin undertook an extensive correspondence with a young English naturalist of Sephardi descent and the grandson of its *haham* (communal leader). Although Raphael Meldola (1849–1915) later became better known as an organic chemist and held a professorship of chemistry, entomology was the subject of his early scientific papers and a topic to which he frequently returned throughout his life. As he later reminisced, "as a youth, I fell into the ranks of Darwinism."[9] Darwin encouraged him and directed his early researches, especially on the subject of mimicry. Darwin also suggested that he translate into English August Weismann's *Studien zur Descendenz-Theorie* and, when it appeared in 1882, wrote a preface to Meldola's translation. Viewing Darwin as his intellectual mentor, Meldola became a staunch defender of Darwin's theory of natural selection not only against anti-evolutionists but also against those who advocated alternative mechanisms to account for evolution.

While specifically Jewish themes were not prominent in Meldola's science, religious issues were crucially important for another of Darwin's Jewish correspondents, a scholar of the Torah and Talmud from Radom, in Russian-occupied Poland, named Naphtali Levy (d.1894). Having studied with several eminent rabbis, Levy was steeped in traditional scholarship but, drawing on the *Haskalah* tradition, he also considered that Torah Judaism should be illuminated by the findings of modern science and that Judaism should address contemporary social issues, including women's rights. Writing to Darwin in 1876, Levy enclosed a book in Hebrew (*Toledot Adam* [Generations of man], 1874), in which he had argued that Jewish thought and Darwin's theory of evolution were in harmony with one another. For example, he conceived Genesis 2:7—"the LORD God formed man from the dust of the ground"—to mean that over a long time inorganic matter had evolved into organisms. Moreover, he conceived that through a teleological process, which he considered to be evolution, successive species had developed, resulting finally in the creation of humankind. As the book was written in Hebrew, Darwin was unable to assess the details of Levy's argument, but he was both surprised and delighted to receive an endorsement of his theory from a religious Jew at a time when he was facing much criticism from Christians. Levy's covering letter (for which Darwin obtained a translation) began with the salutation: "To the Lord, the Prince, who 'stands for an ensign of the people' [Isa. 11:10], the Investigator of the generation, the 'bright son of the morning' [Isa. 16:12], Charles Darwin, may he live long!"[10]

While Levy's unalloyed enthusiasm for Darwin's theory stands out as unusual, a small number of nineteenth-century rabbis did comment on evolution, often positively. For example, from his survey of reactions to evolution by five late-nineteenth-century European Orthodox rabbis, Shai Cherry has noted that those "with the greatest affinities to Kabbalah" have been "most welcoming . . . towards Darwinism."[11] The link with Kabbalah is interesting and perhaps rather unexpected, since Kabbalah is a mystical system of thought and may thus seem opposed to the ethos of modern science. In reacting against the philosophy of materialism, however, some Jewish thinkers have viewed organic evolution within the larger framework provided by the Kabbalistic account of change. On this account all potentialities are imminent at the Creation and the universe unfolds progressively. This general scenario can apply not only to the progress in knowledge of Torah but also to the transformative development of creatures.

We can better appreciate how organic evolution can be related to Kabbalah by examining the views of one of the most influential twentieth-century rabbis, Rabbi Abraham Isaac Kook (1865–1935), who became the first Ashkenazi Chief Rabbi of Israel.[12] He had trained earlier in an eminent Eastern European yeshiva but was also widely read in secular, especially Hegelian, philosophy. Although he frequently appealed to evolutionary notions, he was not evoking the specifically Darwinian mechanism of natural selection; indeed, his account of evolution needs to be located elsewhere—in Jewish philosophy and, more specifically, in Kabbalah. At the heart of his account lies the idea of progressive change in which the world is continually moving from its initial state of *tohu v'vohu* (unformed and void [Gen. 1:2]) toward greater and greater perfection, despite occasional temporary reversals. But this is not a secular notion of progress: by responding to illumination by the divine from above, all lower aspects of the world are drawn upward and eventually achieve perfection. Kook conceived this as involving *teshuva* (return), which he understood as returning to the divine essence. Moreover, through the process of return the world becomes healed (the traditional notion of *tikkun olam*). Thus for Kook the metaphysical notion of progress is endowed with both teleological directionality and also with a mystical meaning involving an ultimate unification in the messianic age with *Ein Sof*, the Kabbalistic notion of God—who possesses such opposing qualities as simplicity and complexity, and reality and illusion, and who encompasses the totality of all being.

According to this Kabbalistic conception, evolution is cosmic and therefore necessarily applies to all domains; indeed, all aspects of the world are ultimately interrelated, which means that all of existence is moving in the same direction. Human history is part of this process, so that we are necessarily moving toward the messianic age. Biological species must likewise evolve along a similar path. This is a specifically Jewish notion of the unity of all creation, but similar ideas of the unity between God and his creation are to be found among Christian and probably Muslim writers. Viewed as a unifying theory, Darwin's theory of evolution has proved attractive to those monotheists who perceive a close unity between God and nature.

Kook was not concerned to show that Jewish philosophy could be reconciled with the doctrines of modern science. Quite the opposite: in adopting Darwin's theory, scientists had only recently come to recognize a small part of the larger philosophy of change that traditional Jewish thinkers had long appreciated. From this perspective Kook could write that "Evolutionary theory which is now achieving such world-wide acclaim coincides with the lofty doctrines of Kabbala."[13] In a similar vein, Carl Feit, an ordained rabbi and currently a professor of biology at Yeshiva College, has argued, "there is no Jewish 'problem' with the science of evolution" since "the two most important and influential Orthodox Jewish thinkers of the twentieth century [Rabbi Kook and Rabbi Joseph B. Soloveitchik], who based their analyses on fairly traditional readings of classic Jewish texts, not only dismissed the notion of any conflict between modern science and Torah, but actually found contemporary scientific notions of evolution and cosmology to be harmonious with classic rabbinic thought."[14]

While some Orthodox rabbis have embraced the theory of evolution, others have adopted the opposite view. Moreover, very many rabbis have remained silent on the subject, leaving the historian with the difficulty of interpreting silence. In the ultra-Orthodox communities, which represent one extreme on the spectrum of Judaism, devotion to Torah study and close attention to performing the duties incumbent on Jews leave little room for secular studies, including not just Darwinism but science in general. Not surprisingly, the ultra-Orthodox rarely comment on evolution but when they do, they generally oppose it. One recurrent strategy has been to identify the shortcomings of science and make it appear of little consequence when compared with the robustness of the Torah. For example, the late Rabbi Menachem Schneersohn, the head of the flourishing messianic Lubavitcher sect, advised an apparently wavering student not to overrate the claims of science because it possesses a very limited factual base. Moreover, he dismissed such speculative theories as the theory of evolution because they were built on sand.[15]

Sections of the Orthodox and ultra-Orthodox communities have recently confronted the theory of evolution in responding to the high-profile activities of Nosson Slifkin, a young Orthodox rabbi. Widely known as the "Zoo Rabbi," Slifkin has written a number of books and conducted educational programs at various zoos in Israel and America. He argues that the pursuit of natural history sits comfortably with Torah study, portrays animals as God's creatures, and accepts evolution as a natural process that God employed in fashioning the species. Moreover, he represents his views as firmly grounded in traditional Jewish texts and the writings of such authorities as Rabbi Samson Raphael Hirsch (who sought to combine secular learning with Orthodox Judaism, 1808–88) and Rabbi Kook. For several years Slifkin and the educational programs proved very popular among the Orthodox and ultra-Orthodox. In the autumn of 2004, however, some leading members of the ultra-Orthodox community condemned his books, claiming that they are "full of heresy, twist and misrepresent the words of our sages and ridicule the foundations of our emunah [faith]. . . . The publication and distribution of these books present a spiritual danger and I fear that people will be adversely influenced by them." Jews were told not to read, own, or distribute these heretical works, and Slifkin was called upon to burn his books and make a public retraction.[16] What is the significance of the Slifkin Affair? It may indicate that the ultra-Orthodox and some sections of Orthodoxy are experiencing difficulty in coping with diversity within their own ranks, especially over an issue that engages an uncomfortable aspect of modernity. Yet it is difficult to determine whether the opposition to Slifkin and his support of the theory of evolution is confined to a few outspoken rabbis or whether their views are widely shared by members of these religious communities.

One final issue raised by the Slifkin Affair possesses much wider significance. Slifkin has been criticized for claiming that the universe is billions of years old, whereas the Torah, if interpreted literally, states that the world was created in six days. In his reply to this charge Slifkin points to the long tradition of nonliteral interpretations of Torah. Hence, the "days" of creation might be taken to mean epochs rather than days of twenty-four-hour duration. To quote Slifkin: "Rambam [Maimonides] interpreted them as a conceptual hierarchy of nature rather than a sequence of time. Rabbi Dovid Tzvi Hoffman [an eminent scholar, 1843–1921] interpreted them as six long eras, each billions of years long."[17] The crucial point is that within Judaism there is a robust dialectical tradition of nonliteral interpretations of Torah.

While it might be assumed that the various progressive movements would have consistently supported evolution, the picture is not so simple.

As Cherry has noted, Abraham Geiger (a leading Reform rabbi in Germany) rejected evolution in the 1860s because of the gap he envisaged between humans and the animals, and also because he could not understand how new species could be formed from existing ones.[18] Likewise, Marc Swetlitz has examined the responses to evolution in late-nineteenth-century America and found that both Conservative and Reform rabbis were divided on this issue. He noted that the varied responses of individuals depended on their attitudes to more pressing concerns, especially the future of their communities and their relations to both Christians and other sections of American Jewry.[19] A similar point about the importance of context emerges from another of Swetlitz's studies. In the early 1980s, he observed, the Central Conference of American [Reform] Rabbis was concerned that the strong advocacy of creationism by the Christian right might pose a severe political challenge to religious toleration within American society. Yet this threat led few of these rabbis to reflect on evolution and, when they did, they tended to oppose creationism by drawing a firm distinction between religion and science. More recently, evolutionary ideas have re-emerged on the coattails of Kabbalah in works by the Reform rabbi Laurence Kushner and the Reconstructionist rabbi Arthur Green. Green is particularly interesting: not only does he present creation as a progressive process occurring over time, but he downplays—though he does not eliminate—the role of natural selection, which he tries to integrate into his theology of development.[20]

Outside ultra-Orthodoxy, rabbis rarely exercise a great deal of influence over their communities, and therefore their views on evolution should not to be taken as reflecting the opinions of the whole Jewish community. We should therefore turn to another group—Jews working in the biological sciences—and ask how they have viewed evolution. One interesting contemporary example is Robert Pollack (b. 1940), professor of biological sciences and director of the Center for the Study of Science and Religion at Columbia University. Describing himself as having only turned to Modern Orthodoxy in recent years, Pollack has also ceased biological research and increasingly directed his thought to the ethical issues raised by science. While he greatly values evolutionary theory for its ability to explain phenomena, he nevertheless recoils from its lack of meaning for our lives, and he is particularly critical of dogmatic evolutionists. He therefore seeks to complement evolution by an ethical Jewish understanding of the human condition. Thus, rather than addressing the theological issues raised by evolution—a topic much discussed by Christian biologists—Pollack is more concerned with the problems of living as a Jew in the age of modern science.[21]

Unlike Pollack, many Jewish biologists are secularists, including such well-known examples as the late Stephen Jay Gould (1941–2002) and the population geneticist Richard Lewontin (b. 1929), both of whom worked at

Harvard University. Despite their commitment to evolutionary theory, they have both been prominent among the critics of the modern synthesis and of sociobiology. While other social, political, and biographical factors may be relevant, it has been claimed that their opposition stemmed in part from their concern that these fields are likely to promote anti-Semitism through the emphasis on genetic determinism and evolutionary progress, which in turn tend to be associated with notions of racial hierarchy.[22] As with Pollack, both Gould and Lewontin have been critical of the extension of evolution as a biological theory into areas with questionable ethical implications.

Given the divisions within the Jewish community and the significance of local context, it is impossible to gain an overall snapshot of Jewish attitudes to evolution. Yet, in the American context it is noticeable that Jews—even those who are critical of evolution—generally try to distance themselves from Christian fundamentalists and oppose the teaching of creationism or intelligent design (ID) in schools alongside evolution. Thus, the New York–based Jewish weekly, the *Forward*, praised Judge Jones's 2005 decision that ID should not be taught alongside evolution in a Dover, Pennsylvania, school. The editor saw the judge's ruling as maintaining the church-state separation and, more importantly, as a ringing endorsement of science. The real issue, he wrote, is "whether we want to prepare the next generation of Americans to pick up the battle against disease and begin solving the puzzles of the ecosphere, or we'd rather train them to accept what they're handed, secure in the faith that some puzzles aren't for unlocking."[23]

A recent investigation indicates that evolution is taught in science classes in most Modern Orthodox high schools, while the implications of the theory are often addressed by a rabbi in a religion class. Moreover, a survey carried out in the late 1980s found that 85 percent of the Modern Orthodox Jews canvassed accepted that evolutionary theory should be taught in schools, with an even higher proportion of less-orthodox Jews supporting this position.[24] A recent survey of American doctors found that Jews who responded were more ready than Catholic and Protestant doctors to accept evolution—94 percent, as against 86 and 59 percent, respectively.[25] Given that most recent surveys of the general American population have reported that half—and in some cases more than half—of the respondents oppose evolution and believe that humans had been created by God in the last 10,000 years, the admittedly sketchy evidence suggests that American Jews are less opposed to evolution than the American population as a whole.

Jewish reactions to the theory of evolution raise one final issue. Although a number of Jews have been opposed to Darwin's theory, there has been no virulent anti-evolutionist movement among Jews comparable with the very hostile creationist opposition by some Christians and Muslims. In part this stems from the Jewish respect for leaning and science. Also, the dialectic tradition in Torah exegesis does not encourage the kind of biblical literalism claimed by many Christian creationists. Finally, outside the messianic ultra-Orthodox sects (which manifest little interest in secular learning), there is in Judaism no close equivalent to the millenarian theologies that have taken firm root in certain Christian denominations, especially in America.

JEWS IN THE MODERN SCIENTIFIC COMMUNITY

After the middle of the nineteenth century, Jews began to attend universities in significant numbers and to move into the professions, principally in the major cities of Germany and Austria. Others of a more entrepreneurial spirit began pursuing technology, especially applied chemistry. Although career advance was often hindered by anti-Semitism—both at institutional and less formal levels—by the closing years of the century Jews were more likely to attend university than their Protestant or Catholic counterparts.[26] A minority also pursued careers in the universities.

The entry of Jews into the universities was in part due to their increasing affluence and security. Typically, they were the sons of businessmen rising through the middle classes. But the position of Jews was also greatly influenced by larger social and political changes in the decades beginning with the French Revolution and by the revolutions that affected much of Europe in 1848–49. Although the call for religious and social toleration was repeatedly challenged, Jews were increasingly able to enter institutions, such as universities, owing to the dismantling of traditional barriers and to greater social equality. It is important to note that these social changes were often perceived as bearing a close relation to the values of science (in the wider sense), since the call for a tolerant, meritocratic society and the rejection of one based on traditional privilege was often portrayed as an aspect of the scientifically sanctioned notion of social progress. One example of this connection is the *Wissenschaft des Judentums* (somewhat anachronistically translated as "the science of Judaism") movement, dating from a Jewish student group in 1819 Berlin that sought to integrate Jews into a wider, unified German society in accordance with the prevalent notions of progress and brotherhood.

In the twentieth century the spotlight turned to America. Despite lagging behind the leading European countries at the start of the century, in many fields America had become the scientific colossus by the outbreak of the First World War. In the rise of American science Jews played a significant role and were recruited through two main demographic routes, although a few Jewish scientists were from earlier generations of immigrant, such as the Nobel Prize–winning physicist Albert Abraham Michelson (1852–1931).[27]

The first main wave comprised the flood of immigrants following the assassination of the czar of Russia, Alexander II, in 1881, which sparked massive anti-Jewish pogroms and resulted in over two million Jews arriving in America in the period 1881–1924. The second occurred during the interwar years, when the scientific community in America (as well as in Britain, Canada, and later Israel) was greatly enriched by a highly educated but largely secular cohort of Jews (and others) who had been forced out of Europe by the fascists in the 1930s.

Most of the immigrants comprising this earlier wave were desperately poor, and they eked out their livelihoods in New York's Lower East Side and the depressed areas of other cities, such as Boston and Chicago. Work in the sweatshop or as a street trader was necessary for survival, but they were determined that they, and especially their children, should better themselves financially, socially, and intellectually. Fired by ambition and through hard work, many moved into the middle classes, and some families even achieved significant wealth over the next couple of generations. These Jewish immigrants also possessed strong intellectual traditions. Many possessed a deep knowledge and respect for Torah and Talmudic scholarship; many were immersed in innovative political ideas, such as communism. Jewish—often Yiddish—literature and theater flourished. Although the Lower East Side was awash with religious organizations—there were about three hundred Orthodox synagogues in 1914—many Jews turned away from their religion and, while remaining strongly committed to certain aspects of Jewish culture, adopted a more secular lifestyle, sometimes mixed with radical politics. As with many other groups of recent immigrants, Jews often tried to succeed by being innovative and were willing to take risks. They also set much store by education, and their determination to succeed was further increased in having to confront anti-Semitism from various sections of the American establishment.

Faced with a rising number of ambitious young Jews seeking entry to universities and particularly medical schools, many institutions imposed quotas on Jewish students during the interwar years. But, as Noah Efron notes, there was also a countervailing force arising from such funding agencies as the Carnegie and Rockefeller Foundations, which supported science in a nondiscriminatory manner and attracted many Jewish scientists. The Institute for Advanced Study at Princeton (founded in 1930), which was funded by Louis Bamberger and his sister Carrie Fuld, provides a particularly important example not only of Jewish philanthropy but also of a research institution where many creative Jews worked, including Albert Einstein (1879–1955).[28]

Although a slow trickle of European-trained Jewish scientists reached America during the first third of the twentieth century, the political successes of the National Socialists in Germany in 1933 and the subsequent dismissal of Jews from university positions resulted in an influx of first-rate and highly trained scientists into America, Britain, and several other countries that allowed immigration from the fascist states. This second wave of immigration added considerably to the luster of American science, yet these refugees often suffered discrimination and were accused of taking jobs from locals. They also played a not insignificant role on the political stage since, having directly experienced anti-Semitism in Europe and suffered frequent persecution by the Nazis, a number of émigré Jewish scientists, such as Hans Bethe and Edward Teller, worked on the Manhattan Project. Another Jew, the American-born J. Robert Oppenheimer, became the project's scientific director, while other Jewish scientists, including Einstein, contributed to the broader history of the atomic bomb.

Many factors attracted American Jews to science, particularly during the interwar period. Most importantly, science was less dominated by the old Protestant ethos than were other areas of either business or academe. Moreover, science was thought to possess an egalitarian ethos implying that anyone could succeed in science through intelligence and hard work (although in practice the playing field often was not entirely level). It is significant that in a much-cited and insightful essay of 1942, the sociologist Meyer R. Schkolnick (better known as Robert K. Merton, 1910–2003) posited four social norms that governed the practice of science—communalism, universalism, disinterestedness, and organized skepticism. His aim was to locate science firmly within an egalitarian and democratic society and wrest it from Nazi attempts to make science subservient to a political ideology. By portraying science—proper science—as objective, beyond interest groups, and subject only to its internal norms, Merton characterized the appeal of science to many Jews who believed that science was both a form of knowledge and a career where the outsider could succeed.[29] Furthermore, science provided a confluence between the ethos of America—a forward-looking country committed to technological progress—and the impetus of mainly second-generation Jewish Americans to set their immigrant past behind them and to play a role in this new world of opportunity.

As David Hollinger has argued, the interwar years saw the rise of the Jewish intellectual in America. This group comprised mainly second-generation Jewish immigrants, who challenged the Protestant hegemony that held sway in the leading American universities, many of which operated a quota system and positively discouraged the integration of Jews. The Jews who entered the intellectual life of America were mostly secular and they "reinforced the most de-Christianized of perspectives already current among the Anglo-Protestants." Such Jewish intellectuals held science in high esteem and many embarked on scientific careers.

As a result of these factors, Jews played a disproportionately large role in American science. To cite just two statistics; by the late 1960s Jews accounted for 17 percent of faculty members of seventeen of the most highly ranked American universities, at a time when Jews constituted only 3 percent of the population.[30] Second, approximately one-third of American winners of the Nobel Prizes in the sciences have been Jewish or possessed at least two Jewish grandparents.[31] By any standard the Jewish contribution to American science has been significant. As Efron has forcefully argued, "Save Vaudeville and then Hollywood, American Jews were nowhere more prominent than in science."[32] This suggests not only that many Jews saw science as a suitable career, but also that the Jewish community was not unwilling to embrace science and scientists.

Although some Orthodox Jews also pursued careers in science, for a significant proportion of the Jews who entered science in the middle decades of the twentieth century, a life in the predominantly secular pursuit of science was in some degree a repudiation of the strict religion of their fathers and grandfathers. Many were secular Jews, while others found progressive forms of Judaism more compatible with modernity and the values of science. One insight into the process of secularization is provided by the American Nobel prize–winning physicist Isidor Isaac Rabi (1898–1988), who grew up in New York's Lower East Side. He had arrived as a baby in 1899 from Rymanow, in Galicia, part of the crumbling Austro-Hungarian Empire. Like many recent immigrants, his family was strict in their traditional Jewish observance and avoided desecrating the Sabbath. They would not, for example, ride on the Sabbath. Yet, having read some introductory science books, the young, questioning Rabi was not satisfied by this restriction. Plucking up great courage, he took a journey on a streetcar one Sabbath and nervously awaited divine retribution. Perhaps the streetcar would crash? It did not. The outcome of this and other empirical tests challenged the religious worldview in which he had been nurtured and opened up the world of science with its secular values.[33]

This anecdote emphasizes one way in which traditional Judaism can be conceived as incompatible with a secular scientific worldview. For Rabi the streetcar experiment was a decisive moment in his life and, despite feelings of betrayal to his family, he proceeded to embrace science and the seductive values of modernity. And yet, as his biographer has noted, "while Rabi substituted scientific for religious explanation and abandon[ed] the practices of Judaism, the religious influences of his early environment remained a vital part of him: God is for Rabi a standard by which ideas and actions are judged." It is also clear that for Rabi, the practice of physics involved a religious duty, bringing him closer to God—although not the God of his childhood.[34]

Einstein's views on religion have been widely discussed. Although he apparently underwent a short period of intense religiosity in his youth, his family was not religious, he did not celebrate his bar mitzvah (which Jewish males traditionally do at the age of thirteen), and he generally paid scant attention to Judaism. Yet, from his many comments on the subject it is clear that he adopted reasoned—although rather idiosyncratic—views on religion. Most importantly, he denied a personal God. As he told one inquirer, he did not believe "in a God who concerns himself with [the] fates and actions of human beings." Given the emphasis that many—but by no means all—Jews and Christians place on God's awareness of our actions and on his ability to intervene in our lives, this view of Einstein's has often been subject to harsh criticism. However, to deny a personal God is not the same as denying God or rejecting religion. Thus Einstein proceeded to elaborate his "cosmic religion." To appreciate this we must turn to Einstein's understanding of causality—he postulated that all phenomena are completely determined by the laws of nature. We humans can grasp these causal relationships only to a very limited extent, whereas God is the creator of these laws. God is thus manifested through "the laws of the Universe as a spirit vastly superior to that of man." For Einstein God is not identical to nature; rather, God transcends nature. Although Einstein considered that we can glimpse God through nature, he also insisted that great music and great art offer similar insights. Einstein stated that he was religious and believed that his "cosmic religion" went far beyond conventional religions by offering a more rational and more intellectually satisfying understanding of God. There are several instances of his rejecting atheism and expressing tolerance and respect for religious Jews and members of other faiths. Yet in his own thinking about religion Einstein departed significantly from many aspects of Jewish tradition. He often stated that his views on religion were similar to those of the seventeenth-century Jewish rationalist and heretic Baruch Spinoza.[35]

In contrast to Einstein, some twentieth-century Jewish scientists have adopted aggressively antireligious positions, none more so than the Nobel Prize–winning physicist Steven Weinberg (b. 1933), who is quoted as claiming: "Religion is an insult to human dignity. With or without it you would have good people doing good things and evil people doing evil things. But for good people to do evil things, that takes religion."[36] Weinberg, who grew up in New York's East Side, has frequently attacked those who claim that physics reveals the religious meaning of the universe. Moreover, he recently signed the "Declaration in Defense of Science and Secularism," issued by the Center for Inquiry in Washington, D.C., which portrays science as necessarily allied with secularism and as opposed to religion.[37]

Sigmund Freud (1856–1939), living in Vienna at the turn of the century, provides another interesting example of an apparently secularized Jew and scientist. Earlier commentators often stressed his commitment to materialist science, his outward appearance as a solid Austrian citizen, and his distance from Judaism, but more recently a number of scholars have uncovered the depth and extent of Freud's Jewishness. Although Freud's father had made a substantial break with Jewish tradition, Freud clearly identified himself as Jewish and aligned himself with the many fairly secular Jews living in Vienna who constituted its intellectual and artistic elite. As a Jew and an outsider to Viennese society, Freud considered that his Jewish background not only freed him from many conventional prejudices but also gave him the emotional strength to put forward challenging ideas and to withstand the not-unexpected opposition to his views, especially his claim about the centrality of human sexual drives.[38]

Issues relating to Jewish identity appear in many of Freud's writings, leading one recent commentator to claim that "Jewish thought, Jewish philosophy and Jewish history flooded . . . [the] foundations [of Freudian psychoanalysis], investing it with the specific inward-consciousness of the Jews, who were newly released in the nineteenth century from their ghettos and at least some of their traditions."[39] More specifically, in arguing that jokes display the role of the unconscious, Freud drew upon the acknowledged heritage of Jewish humor. Moreover, despite his own commitment to science and rationality, Freud felt he had to address a deep-seated irrationality within Judaism and, ultimately, within the human psyche. What emerges clearly from the case of Freud is that he was not confronted by a simple choice between science and religion—between modernity and an ancient tradition—with a clean break from the latter. Instead, religious perceptions and ideals were deeply ingrained in him and affected the kind of science he pursued and the way he pursued it.

However much Freud may have wanted to distance himself from the Orthodox world of his grandparents, the recurrent anti-Semitism in Austria never allowed him to forget that he was a Jew. He repeatedly fought against anti-Semitism and against the Nazis as the purveyors of anti-Semitism. When the situation in Europe deteriorated, he and his daughter Anna fled to England in 1938, a year before his death.

Despite the numerical dominance of secular Jewish scientists, there has also been a sizable Orthodox contingent, especially in Israel. In 1947 the American-based Association of Orthodox Jewish Scientists (AOJS) was founded. By the late 1960s it had grown to nearly 2,000 members, although its membership has subsequently declined. The AOJS's aims include addressing "practical problems encountered by Orthodox Jews and their children in the study or practice of scientific pursuits" and helping to address "the apparent points of conflict between scientific theory and Orthodox Judaism." Moreover, the AOJS offers expert advice to rabbis on "the implications of technological developments for the Jewish religious law." such as in vitro fertilization. Its publications express a range of views about Darwin's theory of evolution, but the predominant position is that the theory is scientifically inadequate.[40]

The charismatic physicist and engineer Herman Branover edits the journal *B'Or Ha'Torah* (By the light of Torah; described on its website as "A journal for the wondering Jew"), subtitled "Science, Art and Modern Life in the Light of the Torah." Many of the articles published here indicate how Orthodox Jews engage the problems raised by modern science. For example, one recent contributor asks how genetic manipulation affects the designation of which foods are kosher. Should, for example, plants genetically engineered with DNA from a nonkosher animal be considered nonkosher?[41] Through such channels as the AOJS, the recently founded Torah Science Foundation, and *B'Or Ha'Torah*, some members of the Orthodox community are in lively debate over the implications for Judaism of modern science and vice versa.

BETWEEN TRADITION AND MODERNITY

Apart from some groups of the ultra-Orthodox, Jews have generally been receptive to modern science. In part this is a continuation of the openness of the medieval tradition discussed in chapter 1, but it should also be understood as a crucial aspect of the Jewish engagement with modernity and (outside Israel) with host communities. As argued earlier, science has played both a direct and an indirect role in how Jews have negotiated the terrain between traditionalism on the one hand and modernity and secularism on the other. The precise form of this engagement depends greatly on local factors, such as the level of discrimination against Jews, although this has often been less in the sciences than in other areas.

In order to explain why so many Jews have entered science, especially over the past century, it has sometimes been claimed that Jews are particularly well suited to the pursuit of science because of the traditional method used in Jewish religious education in which students dispute points of Talmud. This is said to provide a good training for a scientist because students learn to draw logical inferences and to find holes in other people's arguments. Although this claim is not very convincing—many successful Jewish scientists (including Freud and Einstein) did not receive this kind of religious training—other factors have indeed been conducive to a scientific outlook. One is a questioning, anti-authoritarian tradition, which, as Menachem Fisch has argued, is similar to Karl Popper's philosophy of science.[42] Another is the marginalized social position of Jews in many countries, which has impelled them to succeed in areas like science. To combat the anti-Semitic portrayal of Jews as intellectually inferior by members of the host community, success in a rigorously intellectual subject such as science has been of paramount importance. Thus Jews have been attracted to science because it has allowed them not only to demonstrate to the majority culture that Jews can be productive Germans, Americans, or Englishmen, but also to transcend the local to become players on the larger international stage.

With a few interesting exceptions, rabbis have generally paid little attention to the sciences in their sermons and writings.[43] There is no tradition within Judaism comparable to the parson naturalist in Protestant England (who is said to have spent six days of the week collecting the local flora and fauna and the seventh reflecting on the power, wisdom, and goodness of the Creator). In Judaism, the principal role of rabbis is to expound traditional knowledge and values, although they often take on many other responsibilities. Orthodox rabbis have generally insisted on the superiority of Torah and of a religious understanding of the world over that provided by science. Yet this attitude toward science should not be viewed as opposition, since it can incorporate modern science into existing conceptual schemes. Thus, one frequently deployed strategy has been to attempt to understand science through the philosophy of Kabbalah.

Yet, despite the attention paid to science by medieval Jewish thinkers and the many Jews who have pursued careers in science, the modern literature on the relation between Judaism and science is surprisingly thin. A few popular books address this subject,[44] but, as the philosopher Norbert Samuelson has forcefully argued, Jewish thinkers have failed to grapple with developments in the sciences over the past couple of centuries. This failure, claims Samuelson, has rendered Jewish philosophy moribund, and he argues that if it is to revive it must now pay close attention to the sciences.[45] This is a major challenge not only to students of Jewish philosophy but also to the whole Jewish community.

NOTES

For their helpful comments and suggestions on an earlier version of this chapter I would like to express my appreciation to the editors, John Brooke and Ronald Numbers, and to the other participants at the "Science and Religion Around the World" conference held at Green College, University of British Columbia, May 2007.

1. Among the many introductory works on Jewish history are Hilary L. Rubinstein, Dan Cohn-Sherbok, Abraham J. Edelheit, and William D. Rubinstein, *The Jews in the Modern World: A History since 1750* (London: Arnold, 2002); and Paul Kriwaczek, *Yiddish Civilisation: The Rise and Fall of a Forgotten Nation* (London: Weidenfeld and Nicolson, 2005). There are also numerous histories of Jews in specific countries,

such as Todd M. Endelman, *The Jews of Britain, 1656–2000* (Berkeley: University of California Press, 2002); and Hasia R. Diner, *The Jews of the United States, 1654 to 2000* (Berkeley: University of California Press, 2006). On the historical relations of Judaism to science, see items listed in the bibliography.

2. Shmuel Feiner, *The Jewish Enlightenment*, trans. Chaya Naor (Philadelphia: University of Pennsylvania Press, 2004), 21–67.

3. David Ruderman, *Jewish Thought and Scientific Discovery in Early Modern Europe* (New Haven, Conn.: Yale University Press, 1995), 334–38.

4. Ruderman, *Jewish Thought*, 345–68; H. J. Schoeps, "La Vie et l'Oeuvre de Gumpertz Levison: Savant Juif du XVIIIᵉ Siècle," *Revue d'Histoire de la Médicine Hébraïque* 27 (1955): 133–43; H. M. Graupe, "Moredechai Gumpel (Levison)," *Bulletin des Leo Baeck Instituts* 5 (1962): 1–12; Moshe Pelli, "Mordechai Gumpel Schnaber: The First Religious Reform Theoretician of the Hebrew Haskalah in Germany," *Jewish Quarterly Review* 64 (1974): 289–313.

5. Feiner, *Jewish Enlightenment*, 185–290, quotation on 266.

6. Rabbi Formiggini quoted by Naphtali Wessely, *Ein Mishpat* (Berlin, 1784), in Feiner, *Jewish Enlightenment*, 180.

7. Ira Robinson, "Kabbala and Science in 'Sefer Ha-Berit': A Modernization Strategy for Orthodox Jews," *Modern Judaism* 9 (1989): 275–88.

8. Gumpertz Levison, *An Account of the Epidemical Sore Throat: with the Method of Treatment: Illustrated by Cases and Observations* (London: B. White, 1778); Emanuel Mendes da Costa, *A Natural History of Fossils*, vol.1, pt.1 (London: Davies, Reymers, 1757); and *Historia Naturalis Testaceorum Britanniae, or the British Conchology*, 2 vols. (London: Millan, 1778).

9. Raphael Meldola, "The Presidential Address; Delivered . . . at the Annual Meeting, January 27th, 1883," *Transactions of the Essex Field Club* 3 (1884): 59–93, on 75.

10. David Kohn and Ralph Colp, "'A Real Curiosity': Charles Darwin Reflects on a Communication from Rabbi Naphtali Levy," *European Legacy* 1 (1996): 1716–27; Edward O. Dodson, "*Toldot Adam*: A Little-Known Chapter in the History of Darwinism," *Perspectives on Science and Christian Faith* 52 (2000): 47–54.

11. Michael Shai Cherry, "Creation, Evolution, and Jewish Thought," (Ph.D. diss., Brandeis University, 2001), 148.

12. The following discussion is based on Cherry, "Creation, Evolution, and Jewish Thought," 205–24; and Carl Feit, "Modern Orthodoxy and Evolution: The Models of Rabbi J. B. Soloveitchik and Rabbi A. I. Kook," in *Jewish Tradition and the Challenge of Darwinism*, ed. Geoffrey Cantor and Marc Swetlitz, 208–24 (Chicago: University of Chicago Press, 2006).

13. Abraham Isaac ha-Kohen Kook, *Orot HaKodesh*, quoted in Feit, "Modern Orthodoxy and Evolution," 216.

14. Feit, "Modern Orthodoxy and Evolution," 224.

15. Menachem M. Schneersohn, "A Letter on Science and Judaism," in *Challenge: Torah Views on Science and Its Problems*, ed. Aryah Carmell and Cyril Domb, 142–47 (London: Association of Orthodox Jewish Scientists/Feldheim, 1976). See also Michael Rosenak, "Jewish Fundamentalism in Israeli Education," in *Fundamentalisms and Society: Reclaiming the Sciences, the Family, and Education*, ed. Martin E. Marty and R. Scott Appleby, 374–414 (Chicago: University of Chicago Press, 1993).

16. See Nosson Slifkin, *The Science of Torah: The Reflection of Torah in the Laws of Science, the Creation of the Universe, and the Development of Life* (Southfield, Mich.: Targum; Nanuet, N.Y.: Feldheim, 2001), and the documents posted on www.zootorah.com.

17. See Slifkin's "A General Response to the Charge of Heresy" at www.zootorah.com/controversy/scienceresponse.html.

18. Cherry, "Creation, Evolution, and Jewish Thought," 108–11, and 149.

19. Marc Swetlitz, "Responses of American Reform Rabbis to Evolutionary Theory, 1864–1888," in *The Interaction of Scientific and Jewish Cultures in Modern Times*, ed. Yakov Rabkin and Ira Robinson, 103–25 (Lewiston, N.Y.: Edwin Mellen Press, 1995).

20. Marc Swetlitz, "Responses to Evolution by Reform, Conservative and Reconstructivist Rabbis in Twentieth-Century America," in Cantor and Swetlitz, *Jewish Tradition*, 47–70.

21. For example, Pollack's public statement at www.pbs.org/wgbh/evolution/religion/faith/statement_04.html.

22. Michael Ruse, *Mystery of Mysteries: Is Evolution a Social Construction?* (Cambridge, Mass.: Harvard University Press, 1999), 144–45, 165–66, 168.

23. "Dover, Darwin, and the Assault on Science," *Forward*, December 30, 2005; www.forward.com/articles/1852/.

24. Rena Selya, "Torah and Madda? Evolution in the Jewish Educational Context," in Cantor and Swetlitz, *Jewish Tradition*, 188–207. See also Shai Cherry, "Crisis Management via Biblical Interpretation: Fundamentalism, Modern Orthodoxy, and Genesis," in Cantor and Swetlitz, *Jewish Tradition*, 166–87; Ira Robinson, "'Practically I Am a Fundamentalist': Twentieth-Century Orthodox Jews Contend with Evolution and Its Implications," in Cantor and Swetlitz, *Jewish Tradition*, 71–88.

25. This survey of 1,472 physicians was carried out by the Louis Finkelstein Institute for Religious and Social Studies on May 13–15, 2005: www.jtsa.edu/research/finkelstein/surveys/evolution.shtml.

26. Noah J. Efron, *Judaism and Science: A Historical Introduction* (Westport, Conn.: Greenwood, 2006), 170–74.

27. Dorothy M. Livingston, *The Master of Light: A Biography of Albert A. Michelson* (New York: Charles Scribner's Sons, 1973).

28. Efron, *Judaism and Science*, 185–98.

29. Robert Merton, *A Life of Learning* (ACLS Occasional Paper, ca. 1994); Merton, "A Note on Science and Democracy," *Journal of Legal and Political Sociology* 1 (1942): 115–26, reprinted as "The Normative Structure of Science" in Merton, *The Sociology of Science: Theoretical and Empirical Investigations* (Chicago: University of Chicago Press, 1973), 267–78.

30. David A. Hollinger, *Science, Jews, and Secular Culture: Studies in Mid-Twentieth-Century American Intellectual History* (Princeton, N.J.: Princeton University Press, 1996), quotation on 24.

31. See "Jewish Nobel Prize Winners" at www.jinfo.org/. This website also claims that overall 26 percent of Nobel laureates in physics and 20 percent of those in chemistry were Jewish. However, some of those named were not practicing Jews, such as Niels Bohr, whose mother was Jewish but whose father was a Lutheran.

32. Efron, *Judaism and Science*, 178.

33. John S. Rigden, *Rabi, Scientist and Citizen* (New York: Basic Books, 1987), 24.

34. Ibid., x; see also 17–29, 79–80, 234, and 269.

35. Max Jammer, *Einstein and Religion: Physics and Theology* (Princeton: Princeton University Press, 1999), quotations on 49 and 148. See also John Hedley Brooke, "'If I were God': Einstein and Religion," *Zygon* 41 (2006): 941–54. Einstein overstated the similarity between his views and Spinoza's.

36. Quoted in Carey Goldberg, "Crossing Flaming Swords over God and Physics," *New York Times*, April 20, 1999, F, 5.

37. See the Center for Inquiry website, www.cfidc.org/declaration.html.

38. Sigmund Freud to B'nei Brith Lodge of Vienna, May 6, 1926, in *Letters of Sigmund Freud, 1873–1939*, ed. E. Freud, 367–68 (London: Hogarth Press, 1961).

39. Stephen Frosh, *Hate and the "Jewish Science": Anti-Semitism, Nazism and Psychoanalysis* (Basingstoke, Hampshire: Palgrave Macmillan, 2005), 10. A recent and important addition to the literature is Jay Geller, *On Freud's Jewish Body: Migrating Circumcisions* (New York: Fordham University Press, 2008). Scholars, however, remain divided over the significance of Judaism for the history of Freud and psychoanalysis.

40. For current members and other information, see www.aojs.org. Carmell and Domb, *Challenge*, was one of the AOJS's most prominent publications.

41. See www.borhatorah.org/

42. Menachem Fisch, *Rational Rabbis: Science and Talmudic Culture* (Bloomington: Indiana University Press, 1997).

43. For example, Rabbi Israel Lipschitz of Gdansk; see Aryeh Kaplan, *Immortality, Resurrection, and the Age of the Universe: A Kabbalistic View* (Hoboken, N.J.: Ktav, 1993), 115.

44. These include Nathan Aviezer, *In the Beginning . . . : Biblical Creation and Science* (Hoboken, N.J.: Ktav, 1990); Jacob Landa, *Torah and Science* (Hoboken, N.J.: Ktav, 1991); Gerald Schroeder, *The Science of God: The Convergence of Scientific and Biblical Wisdom* (New York: Free Press, 1997).

45. Norbert M. Samuelson, *Jewish Faith and Modern Science: On the Death and Rebirth of Jewish Philosophy* (Lanham, Md.: Rowman and Littlefield, 2009).

3

Early Christianity

Peter Harrison and David C. Lindberg

Three theories have dominated thought and discussion about the relationship between Christianity and the natural sciences in the first seventeen centuries of the Christian era. The first of them, which continues to flourish despite a dearth of supporting historical evidence, maintains that throughout its history the Christian Church has been the enemy of science, consistently erecting theological obstacles to scientific progress. The trial of Galileo and various episodes of medieval conflict are regularly presented as cases in point. This myth originated in the French "Enlightenment" of the eighteenth century. It became common currency in the nineteenth and twentieth centuries through popular books by John W. Draper and Andrew Dickson White and continues to thrive in the present.[1]

A second theory has emerged in the writings of a relatively small scholarly elite of the twentieth century, who maintain (motivated, in some cases, by partisan religious objectives) that Christianity, and only Christianity, was qualified to supply the fundamental assumptions of order and rationality required for the development of modern science.[2]

The third position, which we will defend, acknowledges a more complicated relationship—one of both opposition and encouragement—between Christianity and science. In this view the pattern of interaction has shaped both Christian theology and the natural sciences without exclusively favoring one over the other.[3]

One more preliminary: When did the natural sciences, as an activity or a body of knowledge, make their first appearance? Was there anything that should count as science before, say, the Renaissance of the fifteenth and sixteenth centuries? Absolutely, yes! In antiquity, the patristic period, and the Middle Ages we find the beginnings, the roots, the sources, and ancestors of many modern scientific disciplines and practices, some of which bear a family resemblance to their offspring, others bordering on identity. Many of these early developments were inherited from the "classical tradition" of ancient Greece—a body of philosophical knowledge dealing with the physical world (in both its physical and mathematical garbs), transmitted by a variety of means to the Roman Empire, where it became the intellectual property of scholars, both Christian and pagan.[4]

Our story begins with the advent of Christianity as an organized religion late in the first century CE. Despite serious opposition, Christianity grew from those beginnings as a tiny sect into the state religion of the Roman Empire in a period of just over three hundred years.[5] Along the way it met opposition from an array of competitors, some ready to do battle, including an intimidating collection of pagan cults. These were not the only troublemakers; a variety of Christian heretics had also to be dealt with, including Gnostics and Manichaeans. But religious dispute is not our subject.[6]

Besides the Christian Scriptures, the intellectual landscape of the early centuries of Christendom was defined by the "classical tradition"—by which we mean the accumulated learning of Greek and Roman antiquity, passed vertically downward through time and horizontally across geographical and cultural space. The classical tradition embraced many subjects, including history, drama, poetry, political theory, metaphysics, epistemology, and what we would call the "mathematical and natural sciences."[7] Some of these natural sciences were collectively known as "natural philosophy" rather than "science." More important, for our purposes, these sciences included what we now know as cosmology, astronomy, physics, optics, metallurgy, medicine, botany, zoology, and more. But it was a thin and frequently second- or third-hand version of the classical tradition that was inherited by the early fathers of the Christian Church. Many important Greek originals had been lost along the way, and very little of the remainder was available in Latin translations for Western scholars who did not read Greek. But enough survived (and enough Romans read Greek) to give the early church fathers meat and gristle (depending on your point of view) to chew on; and, of course, there were Roman originals written in Latin, capable of fueling the fires of dissent and debate.

THE PATRISTIC PERIOD

Most of the church fathers were educated, adult converts who had received their education in the pagan schools. In their efforts to create and defend Christian doctrine, it was inevitable that, where relevant, they would employ the logical tools of the classical tradition and its philosophical and scientific content. Some pagan philosophical doctrines could be easily harmonized with Christian theology. Many of the early church fathers found the Platonic tradition (available primarily in its Neoplatonic version) amenable to Christian assimilation. For example, Plato's Demiurge, who constructed the cosmos out of primitive materials, could, without too much twisting, be viewed as a primitive, monotheistic version of the Christian God creating the world out of nothing. The Christian attempt to understand the world in Platonic terms is clearly visible in the writings of such harmonizers as Clement (ca. 150–ca. 220) and Origen (185–253), both from Alexandria, Augustine (354–430), from Hippo in North Africa, and others.[8]

But we also find ample Christian opposition to the classical tradition. Tertullian (fl. 195–215), one of the earliest theologians of Latin Christendom, has become a symbol of the Christian attack on pagan learning and the "battle between faith and reason." Despite his own superior education in the classical tradition, Tertullian bitterly attacked the results of human wisdom. He wrote that the (biblical) apostle Paul, in his visit to Athens, had "become acquainted with that human wisdom which pretends to know the truth, whereas it only corrupts it, and is divided into its own manifold heresies." He continued, explicitly attacking the harmonizers: "There can be no Christianity composed of Stoic, Platonic, and dialectical elements. We have no need for curiosity after Christ Jesus, no investigation after the Gospel. When we believe [the Gospel], we need give credence to nothing else!"[9] But this is Tertullian at his most polemical. In more thoughtful moments, he took a reasoned approach to the classical tradition, going so far as to identify Christianity as the offspring of Greek philosophy and Judaism.[10]

Another oft-cited example of tension between Christianity and pagan learning is the martyrdom of Hypatia (ca. 360–415). Daughter of the mathematician and philosopher Theon of Alexandria, Hypatia was herself a gifted philosopher who became head of the Platonist School in Alexandria. She met a violent death at the hands of a Christian mob, although reports vary on the identity of her killers and their precise motivations. Not surprisingly, perhaps, some have taken this event to typify the hostile relations between Christianity and Greek philosophy during this period.[11] However, it is likely that Hypatia was more a victim of political intrigue than a martyr for science. Among her students were many Christians, including the bishop of Ptolomais, Synseus of Cyrene, with whom Hypatia maintained a correspondence. The Christian writer Socrates Scholasticus, one of our chief sources for the circumstances of Hypatia's death, spoke of her "extraordinary dignity and virtue."[12] Moreover, the Neoplatonist philosophy that Hypatia taught, as already noted, was one which many Christian thinkers found congenial.

The patristic philosopher-theologian who most eloquently and influentially addressed Christian attitudes toward the classical tradition in all of its varieties, including the natural sciences, was St. Augustine of Hippo. Augustine, born nearly a century and a half after the death of Tertullian, and a contemporary of Hypatia, did more to influence Christian attitudes toward scientific knowledge than any theologian of the Middle Ages. Scattered throughout his writings are warnings against overvaluation of the classical tradition. In his *Confessions*, Augustine expressed regret for the effort he had devoted to rhetoric, logic, geometry, music, and arithmetic—studies that "served not to my use, but rather to my destruction," for (as he had come to understand) he had been investigating the Creation rather than the creator. He added astronomy to the list of useless knowledge in his *On Christian Doctrine*, acknowledging that knowing the course of the moon may assist in determining the date of Easter but adding that "knowledge of this kind . . . , although not allied with any superstition, is of very little use in the treatment of the Divine Scriptures and even impedes it through fruitless study."[13]

Here, and in innumerable other passages in his writings, Augustine did not deny that the pagan philosophical writings of the classical tradition contain truth; rather, he questioned the legitimacy of philosophical or scientific study as a matter of misplaced priorities. Insofar as they served Christian religion, the fruits of philosophy should not be feared but accepted and put to work. He delivered the same message when he wrote: "If those who are called philosophers, especially the Platonists, have said things that are indeed true and are well accommodated to our faith, they should not be feared; rather what they have said should be taken from them as from unjust possessors and converted to our use."[14] Pagan knowledge is to serve as the *handmaiden* of Christian religion. It is not to be loved but to be used.

But does this "use" extend to scientific knowledge within the classical tradition? Consider the following example from Augustine's *Literal Commentary on Genesis*:

> Usually, even a non-Christian knows something about the earth, the heavens, and the other elements of this world, about the motion and orbit of the stars and even their size and relative positions, about the predictable eclipses of the sun and moon, the cycles of the years and the seasons, about the kinds of animals, shrubs, stones, and so forth, and this knowledge he holds as certain from reason and experience. Now it is a disgraceful and dangerous thing for an infidel to hear a Christian, presumably giving the meaning of Holy Scripture, talking nonsense on these topics; and we should take all means to prevent such an embarrassing situation, in which people show up vast ignorance in a Christian and laugh it to scorn.[15]

Augustine proceeded to practice what he preached. He discussed Greco-Roman ideas about lightning, thunder, clouds, wind, rain, dew, snow, frost, storms, tides, plants and animals, matter and form, the four elements, the doctrine of natural place, seasons, time, the calendar, the planets, planetary motion, the phases of the moon, astrological influence (which he vigorously condemned), the soul, sensation, sound, light and shade, and number

theory. For all his worry about overvaluing the science of the classical tradition, Augustine applied it with a vengeance to biblical interpretation in the
Commentary.

Augustine's deep ambivalence toward the natural sciences should be
evident. Of marginal applicability to the Christian's terrestrial pilgrimage,
they are of secondary or tertiary importance. Nonetheless, he judged them
indispensable for scriptural interpretation and apologetic efforts. Despite
this ambivalence, it was Augustine's articulation of the handmaiden formula
that would govern attitudes toward the natural sciences to the end of the
Middle Ages and beyond. Though not intrinsically of great value, the natural
sciences of the classical tradition gained extrinsic value insofar as they met
the needs of Christianity and the church.[16]

THE EARLY MIDDLE AGES

As the Roman Empire declined into civil disorder and the chaos of barbarian
invasion and immigration, economic decline, depopulation, and urban
decay, schools disappeared (except in a few of the larger cities), and learning
declined precipitously. Fortunately, a new institution—the monastery—
emerged in time to preserve literacy and keep alive the aforementioned
"thin" version of the classical tradition. Monasteries were not intended to
replace the Roman schools but to serve quite a different clientele—men and
women who wished to withdraw from the world into lifelong pursuit of contemplation and holiness. Important by-products of monasticism were literacy (required for the reading of Scripture and devotional literature) and the
copying of texts.

The majority of this literature was biblical or devotional, and taken as a
whole it included only a modest number of books belonging to the classical
tradition. But there were exceptions. The monastery of Vivarium in southern Italy had a scriptorium for the copying of books, including secular books
belonging to the classical tradition. Its founder, Cassiodorus (ca. 480–ca.
575), wrote a handbook of monastic studies in which he recommended a
substantial number of pagan authors. Another exception is found in Irish
monasteries of the sixth century and following, where the mathematical arts
were seriously pursued.

Such science as we find in the earliest monasteries was mostly related
to practical concerns: medicine, mathematics, timekeeping (to determine
the times for prayer), and regulation of the annual calendar (to fix the
date of Easter and other religious holidays). As monasticism matured in
the seventh, eighth, and ninth centuries, its store of scientific knowledge
increased—though with wide variations. It would typically cover a good bit

of basic astronomy (mostly nonmathematical), including the periods, stations, and retrogradations of planetary motions, phases of the moon, even planetary apsides (positions of closest approach and farthest departure from the earth). All members of the monastic community would know that they lived on a spherical earth, and some would have a pretty good idea of its circumference.[17] Every monastery would have facilities for treating medical ailments of the community and a monk or nun skilled in knowledge of medical remedies and treatments. Finally, botanical knowledge was a necessity for both medical and dietary purposes.

Did the monasteries contribute to the store of scientific knowledge or diminish it? Their mission was religious rather than scientific, and their scientific contribution was primarily one of preservation and transmission during a very dangerous period in the history of European learning. But preservation and transmission are fundamental obligations of any serious scientific tradition, and without the monasteries it seems clear that the quantity and quality of European scientific knowledge in (say) the year 800 would have been less rather than more.

REVIVAL OF LEARNING AND EDUCATION

During the early Middle Ages, as the empire fell apart and Roman authority declined, the Christian Church (the state religion since the late fourth century) became the lone source of centralized authority and order—priests and bishops answering to its demands. Toward the end of the seventh century, an alternative source of authority emerged, in the form of a Frankish dynasty: first the Merovingian kings, followed by the Carolingians. The most important of the Carolingian kings was Charlemagne (or Charles the Great), who ruled over a kingdom embracing much of central Europe (768–814). It was around his court and by his edicts that a resurgence of learning (sometimes called the "Carolingian Renaissance") occurred. He mandated the founding of cathedral and monastic schools, improvement in the education of the clergy, and the copying of books; and he brought together in his court many of the finest European scholars. This scholarly activity, which placed considerable emphasis on astronomical knowledge, laid the foundations for a true revolution in medieval scholarship four hundred years later.[18] The pursuit of scientific knowledge throughout this period was directed toward the recovery of the (mostly) lost scientific knowledge of the classical tradition. This quest was carried out almost exclusively by highly placed literate Christian clerics, who perceived no contradiction between their obligations as Christian leaders and the pursuit of scientific knowledge.

Western recovery continued to accelerate over the next 350–400 years. Europe experienced extraordinary political, social, and economic revival. A population explosion led to reurbanization (undoing the legacy of the barbarian invasions) and economic development, which in turn created opportunities for educated people. Schools multiplied in number and size. The first universities emerged, offering advanced religious, professional, and scientific education. Important above all was the translation of Greek and Arabic sources into Latin by a band of hardy, highly educated European translators. These translations provided educated European scholars with a vastly larger, more complete version of the classical tradition (the "thick" version), including the major scientific achievements of Greek antiquity, to which Islamic improvements and original additions had been made.[19] The time was ripe for serious scientific effort; but before that could flourish, a now powerful church bureaucracy needed to come to terms with the contents of the classical tradition, newly regained and not entirely benign from a theological standpoint.

CONFLICT AND ASSIMILATION

One of the major turning points in the intellectual history of western Europe was the acquisition (in the twelfth century, continuing in the thirteenth) of the "thick version" of the classical tradition in Latin translation.[20] New learning, astonishing in breadth, depth, and quantity, charged onto the stage, demanding to be heard. It made its way to centers of learning, where it revolutionized the curriculum of the universities and set the intellectual agenda for the thirteenth century and beyond. The task was to master a body of knowledge, pagan in origin and vast in scope, to assess its compatibility with a (by now) well-developed Christian theology, and (following Augustine's advice) to appropriate for religious purposes whatever proved useful.

Most of the newly translated literature was theologically benign. Technical treatises that dealt with such scientific subjects as mathematics, astronomy, optics, statics and dynamics, meteorology, and medicine were superior to any previously existing European knowledge on their subjects and were received with enthusiasm. They filled an intellectual void and were soon being lectured on in the universities, without opposition or disapproval. Trouble arose with regard to broader subjects that had implications for theology and the dominant worldview: cosmology, metaphysics, epistemology, psychology, and of course theology itself.

Opposition focused primarily on the works of Aristotle (d. 322 BCE, the towering figure of ancient Greek philosophy) and his commentators. Most of the Aristotelian corpus proved not only unproblematic but overwhelmingly persuasive, capable of teaching scholars how to think about all manner of subjects; and it is this, rather than coercion from the church, that explains the dominance of Aristotelian philosophy and science in the later Middle Ages. Alongside these benefits, however, Aristotelian metaphysics and epistemology raised a collection of serious problems for Christian theology. These included Aristotle's claim that the universe was eternal, without beginning or end; his denial of personal immortality, divine providence, and free will; his stubborn naturalism and materialism; and his exclusive reliance on sense perception and rational inference in the pursuit of truth. The dilemma confronting the intellectual leaders of Christendom is obvious: Aristotelian philosophy was both dangerous and valuable. It was not to be repudiated but to be disciplined—to be domesticated without being emasculated.

Surviving historical documents tell us how the problem was managed at one institution: the University of Paris, Europe's premier university at the time. In 1210, Aristotle's writings on natural philosophy were banned from the undergraduate faculty by a committee of local bishops. In 1215, the ban was reaffirmed. In 1231, the ban was qualified by the pope: Aristotle's works were to be purged of error, so that the remainder could be put to use (an acknowledgment of the high value placed on that remainder). However, the commission charged with this task apparently never met, and no purged version of Aristotle has been found. In 1255, the faculty of arts at the University of Paris passed new statutes that required the teaching of all known works by Aristotle, apparently making mandatory what was already the practice. In the next few decades, we find massive attempts by scholars such as Albertus Magnus and Thomas Aquinas to Christianize Aristotle—and at the same time to Aristotelianize Christianity—by weeding out Aristotelian errors, crafting compromises, and defining the proper relationship between Christian theology and this important collection of pagan learning. These efforts were driven by the belief that Aristotelian philosophy and Christian theology, properly interpreted, are complementary roads to truth.

The events in this Parisian tale came to a head in 1270 and 1277, when the bishop of Paris, Etienne Tempier, condemned a collection of theological propositions (13 and 219 propositions, respectively) allegedly being taught in the faculty of arts. The crucial propositions for our purposes addressed things that God could not do, because Aristotle's philosophy ruled them impossible—for example, that God could not create multiple worlds or qualities without a subject, because within the framework of Aristotelian philosophy these things are impossible. Tempier's purpose in issuing the condemnations was not to destroy Aristotelian philosophy and science but to proclaim unequivocally that limits may *not* be placed on the creative acts of an omniscient, omnipotent God (exempting only those that involve a self-contradiction). God's freedom to act may not be limited by the dictates of Aristotelian philosophy. Finally, fifty years later, in 1325, the numerous articles of the condemnations pertaining to the teachings of Thomas Aquinas were revoked.

The Middle Ages saw many instances of condemnation of doctrinal stances directed toward a single individual; the condemnations of 1270 and 1277 were exceptional in their focus on content rather than culprit. Any scholar who had violated these condemnations was to report to Tempier for punishment. A dominant interpretation of the condemnations of 1270 and 1277, proposed by the early-twentieth-century historian and philosopher Pierre Duhem, who first gave them notoriety, is that Tempier's act freed scholars from the bonds of Aristotelian orthodoxy, opening the door to alternative theoretical schemes, thereby allowing scholars to take their first steps toward modern science.[21] This is a seductive interpretation until one surveys scientific activity in the aftermath of the condemnations. What we find is an attempt to complete the work of accommodating Aristotle within a Christian framework begun in the middle of the thirteenth century by Albertus Magnus, Thomas Aquinas, and others. We do find a new willingness on the part of university scholars to explore hypothetical non-Aristotelian possibilities now declared to be within God's power to create, without any suggestion that he had actually created them. But we *do not* find a sea change in the sciences, a widespread abandonment of Aristotelian metaphysics, cosmology, and natural philosophy. Albert and Aquinas had done their work well, and Aquinas's philosophy, with its Aristotelian accommodations, was on its way to becoming the official philosophy of the Catholic Church. Modern science would come several centuries later.

THE MEDIEVAL SCIENTIFIC ACHIEVEMENT

If the Christian Middle Ages truly possessed a scientific tradition, what did it accomplish scientifically? In the first place, it preserved and transmitted the classical scientific tradition through a dangerous period in which literacy itself was at stake, thus fulfilling that fundamental disciplinary obligation. Second, for the first time in history a culture supported universities (of which there were between thirty and fifty, depending on how and when you count), permanent institutions sharing common curricula, turning out hundreds of thousands of students equipped epistemologically, methodologically, and mathematically to investigate the nature of the cosmos in which they lived. Most of the universities had the support of patrons, and what is quite astonishing (in light of the conflict myth) is that by far the greatest patron of the medieval universities was the Christian Church, which worried, on occasion, about the theological dangers of liberal higher education but was aware of the practical and scientific benefits to the point of protecting and supporting these institutions.[22]

What was the payoff in scientific terms? We have space only to hint at a few. The ancient Greek classical tradition was widely available in its thick version, and it inspired much scientific effort and innovation. In the early medieval history of the eastern (Greek) half of the Roman Empire,[23] we find John Philoponus, Neoplatonic Christian of the seventh century, testing Aristotle's theories of motion. In one experiment, he dropped two objects simultaneously, one light and the other heavy, from a high place in order to demonstrate that the speeds were not proportional to the weights but nearly identical. More typical of this early period was the strong medical tradition, built on foundations laid by Galen and his Greek predecessors. This included medical theory and practice, both traditional and innovative. New techniques of diagnosis, prognosis, and therapeutics were developed. Drug therapy and other traditions of medical theory and practice emerged. Professionalization and enlargement of the medical profession took place; in 1338 Florence had sixty licensed physicians. Women practitioners made an appearance (Trotula is the best-known name), specializing mainly in obstetrics and gynecology. Hospitals, as institutions where the object was healing, became numerous; and the institutionalization of medical education in the universities brought medical theory into contact with broader traditions of natural philosophy. Invasive surgery was not uncommon, and it employed new (or newly adapted) surgical instruments. A tradition of human dissection for pedagogical purposes was developed, which continued into the early modern period. And finally, medical manuals were written or adapted, some of which remained in use into the seventeenth century.

Quite a different sort of scientific achievement emerged in medieval universities of the fourteenth century. A group of outstanding mathematicians at Merton College, Oxford University, developed mathematical techniques for representing uniform motion, uniformly accelerated motion, and nonuniformly accelerated motion. Their "mean-speed theorem" stated that a body, starting from rest and moving with a uniformly accelerated motion, would cover, in a given period of time, the same distance as if it were to move for that entire time with the mean speed of the accelerated motion—a theorem that was appropriated by Galileo 250 years later, as proposition 1, theorem 1, of his discussion of the kinematics of uniformly accelerated motion. One member of this Merton College group, Thomas Bradwardine (d. 1349), subsequently Archbishop of Canterbury, developed a theory of the dynamic relationship between force, speed, and resistance that was widely held and remained a topic of discussion as late as the sixteenth century. An important aspect of these efforts was the making of a distinction between kinematics and dynamics, and recognition that the answers were necessarily mathematical functions applied to the behavior of physical bodies. Later in the fourteenth century Nicole Oresme (ca. 1320–1382), Parisian scholar-theologian and future bishop, developed graphical representations of motion and other variable qualities that anticipated Cartesian coordinates.[24]

Much more could be written. Mathematical astronomy, built on the foundation laid by Ptolemy in the second century CE, flourished throughout the Middle Ages and paved the way for Copernicus. The *Alfonsine Tables*, produced at the court of Alfonso X of León and Castile in the thirteenth century, were still the best available astronomical tables as late as the sixteenth century when they were employed by Copernicus in his creation of heliocentric astronomy.[25]

From the early church fathers to the end of the Middle Ages, we find episodes of conflict as Christianity and the natural sciences attempted to occupy the same intellectual ground. We also see the efforts of Albertus Magnus, Thomas Aquinas, Roger Bacon, and many more like them to mediate between the claims of theology and those of the natural sciences. In the end, the protagonists on both sides preferred compromise to conflict, peace to warfare; in nearly every case they found or created the means for peaceful coexistence. It does not follow that they were equals. The sciences were handmaidens to theology, as Augustine had proposed. And so they would remain for several centuries more. But they had become trusted members of the household and had earned the right to pursue tasks outside the household without unduly close supervision and only an occasional reprimand.

SCIENCE AND THE RENAISSANCE

Traditionally, historians have considered the modern period to have been inaugurated by three successive events—the Renaissance, the Reformation, and the Scientific Revolution. While in recent years there has been much discussion about whether these three labels are the best way to categorize the dramatic changes that took place at the dawn of the modern age, in many respects they still provide a helpful guide to understanding the transformation of intellectual life that occurred during the sixteenth and seventeenth centuries. As it relates to the relationship between science and Christianity, the Renaissance is significant because it was the occasion of an even deeper and more comprehensive engagement with classical learning than that witnessed in the twelfth through the fourteenth centuries. This afforded Christian thinkers the opportunity to reflect on whether some of the newly revived philosophical approaches might provide a better partner for Christian theology than the prevailing Aristotelian tradition. At the same time, the Protestant Reformation offered its own challenges to Aristotelian science. Prominent Protestant reformers—and Martin Luther (1483–1546) in particular—were sharply critical of the dominant role played by Aristotelian thought in Christian theology and in the university curriculum. Moreover, the Protestant Reformation, although it was by no means a monolithic phenomenon, eroded the centralized authority of the Catholic Church, not only making possible the cultivation of heterodox religious positions but also allowing departures from the officially sanctioned range of scientific doctrines. In these ways, the new science of the seventeenth century was facilitated, to a significant degree, by the Renaissance and Reformation.

The Renaissance witnessed the revival of a number of strands of ancient thought that were of great importance for the development of modern science and for the relationship between science and Christianity. Atomism—the view that the phenomena of the material world are best understood in terms of the interactions of tiny, indivisible particles—had first been proposed by the pre-Socratic philosophers Leucippus (fl. fifth century BCE) and Democritus (b. ca. 460 BCE). Almost from the first, however, this view was considered to be incipiently atheistic, and its subsequent espousal by the Epicurean poet Lucretius (d. ca. 50 BCE) further reinforced the association between atheism and atomism. For a number of early modern thinkers, however, atomism was potentially more compatible with Christianity than Aristotelian matter theory. According to the Aristotelian view, change and motion in the cosmos were to be understood in terms of the intrinsic powers of natural objects. God was understood to *concur* in the motions of natural objects—that is to say, permit them to take place—but the immediate cause of motion was the active power of things themselves. On the atomistic account, by way of contrast, natural things were thought to be composed of fundamental units of matter that were essentially inert and hence lacking any causal efficacy of their own. Seventeenth-century advocates of "the corpuscular hypothesis"—a view that drew its inspiration from ancient atomism—claimed that their approach to nature was more in keeping with Christian theology because on such an account motion was possible only if God acted directly in nature as the source of motion of inert matter.[26] The corpuscular hypothesis, its advocates claimed, allowed God to be more intimately involved with nature than did traditional Aristotelianism.[27]

Hand in hand with this new theory of matter came the idea that the regularities observed in the natural world were to be thought of as laws imposed by God.[28] Prior to the seventeenth century, the sphere in which natural laws were thought to operate was the moral realm. Laws of nature had typically been understood to consist in divine commands of the kind "Thou shalt not kill." The notion that the divine lawgiver might also issue decrees in the natural realm was a concomitant of corpuscular matter theory. On this account, the orderly patterns of motion and change that we observe in the world are not to be explained in terms of the internal properties of natural things, but rather in terms of God's direct willing of events. Thus, accompanying the idea that God was immediately involved in natural motion was the further notion that God's willing in the realm of nature was also regular and lawful. This new understanding of God's relation to the natural world was first developed by the French philosopher René Descartes (1596–1650).

While Descartes is perhaps best known as the father of modern philosophy and of the dictum "I think, therefore I am," he was an important figure in the scientific community of the seventeenth century. In his *Principles of Philosophy* (1644), Descartes set out three laws of nature. He explained that "God imparted various motions to the parts of matter when he first created them, and he now preserves all this matter in the same way, and by the same process by which he originally created it."[29] The lawful motions of material bodies are thus understood as nothing other than the continuous lawlike acts of the Deity. This conception of natural law was to provide the foundation of the Newtonian worldview. As is well known, Isaac Newton (1642–1727) articulated three laws of motion, following the lead of Descartes. In an. explicit rejection of the older idea of active powers, Newton declared that phenomena such as gravity do not reside in "the specific forms of things" but arise out of "the general laws of nature." His follower Samuel Clarke (1675–1729) explained that these laws of nature were to be understood as God's direct commands: "the Course of Nature, cannot possibly be any thing else, but the Arbitrary Will and pleasure of God exerting itself and acting upon Matter continually."[30] The idea that science seeks to uncover the laws of nature thus owes its origin to this new theological understanding of God's relation to the natural world.

If ancient atomism had an important bearing on the content of new scientific approaches to nature, other ancient philosophical traditions such as Platonism, Neoplatonism, and Pythagoreanism also played a role in the new sciences of the seventeenth century. Renewed interest in Plato was inspired by the recovery, over the course of the fifteenth century, of virtually the entire corpus of Platonic works, along with a body of magical, astrological, and alchemical Neoplatonic writings known as the "hermetic" literature. While it is true that aspects of Platonism had been incorporated into Christian theology almost from the inception of Christianity—and, as we have seen, the Platonists were thought by Augustine to have represented the best of what pagan philosophy had to offer—many Renaissance thinkers came to the view that medieval thinkers had been wrong to privilege Aristotle over Plato.[31] The magical ideas associated with Neoplatonism and the hermetic writings may seem a world away from modern "science," yet arguably they inspired an interest in the manipulation of nature and stimulated the practical orientation of much early-modern natural philosophy. Hermetic notions also had an important formative influence on the medical reforms advocated by the so-called Luther of medicine, Theophrastus Phillippus Aureolus Bombastus von Hohenheim, better known as Paracelsus (1493–1541).[32]

Some historians of science have also suggested that the sixteenth-century resurgence of interest in Platonic and Pythagorean ideals played an important role in the mathematization of nature that is characteristic of the new sciences.[33] This view is now less credible than when first advanced, yet it is significant that proponents of the new astronomy often represented themselves as Platonists or Pythagoreans. At the very least it can be said that appeals were frequently made to the authority of these philosophers by those promoting new scientific positions. The heliocentric view, articulated by Nicholas Copernicus (1473–1543), was often referred to as the "Pythagorean hypothesis," and the name of Plato was commonly associated with mathematical and geometrical accounts of astronomy. Galileo suggested that a sun-centered system had been implicit in Plato's philosophy, although Plato had remained silent about its mathematical foundations.[34] As in the case of atomism, these Platonic and Neoplatonic ideas were argued to be more consistent with Christian theism than the available alternatives. The astronomer Johannes Kepler (1571–1630), who uncovered three laws of planetary motion, described God as the eternal geometer who had created the world according to a mathematical plan that human minds could discover: "For the Creator, who is the very source of astronomy and, as Plato wrote 'practices eternal geometry' does not stray from his own archetype."[35] In contrasting his view with that of Aristotle, Kepler also cited the biblical proof text—one of Augustine's favorites—describing God as having created the world according to "weight, measure and number."[36]

The idea of God as the divine mathematician also meshed neatly with the developing notion of God as the divine lawgiver. Newton spoke of "an infinite and omnipresent spirit in which matter is moved according to mathematical laws."[37] Laws of nature, henceforth, were understood as *mathematical* laws. It may seem that the idea of mathematical laws of nature was not entirely unprecedented. As we have already seen, as early as the fourteenth century scholars at Merton College had applied mathematics to motion to arrive at the mean-speed theorem. However, such formulations were regarded more as "rules of calculation" (*regulae*) than laws of nature in the modern sense. Moreover, God was not understood to be the author of these rules. The new early-modern understanding of laws of nature—as universal, invariant, and mathematical—provided one of the important presuppositions of modern mathematical physics.

NATURAL PHILOSOPHY AND THE REFORMATION

The Protestant Reformation was a sixteenth-century movement that began as an attempt to reform the Catholic Church. It had far-reaching consequences for the political and intellectual life of Europe and indirectly affected the development of the new sciences in a number of different ways. Protestant reformers often expressed reservations about the role played by Aristotelian philosophy in the development of Christian theology, and this negative view, although not universal among Protestants, carried the implicit assumption that natural philosophy also needed to be reformed. Martin Luther, who initiated the Protestant Reformation in 1517, was a vociferous critic of Aristotle. In tones reminiscent of Tertullian, he railed against the admixture of pagan philosophy with Christian teaching and castigated Thomas Aquinas for having introduced Aristotle's "unchristian, profane, meaningless babblings" into theology. Luther's main criticism centered on Aristotle's moral teaching. He complained bitterly that the Greek philosopher had been accorded the status of a Christian saint, and also mocked his natural philosophy, referring to "the great famous Aristotle, who taught and still teaches them that a stone is heavy, that a feather is light, that water is wet and fire dry."[38] The other leading Protestant reformer, John Calvin (1509–64), was more moderate in his views and more ambivalent about the merits of Aristotle's philosophy. The ancient philosopher was described as "a man of genius and learning," yet at the same time "a heathen whose heart was perverse and depraved" and who "employed his naturally acute powers of mind to extinguish all light."[39] These criticisms of Aristotelian thought reinforced those of the Renaissance Platonists and added weight to growing calls for alternative conceptions of nature and its operations.

The sixteenth-century reformations of religion also led to a diminution in the authority of the Catholic Church, most obviously in those territories that now identified themselves with one or another version of Protestantism. On the one hand, again, this meant that natural philosophers in those provinces enjoyed a greater degree of freedom to speculate on alternatives to the officially sanctioned Aristotelianism. On the other hand, in those regions that remained under its control, the Catholic Church sought actively to reassert its authority in the face of the threats posed by Protestantism. This accounts, in part, for the Church's interest in Galileo and the heliocentric hypothesis. While the Roman Church had initially been quite sanguine about Copernicus's radical thesis that had the earth moving around a stationary sun, in the heightened tensions of the post-Reformation period, when controversies about the interpretation of Scripture were at their height, the Holy Office was concerned to impose its authority on questions of biblical interpretation.[40] Hence, its well-known censure of Galileo in

1633 and its declaration that the Copernican hypothesis was contrary to the teaching of Scripture.

It should not be concluded from this single unhappy episode, however, that the Catholic Church was implacably opposed to science. After all, in upholding the truth of the Ptolemaic, earth-centered cosmos, the Holy Office was in fact endorsing the prevailing scientific consensus. Moreover, it is clear that the Catholic Church had been, and continued to be, a major supporter of scientific activity. If we consider the case of astronomy, for example, the historian of science John Heilbron has plausibly suggested that "the Roman Catholic Church gave more financial and social support to the study of astronomy for over six centuries, from the recovery of ancient learning during the late Middle Ages into the Enlightenment, than any other, and, probably, all other, institutions."[41] An important Catholic contribution to the sciences also came from the Society of Jesus, founded in 1540. The role of Jesuit educational institutions in promoting mathematical and experimental sciences is only now beginning to be fully appreciated.[42]

In the light of more recent controversies about evolutionary theory, an insistence on the authority of the Bible in scientific matters may not seem particularly conducive to the practice of good science. It is clear that in the sixteenth and seventeenth centuries, however, the elevation of biblical authority had a quite positive impact on the developing natural sciences, and in a number of different ways. First, the authority of the Bible was used as a weapon to demolish Aristotelian science, which, it could be argued, was inconsistent with Scripture. Some Protestant philosophers argued that just as Luther and Calvin had sought, by appeals to Scripture, to reform a Christianity that had been corrupted by pagan philosophy, so natural philosophy might be similarly reformed, by purging it of its pagan elements and aligning it with scriptural truths. One of Calvin's students, Lambert Daneau (1530–95), wrote a work titled *Physica Christiana* (*Christian Physics*), the goal of which was "to reform the opinions of the Philosophers by the word of God."[43]

This reformation of natural philosophy was to be accomplished by showing the conformity of new scientific models with the biblical writings, in particular the book of Genesis. Such exercises were typically based on the assumption that Moses—the biblical patriarch then assumed to have written the first five books of the Bible—had possessed an acute scientific knowledge of the world. Traces of this knowledge, it was thought, could still be found in the Bible if one looked hard enough. The Platonist philosopher Henry More (1614–87), who in the middle decades of the seventeenth century introduced the teachings of Descartes to students at the University of Cambridge, insisted that Descartes had revived the ancient scientific views of Moses. More believed that Moses had subscribed to a heliocentric view of the cosmos along with an atomic theory of matter. These views in turn had been passed onto the Greek thinkers with whom they are more commonly associated—Pythagoras, Leucippus, and Democritus. So Descartes's assertion of the earth's motion along with his advocacy of atomic theory could be regarded as the revival of a true biblical natural philosophy, one originally taught by Moses and other biblical patriarchs.

Descartes himself remarked on the congruity between his view of the universe and the biblical writings, confiding to a correspondent:

> I am about to describe the birth of the world, in which I hope to comprehend the greatest part of physics. And I will tell you that after four or five days, in re-reading the first chapter of Genesis, I have found, as if by a miracle that it can all be explained according to my imagination. . . . My new philosophy is in much better agreement with all the truths of faith than that of Aristotle.[44]

Many other writers commented on the agreement between the new sciences and the ancient biblical teachings. In what was one of the most popular scientific works of the seventeenth century, the clergyman Thomas Burnet (ca. 1635–1715) set out a geological history of the earth, demonstrating how the biblical accounts of the Creation and deluge, along with prophecies concerning the final conflagration of the world, were consistent with the new cosmology of Descartes.[45] In time, similar exercises were conducted for the Newtonian cosmology that was eventually to supersede the Cartesian account.[46] Isaac Newton himself believed that many of the ideas central to his account of the universe, including atomism and the theory of universal gravitation, had been known to Moses and other ancient sages, such as Pythagoras and Democritus.[47]

A second way in which the Bible was involved in the new sciences was in the sphere of biblical interpretation. New literal approaches to the Bible, promoted by Renaissance and Protestant thinkers, had an indirect bearing on approaches to the natural world. It was a commonplace in the Middle Ages and early-modern period that God had written two "books"—the book of nature and the book of scripture.[48] It is not surprising, then, that changes to the reading of one of these "books" would have implications for the reading of the other. The sixteenth-century emphasis on the literal sense of scripture and a corresponding skepticism about the value of allegory and symbolism were accompanied by a new, literal reading of the world. Whereas once the natural world had derived intelligibility from the rich symbolic associations of plants and animals, with the collapse of medieval symbolism its intelligibility was perceived to lie elsewhere, in more abstract mathematical relations or in schemes of classification.[49]

Finally, certain biblical narratives, now read in their literal or historical sense, provided important motivations for scientific activities. Perhaps the best-known instance of this is the work of the English philosopher Francis

Bacon (1561–1626), whose conception of the goals and methods of science was enormously influential during the seventeenth century and beyond. In his writings Bacon frequently alluded to the Genesis narrative of the Creation, and to the fact that Adam had once enjoyed dominion over the whole of nature. According to the biblical account, however, Adam had lost much of this power over nature as a consequence of his fall from grace in the garden of Eden. Bacon argued that science was to be the means by which the human race regained the control over nature that Adam had once enjoyed in paradise: "For man by the fall fell at the same time from his state of innocency and from his dominion over creation. Both of these losses however can even in this life be in some part repaired; the former by religion and faith, the latter by arts and sciences."[50] While it is often assumed that an insistence on the primacy of biblical authority would be a serious impediment to the development of science, close examination of the role played by the Bible in the sciences of the sixteenth and seventeenth centuries shows this assumption to be ill-founded. It is undoubtedly true that passages of Scripture were deployed against Copernicanism. Yet this is but a small part of a much larger picture in which, in various ways, the Bible provided support for new scientific views and motivated scientific enquiry.

If the religiously inspired debates about authority had an important role in the development of the sciences, it is equally true that the *content* of the religious ideas of the early-modern period was important for new avenues of investigation. One example of the influence of particular religious doctrines at this time relates to the emergence of experimental methods. The sixteenth and seventeenth centuries saw a resurgence of interest in Augustinian theology, and indeed the religious controversies of the period have been explained in terms of a conflict between Augustine's doctrine of grace and his doctrine of the Church.[51] One feature of Augustine's thought that came to prominence at this time was his doctrine of original sin, according to which once-perfect human beings had fallen from grace, irremediably damaging both their moral and intellectual capacities. It was this latter aspect—the wounding of human reason—that was taken up with great enthusiasm by a number of advocates of "experimental natural philosophy."

Those who held to a strong view of human incapacity argued that Aristotelian science, which was based on commonsense observations and generalizations based on those observations, assumed too optimistic a view of human nature. Aristotelian science, moreover, aimed at certainty and sought the true causes of things. For those who subscribed to an Augustinian view of human nature, such an approach was far too optimistic, presupposing as it did that human mental and sensory powers were capable of arriving at accurate knowledge of the world. The experimental approach to science, which has been accurately characterized as a "probabilistic and fallibilistic conception of man's natural knowledge," accords far better with a pessimistic view of human nature.[52] The concern of the seventeenth century with questions of method and theories of knowledge was thus motivated to a large degree by theological concerns about the extent to which human minds were capable of generating reliable knowledge. The human propensity for error—understood as a consequence of original sin—was the starting point for such discussions, which often concluded with an endorsement of experimental methods and a censure of overoptimistic Aristotelianism. Robert Hooke, first curator of experiments at the Royal Society—founded in the 1660s and hence one of the very first scientific associations—summed up this general sentiment: "every man, both from a deriv'd corruption, innate and born with him, and from his breeding and converse with men, is very subject to slip into all sorts of errors. . . . These being the dangers in the process of humane Reason, the remedies of them all can only proceed from the real, the mechanical, the experimental Philosophy."[53]

The religious upheavals of the sixteenth and seventeenth centuries had both direct and indirect influences on the development of new scientific methods and theories. As early as the seventeenth century, the proximity of these two revolutions—one religious and one scientific—had led some to speculate about possible connections between them. Francis Bacon, for example, contended that the sixteenth-century reformations of religion had provided the inspiration for the subsequent reformations in the sphere of learning. Other leading figures in the new sciences also pointed to the revolution that had taken place in the religious sphere as justification for the pursuit of new avenues of scientific investigation.[54] From the more distant perspective of the twentieth century, the general tenor of these earlier assessments about the role of religion in the scientific revolution can be cautiously endorsed.

BEYOND THE HANDMAIDEN METAPHOR

While it is still common to encounter the idea that the rise of science in the West was necessarily accompanied by a decline in religion, this is no longer a view that finds serious support among historians of science, and we are now in a position to see why.

Most obviously, perhaps, scientific activity flourished during a Middle Ages that was dominated by ecclesiastical institutions and an intellectual culture that was oriented primarily toward theology. Almost of necessity there were boundary disputes, but these should not be taken to typify the relations between science and Christianity. This amicable relationship was not to change significantly with the well-known scientific innovations of early-modern figures such as Galileo, Descartes, and Newton. In fact, it could be argued that the connections between natural philosophy and Christianity became even more intimate during the course of the sixteenth and seventeenth centuries than they had been during the Middle Ages. Certainly it was the explicit intention of many figures involved in the new sciences of the seventeenth century to develop approaches to nature that were consistent with Christian belief. As we have seen, some suggested that natural philosophy might be built anew on biblical foundations, and many of the approaches to nature that emerge in the sixteenth and seventeenth centuries sought to present themselves as more truly Christian philosophies than anything that had come before.

In some sense, the idea that natural philosophy was pursued primarily to serve as a handmaiden to theology remained a guiding principle. Isaac Newton wrote in his *Opticks* (1704) that one of the goals of natural philosophy was to expand the bounds of moral philosophy and ultimately to shed light on the nature of the "first cause"—God.[55] It was widely assumed during the seventeenth and eighteenth centuries that the study of nature revealed the wisdom and goodness of God. The pious Robert Boyle (1627–91)—often referred to as "the father of modern chemistry"—endowed an eponymous lecture series whose aim was "to prove the truth of the Christian religion against infidels." Many of the distinguished Boyle lecturers used recent developments in natural history and natural philosophy to demonstrate the reasonableness of theistic belief.

But beyond this, some seventeenth-century figures argued that the pursuit of science was itself a form of religious activity. Francis Bacon, as noted, suggested that the contemplation and control of nature had been the original occupation of Adam. Although, like a number of his contemporaries, Bacon insisted that natural philosophy and theology should not be combined in an inappropriate way, he nonetheless implied that the pursuit of science was a religious vocation and that the benefits provided by science were nothing other than Christian charity in action.[56] Johannes Kepler, who had originally considered a career in the church, also came to the conclusion that the study of nature was a religious occupation: "I wished to be a theologian; for a long time I was troubled, but now see how God is also praised through my work in astronomy."[57] Boyle himself used Kepler's expression "priests of nature" for those engaged in scientific activities, describing the rational contemplation of nature as "the first act of religion" and "philosophical worship of God."[58] The English naturalist John Ray, one of the originators of modern biological taxonomy, also regarded the study of nature as a form of religious worship. His best-known work—*The Wisdom of God Manifested in the Works of Creation* (1691), compiled from sermons delivered in the chapel of Trinity College, Cambridge—proposed that Sundays be set aside not only for formal worship but for the contemplation of nature.[59]

Natural history and natural philosophy, for these individuals, were more than mere aids to religion, they were an integral part of it.

It must be said, in conclusion, that the history of the association between science and Christianity from the patristic period and through the Middle Ages is not simply the story of shifting relations between two distinct entities. Part of the complexity of the history that we have considered here is owing to the fact that the mutual interactions of science and Christianity wrought fundamental changes in both enterprises. This means that the exercise we are engaged in is not simply about the relationship between unchanging and static entities—science and Christianity—but rather concerns two dynamic activities and sets of practices that mutated over historical time. In the sixteenth and seventeenth centuries, Christianity took on some of the features of the natural sciences. By the same token, the natural sciences were shaped by theological influences. Indeed, there is a sense in which the emergence of scientific activity as a characteristic feature of Western modernity is a consequence of the fact that it was constructed, to an important degree, in the image of religion.[60]

In the light of these intimate interactions it is clear that there is little historical evidence to support the surprisingly widespread sentiment that the medieval church stifled the development of science *or* the common contention that the triumph of Copernicanism and Newtonianism were possible only because of the waning of religious authority. There were, to be sure, episodes during which scientific doctrines conflicted with religious beliefs, and moments when ecclesiastical authorities were ranged against individual natural philosophers. It can be said, however, that for the most part relations between science and religion during this period were peaceful and, beyond this, that Western Christendom actually provided the institutional and intellectual settings that made possible the emergence of modern science.

NOTES

1. John William Draper, *History of the Conflict between Religion and Science* (New York: D. Appleton, 1874); Andrew Dickson White, *A History of the Warfare of Science with Theology in Christendom*, 2 vols. (New York: D. Appleton, 1876).

2. Reijer Hooykaas, *Religion and the Rise of Modern Science* (Grand Rapids, Mich.: Eerdmans, 1972); Stanley L. Jaki, *The Savior of Science* (Washington, D.C.: Regnery Gateway, 1988); Rodney Stark, *For the Glory of God: How Monotheism Led to Reformations, Science, Witch-Hunts, and the End of Slavery* (Princeton, N.J.: Princeton University Press, 2003), chap. 2.

3. John Hedley Brooke, *Science and Religion: Some Historical Perspectives* (Cambridge: Cambridge University Press, 1991); David C. Lindberg and Ronald L. Numbers, eds., *When Science and Christianity Meet* (Chicago: University of Chicago Press, 2003).

4. Pagans were practitioners of non-Abrahamic religions (neither Christians nor Jews), of which the Roman Empire had an abundance. See Ramsay MacMullen, *Paganism in the Roman Empire* (New Haven, Conn.: Yale University Press, 1981).

5. The emperor Constantine was converted to Christianity about 312. Christianity became the state religion before the end of the century.

6. MacMullen, *Paganism in the Roman Empire*; Ramsay MacMullen, *Christianizing the Roman Empire, A.D. 100–400* (New Haven, Conn.: Yale University Press, 1984).

7. Dispute about the proper nomenclature for what we refer to as "science" or "natural science," which is plentiful, revolves around a disagreement over whether to employ the ancient terminology or the modern equivalent. Aristotle's two major expressions were "mathematics" and "natural philosophy," best translated as "mathematical science" and "nonmathematical science." Ancient and medieval writers were not entirely consistent, however; we consider this a semantic quibble that would confuse more often than it would clarify for readers of this chapter. We will therefore employ the common expressions "science," "natural science," and "mathematical science," all with their contemporary meanings, but readers should bear in mind that these terms are not exact equivalents of the relevant ancient expressions. Many scientific disciplines have specific names ("astronomy," "botany," "mechanics," and the like), and we will employ these whenever available.

8. See the indices of Henry Chadwick, *The Early Church* (New York: Dorset, 1986); W. H. C. Frend, *The Early Church* (Philadelphia: Fortress Press, 1982); Stephen Benko, *Pagan Rome and the Early Christians* (Bloomington: Indiana University Press, 1984); and innumerable other works on the early Christian Church. On Augustine, who deserves special attention, see Peter Brown, *Augustine of Hippo: A Biography* (New York: Dorset, 1967).

9. Tertullian, *On Prescription of Heretics*, trans. Peter Holmes, in *The Ante-Nicene Fathers* (Grand Rapids, Mich.: Eerdmans, 1986), vol. 3, pts. 1–3, chap. 7, col. 246b; Tertullian, *De praescriptione hereticorum*, chaps. 7–8, in *Tertulliani opera*, ed. Nic Rigaltius, 205 (Paris, 1664) (here I prefer my translation to that of Holmes).

10. Eric Osborn, *Tertullian, First Theologian of the West* (Cambridge: Cambridge University Press, 45). Osborn offers a refreshing, balanced portrayal of Tertullian's attitudes toward the classical tradition.

11. See, e.g., Draper, *Conflict between Religion and Science*, 56f.

12. Socrates Scholastica, *Ecclesiastical History*, 7.xv.

13. St. Augustine, *Confessions*, 4.16, trans. Whitney J. Oates, *Basic Writings of Saint Augustine* (New York: Random House, 1948), 1:55–56; *On Christian Doctrine*, trans. D. W. Robertson (Indianapolis, Ind.: Bobbs-Merrill, 1958), 29.65–6.

14. St. Augustine, *On Christian Doctrine*, 40, 75.

15. St. Augustine, *Literal Commentary on Genesis*, trans. John Hammond Taylor, in *Ancient Christian Writers*, vol. 41 (New York: Newman Press, 1982), 42–43, with modest improvements. The term "literal (*ad litteram*)" did not have the same meaning for Augustine's readers as it does for us. See the translator's discussion of this expression in 41:7–12.

16. David C. Lindberg, "The Medieval Church Encounters the Classical Tradition: Saint Augustine, Roger Bacon, and the Handmaiden Metaphor," in Lindberg and Numbers, *When Science and Christianity Meet*, 7–32.

17. The myth that medieval people believed in a flat earth was the invention of Washington Irving in his four-volume biography of Christopher Columbus (Paris, 1828). We know of no medieval person in western Europe who held this opinion. Estimates of its circumference were about equivalent to the modern value. On

astronomy in the early Middle Ages, including the monasteries, see Stephen C. McCluskey, *Astronomies and Cultures in Early Medieval Europe* (Cambridge: Cambridge University Press, 1998).

18. McCluskey, *Astronomies*, chap. 8; Heinrich Fichtenau, *The Carolingian Empire: The Age of Charlemagne* (Oxford: Basil Blackwell, 1957).

19. On the translations, see Charles S. F. Burnett, "Translation and Transmission of Greek and Islamic Science to Latin Christendom," in *The Cambridge History of Science*, vol. 2: *The Middle Ages*, ed. David Lindberg and Michael Shank (Cambridge: Cambridge University Press, forthcoming); and David C. Lindberg, "The Transmission of Greek and Arabic Learning to the West," in *Science in the Middle Ages*, ed. David C. Lindberg, 52–90 (Chicago: University of Chicago Press, 1976).

20. What follows in this section is a drastically abbreviated version of David Lindberg, *The Beginnings of Western Science: The European Scientific Tradition in Philosophical, Religious, and Institutional Context, 600 B.C. to A.D. 1450* (Chicago: University of Chicago Press, 1992), chap. 10 ("The Recovery and Assimilation of Greek and Arabic Science").

21. Pierre Duhem, *Etudes sur Léonard de Vinci* (Paris: F. De Nobele, 1906–13; 1955), 2:412.

22. Edward Grant, *God and Reason in the Middle Ages* (Cambridge: Cambridge University Press, 2001), deals with the universities throughout. My colleague Michael Shank has correctly referred to the status of science in the medieval universities as an act of scientific education unprecedented in human history.

23. Eastern (Greek) portions of the Roman Empire separated themselves from Rome and the Latin West in fits and starts, between about 330 and 650 CE, and came to be known as the Byzantine Empire. Apart from early controversy over the interpretation of the six days of creation as described in the Bible and the murder of Hypatia, the relations between science and religion in the Byzantine Empire have been little studied and will not be further discussed here.

24. See Lindberg, *Beginnings of Western Science*, especially chap. 12, 290–307.

25. The best single source on medieval astronomy is J. D. North, *The Norton History of Astronomy and Cosmology* (New York: W. W. Norton, 1995).

26. Strictly speaking, atomism, which posits indivisible particles and the existence of a void for them to move in, should be distinguished from the corpuscular hypothesis, which holds that matter is made of invisible, but not necessarily indivisible, particles. Some corpuscularians (e.g., René Descartes) also denied the existence of the void.

27. See Stephen Gaukroger, *Descartes: An Intellectual Biography* (Oxford: Oxford University Press, 1997), 146–52; Margaret Osler, ed., *Atoms, Pneuma, and Tranquility: Epicurean and Stoic Themes in European Thought* (Cambridge: Cambridge University Press, 1991).

28. John Henry, "Metaphysics and the Origins of Modern Science: Descartes and the Importance of Laws of Nature," *Early Science and Medicine* 9 (2004): 73–114; Francis Oakley, "Christian Theology and the Newtonian Science: The Rise of the Concept of Laws of Nature," *Church History* 30 (1961): 433–57; M. B. Foster, "The Christian Doctrine of Creation and the Rise of Modern Natural Science," *Mind* 18 (1934): 446–68; Peter Harrison, "The Development of the Concept of Laws of Nature," in *Creation: Law and Probability*, ed. Fraser Watts, 13–36 (Aldershot: Ashgate, 2007).

29. Descartes, *Principles of Philosophy*, §61, *The Philosophical Writings of Descartes*, 2 vols., ed. J. Cottingham, R. Stoothof, and D. Murdoch (Cambridge: Cambridge University Press, 1984), 1:240.

30. Isaac Newton, *Opticks*, 4th ed. (New York: Dover, 1979), 401; Samuel Clarke, "The Evidences of Natural and Revealed Religion," *The Works of Samuel Clarke, D.D.*, 2 vols. (London, 1738), 2:698.

31. James Hankins, "Plato's Psychogony in the Later Renaissance: Changing Attitudes to the Christianization of Pagan Philosophy," in *Ancient and Medieval Philosophy*, vol. 32, ed. Thomas Leinkauf and Carlos Steel, 393–412 (Leuven: Leuven University Press, 2005).

32. John Henry, *The Scientific Revolution and the Origins of Modern Science* (London: Palgrave, 2001), chap. 4; Francis Yates, *Giordano Bruno and the Hermetic Tradition* (Chicago: University of Chicago Press, 1991), chap. 8; Brian P. Copenhaver, "Natural Magic, Hermeticism, and Occultism in Early Modern Science," in *Reappraisals of the Scientific Revolution*, ed. Robert S. Westman and David C. Lindberg (Cambridge: Cambridge University Press, 1990), 261–302.

33. Daniel Garber, "Physics and Foundations," in *The Cambridge History of Science*, vol 3, *Early Modern Science*, ed. Katherine Park and Lorraine Daston, 21–69 (Cambridge: Cambridge University Press, 2006); Joseph C. Pitt, "Apologia pro Simplicio: Galileo and the Limits of Knowledge," in *An Intimate Relation: Studies in the History and Philosophy of Science*, ed. J. R. Brown and J. Mittelstrass, 1–22 (Dordrecht: Kluwer, 1989). For the earlier and more controversial views of the influence of Platonism, see Alexander Koyré, "Galileo and Plato," in *Metaphysics and Measurement: Essays in the Scientific Revolution* (London: Chapman and Hall, 1968); E. A. Burtt, *The Metaphysical Foundations of Modern Science* (New York: Dover, 2003), 22.

34. James Hankins, "Galileo, Ficino, and Renaissance Platonism," in *Humanism and Early Modern Philosophy*, ed. Jill Kraye and M. W. F. Stone (London: Routledge, 2000), 209–37 (210).

35. Johannes Kepler, *The Harmonies of the World*, trans. Charles G. Wallis (Chicago: Encyclopedia Brittanica, 1952), 1017.

36. Johannes Kepler, *The Harmony of the World*, trans. E. J. Aiton, A. M. Duncan, J. V. Field (Philadelphia: American Philosophical Society, 1997), 115. Cf. Augustine, *Trinity* 11.iv; *Wisdom*, 11.20.

37. Draft corollary to Proposition 6 of the *Principia*, quoted in John Brooke, "The God of Isaac Newton," in *Let Newton Be*, ed. John Fauvel et al., 172 (Oxford: Oxford University Press, 1990).

38. "Sermon for Epiphany," 1, 23 in *Sermons of Martin Luther*, 8 vols., ed. and trans. John N. Lenker et al. (Grand Rapids, Mich.: Baker Book House, 1983), 1:332.

39. Calvin, *Commentary on the Psalms* 107:43, *Calvin's Commentaries*, 22 vols. (Grand Rapids, Mich.: Baker Books, 1984), 6:266.

40. David Lindberg, "Galileo, the Church and the Cosmos," in Lindberg and Numbers, *When Science and Christianity Meet*, 33–60 (45).

41. John Heilbron, *The Sun in the Church: Cathedrals as Solar Observatories* (Cambridge, Mass.: Harvard University Press, 1999), 3. For Jesuit contributions to seventeenth-century science, see Mordechai Feingold, ed., *The New Science and Jesuit Science: Seventeenth-Century Perspectives* (Dordrecht: Kluwer, 2003).

42. Mordechai Feingold, ed., *Jesuit Science and the Republic of Letters* (Cambridge, Mass.: MIT Press, 2002); Marcus Hellyer, *Catholic Physics: Jesuit Natural Philosophy in Early Modern Germany* (Notre Dame, Ind.: University of Notre Dame Press, 2005).

43. Lambert Daneau, *The Wonderfull Woorkmanship of the World* (London, 1578), sig. A3v. On biblical natural philosophy, see Ann Blair, "Mosaic Physics and the Search for a Pious Natural Philosophy in the Late Renaissance," *Isis* 91 (2000): 32–58; Peter Harrison, *The Bible, Protestantism and the Rise of Natural Science* (Cambridge: Cambridge University Press, 1990), chap. 4.

44. Descartes to William Boswell, 1646, *Oeuvres de Descartes*, 11 vols., ed. Charles Adam and P. Tannery (Paris: Cerf, 1897–1913), 4:698.

45. Peter Harrison, "The Influence of Cartesian Cosmology in England," in *Descartes' Natural Philosophy*, ed. S. Gaukroger, J. Schuster, and J. Sutton, 168–92 (London: Routledge, 2000).

46. William Whiston, *A New Theory of the Earth* (London, 1696).

47. J. E. McGuire and P. M. Rattansi, "Newton and the 'Pipes of Pan,'" *Notes and Records of the Royal Society of London* 21 (1966): 108–43.

48. K. van Berkel and A. Vanderjagt, eds., *The Book of Nature in Early Modern and Modern History* (Leuven: Peeters, 2006).

49. Harrison, *Bible, Protestantism, Rise of Natural Science*; Kevin Killeen and Peter Forshaw, eds., *The Word and the World: Biblical Exegesis and Early Modern Science* (London: Palgrave, 2007).

50. Bacon, *Novum Organum* II §52, in *The Works of Francis Bacon*, ed. James Spedding, Robert Ellis, and Douglas Heath, 14 vols., 4:247.

51. Benjamin B. Warfield, *Calvin and Augustine* (Philadelphia, Pa.: Presbyterian and Reformed, 1956), 321–22.

52. The description is that of Steven Shapin and Simon Schaffer, *Leviathan and the Air Pump: Hobbes, Boyle, and the Experimental Life* (Princeton, N.J.: Princeton University Press, 1985), 1.

53. Robert Hooke, *Micrographia* (London, 1665), preface. On this general theme see Peter Harrison, *The Fall of Man and the Foundations of Science* (Cambridge: Cambridge University Press, 2007).

54. Francis Bacon, *The Advancement of Learning*, ed. Arthur Johnston (Oxford: Clarendon Press, 1974), 42; Thomas Sprat, *History of the Royal Society* (London, 1666), 371. See also Charles Webster, *From Paracelsus to Newton* (Cambridge: Cambridge University Press, 1982), 4.

55. Newton, *Opticks*, Query 31, 405.

56. Bacon, *Valerius Terminus*, in *The Works of Francis Bacon*, 3:221f. Benjamin Milner, "Francis Bacon: The Theological Foundations of *Valerius Terminus*," *Journal of the History of Ideas* 58 (1997): 245–64.

57. Johannes Kepler, *Gesammelte Werke*, 20 vols. (Munich, 1937–45), 8:40.

58. Boyle, *Usefulness of Natural Philosophy*, in *The Works of the Honourable Robert Boyle*, ed. Thomas Birch, 6 vols. (Hildesheim: George Olms, 1966), 2:62f.

59. John Ray, *The Wisdom of God Manifested in the Works of Creation* (London, 1691), 124.

60. On this theme see Stephen Gaukroger, *The Emergence of a Scientific Culture: Science and the Shaping of Modernity, 1210–1685* (Oxford: Oxford University Press, 2007).

4

Modern Christianity

John Hedley Brooke

Ongoing battles between creationists and evolutionists in the United States might suggest that the relations between Christianity and science have been continuously fraught and dominated by opposing interests. Conflicts there certainly have been, but there have also been instances of intimacy, cooperation, and mutual respect. Scientists with Christian convictions have generally been able to marry their faith with their science, and theologians have often been ready, sometimes too ready, to reinterpret their theology in the light of scientific theory. There has been peace as well as war.

There is no single "Christian tradition." The forms of Christian life, worship, and church governance in the Latin West differed from those of Eastern Orthodox Christianity, and further divisions ensued following the Protestant Reformation, when the problem of authority and how it was to be constituted became matters of political urgency. There could be very different understandings enshrined in doctrines such as the Fall of humankind and on issues such as whether the study of nature might itself be a form of worship.[1] One difference, as perceived by the Patriarch Jeremias II of Constantinople in 1590, was that "it is not the practice of our Church to innovate in any way whatsoever, whereas the Western Church innovates unceasingly."[2] The pace of innovation increased within the Protestant churches, whose lack of a sufficiently powerful centralized authority contributed to conditions in which a proliferation of sects soon occurred, the diversification continuing to the present day. Each of the three main branches of the Christian Church experienced the rationalism of the Enlightenment in different ways. It was in Russia in the nineteenth century that Eastern Orthodoxy first seriously engaged modern philosophical critiques. And whereas Catholicism bore the brunt of eighteenth-century attacks, especially in France, Protestant dissenting movements tended to be more accepting of a scientific culture, especially in England. The most fundamental of Christian doctrines, such as the Resurrection of Jesus

Christ, has been shared by all three traditions, but the importance attached to the intensive study of nature has been a subject of controversy within each of them.

Conflicts, when they have arisen, have sometimes been between Christian thinkers unable to agree on the best strategy for achieving peace. In a famous controversy of the early eighteenth century between Samuel Clarke (1675–1729) and the German philosopher Gottfried Leibniz (1646–1716), part of their debate revolved around the suggestion of Isaac Newton (1642–1727) that cumulative irregularities in the planetary orbits were correctable through divine initiative. Both were Christian philosophers— Clarke, an Anglican clergyman attracted to Newton's science, Leibniz, an expert in both mathematics and metaphysics who was committed to finding ways of reconciling the Catholic and Protestant churches. Clarke saw no problem in placing physical events under immediate divine control. Surely, he reasoned, it would detract from divine power and freedom if God were unable to intervene in the world? For Leibniz the very idea of a deity having to remedy deficiencies in Creation was insulting to a God of wisdom and foresight, who could not possibly have created a clockwork universe of second-rate quality.[3] Their respective positions have modern counterparts in debates within Christianity concerning intelligent design,[4] where the suggestion that divine enhancement of the natural order had to make up for supposed deficiencies in Darwinian evolution is met with the reply that to suppose the deity incapable of achieving purposes through processes internal to the natural order is bad theology—as well as bad science.

Although determined efforts were made, especially by the Roman Catholic Church, to control what was permissible in printed texts, it had proved difficult, even during the seventeenth century, to achieve unanimity in constructing a theology of nature. Catholic natural philosophers such as Marin Mersenne (1588–1648), Pierre Gassendi (1592–1655), René Descartes (1596–1650), Blaise Pascal (1623–62), and Nicolaus Steno (1638–86) integrated their science with their faith in contrasting ways, with as much variety as among Protestant Christians less subject to a centralized authority. This absence of pattern means that "nothing was inherently denied to the Catholic scientist by his personal faith."[5] Within later Protestant cultures there were disparate attitudes toward innovative science, even within the same Christian tradition. One reason for this diversity stems from the possibility of interpreting Christian doctrines in ways that could be either auspicious for the sciences or obstructive. A doctrine of Creation, for example, underpinned the belief that in uncovering regularities in nature one was discovering the *laws* that a Creator had impressed on the world. Accordingly, Newton discerned in the mathematical elegance of the solar system evidence of a deity "very well skilled in mechanics and geometry."[6] However, concepts of Creation have also been used to oppose important innovations, particularly in reactionary responses to the concept of evolution. Similarly, reference in the book of Genesis to humans being granted *dominion* over nature has sometimes sanctioned anthropocentric exploitation of nature; but, especially in the context of current environmental concerns, it has also been used to emphasize the need for stewardship and responsibility.[7] Diversity also stems from the role of local circumstances and events in shaping religious attitudes. Recent research on Presbyterian responses to the evolutionary theory of Charles Darwin (1809–82) characterizes the reaction as largely hostile in Belfast, almost indifferent in Edinburgh, and relatively receptive in Princeton.[8]

In evaluating the relevance of scientific culture to the Christian faith it is often necessary to distinguish opinions formulated by an intellectual elite and by relatively unsophisticated members of the public. This distinction has been particularly significant in disputes over human evolution, where theologically informed understandings of God have often diverged from popular notions. Opinions have been divided, too, on the value of one of the most enduring links between science and the Christian religion—that forged by arguments for design. Newton, for example, ascribed the beauty of a solar system in which the planets orbited the sun in the same direction and in roughly the same plane to God's original design. Scientific knowledge, certainly until the time of Darwin, was often used to substantiate evidence of a designer, who in Christian literature would be identified with the God of Abraham, Isaac, and Jacob—the God whose nature had been definitively revealed in the person of Jesus Christ.[9] Whether the argument affords a formal *proof* of God's existence, whether it rather serves to confirm an existing faith, or whether its value consists in capturing the attention of the atheist is a question on which Christian apologists have diverged. Some, indeed, have considered the design argument largely valueless, for the reason given in the mid-nineteenth century by John Henry Newman (1801–90): it simply had nothing to say about the fundamental tenets of Christianity—those concerning the relationship between a God of love and mercy to a willful humanity in need of redemption. Newman, who famously deserted the Church of England for the Church of Rome, also articulated a question that must haunt the discussion of science and religion within any theistic tradition: "It is indeed a great question whether atheism is not as philosophically consistent with the phenomena of the physical world, taken by themselves, as the doctrine of a creative and governing power."[10] Without cognizance of a Providence revealed in human *history*, natural phenomena and their scientific explanations could not adjudicate between theism and atheism.

A less subtle account of the effects of scientific naturalism on religious mentalities is often heard. Surely, as increasing numbers of phenomena were satisfactorily explained by *natural* causes, references to a deity became redundant? They may indeed have become so in the context of scientific explanation; but a deity devised merely to fill gaps in scientific knowledge is precisely that—a god-of-the-gaps—not the God of Christian theology on whom the whole universe, or indeed all universes, are deemed to depend for their being and continuing existence. Scientists holding a Christian faith, such as the twentieth-century Oxford chemist and Methodist preacher Charles Coulson (1910–74), have insisted that those two ideas of God should not be confused and conflated.[11]

THE SANCTIONING OF SCIENCE BY CHRISTIAN THEOLOGY

Such was the expansion of scientific activity in sixteenth- and seventeenth-century Europe that many ways had been found for presenting the empirical study of nature consistently with Christian beliefs and virtues. Belief in the unity of a universe governed by a unique set of laws sat comfortably, as it did for Newton, with belief in an intelligent Creator whose will had been impressed on the world. The Christian deity was frequently described as the author of two books: the book of God's words and the book of God's works. The obligation to study the former was matched, as Francis Bacon (1561–1626) had urged, by an obligation to study the latter. Bacon had also argued that the acquisition of firsthand knowledge of God's Creation showed a greater piety and humility than an overdependence on ancient texts and scholastic commentaries on them. The Christian doctrine that all humankind had been tainted by the fall from grace of Adam and Eve featured in many discussions of the fallibility of the human intellect and by what means the knowledge originally granted to Adam might, to some degree, be regained.[12]

During the second half of the seventeenth century, especially in England, scientific activity had been defended on the ground that it furnished evidence for the power and wisdom of God. This genre of natural theology was a response to concerns that atomistic and mechanistic models for the workings of nature would have connotations of atheism. But it also reflected a genuine wonder at the intricate craftsmanship displayed in the minutest organisms newly revealed by the microscope. From the microscopic world studied by Robert Hooke (1635–1702) and Robert Boyle (1627–91) to the macroscopic world of Newton's divinely calculated planetary orbits, the evidence appeared to corroborate belief in a Creator. In new readings of the early chapters of Genesis justification had also been found for viewing

the natural world not only as a source of pious reflection but also a resource—
a divine gift that, when properly investigated, would yield knowledge that
could enhance the quality of human life.[13] The archetypal example of Jesus
Christ as healer could always be used to sanction the quest for medical
improvements.

During the seventeenth century the dream of power over nature, once
the preserve of the magician, became socially respectable. Legitimation
from Christian theology helped to consolidate the process, though not
without anxiety.[14] Christian clergy captivated by a detailed study of nature
sometimes found it difficult to justify their devotion to it when their first
loyalty was to their pastoral responsibilities.[15] The Copernican innovation
had raised serious questions about the interpretation of biblical texts that,
when taken literally, jarred with the new science. Although a universe that
ran according to mechanical laws still allowed one to see the general Providence of God in the design of the system, was there still space for a special
Providence responsive to human needs and intimately involved in the
events of human history?[16]

Such problems can be exaggerated. With reference to biblical interpretation, Christian astronomers committed to the Copernican scheme drew on
an additional resource—the concept of biblical accommodation. In one
form, this was the doctrine that the language of Scripture had been deliber-
ately accommodated by the Holy Spirit to the needs of even the simplest
reader. To have employed language in accord with esoteric scientific theories
would have rendered it unintelligible, with the consequence that its primary
message of salvation would be obscured. A corollary was that biblical texts
should not be used to outlaw conclusions drawn from serious science. This
was not just an artifice to defuse an existing problem. The principle of
accommodation had been countenanced by John Calvin (1509–64), one of
the leaders of the Protestant Reformation. Calvin had explicitly said that the
Bible was not the place to look if one wished to learn astronomy.[17] The
principle was familiar enough for Galileo Galilei (1564–1642) to deploy it in
self-defense, though the political circumstances surrounding his tragic
alienation of Pope Urban VIII meant that it was not sufficient to earn him a
reprieve.[18]

There were additional resources, too, to protect belief in a God who could
answer prayers, work miracles, and take an interest in every human life.
Both Boyle and Newton entertained an analogy between the relation of
mind to body in humans and the relation of God to the physical world. Every
time we move a limb there is proof that mind can act on matter. Why, by
analogy, should not God, as mental agency, be able to influence the material
world? One of Newton's aims was to show that it was easier for God to move
matter than for us to move our limbs.[19] This image of the universe as the

body of God is still to be found in works of Christian theology that address the challenge of a naturalistic worldview.[20] Though it was offensive to Leibniz because it implied the corporeality of God, the analogy sanctions the possibility of immediate divine control without recourse to the language of intervention. For Boyle, whose Christianity was less heterodox than Newton's, science had done nothing to dispel belief in the reality of a world of spirit complementing the visible world.[21] The regularities uncovered by the natural philosopher did not ultimately dictate what was or was not possible in the world. As Samuel Clarke put it, the course of nature was "nothing else but the will of God producing certain effects in a continued, regular, constant, and uniform manner."[22]

CHRISTIANITY UNDER ATTACK

Although the problems raised for Christian belief by the scientific move-ments of the seventeenth century can be exaggerated, it was possible for critics of the established churches to build on them. During the eighteenth century many attacks on the Christian faith were launched, variously capi-talizing on biblical criticism and the philosophies of John Locke (1632–1704) and Benedict (Baruch) de Spinoza (1632–77).[23] They were often inspired by the lack of toleration shown by the churches to those who would not con-form to their discipline and doctrine. The Catholic Church was the major target because, in an age that came to value the powers of human reason, several of its teachings and rituals could be dismissed as superstitious. The belief that during the Eucharist the bread and wine were miraculously turned into the body and blood of Christ was unpalatable to many Protes-tant Christians, let alone to more radical critics of religious ritual. The power of the Catholic Church was deeply resented by dissidents such as the deist Matthew Tindal (1657–1733), who complained in 1730 that Catholic priests had gained their power through claiming a divine right to hear confessions, thereby learning the secrets of all they absolved.

The word "deist" deserves clarification because it was a description given—usually by Christian thinkers—to those who, without denying the existence of a deity, would not accept statements based on revelation that were not independently supported by reason. In England, these critics of the Anglican Church usually presented themselves as advocates of an enlight-ened Christianity rather than as an enemy of the faith. The title of John Toland's book, *Christianity Not Mysterious* (1696), epitomized a politically motivated critique that could also pass for an attempt to make Christianity more credible by sanitizing it of mystery. Whereas Boyle had considered that certain Christian teachings, concerning the afterlife for example, were "above reason," this was a category that shrank during the eighteenth century.

It would, however, be incorrect to say that it was developments in science that led to deism because the science often had to be reinterpreted to bolster the attack. Toland's use of Newton is a case in point. Toland (1670–1722) wished to have powers such as gravity recognized as basic properties of matter; but he knew that Newton himself had rejected that materialist view. For Newton the gravitational force was not innate to matter but an additional power ultimately operative through the will of the deity. A reinterpretation favorable to Toland's opinion was required.[24]

Toland's requirement underlines a point of great importance for discussions of science and religion. In contests concerning the cultural meanings of science, everything hinges on the interpretation placed on scientific knowledge, which has repeatedly been a resource for both Christian and anti-Christian activists who have appropriated it for their purposes. By the 1740s it is possible to point to scientific discoveries that were exploited, especially in France, to support a materialist, anti-Christian philosophy. But these same discoveries were also susceptible of less damaging interpretations.[25] When the English Catholic priest John Needham (1713–81) reported the spontaneous generation of microscopic creatures from both vegetable- and meat-based infusions, it seemed that the power of matter to organize itself into living systems had been underestimated. Yet Needham himself saw no threat to his religion, and the archetypal French deist François-Marie Arouet de Voltaire (1694–1778) declined to exploit it, preferring to dismiss the experimental results as fraudulent miracle-mongering!

There were materialists and atheists in eighteenth-century Europe who, had they openly published their views, as distinct from circulating them clandestinely, would certainly have been vilified or prosecuted. One of the more visible atheists in France was Denis Diderot (1713–84), who during the 1740s deserted a deistic position for one bordering on atheism. Mastermind of the *Encyclopédie*, a cornucopia of secular knowledge, Diderot speculated that the striking adaptation of living things to their mode of life might only reflect nature's experimentation with many combinations of animal parts, the nonviable combinations having perished. A similar conjecture was made by the Scottish philosopher David Hume (1711–76), whose posthumous *Dialogues Concerning Natural Religion* (1779) exposed a fundamental flaw in arguments for design. According to Hume, the analogy between organisms and human artifacts, on which the argument depended, was too fragile to yield any knowledge of the cause of the universe. The analogy did not even exclude the possibility of polytheism, since human constructions, such as ships, were the work of many hands. Hume never denied that the universe had a cause; it was simply that nothing could be known about it. In a famous essay that attracted many rejoinders from Christian apologists, Hume was also skeptical of miracles, arguing that it was always more probable that those who reported them were deceived or deceptive than that the event had occurred as they reported it.[26]

CHRISTIAN INVOLVEMENT IN ENLIGHTENMENT SCIENCE

The fact that scientific discoveries were sometimes implicated in Enlightenment attacks on Christianity does not mean there was a general Christian retreat from involvement in scientific activity. In contexts remarkable for their diversity, knowledge of the natural world was valued and encouraged. The eighteenth century saw a significant expansion in the number of European scientific societies and, while a precedent had been set in the Royal Society of London and the Paris Academy of Sciences for excluding the discussion of religion, individual members rarely had to compromise their religious convictions. The value of competence in the sciences was also recognized by Catholic and Protestant educators, though the emphasis and the particular sciences favored varied from place to place.

Within Catholic Christianity the Jesuits had become the most influential teaching order and could boast a lineage of prominent astronomers and mathematicians. It was members of the Jesuit order who had found ways of commending the Copernican system despite the tightened ban following Galileo's condemnation. The mathematicians of the Order, after ca. 1670, "seldom bothered to try to refute Copernicanism, taught mathematics and mechanics in the style of the Galileo school, and made useful contributions to geometry, positional and physical astronomy, and applied mathematics."[27] Papal patronage sometimes flowed from a strong personal interest in experimental science. Following his accession to the papacy in 1740, Benedict XIV gave direct support to the Academy of Sciences in Bologna and to scientific work undertaken at the University of Rome, where a Jesuit mathematics professor, Roger Boscovich (1711–87), was commissioned to complete a meridian project involving measurements from Rimini to Rome.

Boscovich provides a striking example of a Jesuit mathematician steeped in scientific enquiry. He is noted for a dynamic theory of matter in which Newton's solid impenetrable atoms were replaced by immaterial points surrounded by spheres of attractive and repulsive forces. On this model, the resistance experienced when one body was pressed against another was due not to an intrinsic solidity of atoms but to the repulsive forces operating at short range. This nonmaterialistic model was to find particular application in the explanation of electrical phenomena. In various modifications, it appealed to a succession of British physical scientists: Joseph Priestley

(1733–1804), Humphry Davy (1778–1829), Michael Faraday (1791–1867) and William Thomson (Lord Kelvin 1824–1907).[28]

In the English-speaking world, there were clergy suspicious and sometimes resentful of the way a new breed of popular science lecturers displayed and manipulated the forces of nature with a showmanship that seemed to suggest it was their prerogative rather than God's to control the workings of nature.[29] At the same time a prevalent natural theology could make scientific knowledge attractive as a stick with which to beat atheists and deists. Just as the Reverend Richard Bentley (1662–1742) used Newton's science to contest the Epicurean view that the universe is the result of chance collisions of atoms, so other Christian apologists followed the example of John Ray (1627–1705)—whose *The Wisdom of God Manifested in the Works of Creation* (1691) had displayed many marvels, such as the migrating instincts of birds—to excite a reverent belief in Providence. These works of natural theology were not confined to the Anglophonic world; but, in Britain, clerical involvement in the practice of natural history constituted something of a tradition. A prominent example would be Stephen Hales (1677–1761), whose *Vegetable Staticks* (1727) recorded his pioneering experiments on the rise of sap in trees and an early attempt to analyze the composition of the air. Hales is credited with the invention of the pneumatic trough, which was later to play a crucial role in the isolation of distinctive gases. In his introduction he aligned his quantitative approach with the biblical image of an all-wise Creator who had "observed the most exact proportions, *of number, weight and measure*, in the make of all things."

An heir to Hales's work was another minister, Joseph Priestley, famous for the isolation of a gas that the French chemist Antoine Lavoisier would call oxygen. Priestley illustrates another strand in the evolving relations between scientific and religious thought—that between science and religious dissent. Priestley's theology was Unitarian; in fact he coined the word. Like Newton, he rejected conventional accounts of the Trinity, declining to identify Christ with the Godhead and refusing to accept his preexistence before his earthly life. By orthodox Christians Priestley was not considered a Christian at all; but, again like Newton, he fervently believed he was defending a purified, rational Christianity. Both believed that, early in its history, Christian faith had been corrupted by contamination with Platonist philosophy and that biblical texts conventionally used to authenticate a Triune God were themselves corruptions. Priestley reacted against other doctrines, particularly those associated with Calvinist theology. He considered it irrational to believe that all humankind deserved punishment because of the sin of one man, Adam. The doctrine that because of God's sovereignty it was effectively decreed who would be among the elect and who would face eternal damnation struck him as morally indefensible. Having rejected the doctrine of original sin, he also rejected the idea that Christ's death had been an atoning sacrifice, making possible divine forgiveness. Other Christian doctrines, such as bodily resurrection in a life after death, Priestley considered perfectly reasonable as well as indispensable for social control.[30]

In this culture of rational dissent, as it came to be known, science was an important constituent. It provided both a model *of* progress and a means *to* social progress. For Priestley it was on the same side as rational religion in the fight against popular superstition. In some dissenting academies, as at Warrington, the teaching of science gained a higher profile than in the universities of Oxford and Cambridge. In manufacturing towns in the north of England, discussion of science, medicine, and technology was facilitated by literary and philosophical societies, which in Manchester and Newcastle were dominated by Unitarians. Priestley belonged to the Lunar Society of Birmingham, which profitably brought together entrepreneurs, scientists of the caliber of James Watt (1736–1819), and industrialists such as the pottery manufacturer Josiah Wedgwood (1730–95). Typifying a philosophy of improvement, Priestley expected that the gases he identified would find medical application; for example, he hoped that what we know as carbon dioxide, when dissolved in water, might remove the scourge of scurvy.

Priestley personified a connection between radical Christianity and a growing scientific culture.[31] He wrote on electricity and optics, outlining experiments that his readers could perform for themselves. At a serious philosophical level, he reformed discussion of the relationship between mind and body, rendering possible a science of the brain. Rejecting the belief that mind is made of other stuff than matter—a belief Descartes had defended—Priestley forsook a duality of matter and spirit, preferring a monism in which mind and brain were in intimate union. A presupposition of modern neuroscience, that it is the brain that thinks, was first made explicit by Priestley in his *Disquisitions Relating to Matter and Spirit* (1777). In the defense of monism, Priestley's radical theology played a key role: he argued that it fitted a biblical understanding of the human person as a unified psychosomatic whole better than the prevalent Catholic view that humans have immortal souls that automatically survive death. The correct view, Priestley insisted, was one of bodily resurrection, which he considered more theologically sound because it restored sovereignty to God in this future dispensation.[32] Priestley's version of Christianity was extreme among dissenters. He paid a heavy price for his political sympathies when, in the conservative reaction following the French Revolution, an angry mob burned his house and laboratory. He himself valued his ministry more highly than his scientific vocation, but in that combination of interests is a telling example of how dialogue between radical and traditional forms of Christianity could generate intellectual ferment propitious for the sciences.

An absorbing question is whether distinctive forms of Christianity correlated with involvement in particular sciences. A special preoccupation with mathematics and astronomy among the Jesuits has already been noted. Research on a minority dissenting sect, the Quakers, has shown a recurring predilection for observational sciences, especially botany, and a propensity for careers in medicine as physicians, surgeons, and apothecaries. For a relatively small constituency, a surprisingly large number of Quakers and ex-Quakers were elected to the Royal Society. Their number included such major scientific figures as Thomas Young (1773–1829) and John Dalton (1766–1844), the former associated with the wave theory of light, the latter with the chemical atomic theory.[33]

During the second half of the eighteenth century, a taste for some sciences more than others accompanied the successful efforts of John Wesley (1703–91) to revitalize Christian faith through his evangelical preaching. Keeping abreast of the latest developments through reading the transactions of the Royal Society, Wesley was particularly engaged by the medical applications of electricity, on which he published in 1760, taking cognizance of Benjamin Franklin's work on the nature of lightning and electrical conductivity. Wesley was less enamored of ambitious theoretical systems. Aware that Newton's science had been commandeered by freethinkers to injure the faith, he shared with Jonathan Edwards (1703–58), one of the catalysts of American evangelicalism, a suspicion of presumptuous forms of science that kept the God of love and mercy at arms length. Such selectivity has been a recurring feature of clerical interest in the sciences, and Wesley would cede no ground to any who wished to affirm the full autonomy, or full comprehensibility, of nature. On the subject of miracles, for example, his starting point was very different from Hume's. Whereas Hume pressed his probability argument, insisting that reports of miracles were to be mistrusted, Wesley contended that a God powerful enough to make as wondrous a world as this could surely not be incapable of working lesser miracles.[34]

CHANGING SENSIBILITIES AND A CHANGED EARTH

In discourses that brought science and Christian theology together the terms of the discussion were deeply affected, if not always immediately, by changes in the content and scope of scientific theory. By the end of the eighteenth century exciting or (for some) disturbing contrasts could be drawn between how the world was seen then and the world picture a hundred years earlier. Whereas Newton had required a deity to calculate initial planetary velocities to ensure a viable system, and subsequently to keep them under review, the French mathematician Pierre-Simon Laplace (1749–1827) now managed without. Laplace explained planetary orbits by suggesting the planets had originally condensed from a rotating nebular atmosphere encircling the sun. He also showed that the instabilities that had concerned Newton were self-correcting.[35] Whereas Robert Boyle had collated evidence for a spirit world behind visible material phenomena, even suggesting that alchemical secrets might be discovered through communion with higher powers, a hundred years later Priestley was banishing the word "spirit" altogether from both chemistry and theology. Late in the seventeenth century Thomas Burnet (ca.1635–1715) had published his *Sacred Theory of the Earth* (1684), in which physical mechanisms were invoked to explain the Flood in Genesis. But Burnet had still divided Earth history into separate phases in accord with events described and foretold in Scripture. A hundred years later the Scottish landowner James Hutton (1726–97) published his *Theory of the Earth* (1795), in which the geological processes that created mountains and eroded them in producing soils were cyclic, furnishing no evidence of a beginning or end.[36]

In another respect, the contrast is particularly striking. In *Wisdom of God Manifested in the Works of Creation*, Ray had explained that what he meant by "Creation" was a world that had not significantly changed since it had been created. By the end of the eighteenth century, the French naturalist Georges-Louis LeClerc, Comte de Buffon (1707–88), had conjectured that as the Earth had gradually cooled from an original molten mass, the flora and fauna it could support had changed. Large mammals now living in equatorial regions had once roamed at the poles—hence the frozen mammoths found in Siberia. Earth history and human history were no longer coextensive.[37] Potentially more disturbing were the speculations of Erasmus Darwin (1731–1802) in Britain and Jean-Baptiste Lamarck (1744–1829) in France, both of whom proposed that living things had been transformed by nature over the course of time.[38]

Such contrasts show how knowledge of nature that had once been sacred could be displaced by reconstructions in which the sacred became less conspicuous. Laplace's nebular hypothesis, initially highly speculative, provided a template for future naturalistic accounts of the origins of the solar system. It did not prove difficult to harmonize this new cosmology with the account of Creation in Genesis,[39] but was there conceivably an absence of design in the emergence of the solar system and consequently in Earth history? When the French paleontologist Georges Cuvier (1769–1832) demonstrated that large quadrupeds had become extinct, there was a new worry: Was humankind itself destined for destruction?[40]

CHRISTIANITY AND THE HISTORICAL SCIENCES
IN THE NINETEENTH CENTURY

The biggest intellectual threat to the Christian churches came during the nineteenth century—not only from the historical sciences of geology and evolutionary biology but also from the practice of history itself. To relate biblical writings to the contexts in which they had been written was envisaged by leading Christian scholars as a way of enhancing religious understanding. But in its most radical form, as in David Friedrich Strauss's *Life of Jesus* (1835), a historical methodology was associated with attacks on the veracity of the gospel narratives. Strauss argued, for example, that miracles were ascribed to Christ by the gospel writers because such powers had been expected of the Messiah. Even in less radical forms the "higher criticism," as it became known, could be troubling to conservative Christians because a primary assumption was that the books of the Bible derived from many documentary sources and should not be regarded as conveying a seamless truth. When Bishop John Colenso of Natal challenged a conventional belief that Moses was the author of the first five books of the Old Testament, he was dismissed from his post by a synod of bishops in South Africa. This was shortly after the appearance in England of a controversial volume of *Essays and Reviews* (1860) in which several Anglican clergy argued that the Bible must be read like any other book—a product of its time and therefore fallible in its cosmology. Attacking this book, the bishop of Oxford, Samuel Wilberforce, was far more indignant than in his review of Darwin's *Origin of Species* (1859), which had appeared a few months earlier.[41]

During the preceding half-century there had been elaborate attempts to harmonize science and Scripture. How might the great age of the Earth be squared with the few thousand years inferred from Old Testament genealogies? An early move favored by the Scottish evangelical Thomas Chalmers (1780–1847), by Oxford's foremost geologist William Buckland (1784–1856) and by Edward Hitchcock (1793–1864), a Congregational minister in America, was to expand the time-gap between "In the beginning" and the events of the first "day" in Genesis. During the 1830s there was, as yet, no conclusive evidence to suggest the human race itself was other than of recent origin.[42]

A prolific popularizer of geology, Hugh Miller (1802–56), elaborated an alternative harmonizing strategy. Miller was editor of *The Witness*, principal newspaper of the Free Church of Scotland. His argument was that the sequence of creation in Genesis broadly matched that of the fossil record. The vast age of the Earth was no problem as Miller followed earlier precedents in equating the Genesis "days" with long geological epochs. He proposed that the "days" could also refer to successive days in which the biblical author had received visions of what the Earth had been like during each of its phases. Ingeniously, he constructed an interpretation of the fossil record that revealed both progress and degeneration. At the beginning of each epoch creatures more complex than their predecessors had been introduced by their Creator. But believing in the Fall and battling against theories of progressive evolutionary transformation, Miller insisted that within each epoch there was evidence of degeneration. He rejected the mutability of species because, if humans derived from animal ancestors, their unique-ness as moral beings blessed with aesthetic sense and immortal soul would be compromised.[43]

One of Miller's targets was a sensational book that argued a case for bio-logical evolution fifteen years before Darwin. This was *Vestiges of the Natural History of Creation* (1844), written by the Edinburgh publisher Robert Cham-bers (1802–1871), whose authorship was successfully concealed for many years. Chambers claimed to see evidence of design in the laws governing the development of life, but his thesis was frequently attacked for its mate-rialism. This was because his account of the relationship between mind and brain appeared to strike at notions of free will and individual responsibility. He was sympathetic to a voguish phrenology, the view that personality and behavioral characteristics could be correlated with specific parts of the brain and their reflection in the contours of the skull. The phrenological circle in Edinburgh to which Chambers belonged was dominated by anticlericalism, political liberalism, and religious indifference.[44] The problem perceived by Christian observers was not merely a materializing of the soul but the corol-lary that the autonomy of the human subject was thrown into jeopardy. Christian theology has generally resisted deterministic accounts of human behavior, whether the determinism has been placed in the stars, in statis-tical regularities, in physical or psychological descriptions of brain-states or, as in contemporary debates, in our genes.

The fact that Darwin made a far stronger case for the transformation of species, encouraging its extension to human evolution, has meant that his work is routinely seen as a watershed in the historical relations between science and Christianity. Reconstructions of the past, it is often assumed, would no longer need to defer, or even refer, to a Creator. It is, however, important to recognize that questions about origins were also arising from the physical sciences, particularly the science of thermodynamics. Among the pioneers of this new science were committed Christians such as Michael Faraday and William Thomson, whose religious convictions found expres-sion in their science. Faraday was a conscientious member of a small Chris-tian sect, the Sandemanians, and is renowned for research that eventually led to the electric motor. He succeeded in correlating quantitatively the forces of electricity, magnetism, and chemical affinity, and he also pursued, though unsuccessfully, an attempt to convert gravitational into electrical forces. His conviction that the different forces of nature were all interrelated appears to have been underpinned by his monotheistic belief in the ultimate unity of nature.[45] With the science of thermodynamics a discourse about *forces* was displaced by a discourse of *energy*. For William Thomson, the principle of energy conservation testified that only God could create and destroy the energy inherent in the universe. Energy, however, was continually being dissipated. Thomson wrote of a "tendency in the material world for motion to become diffused" and this he saw as consonant with Psalm 102, which spoke of the earth and the heavens eventually perishing.[46] In later formulations, the second law of thermodynamics referred to an inexorable tendency in closed physical systems for entropy (a measure of the disorder in the system) to increase. Applying this principle to the universe as a whole was problematic, but it gave rise to an argument for an ultimate Creation sufficiently persuasive to worry the atheist Friedrich Engels (1820–95). If entropy was continually increasing, a backward extrapolation implied a moment of beginning and refuted a universe of infinite duration that had always existed. This was no *proof* of a Creator, but it promised support for Christian belief in a universe having an origin and direction.[47]

Darwin's theory of evolution by natural selection had nothing to say about the origin of the universe, the origin of the earth or even the origin of life. He did not compromise its rigor by indulging in speculation about spontaneous generation, which had damaged the scientific credibility of *Vestiges*. By explaining how new species could emerge from pre-existing species over long periods of time, during which advantageous variations were preserved and transmitted in a competitive struggle for survival, Darwin nevertheless challenged long-cherished understandings of God's relationship to nature. The origin of species was no longer the "mystery of mysteries" it had formerly been. If humans shared ancestors with other primates, could they still be accorded the dignity that derived from their having been made in the image of God? Could Genesis still be said to convey spiritual insight if, in detail, it was no longer historically or scientifically credible? What of the status of the human soul that had so worried Hugh Miller and continued to be of primary importance in Catholic theology? What of the argument for design, made by English theologian William Paley (1743–1805), based on the many contrivances in nature whereby organic structures were so wonderfully adapted to their functions? The presentation of natural selection as a perfecting mechanism suggested that the appearance of design might be an illusion. This was in marked contrast to a theology of nature as epitomized by the Cambridge philosopher William Whewell (1794–1866), who had argued that, unlike physical systems, living systems could not be analyzed *scientifically* without reference to the "final causes" in which he saw indications of a Creator. By the end of the century it would be rare to find theological references in technical scientific treatises. Darwin's science did not cause this transformation, but with its excision of final causes it was certainly a catalyst.[48]

This transition was fraught because it accompanied a social transformation in which the clergy, certainly in Britain, had their cultural authority and control over education challenged by a generation of naturalists typified by Darwin's "bulldog," Thomas Henry Huxley (1825–95).[49] More anti-clerical than anti-religious, Huxley resented the privileges bestowed by membership in the established church and the ancient universities of Oxford and Cambridge. In 1860 he pointedly declared that "extinguished theologians lie about the cradle of every science like the strangled snakes beside that of Hercules."[50] Huxley nevertheless conceded that Darwin's theory did not preclude the possibility that an initial configuration of the universe had been designed in such a way that the evolutionary process would eventuate in human beings. Christians receptive to Darwin's science would increasingly argue that design was to be seen not so much in specific structures, such as the beak of the woodpecker, but in the *laws* (in Darwin's own words) "impressed on matter by the Creator."[51] And because they could also apply a concept of evolution to biblical exegesis, arguing that the Scriptures revealed a developing and increasingly refined understanding of God, the religious response to Darwin's theory was far from uniformly oppositional.

A DIVISIVE FORCE WITHIN CHRISTENDOM

From 1859 to the present, Darwin's naturalistic account of the origin of species has been a valuable resource for atheists, materialists, and freethinkers eager to exclude references to the supernatural from their worldview. When Richard Dawkins says that Darwin made it possible to become an intellectually fulfilled atheist, he has in mind Darwin's demonstration that nature could counterfeit design.[52] Because the theory quickly appealed to critics of Christianity, gaining ground in France during the prevailing secular ethos of the Third Republic and in Germany through a popular movement that almost turned belief in evolution into an alternative religion, Christian thinkers have not always known how best to respond. Attitudes have been colored by events having high public profile. Such an event was the physicist John Tyndall's presidential address before the British Association for the Advancement of Science, delivered in Belfast in 1874. Provoked by the refusal of Catholic authorities in Ireland to bring science into their curricula, Tyndall (1820–93) invoked Darwin's theory in an aggressive attack on the pretensions of theology: "we claim, and we shall wrest, from theology the entire domain of cosmological theory."[53]

In such public contexts, Darwinism came to be linked with anti-Christian sentiments. Tyndall shared with Darwin's cousin Francis Galton (1822–1911) a scornful attitude toward the effectiveness of prayer—an issue publicized by Galton's skeptical attempt to gauge its efficacy by checking whether the much-prayed-for kings and queens of England had enjoyed a greater longevity than those less privileged. Whether the deity would consent to be trapped by such a crude, mechanical experiment was a subject of great controversy; but it transpired that they had not.[54] The 1870s also saw the publication of John William Draper's *History of the Conflict between Religion and Science* (1874), which, having enjoyed many reprintings, has reinforced popular perceptions of polarization. Draper's venom was directed against the Roman Catholic Church, which in the preceding decade had reaffirmed its jurisdiction over the teaching of literature and science, and had asserted papal infallibility on matters of faith and morals. The rewriting of history to demonstrate unrelenting conflict was consummated twenty years later, when Andrew Dickson White, first president of Cornell University, published *A History of the Warfare of Science with Theology in Christendom* (1896), in which the villain was declared not to be religion as such but dogmatic theology. Despite its lack of discrimination, White's revenge on the New York clergy who had opposed a secular curriculum for Cornell continues to fuel public perceptions of antagonism between science and Christian belief.

The history of Darwinism within Christendom is, however, far richer than such polarities suggest. One of Darwin's earliest converts was Charles Kingsley (1819–75), a Christian clergyman willing to accept that a God able to make things *make themselves* was more deserving of admiration than one who separately conjured creatures into existence like a magician. Such an affirmative response underlines the fact that within Christendom the Darwinian theory would prove more divisive than destructive.[55]

The reaction of Samuel Wilberforce (1805–73) is often taken to typify Christian resistance. At the 1860 Oxford meeting of the British Association, the bishop allegedly baited Huxley by asking whether he would prefer to have an ape for an ancestor on his grandfather's or grandmother's side. Legend has it that he got an immediate comeuppance when Huxley declared he would rather have an ape in his ancestral line than a person (meaning the bishop) who used his intellectual gifts to obscure the truth. The anecdote flourishes as a foundation myth of scientific professionalism, but Wilberforce was undoubtedly aggrieved that Darwin had threatened human dignity.[56] He simply could not accept that human beings, for whom Jesus Christ had lived and died, had an animal ancestry. And yet at the same meeting of the British Association, one of Wilberforce's own ordinands and a future archbishop of Canterbury, Frederick Temple, preached a sermon in which he welcomed the expansion of naturalistic explanation. The greater the number of phenomena brought under the reign of physical law, Temple argued, the stronger the case for asserting, by analogy, the existence of moral laws to which humans were subject. There were many such divisions of opinion among Christian clergy. Darwin was stung by his old friend Adam Sedgwick, who reproached him for denying a role for final causes, for purposive direction, in the process of evolution. Yet another old friend, John Henslow, reproached Sedgwick and vindicated Darwin. According to Henslow, it was not Darwin's intention to demean the role of God in the world but simply to show that divine purposes could be effected through laws in the animate world as they were already acknowledged to be in the inanimate.[57]

In North America there was considered opposition to Darwin's theory in Princeton's Theological Seminary from Charles Hodge, whose book *What Is Darwinism?* (1874) did not so much pit the Bible against evolution as take issue with the specific mechanism of natural selection, which Hodge, following Darwin, deemed incompatible with prevailing understandings of design. Yet Princeton College would have a Presbyterian president, James McCosh, who boldly endorsed the idea of evolution and saw no difficulty in the roles accorded to chance and accident in the process. At Harvard, Louis Agassiz (1807–73) resisted Darwin's theory, rejecting material connections between species. But if Harvard's professor of geology and zoology saw in the fossil record a progressive instantiation of divine ideas, her professor of botany, Asa Gray (1810–88), became Darwin's chief advocate in North America. Gray saw in the new science a valuable resource for Christian theology. To the old question why a benevolent God would allow so much pain and suffering there was the prospect of a new answer. They were concomitants of a struggle for existence without which there would have been no motor for evolutionary change, no possibility of human beings emerging at all. Diverging from Darwin's agnosticism, Gray considered that the variations on which natural selection worked could still be understood as under divine control. Their origins were as yet unknown, and in those that had made possible complex organs, and especially in those that marked the transition from pre-human to human, Gray saw a special role for divine action.[58]

There are many reasons why Darwinism in America developed a high public profile. It was drawn into discussions about race when, in the 1860s, the Civil War elevated the issue, and well into the twentieth century, it was also invoked to support highly controversial eugenic proposals. Biblical support for the unity of the human race had been challenged in the mid-nineteenth century by advocates of multiple origins, such as Robert Knox in Britain and Samuel Morton in America, whose polygenism was a serious threat to both Catholic and Protestant theology.[59] Measuring representative skulls, Morton appealed to phrenology to display the moral and intellectual differences between the races. A compelling attraction of Darwin's theory for Asa Gray was the implication that all members of the human species ultimately had a common origin, thereby challenging the polygenism to which Morton and Agassiz subscribed and which could provide additional justification for slavery and racial stereotyping. The monogenism approved by Darwin in *The Descent of Man* (1871) was, however, a novel form because, unlike its earlier Christian instantiation, it did not presuppose an equality or potential equality among the human races. The polygenists' belief in separate, primordial, and immutable species was shaken; but the continuous action of natural and cultural selection had irreversibly and indelibly produced races with different characteristics. Because natural selection provided a "monogenist base for what was a practical polygenism,"[60] the Darwinian theory, in some contexts (as in New Zealand), was unashamedly used to justify colonial displacement of indigenous peoples.[61]

The question of racial *improvement* was addressed in many eugenic proposals during the late nineteenth and early twentieth centuries. Here again was a hugely divisive issue. It even featured marginally in what became perhaps the most emblematic event in America's struggle to come to terms with Darwinism—the trial of biology teacher John Scopes in 1925 in Dayton, Tennessee. The association of Darwinism with eugenics was strong in Britain, represented by the geneticist Ronald Fisher (1890–1962) for whom it was a practical Christian duty to encourage breeding among those of "higher ability, richer health, and greater beauty."[62] American evangelicals, many suspicious of attempts at racial engineering, were apt to see Darwinism as villain and partner in crime. This was true of William Jennings Bryan, who was pitted against Clarence Darrow, defender of Scopes and of his liberty to teach evolution against a Tennessee law banning the teaching of human evolution—a law that the American Civil Liberties Union wished to test.[63] Later dramatization of the trial in the film *Inherit the Wind* (1860) contributed to a mythology described by Stephen Jay Gould: "John Scopes was persecuted, Darrow rose to Scopes's defense and smote the antediluvian Bryan, and the anti-evolution movement then dwindled or ground to at least a temporary halt." Gould then added: "All three parts of this story are false."[64] The resurgence of a young-earth creationism in the wake of Henry Morris and John Whitcomb's *The Genesis Flood* (1961) demonstrated a vitality in fundamentalist opposition to Darwin, albeit earthed in archaic ideas long abandoned by respected geologists.

Christian attitudes toward Darwinism must not, however, be judged by the reactions of extremists. In early debates over the mechanism of evolution, natural selection was complemented by other contributing factors, especially when explaining how the human mind had developed. This created space for many versions of theistic evolution.[65] A well-known example from the twentieth century was the visionary scheme of the Jesuit scientist and theologian Teilhard de Chardin (1881–1955), who saw in the exemplary character and perfections of Jesus Christ a prefiguring of the goal toward which human evolution was progressing. As with many mediators, Teilhard's theologizing did not endear him to the Catholic authorities. His invocation of tendencies toward greater complexity *inherent* within living organisms meant that his poetic synthesis was also marginalized by a scientific community excited by an alternative neo-Darwinian synthesis of genetics and natural selection.[66] Various forms of theistic evolution are, however, very much alive among liberal Christian thinkers and within some evangelical institutions, such as the American Scientific Affiliation.[67] Nonpartisan philosophers have acknowledged that, despite genuine problems, it is not impossible to be a Darwinian and a Christian.[68]

THE ENGAGEMENT OF CHRISTIANITY AND SCIENCE
IN THE TWENTIETH CENTURY

Commentators on the mutual bearings of science and religion have repeatedly asked whether their respective spheres of authority should be disengaged or allowed to interpenetrate. For much of the twentieth century there were serious deterrents to combining Christian theology with scientific discourse. Within the culture of science, religion was increasingly seen as a private matter having no bearing on scientific practice. A legacy from the territorial squabbles of the nineteenth century was the conclusion favored by T. H. Huxley—that science was neither Christian nor un-Christian but "extra-Christian," simply outside and beyond religious discourse. A sophisticated case for separation was made by the philosopher Ludwig Wittgenstein, who argued that distinctive linguistic discourses reflected distinctive ways of life and should not be confused: religious and scientific *practices*, and their respective goals, were unmistakably different. From the controversies of the nineteenth century some Christians at least had learned the lesson commended by the great physicist James Clerk Maxwell (1831–79) that it was a mistake to base biblical exegesis on the latest scientific theory: to do so was to be embarrassed when the science changed. Within Protestant theology a powerful influence was the critique of natural theology pressed by Karl Barth (1886–1968), who emphasized God's grace and initiative in self-revelation, inviting a human commitment in response. To reason one's way to the existence and attributes of God, as many had who drew their arguments from the sciences, was for Barth misguided and presumptuous. Barth published between the two World Wars, which themselves inflicted serious damage on optimistic fusions of human evolution with divine providence.[69]

There was, however, a recurring obstacle to disengagement in the shape of attacks on religious belief from scientists convinced that their science *was* relevant to religious concerns, albeit destructively. A well-known example would be the analytical psychology of Sigmund Freud (1856–1939), for whom belief in a caring God was an infantile projection of a father figure. A Christian understanding of guilt, release from which could come only from divine forgiveness, was replaced by therapeutic techniques designed to help patients understand the natural origins of their guilt feelings and so achieve liberation from them.[70] A decisive relevance of science to religion was also enshrined within fashionable schools of academic philosophy, notably logical positivism, in which no room was left for religious discourse since it was judged not to conform to the strict canons of verifiability operative in the sciences.

With the throwing down of such a gauntlet, it is not surprising that Christian apologists sought reengagement with the sciences rather than disengagement. At least three twentieth-century developments provided irresistible temptation: the indeterminacy introduced by quantum mechanics; a new cosmology in which the universe ceased to be in steady state but was rather expanding from an original "Big Bang"; and, most recently, the realization that for carbon-based life to be possible, extremely stringent conditions have to be satisfied in the underlying laws of physics. For Christians considering how a deity might act in the world, each of these innovations has provided a platform for theological speculation.

A feature of the quantum mechanics developed by Max Planck (1858–1947), Werner Heisenberg (1901–76), and Niels Bohr (1885–1962) was a concept of indeterminacy in nature, which seemed to offer liberation from the mechanistic, deterministic universe against which romantic spirits had traditionally rebelled. In the new physics it still made sense to say that one state of a subatomic system gives rise to the next. But because a quantum-mechanical description could not be given without reference to probabilities, it appeared that each state was only one of several possibilities permitted by its antecedent. Why then would one state be instantiated rather than another? Without postulating any kind of divine intervention, could one simply identify the actual outcome, when others had been possible, with the will of a providential God?[71] If one wished to go further and make room for an intervening deity, there was the tantalizing possibility that direct divine involvement in the instantiation of one state rather than another would not be detectable—a rather curious advantage for those theologians whose aesthetic sensibilities precluded visible signs of interference.[72] There are major problems with such theologizing; but the license to reject a rigidly deterministic universe has appealed to Christian and secular thinkers alike, particularly in the context of rationalizing the possibility of free will.

The idea that the universe has expanded from an original explosion was proposed in 1927 by the Belgian Catholic priest and astrophysicist Georges Lemaître (1894–1966). Although Lemaître himself refrained from speaking of the universe's beginning as a creation, other Christians have celebrated the Big Bang as confirmation of the kind of beginning they envisage from their doctrine of Creation, one in which time itself, as for Saint Augustine, is a created product. The congruence was irresistible to Pope Pius XII, who rejoiced that astronomers and physicists now regarded the idea of Creation as "quite compatible with scientific conceptions." The dangers in appropriating the latest science were rather clearer to a later pope, John Paul II, who, in 1988, explicitly warned against making "uncritical and overhasty use for apologetic purposes of such recent theories as that of the 'Big Bang' in cosmology."[73]

The recognition during the second half of the twentieth century that a minuscule change in the balance of the fundamental forces that have governed the formation of chemical elements would translate into a universe in which carbon-based life would be impossible poses a very peculiar enigma: why is our universe "so uncannily fit for life"?[74] One response might be to shrug one's shoulders and simply accept that this is how it is. For Christians who believe that the universe is the result of a loving and intelligent deity, the temptation is to see in the finely tuned universe evidence of a fine-tuner. Those who adopt that position, like the Cambridge physicist-turned-theologian John Polkinghorne, concede that the inference to an intelligent creator does not constitute a proof. Rather, the scientific data are consonant with belief in such a Being. In more skeptical lines of argument the possibility is entertained of an enormous number of universes, each having a different balance of fundamental parameters. Given a sufficiently large number, the argument goes, it becomes less surprising that one has the necessary prerequisites—the one in which we find ourselves. Christian philosophers sometimes suggest that the postulation of a multiverse is merely a device to evade their argument; but that criticism in turn may be too severe, since cosmological models involving a multiverse have not been scientifically sterile.[75] The problem of access to other universes is, however, formidable, and it is not clear that there can be a decisive disproof of the theistic option. On such matters aesthetic sensibilities and religious predispositions tend to be paramount.

Nothing in this survey should be taken to imply that in the practice of the sciences Christians have outnumbered non-Christians or that Christian presuppositions have conferred a decisive advantage in pursuing scientific research.[76] Nevertheless, because the great expansion of modern science has taken place predominantly in cultures profoundly influenced by Christian teaching, there have been many points of contact and exchanges of the kind we have been examining. In the modern period Christianity, as well as science, has undergone many changes, notably through contact with other cultures and, more recently, through both globalization and fragmentation. Christianity is an evangelistic religion: over the centuries it has been spread by missionary activity, much of which was at its height at the very time when scientific agnosticism was supposedly sapping its intellectual foundations. Interestingly, recent research has revealed the crucial role played by missionaries in introducing Western science to other civilizations and in promoting collection of valuable specimens and data from foreign soil.[77] One example, among many, would be the activities of three Baptist missionaries in India. These are William Carey, William Ward, and Joshua Marshman, who in the late eighteenth and early nineteenth centuries endeavored to bring indigenous Indian philosophy into dialogue with European science, in the belief that the superiority of Western science would be revealed in ways that would also commend the virtues of Christian civilization. The interest of this particular case lies in the fact that the Baptist trio did far more than simply diffuse a London-centered science. Carey established an impressive botanical garden and was instrumental in the formation of the Agricultural Society of India. They were willing to teach Sanskrit science alongside European science and hoped to enlist European residents in India in furthering their scientific projects.[78]

The spread of Christianity in the Southern Hemisphere has been marked in recent years by the diffusion of Pentecostalism and other charismatic movements, to such an extent that it is said by 2000 a quarter of all Christians identified with these radically supernatural forms of spirituality. This has undoubtedly created larger audiences for messages either indifferent toward the sciences or critical of their naturalistic presuppositions. The rapid spread of intelligent design theory, with its message of an irreducible complexity in organic structures that supposedly defies explanation in Darwinian terms, is indicative of a widespread popular disenchantment with liberal values associated with Darwinism and especially with the materialism superimposed on it. Another consequence has been to magnify divisions within Christendom on such sensitive issues as homosexuality, abortion, and the cloning of embryonic stem cells for medical research. The ritualistic accusation that scientists are "playing God" when they seek to enhance human attributes often has its roots in religious scruples about interfering with the "natural." At the same time Christian theology, both Catholic and Protestant, has provided resources for a more affirmative response in its portrayal of humans as collaborators, sometimes even co-creators, with the deity in improving the world.[79]

NOTES

1. Alexei V. Nesteruk, *Light from the East: Theology, Science, and the Eastern Orthodox Tradition* (Minneapolis: Fortress Press, 2003), 36–40; Christopher C. Knight, "The Fallen Cosmos: An Aspect of Eastern Christian Thought and Its Relevance to the Dialogue between Science and Theology," *Theology and Science* 6 (2008): 305–17.

2. Cited by Kallistos Ware, "Eastern Orthodox Theology," in *The Oxford Companion to Christian Thought*, ed. Adrian Hastings, Alistair Mason, and Hugh Pyper, 184–87, on 185 (Oxford: Oxford University Press, 2000).

3. H. G. Alexander, ed., *The Leibniz-Clarke Correspondence* (Manchester: University of Manchester Press, 1956).

4. Ronald L. Numbers, *The Creationists: From Scientific Creationism to Intelligent Design*, expanded ed. (Cambridge, Mass.: Harvard University Press, 2006), chap. 17.

5. William B. Ashworth Jr., "Catholicism and Early Modern Science," in *God and Nature: Historical Essays on the Encounter between Christianity and Science*, ed. David C. Lindberg and Ronald L. Numbers, 136–66, 147 (Berkeley: University of California Press, 1986).

6. Isaac Newton, Letter to Richard Bentley, December 10, 1692, in *Newton's Philosophy of Nature*, ed. H. S. Thayer, 46–50, 49 (New York: Hafner, 1953).

7. Peter Harrison, "Subduing the Earth: Genesis 1, Early Modern Science, and the Exploitation of Nature," *Journal of Religion* 79 (1999): 86–109; Jürgen Moltmann, *God for a Secular Society* (London: SCM Press, 1997), 92–116.

8. David N. Livingstone, *Putting Science in Its Place: Geographies of Scientific Knowledge* (Chicago: University of Chicago Press, 2003), 116–23.

9. John Hedley Brooke, *Science and Religion: Some Historical Perspectives* (Cambridge: Cambridge University Press, 1991), chap. 6; and with Geoffrey Cantor, *Reconstructing Nature: The Engagement of Science and Religion* (Edinburgh: T and T Clark, 1998), chaps. 5–7.

10. Cited by Jack Morrell and Arnold Thackray, *Gentlemen of Science* (Oxford: Clarendon Press, 1981), 241.

11. Arie Leegwater, "Charles Alfred Coulson (1910–74)," in *Eminent Lives in Twentieth-Century Science and Religion*, ed. Nicolaas A. Rupke, 47–77 (Frankfurt: Peter Lang, 2007).

12. Peter Harrison, *The Fall of Man and the Foundations of Science* (Cambridge: Cambridge University Press, 2007).

13. Peter Harrison, *The Bible, Protestantism, and the Rise of Natural Science* (Cambridge: Cambridge University Press, 1998), chaps. 5–6.

14. Stephen Gaukroger, *The Emergence of a Scientific Culture: Science and the Shaping of Modernity* (Oxford: Clarendon Press, 2006).

15. Mordechai Feingold, "Science as a Calling? The Early Modern Dilemma," *Science in Context* 15 (2002): 79–119.

16. Richard S. Westfall, *Science and Religion in Seventeenth-Century England* (New Haven, Conn.: Yale University Press, 1958).

17. Kenneth J. Howell, *God's Two Books: Copernican Cosmology and Biblical Interpretation in Early Modern Science* (Notre Dame, Ind.: University of Notre Dame Press, 2002), 140–54.

18. Ernan McMullin, "Galileo's Theological Venture," in *The Church and Galileo*, ed. Ernan McMullin, 88–116 (Notre Dame, Ind.: University of Notre Dame Press, 2005).

19. Brooke, *Science and Religion*, 139, 144–51.

20. Philip Clayton and Arthur Peacocke, eds., *In Whom We Live and Move and Have Our Being: Panentheistic Reflections on God's Presence in a Scientific World* (Grand Rapids, Mich.: Eerdmans, 2004).

21. Lawrence M. Principe, *The Aspiring Adept: Robert Boyle and His Alchemical Quest* (Princeton, N.J.: Princeton University Press, 1998), 201–8.

22. Cited by Margaret C. Jacob, *The Newtonians and the English Revolution 1689–1720* (Ithaca, N.Y.: Cornell University Press, 1976), 188.

23. James Dybikowski, "The Critique of Christianity," in *The Enlightenment World*, ed. Martin Fitzpatrick, Peter Jones, Christa Knellwolf, and Iain McCalman, 41–56 (London: Routledge, 2004).

24. Brooke, *Science and Religion*, 167–71.

25. Ibid., 171–80.

26. David Wootton, "Hume's 'Of Miracles': Probability and Irreligion," in *Studies in the Philosophy of the Scottish Enlightenment*, ed. M. A. Stewart, 191–229 (Oxford: Oxford University Press, 1990).

27. John L. Heilbron, *The Sun in the Church* (Cambridge, Mass.: Harvard University Press, 1999), 191.

28. Robert E. Schofield, *The Enlightenment of Joseph Priestley* (University Park: Pennsylvania State University Press, 2004), 71–72.

29. Simon Schaffer, "Natural Philosophy and Public Spectacle in the Eighteenth Century," *History of Science* 21 (1983): 1–43.

30. John Hedley Brooke, "Joining Natural Philosophy to Christianity: The Case of Joseph Priestley," in *Heterodoxy in Early Modern Science and Religion*, ed. John Brooke and Ian Maclean, 319–36 (Oxford: Oxford University Press, 2005).

31. Paul Wood, ed., *Science and Dissent in England, 1688–1945* (Aldershot: Ashgate, 2004).

32. Fernando Vidal, "Brains, Bodies, Selves and Science: Anthropologies of Identity and the Resurrection of the Body," *Critical Inquiry* 28 (2002): 930–74.

33. Geoffrey Cantor, *Quakers, Jews, and Science* (Oxford: Oxford University Press, 2005).

34. Brooke, *Science and Religion*, 189–91.

35. Roger Hahn, "Laplace and the Mechanistic Universe," in Lindberg and Numbers, *God and Nature*, 256–76.

36. Martin J. S. Rudwick, *Bursting the Limits of Time: The Reconstruction of Geohistory in the Age of Revolution* (Chicago: University of Chicago Press, 2005), 158–72.

37. Ibid., 139–50.

38. Ludmilla Jordanova, "Nature's Powers: A Reading of Lamarck's Distinction between Creation and Production," in *History, Humanity, and Evolution*, ed. James R. Moore (Cambridge: Cambridge University Press, 1989), 71–98.

39. Ronald L. Numbers, *Creation by Natural Law: Laplace's Nebular Hypothesis in American Thought* (Seattle: University of Washington Press, 1977), 88–104.

40. Rudwick, *Bursting the Limits*, 505–10.

41. Brooke, *Science and Religion*, 263–74; Samuel Wilberforce, *Essays Contributed to the Quarterly Review*, 2 vols. (London: Murray, 1874), 1:52–103 and 104–83.

42. Martin J. S. Rudwick, "The Shape and Meaning of Earth History," in Lindberg and Numbers, *God and Nature*, 296–321; Mott T. Greene, "Genesis and Geology Revisited: The Order of Nature and the Nature of Order in Nineteenth-Century Britain," in *When Science and Christianity Meet*, ed. David C. Lindberg and Ronald L. Numbers, 139–59 (Chicago: University of Chicago Press, 2003).

43. John Hedley Brooke, "Like Minds: The God of Hugh Miller," in *Hugh Miller and the Controversies of Victorian Science*, ed. Michael Shortland, 171–86 (Oxford: Clarendon Press, 1996).

44. James A. Secord, *Victorian Sensation: The Extraordinary Publication, Reception, and Secret Authorship of Vestiges of the Natural History of Creation* (Chicago: University of Chicago Press, 2000).

45. Geoffrey Cantor, *Michael Faraday: Sandemanian and Scientist* (London: Macmillan, 2001).

46. Crosbie Smith and M. Norton Wise, *Energy and Empire: A Biographical Study of Lord Kelvin* (Cambridge: Cambridge University Press, 1989), 317, 330–31.

47. Helge Kragh, "Cosmology and the Entropic Creation Argument," *Historical Studies in the Physical and Biological Sciences* 37 (2007): 369–82.

48. For historical perspectives on the theological issues raised by Darwin's theory, see David N. Livingstone, "Re-placing Darwinism and Christianity," in Lindberg and Numbers, *When Science and Christianity Meet*, chap. 8; James R. Moore, *The Post-Darwinian Controversies* (Cambridge: Cambridge University Press, 1979); and Jon H. Roberts, *Darwinism and the Divine in America* (Madison: University of Wisconsin Press, 1988).

49. Frank M. Turrner, *Contesting Cultural Authority* (Cambridge: Cambridge University Press, 1993).

50. Bernard Lightman, "Victorian Sciences and Religions: Discordant Harmonies," *Osiris* 16 (2001): 343–66, especially 343.

51. Charles Darwin, *On the Origin of Species* (London: Murray, 1859), 488.

52. Richard Dawkins, *The Blind Watchmaker* (New York: Norton, 1986).

53. John Tyndall, "The Belfast Address," in Tyndall, *Fragments of Science* (London: Longmans, 1879), 2:137–203, 199.

54. Robert Bruce Mullin, "Science, Miracles, and the Prayer-Gauge Debate," in Lindberg and Numbers, *When Science and Christianity Meet*, chap. 9.

55. John Hedley Brooke, "Darwin and Victorian Christianity," in *The Cambridge Companion to Darwin*, ed. Jonathan Hodge and Gregory Radick, 192–213 (Cambridge: Cambridge University Press, 2003).

56. David N. Livingstone, "The Bishop and the Bulldog," in *Galileo Goes to Jail and Other Myths in Science and Religion*, ed. Ronald L. Numbers (Cambridge, Mass.: Harvard University Press, 2009).

57. Frederick Burkhardt, ed., *The Correspondence of Charles Darwin*, vol. 8 (Cambridge: Cambridge University Press, 1993), 200 and 218.

58. Asa Gray, *Darwiniana*, ed. A Hunter Dupree (Cambridge, Mass.: Harvard University Press, 1963), 72–145 and 293–320; David N. Livingstone, *Darwin's Forgotten Defenders* (Grand Rapids, Mich.: Eerdmans, 1987), 60–64.

59. David N. Livingstone, *Adam's Ancestors: Race, Religion and the Politics of Human Origins* (Baltimore, Md.: Johns Hopkins University Press, 2008), chaps. 5–7.

60. Robert Kenny, "From the Curse of Ham to the Curse of Nature: The Influence of Natural Selection on the Debate on Human Unity before the Publication of *The Descent of Man*," *British Journal for the History of Science* 40 (2007): 367–88, 382.

61. John Stenhouse, "Darwinism in New Zealand, 1859–1900," in *Disseminating Darwinism: The Role of Place, Race, Religion, and Gender*, ed. Ronald L. Numbers and John Stenhouse, 61–89 (Cambridge: Cambridge University Press, 1999).

62. James R. Moore, "Ronald Aylmer Fisher: A Faith Fit for Eugenics," in Rupke, *Eminent Lives*, 103–38, 118.

63. Edward Larson, *Summer for the Gods: The Scopes Trial and America's Continuing Debate over Science and Religion* (Cambridge, Mass.: Harvard University Press, 1997), 28 and 115.

64. Cited by Larson (*Summer for the Gods*, 245), who discusses the many echoes of the trial in "The Scopes Trial in History and Legend," in Lindberg and Numbers, *When Science and Christianity Meet*, chap. 11.

65. Peter J. Bowler, *Reconciling Science and Religion* (Chicago: University of Chicago Press, 2001).

66. Ibid., 413–14.

67. Illustrative examples include Ian G. Barbour, *Religion in an Age of Science* (London: SCM Press, 1990), chaps. 5–7; John F. Haught, *God after Darwin: A Theology of Evolution* (Boulder: Westview Press, 2000); and Arthur Peacocke, *Creation and the World of Science* (Oxford: Oxford University Press, 2004).

68. Michael Ruse, *Can a Darwinian Be a Christian?* (Cambridge: Cambridge University Press, 2001).

69. Barbour, *Religion in an Age of Science*, 10–16, provides a fuller summary of these pressures.

70. Jon H. Roberts, "Psychoanalysis and American Christianity," in Lindberg and Numbers, *When Science and Christianity Meet*, chap.10.

71. William Pollard, *Chance and Providence* (New York: Scribner, 1958).

72. As exemplar: Robert J. Russell, "Special Providence and Genetic Mutation: A New Defense of Theistic Evolution," in *Evolutionary and Molecular Biology: Scientific Perspectives on Divine Action* (Vatican City: Vatican Observatory Publications, 1998), 191–223.

73. Christopher Southgate, ed., *God, Humanity, and the Cosmos*, 2nd ed. (London: T and T Clark International, 2005), 27.

74. Paul Davies, *The Goldilocks Enigma: Why Is the Universe Just Right for Life?* (London: Allen Lane, 2006), 3.

75. Richard G. Swinburne, *The Existence of God*, rev. ed. (Oxford: Clarendon Press, 1991), 300–322.

76. For more strident claims, compare Rodney Stark, *For the Glory of God: How Monotheism Led to Reformation, Science, Witch-Hunts, and the End of Slavery* (Princeton, N.J.: Princeton University Press, 2004).

77. Sujit Sivasundaram, *Nature and the Godly Empire: Science and Evangelical Mission in the Pacific, 1795–1850* (Cambridge: Cambridge University Press, 2005).

78. Sujit Sivasundaram, "'A Christian Benares': Orientalism, Science, and the Serampore Mission of Bengal," *Indian Economic and Social History Review* 44 (2007): 111–45.

79. Philip J. Hefner, *The Human Factor: Evolution, Culture, and Religion* (Minneapolis, Minn.: Fortress Press, 1993); John Hedley Brooke, "Detracting from Divine Power? Religious Belief and the Appraisal of New Technologies," in *Re-Ordering Nature: Theology, Society and the New Genetics*, ed. Celia Deane-Drummond, Bronislaw Szerszynski, and Robin Grove-White, 43–67 (London: T and T Clark, 2003).

5

Early Islam

Ahmad S. Dallal

With a few recent exceptions, studies of the Islamic sciences assume an opposition between science and religion. According to these accounts, interest in science in the Islamic world resulted from a massive translation movement during the ninth century, through which the body of Greek scientific knowledge was passed to the Arabs. The Greek legacy was then preserved by the Arabs until Islam came of age and defined its tenets. The consolidation of a traditional religious worldview around the eleventh century (as reflected in the works of al-Ghazali, d. 1111) sealed the fate of the rational sciences and marked the beginning of their steady decline. This theory even posits an essential contradiction between science and Islam; it is part of a larger contention in post-Enlightenment historiography that opposes science and religion in general in post-medieval civilizations. Thus, according to various accounts based on this theory, scientific activities in Muslim societies were consistently opposed (ostensibly by religious authorities or Islam), and they survived despite, and not as a result of, Islamic culture. While the grand narratives of the history of the relationship between science and religion celebrate the triumph of science in Europe, they often assert that the irreversible decline of science in the Muslim world was due to the victory of religion.[1]

The rapid establishment of a unified Muslim empire over the previous territories of the Byzantine and Sassanid (Persian) empires was coupled with a gradual but deliberate effort to appropriate the cultures of these ancient civilizations. As early as the eighth century, scientific works were translated into Arabic. Translation, however, was not the source of the growing interest in science at the time but a consequence of this interest. One factor that contributed to the Islamic interest in science was the growing awareness of the status of the emerging Islamic civilization as heir to world civilizations. At a more tangible level, the increasing complexity of social organization and the subsequent demand for professional expertise provided both opportunities as well as incentives for aspiring professionals to culti-vate scientific knowledge.

Most of the translations of scientific works into Arabic were produced in Baghdad in the course of the ninth century. They were frequently produced at the request of patrons who commissioned them. These patrons included rulers, government officials, and civil servants, as well as scientists and physi-cians often employed by members of the political elite. Some translations were also prepared for members of the social elite. An official library, *Bayt al-Hikma* (House of wisdom), was established in Baghdad under the Caliph Harun al-Rashid (r. 786–809 CE), but it gained its reputation in the context of the trans-lation movement during the reign of his son al-Ma'mun. Many acquired and translated scientific and philosophical works were collected in this library and were in turn made available to the researchers and translators of the period.

The most influential body of scientific knowledge translated into Arabic was undoubtedly the Greek, yet the context for ninth-century scientific translations was decidedly Islamic. Arabic science did more than simply preserve the Greek scientific legacy and pass it to its European heirs. The inherited legacy came in a package, which included science and philosophy, astrology and astronomy, medicine and alchemy. Part of this package con-tradicted the teachings of Islam by compromising the unique position reserved for the One Omnipotent Creator. Muslims, for several centuries, tried to sort out the part that contradicted their faith. The process of subject-ing the Greek inheritance to scrutiny resulted in what may be called the Islamization of science, which is not to say that science was censored by a religious institution. Rather, Islamization meant identifying and isolating those parts of the inherited legacy that were not universal and that carried the imprints of the culture that produced them. Seeking to eliminate such cultural infusion, Muslims allowed what they considered to be the neutral and value-free sciences to flower freely, without interfering in their develop-ment. Thus, after astrology, philosophy, and certain elements of the philo-sophical underpinnings of the natural sciences were singled out as targets of attack, the supposed neutrality of the rest of scientific knowledge was widely accepted. Once neutral science was defined, as science less astrology and philosophy, it became a valid field of knowledge. Since this science had no moral claims to make, it had no quarrel with religion, just as religion had no claims on the "value-free" parts of the natural sciences.

CLASSIFICATIONS OF THE SCIENCES

In Muslim societies a genre of science classification proliferated that illus-trates this trend. Both in scope and number, these classifications surpassed the Greek originals. Most studies of the subject assume the existence of two incompatible epistemic systems of knowledge—religious and ratio-nalist—which the classifications attempt to reconcile, unify, lay side by side, or simply reflect.[2] Perhaps one reason for this assumption is that most Islamic classifications do include some overall division into either philo-sophical, rational, foreign, ancient, Greek, universal, intellectual, or positive (*wad'iyya*) classes, on the one hand, or Arabic, Islamic, traditional, trans-mitted, specific, or religious classes, on the other. Islamic classification schemes, however, are not the only, and perhaps not even the most impor-tant, rationale for positing a reason/belief dichotomy. For this dichotomy was itself deployed by the Enlightenment to denote the targets of its po-lemics, and ever since this paradigm was developed it has exerted great influence on historians of Western and non-Western civilizations alike. But when the terms "reason" and "tradition" are used in the Islamic classification schemes, they do not carry the value judgment attached to them in modern studies. Being rational or traditional does not indicate whether a certain discipline is commendable or reprehensible, nor does it impinge on the validity of the discipline. Moreover, reason is a given whose use is presup-posed in all disciplines of learning. For example, the celebrated eleventh-century scholar al-Ghazali states that "most of the branches of religious knowledge are intellectual for one who comprehends them, and most of the branches of intellectual knowledge are religious for one who knows them."[3]

The first Islamic classifications we have are those of the Muslim philoso-phers al-Kindi (d. 873) and al-Farabi (d. 950), in which all the sciences are subsumed under one general system of knowledge. Soon after, a type of classification emerges in which sciences are divided into traditional and intellectual, and in which comparisons are made and structural parallels drawn between these two general groups.[4] One main purpose of these com-parisons is to defend the legitimacy of the rational sciences, either because they are structurally similar to the religious sciences or because of their practical and religious utility. Interestingly, however, such apologetic com-parisons are abandoned in most classification schemes that emerge soon after the eleventh century. Ghazali, for example, argued that any knowledge is noble in itself and that there is no need theoretically to justify one kind of knowledge on the basis of another.[5] In theory, all that is knowable should be investigated unless it is harmful. Elsewhere Ghazali adds that one should not blame knowledge if it happens to be abused.[6]

Along similar lines, the fourteenth-century historian and religious scholar Ibn Khaldun (d. 1406) went even farther when he argued that there is no common hierarchy of religion and natural science because these are two separate spheres of knowledge, and because the knowledge of the causal chain is natural and need not be introduced by religious dogma. Science was studied and classified by Ibn Khaldun in the context of human civilization, itself being a manifestation of civilized living. Religious knowledge, on the other hand, is a matter of transmission and instruction, and is clearly different from the sciences in the kinds of evidence it employs and in the way it is justified. Ibn Khaldun's classification, therefore, does not serve as a basis for deciding the relative merits of science. There are two criteria for passing such a judgment: one is the use to which each science is put (i.e., whether or not it has harmful results). This is an external criterion that has nothing to do with the epistemological status of the science. The second criterion is the internal coherence of the science and the appropriateness of the procedures used for inquiring into its subject matter. Ibn Khaldun's critique of philosophy, for example, is quite consistent with these general principles. Instead of criticizing philosophy on religious grounds, because of the presumed conflict between reason and religious belief, Ibn Khaldun argued that philosophy, which he equated with metaphysics, treats questions that are not perceivable by the senses. Consequently it is neither an empirical nor a demonstrable science. Thus, philosophy according to Ibn Khaldun cannot claim to be an intellectual science—that is, a science that grounds itself on the authority of rational principles— when these principles are by definition nondemonstrable and therefore nonrational. The only kind of authority that is valid for metaphysics is an external, transmitted textual authority. In short, according to Ibn Khaldun, philosophy is defective because of the incompatibility between its subject matter and its procedures.[7]

PHILOSOPHY VERSUS SCIENCE

Parallel to this epistemological critique of Greek philosophy, the natural-philosophical principles underlying Greek astronomy were also criticized.[8] Aristotelian philosophical principles of motion, underlying Ptolemaic astronomy and the astronomy of its Islamic successors, were not completely abandoned. The attacks on philosophy, however, emboldened Islamic astronomers, allowing them to question freely the connections between the Ptolemaic planetary models and the physical world they purported to represent. Many original contributions to planetary theories resulted from such philosophical considerations. Some scientists conceived of a difference between philosophical and mathematical problems, restricting themselves to the solution of the mathematical ones. One such scientist is Abu Rayhan al-Biruni (973–ca. 1048). In a work on the construction of astrolabes, Biruni refers to one known as the boat-like astrolabe constructed by Abu Sa'id al-Sizji. Biruni continues:

I liked it immensely as he [al-Sizji] invented it on the basis of an independent principle, which is in turn extracted from what some people hold to be true, namely that the absolute eastward visible motion is that of the earth rather than the celestial sphere. I swear that this is an uncertainty which is difficult to analyze or resolve. The geometricians and astronomers who rely [in their work] on lines and planes have no way of contradicting this [theory]. However, their craft will not be compromised, irrespective of whether the resulting motion is assigned to the earth or to the heavens. If it is at all possible to contradict this belief [in the motion of the celestial sphere] or to resolve this uncertainty, then such [a duty] will have to be assigned to the natural philosophers.[9]

Here Biruni indicated that, as far as mathematical astronomy is concerned, it does not matter whether the astronomer uses a geocentric or a heliocentric model. This is so because the relative motions will be the same. The observational technology available at the time of Biruni (and indeed Copernicus) was not accurate enough to provide a satisfactory answer to this question on the basis of mathematical astronomy. Therefore, the discussion pertaining to the nature of the motion of heavenly bodies was primarily philosophical, not mathematical. Thus Biruni, who thought of himself as a mathematical astronomer, did not feel it was his responsibility to address such a philosophical question.

Biruni's subtle distinction between science and philosophy is confirmed in an exchange titled "the Questions and Answers" in which he presented Ibn Sina (d. 1037), the greatest Muslim Aristotelian philosopher, with a number of criticisms of Aristotle's *De Caelo* and then responded to Ibn Sina's answers to those criticisms. In almost all of these criticisms (eighteen in number), Biruni did not disagree with the final descriptions provided by Aristotle; his objections, however, were to Aristotle's methods of proof. So, for example, although Biruni did not deny the circular motion of the planets or the sphericity of the celestial sphere, he explicitly disagreed with Aristotle's proofs of these observable facts. Biruni rejected the following Aristotelian principles: that celestial spheres have no gravity nor levity, that the circular motion of the planets is due to the nature of heavenly bodies (rather than being accidental), that an elliptical motion of the planets is a natural impossibility, and that there can be no vacuum or void in the universe. Throughout this debate Biruni rejected the metaphysical axioms and not the final conclusions of Aristotelian physics. Furthermore, he justified his rejection by arguing that none of these axioms can be proven by using the techniques of mathematical astronomy. We thus have the seeds of a conceptual separation between the profession of a philosopher and that of a scientist and, more importantly, the conceptual transformation of physics from a philosophical/metaphysical discipline to a mathematical one, itself a major step toward the mathematization of nature.

KEY CONTRIBUTIONS OF ARABO-ISLAMIC SCIENCE

The conceptual development reflected in the work of Biruni was only one of various modes of transforming and reformulating the Greek scientific legacy, even as its texts were being translated. Simultaneous research and translation did not take place in just one field; rather, such research was the driving force behind the translation of numerous astronomical, mathematical, and medical texts. The Arabic scientific traditions were also characterized by a large degree of coherence and continuity. For example, the tradition of reforming Ptolemaic astronomy, which started in the eleventh century, continued until at least the sixteenth, and it spanned most of the Islamic world. Similarly, in the various disciplines of Arabic mathematics, for each instance of seemingly isolated scientific breakthrough there are precedents and successors, as well as a community of interested scholars and intellectuals. To summarize the main contributions of Islamic science, I provide in this section a brief overview of key developments in the main scientific disciplines.

ASTRONOMY in the Islamic tradition was unambiguously differentiated from astrology. Although astrology had its appeal, astronomy dominated an extensive literature. Many astronomers served as court astrologers, but many more condemned astrology and distanced themselves from it. Arab astronomers were first exposed to Persian and Indian astronomy, and they continued to use some of the parameters and methods of these two traditions. Yet the greatest formative influence on Arabic astronomy was undoubtedly Greek. Ptolemy's *Almagest* exerted a disproportionate influence on all of medieval astronomy throughout the Arabic period. The main purpose of the book is to establish the *geometric* models that would accurately account for observational phenomena. A Greek tradition of *physical* astronomy is also reflected in the *Almagest* and in Ptolemy's other influential work, the *Planetary Hypothesis*. According to this predominantly Aristotelian tradition, the universe is organized into a set of concentric spheres and, in contrast to sublunary rectilinear motion, the heavenly bodies move in perfect uniform circular motions. Ptolemy adopted, at least in theory, the two basic Aristotelian principles: that the earth is stationary at the center of the universe and that the motion of heavenly bodies ought to be represented by a set of uniform circular motions. In practice, however, mathematical considerations often forced Ptolemy to disregard these principles.

The first extant original work of Arabic astronomy is Khwarizmi's (fl. 830) *Zij al-Sindhind*. It contains tables for the movements of the sun, moon, and five planets, with introductory explanatory remarks on how to use them. Most of the parameters used by al-Khwarizmi are of Indian origin, but some are derived from Ptolemy with no attempt to harmonize the two sources. Such selective use of parameters, sources, and methods of calculation from different scientific traditions had the consequence that the Ptolemaic tradition was made receptive to the possibility of observational refinement as well as mathematical restructuring.

From its beginnings, Arabic astronomy set out to rectify and complement Ptolemaic astronomy. Under the Caliph al-Ma'mun, a program of astronomical observations was organized in Baghdad and Damascus, which endowed astronomical activity in the Islamic world with formal prestige. It also set a precedent for future patronage of science. The professed purpose of this program was to verify the Ptolemaic observations by comparing the results derived by calculation, based on the Ptolemaic models, with actual observations conducted in Baghdad and Damascus some seven hundred years later. This program stressed the need for continuing verification of astronomical observations and for the use of more precise instruments. It also represents the first recorded instance in history of a collective scientific undertaking.

Already in the ninth century, Arabic astronomy struck deep roots: it integrated all previous knowledge and was positioned to surpass it. The achievements of the ninth century laid the foundation for high-quality work in the following two centuries, which witnessed important developments in the science of trigonometry, with dramatic effects on the accuracy and facility of astronomical calculations. In this period steps were taken toward the formal establishment of large-scale observatories. Moreover, the earlier examinations of Ptolemaic astronomy led to systematic projects, which, rather than addressing the field in its totality, focused on specific aspects of the science on which exhaustive, synthesizing works appeared. This trend culminated in the work of the illustrious al-Biruni, who wrote over 150 works on most of the known sciences of his time, including astronomy, mathematics, mathematical geography, mineralogy, metallurgy, pharmacology, history, and philosophy. Like many of his predecessors and contemporaries, Biruni provided exhaustive studies of specialized topics within astronomy. With his command of Greek, Indian, and Arabic traditions, his treatises represent a critical assessment of the state of the science of mathematical astronomy up to his own time.

After the eleventh century, the efforts of most theoretical astronomers were directed toward providing a thorough evaluation of the physical and philosophical underpinnings of Ptolemaic astronomy and proposing alternatives to it. The most important work of this genre was written by Ibn al-Haytham (d. 1039). In his celebrated work *Al-Shukuk 'ala Batlamyus* (Doubts on Ptolemy), Ibn al-Haytham summed up the physical and philosophical problems inherent in the Greek astronomical system and provided an inventory of the theoretical inconsistencies of the Ptolemaic models. This tradition of astronomical research thrived in the thirteenth century, climaxed in the fourteenth, and continued well into the fifteenth and sixteenth centuries. Most astronomers of this period took up the theoretical challenge outlined by Ibn al-Haytham, attempted to rework the models of Ptolemaic astronomy and to provide, with varying degrees of success, alternatives to them.

The astronomers who attempted to solve the problems deriving from the Ptolemaic legacy can be classified into two general schools: a mathematically oriented school, predominantly in the eastern parts of the Muslim world, and a philosophically oriented school based in the western regions of the empire. The name "Maragha school" is often given to the eastern reformers in recognition of the achievements of astronomers working in an observatory established at Maragha. The eastern reform tradition, however, was too diffused to be associated with any one geographical area or period, and it spanned several centuries of Arabic astronomical research throughout the eastern domains of the Muslim world.[10] One of the main objectives of reform was to devise models that could generate planetary motions from combinations of uniform circular motions while simultaneously conforming to the accurate Ptolemaic observations. The most comprehensive and successful of these were introduced in the fourteenth century by the Damascene astronomer Ibn al-Shatir (d. 1375), whose models for all the planets utilized combinations of perfect circular motions, with each circle rotating uniformly around its center. Ibn al-Shatir was also able to solve problems of planetary distances, accounting more accurately for observations. A number of Ibn al-Shatir's models were reproduced a century and a half later by Copernicus, thereby situating the latter within the eastern Arabic tradition of astronomical reform.

The development of Arabic astronomy in al-Andalus and North Africa followed different routes.[11] The aim of the western school was to reinstate Aristotelian homocentric spheres and to eliminate completely any use of the eccentrics and epicycles employed by Ptolemy. In accordance with the most stringent and literal interpretations of Aristotelian principles, the western researchers demanded that the heavens be represented exclusively by nested homocentric spheres and perfect uniform circular motions. Even epicycles and deferents that rotated uniformly around their centers were not tolerated, because their use entailed an attribution of compoundedness to heavenly phenomena. However, since the predictive power of the Ptolemaic models and their ability to account for the observed phenomena relied on the use of epicycles and eccentrics, the western models were strictly qualitative and philosophical—and were completely useless from a mathematical point of view. Consequently, the western Islamic reform tradition was a failure scientifically, driven as it was by the then-outdated Aristotelian philosophical concerns that proved incompatible with the advanced mathematical and scientific aspects of astronomy. On the other hand, the success of the eastern reform tradition was predicated on the gradual loosening of the hold of Aristotelian natural philosophy on mathematical astronomy.

MATHEMATICS underwent its own cycle of reorganization and reconstruction of disciplines by cross-application. The foundations of each discipline were thoroughly reorganized by systematically applying other fields to it and by generalizing its concepts and methods. The three mathematical disciplines that interacted in this generative way were arithmetic, algebra, and geometry. A central role in this process was played by the new Arabic discipline of algebra. The first work to consider algebraic expressions irrespective of what they may represent was *Kitab al-Jabr wal-Muqabala* by al-Khwarizmi. This book, written in the first quarter of the ninth century, is generally considered an outstanding achievement in the history of mathematics. Al-Khwarizmi was aware of the novelty of his work, providing, for the first time, a theory for the solution of all types of linear and quadratic equations by radicals without restricting the solution to any one particular problem. His achievement was only the first in a long and increasingly more sophisticated tradition of algebraic research. In the tenth and eleventh centuries, a new research project focused on the systematic application of the laws of arithmetic to algebraic expressions. In the following six centuries, central efforts in algebraic research focused on the arithmetization of algebra and the study of arithmetical operations on polynomials.

While the application of arithmetic to algebra occupied center stage in algebraic research, the theory of algebraic equations also continued to develop. Mathematicians increasingly resorted to conic sections to solve cubic equations that could not be solved by radicals. A continuous tradition of contributions to this field began in the ninth century and culminated in the systematic work of al-Khayyam (1048–1131), who elaborated a geometrical theory for equations of degree equal to or less than three. For all types of third-degree equations, he provided a formal classification according to the number of terms and then solved these equations by means of the intersection of two conic sections. Al-Khayyam's monumental contribution to the theory of algebraic equations marked the beginning of a long and continuous tradition that was further transformed, a half-century later, by Sharaf al-Din al-Tusi. In its analytic approach, the work of Tusi on equations marks the beginning of the discipline of algebraic geometry: the study of curves by means of equations. Tusi was original in proving the intersection of curves algebraically by means of their respective equations. He also introduced several new concepts usually attributed to later European mathematicians. He was the first to formulate the concept of a maximum of an algebraic expression. Although he does not use a distinct term for the word "derivative," Tusi clearly introduced local analysis, the study of maxima, and the notion of a derivative.

Mathematicians such as al-Khwarizmi, al-Khayyam, and Tusi were fully aware of the novelty of their work. They concocted unfamiliar titles for their books, coined technical terminology unique to their disciplines, organized their works in decidedly different ways, and invented original mathematical algorithms to solve the problems of their disciplines; above all, they conceived of totally new subjects and mathematical concepts. Such innovations were made possible by the deliberate and systematic application of three mathematical disciplines to each other: algebra, arithmetic, and geometry. The effect of these trends was not restricted to the restructuring of Hellenistic mathematical knowledge but extended to the creation of new mathematical disciplines.

Trigonometry provided a means by which Arab scientists enriched and eventually reoriented earlier scientific knowledge. It was initially developed in conjunction with research in astronomy but finally became an independent mathematical discipline in its own right. Ptolemaic astronomical computations were based on a single function, the chord of a circular arc; moreover, the only tool for spherical computation was Menelaus's theorem. The latter is a cumbersome formula for the relationship between the six segments that result from the intersection of four arcs in a complete quadrilateral. Soon after translating Ptolemy and adopting his models, Arab astronomers augmented his geometry with the powerful sine function of Indian trigonometry. In the ninth century, the tangent function was also introduced. The emergence of trigonometry as an independent science, however, required two additional developments: first, identifying the spherical triangle as the object of study (as opposed to the calculus of chords on the spherical quadrilateral); second, including the angles of triangles in this calculus and not restricting it to the sides. The first accounts of the spherical triangle appeared by the end of the tenth century. In the thirteenth century, Nasir al-Din al-Tusi wrote the first independent treatise on trigonometry without reference to astronomy, thus sealing the process by which another independent discipline was created.

OPTICS is another field advanced by Muslim scholars during the medieval period. The Arabs inherited a large body of Hellenistic optical knowledge encompassing the physical as well as geometric study of vision, the reflection of rays on mirrors (catoptrics), burning mirrors, and atmospheric phenomena such as the rainbow. Within two centuries, however, the field of optics was radically transformed, and Arabic optics acquired the characteristics of a new field of study. One feature of optical research in this formative period was an integration of the geometry and the physiology of vision. Building on this integrated approach, the greatest work of Arabic optics was undoubtedly *Kitab al-Manazir* of Ibn al-Haytham.

Ibn al-Haytham rejected the Hellenistic theories of vision and introduced a radically different one. Vision, according to earlier theories, was considered a result of contact between the eye and the object either through a ray emitted from the eye to the object—as in the extramission theories of Euclid and Ptolemy—or through the transmission of a "form" from the object to the eye—as in the intromission theories of Aristotle and the atomists. Rejecting these theories, Ibn al-Haytham argued that what is sensed is not the object itself, that an image of the object is formed as a result of the reflection of light from the object to the eye. Ibn al-Haytham could thus proceed to study the geometric aspects of the visual cone theories without having to explain at the same time the psychology of perception. He also benefited from advances in the study of the physiology of the eye, thus integrating into his theory of vision the cumulative results of mathematical, physical, and medical research. Ibn al-Haytham's innovative conceptualization and approach also led to the adoption of controlled experimentation as a practice of investigation as well as the norm for proofs in optics and more generally in physics. More systematic experimentation was employed by Kamal al-Din al-Farisi (d. 1319), who pursued Ibn al-Haytham's project of reforming optics. To explain the rainbow, Farisi introduced an experimental setup in which a glass sphere filled with water simulated the droplets of water suspended in the atmosphere. He then proceeded mathematically to justify the analogy between this artificial model and nature, by arguing that a sufficiently thin glass sphere would produce negligible additional refraction. By controlling the medium in which the experiment was conducted, Farisi was successful in explaining the shapes of the principal arc and the secondary arc of the rainbow as resulting from two refractions and one or two reflections inside the sphere.

MEDICINE in Islam was based on a shared Hellenistic medical legacy, which may account for the apparent uniformity of Arabic medicine. However, the actual practice of medicine produced diverse and at times competing tendencies within this tradition. The Abbasid caliphs of Baghdad employed Nestorian physicians from the city of Gundishapur. In addition to the learned practice of medicine, translations of medical texts as well as new medical writings started to appear in the ninth century. Most of the new writings were based on Hellenistic medicine, but even in the very early period some new treatises contained original features. The first comprehensive work of Arabic medicine that integrated and compared the various medical traditions of the time was 'Ali ibn Sahl al-Tabari's (fl. mid-ninth century) Firdaws al-Hikma (Paradise of wisdom). This book contains a section on Indian medicine, which provides valuable information on its sources and practices. In general, however, Indian medicine was far less crucial than Hellenistic medicine in shaping the Arabic medical tradition. Yet a mere awareness of more than one available tradition encouraged a critical and selective approach that pervaded all fields of Arabic science.

By the end of the ninth century, the Galenic humoral system of pathology was completely integrated into Arabic medicine. This medical system employed a significant degree of logical reasoning alongside medical observation to explain illness and to devise treatment. Arabic medicine further developed this tendency to systematize and rationalize. For the first time, attempts were made to organize the vast body of medical knowledge into one comprehensive, logical structure. An equally important trend focused on expanding empirical medical knowledge—with emphasis on clinical or case medicine—and on practical procedures for treatment, as opposed to the theoretical reflections on illness and health. One of the greatest representatives of this trend is Abu Bakr al-Razi (d. 925). Throughout his work, al-Razi put more emphasis on observational diagnosis and therapy than on the theoretical diagnosis of illnesses and their cures. His experience as a clinician was undoubtedly wide and rich, and was acquired in the course of a long career as the head of hospitals in Rayya and Baghdad. Al-Razi wrote numerous medical treatises of considerable originality, including the first thorough account of the diagnosis and treatment methods of smallpox and measles. His most important work is his *al-Hawi fi al-Tibb* (The comprehensive book on medicine). In this encyclopedic work al-Razi criticized Galen and stated clearly that the reason for his criticism was that his own clinical observations did not conform with Galen's assertions.

The *al-Hawi* of al-Razi was not without fault. Its main weakness was its sheer size and poor organization. This made the work inaccessible even to expert physicians, and the demand for comprehensive but structured medical handbooks was not fulfilled by it. Later in the tenth century, 'Ali Ibn 'Abbas al-Majusi wrote his *Kitab al-Kamil fi al- Sina'a al-Tibbiya* (The complete book of the medical art), also known as *Kitab al-Malaki* (The royal book), with the explicit intention of filling this gap. Although the book of al-Majusi served as a popular handbook of medicine, it was soon replaced by what became the single most influential book on theoretical medicine in the Middle Ages and up to the seventeenth century. This is *al-Qanun fi al-Tibb* (The canon of medicine) by the celebrated Muslim philosopher and physician Ibn Sina, otherwise known as Avicenna. Ibn Sina's magnum opus *al-Qanun* was written with the intention of producing the definitive canonical work on medicine, both in terms of comprehensiveness and theoretical rigor. In this book, Ibn Sina provided a coherent and systematic theoretical reflection on the inherited medical legacies, starting with anatomy, followed by physiology, then pathology, and finally therapy. Although he included many bedside observations and a few original contributions of a purely practical nature, Ibn Sina's main achievement was not primarily in the clinical domain. Rather, he produced a unified synthesis of medical knowledge that derived its coherence from the relentlessly systematic application of logical and theoretical principles.

The fame of Ibn Sina's school of medical research often overshadows a significant tradition in Arabic medicine, which, though not completely innocent of philosophy, practiced medicine essentially as a practical art. The careers of many physicians seem to be disproportionately devoted to the cultivation of medicine as a practical scientific discipline. In al-Andalus and North Africa, for example, many physicians after the end of the tenth century were also pharmacologists. The first criticism of Ibn Sina's *Qanun* was written in al-Andalus by Ibn Zuhr (d. 1131), who objected mainly to the section of *al-Qanun* dealing with pharmacology because its exclusively theoretical nature reduced its practical usefulness. Another field where strong empirical tendencies were manifest is anatomy. Modern studies on Islamic medicine often assert that because of cultural taboos and religious restrictions, anatomy was not pursued by Arab physicians, and that the notable anatomical observations were mere theoretical speculations on inherited anatomical knowledge. The most debated example of Arabic anatomy is the thirteenth-century discovery by Ibn al-Nafis of the pulmonary circulation of the blood. After obtaining his initial education in Syria, Ibn al-Nafis moved to Cairo, where he pursued a career in Islamic law and medicine. Ibn al-Nafis wrote several commentaries on Ibn Sina's *Qanun*. In a book titled *Sharh Tashrih al-Qanun* (Commentary on the anatomy of the canon), he noted that Galen's and Ibn Sina's assertions that blood moves between the right and left ventricles of the heart through a hole between them is not correct. Anatomy, Ibn al-Nafis maintains, refutes this assertion because no such hole is detectable through anatomical observation. Ibn al-Nafis then argued that blood reaches the left ventricle through the lungs, thus providing the first explanation of the minor circulation of the blood. This and many other examples suggest that, despite some restrictions, Arab physicians performed anatomical dissections to develop medical knowledge.

The significant contributions of Arab and Muslim physicians did not occur in a vacuum. The twelfth and thirteenth centuries witnessed a surge in medical activity as physicians from all over the Muslim world sought careers in the medical institutions of Damascus and Cairo. At the social level, physicians of the period were closely integrated with the rest of society, and many of them were leading authorities in the religious disciplines, especially law and *hadith* (traditions of the prophet Muhammad) scholarship. As a result of the enhanced social status of physicians in this period, a thirteenth-century physician, Ibn Abi Usaybi'a, compiled a bibliographical dictionary for physicians, now fully recognized as members of the social elites.

The prestige of the medical profession was closely dependent on mechanisms of social and professional integration, most notably through hospitals and, later, medical schools. The hospital is one of the greatest institutional achievements of medieval Islamic societies. Between the ninth and the tenth centuries, five hospitals had been built in Baghdad alone, and several others were built in other regional centers. The most famous of these is the 'Adudi hospital established under Buwayhid rule in 982. After this period, the numbers of hospitals increased significantly when such famous institutions as the Nuri hospital of Damascus (twelfth century) and the Mansuri hospital of Cairo (thirteenth century) were built along with others in Qayrawan, Mecca, Medina, Rayy, and many more. These institutions were open to everyone who needed medical care, regardless of sex, religion, age, or social class and wealth. In the thirteenth century schools were endowed for the exclusive teaching of medicine. One such, established in Damascus, was inaugurated by the leading religious authorities of the city and attracted many religious scholars as students; leading religious figures of the city filled the prestigious position of head administrator of this school. There are also several references in the historical sources to medical instruction in religious schools. Taken together, these and other institutional structures and practices afforded Arabic medicine an unprecedented level of organization, contributing to its further development and its social integration.

Science was definitely not marginal in Muslim culture. It struck deep roots and continued to flourish from the late eighth century through at least the sixteenth century, way past the crystallization of an Islamic religious worldview. The suggestion that the rational sciences declined as a result of religious opposition around the eleventh century is no longer tenable. In fact, all recent research by historians of Islamic science demonstrates a vibrant scientific activity that culminated in what was previously assumed to be the age of decline.[12] Yet before revisiting the relationship between science and religion in Muslim societies, a word about scientific education is in order.

INSTITUTIONS OF LEARNING

General histories of science often assert that the lack of institutional support in Muslim societies for the rational sciences is responsible for their marginalization and eventual demise.[13] This argument draws on the classic work on Islamic educational institutions by George Makdisi. Makdisi contended that the quintessential institutions of learning in Muslim societies, the *Madrasa* and its antecedent and cognate institutions, were exclusively devoted to the study of the legal sciences and other ancillary religious and philological disciplines, with no room for the rational sciences. According to Makdisi, this dichotomy between the two sets of sciences was maintained and was matched by a dichotomy in the institutions of learning.[14] Because of their exclusion from the formal curricula of the institutions of learning, the rational sciences supposedly remained alien to Muslim culture. Initially they thrived despite and not because of their cultural context, but eventually their marginality led to their stagnation and decline.[15] However, recent research has provided a compelling critique of this thesis of marginality, by comparing the medieval Islamic biographical accounts about education in the rational sciences with those about education in the religious sciences. Among other things, this comparison shows a shift in the use of the terms *'ulum al-awa'il* (the sciences of the ancients) and *al-'ulum al-'aqliyya* (the rational sciences) and the gradual emergence of alliances between secular and religious sciences.[16]

It is possible to identify manifold evidence that undermines the thesis of marginality and illustrates the integration of the rational sciences into the larger intellectual landscape of Muslim societies. Historical and literary sources provide abundant evidence for the respectability of many branches of the rational sciences, such as logic, arithmetic, medicine, geometry, astronomy, algebra, and philosophy. For example, the biographical dictionaries of religious scholars often celebrate their knowledge of the rational sciences. Many of these scholars combined expertise in the religious and rational sciences. Furthermore, specialized biographical dictionaries, which served the important function of identifying and sanctioning communities of scholars, were compiled to celebrate scientists. Another indicator of the respectability of rational sciences is the use of the same discourse and idioms in praising knowledge in rational as well as religious sciences. Finally, the constant presence of the rational sciences in all classifications of the sciences reflects not just their social but also their epistemological sanction.

The twelfth and thirteenth centuries witnessed a shifting professional alliance between various religious and rational disciplines, providing new space for the intersection of rational and religious sciences, and thereby lending the former added prestige and respectability. As of the twelfth century, numerous scholars specialized in *hadith* and medicine, including the famous thirteenth-century scholar Ibn al-Nafis, who discovered the pulmonary circulation of blood.[17] The subjects of *usul al-din* (principles of religion), *usul al-fiqh* (principles of jurisprudence), and logic were combined in this period, as were theology *(kalam)*, logic, and astronomy. Further evidence suggests that scientific education was pervasive and widespread through at least the sixteenth century and was central to mainstream intellectual life in Muslim societies. This integration is reflected in the large number of religious scholars who were also competent and original scientists.[18]

In addition to the combination of specific scientific and religious disciplines in the persons of individual scholars, several scientific subfields were
integrated into the standard curriculum of religious educational institutions.
These include the fields of *fara'id* (inheritance algebra), a subfield of algebra
dealing with inheritance law; *'ilm al-miqat* (timekeeping), a subfield of practical astronomy dealing with such questions as keeping time, finding the
direction of prayer, and computing lunar visibility. To take one example, the
qibla is the sacred direction that Muslims face during prayer and other ritual
acts. Finding the direction of the *qibla* was a favorite problem for medieval
astronomers. It was treated in separate works, in sections of astronomical
handbooks, or in manuals for timekeeping. Some of the greatest Muslim
astronomers addressed this problem and devised solutions of considerable
sophistication. Moreover, numerous tables giving the direction of the *qibla*
for different localities were computed on the bases of their respective
methods.[19] The integration of these subfields of science into the curriculum
of religious education did not undermine their autonomy. Rather, it
enhanced the standing of astronomy and mathematics in general without
inhibiting the pursuit of other branches of these sciences that were not
integrated into the religious curriculum.[20] Their integration also provided
institutional support to these disciplines. As early as the twelfth century, the
office of timekeeper (*mu'aqqit*) was established in most major mosques to
solve problems of mathematical astronomy emerging from an Islamic cultural context. As noted above, these included finding the direction of *qibla*,
determining times of prayer, and lunar visibility. Astronomers occupying
this office attended to these practical needs, but in their spare time they
pursued independent research agendas. Some of the most original research
in planetary theory was done by timekeepers, including the famous work of
the fourteenth-century Damascene astronomer Ibn al-Shatir.

Given the demonstrable vibrancy of Islamic scientific culture and the multiple ways in which the rational sciences were integrated into the intellectual
landscape, it is logical to assume that the Islamic sciences thrived because of,
and not despite, the larger cultural forces at work in these Muslim societies.
But how are we to characterize the relationship between science and religion
in light of the actual history of the Islamic sciences? To answer this question,
in the following sections I examine the ideas of four major Muslim thinkers
in four respective fields at the intersection of science and religion.

Generally speaking, religious assessments of the epistemic value of various kinds of scientific knowledge were nuanced and diverse. Although one
cannot adduce a direct correlation between the religious arguments and the
ways in which scientists perceived and theorized their own scientific disciplines, it is abundantly clear that the views of scientists were also manifold.
Furthermore, since they were inspired by a variety of cultural factors, these

articulations by scientists are tangible expressions of what "Islamic" science actually meant to living scientists and are as indicative of the Islamic dimension as the views expressed by religious scholars.

BIRUNI ON THE RELATIONSHIP BETWEEN SCIENTIFIC AND RELIGIOUS KNOWLEDGE

In his anthropological history of India,[21] al-Biruni starts a chapter "On the Configuration of the Heavens and the Earth According to [Indian] Astrologers" with a long comparison between the cultural imperatives of Muslim and Indian sciences. The views of Indian astrologers, Biruni maintained, "have developed in a way which is different from those of our [Muslim] fellows; this is because, unlike the scriptures revealed before it, the Qur'an does not articulate on this subject [of astronomy], or any other [field of] necessary [knowledge] any assertion that would require erratic interpretations in order to harmonize it with that which is known by necessity." The Qur'an, added Biruni, does not speak on matters that are subjects of hopeless differences, such as history. To be sure, Islam has suffered from people who claimed to be Muslims but retained many of the teachings of earlier religions, claiming that these teachings are part of the doctrines of Islam. Such, for example, were the Manichaeans, whose religious doctrines, together with their erroneous views about the heavens, were wrongly attributed to Islam. Such attributions of scientific views to the Qur'an are, according to Biruni, false claims of un-Islamic origins. In contrast, all the religious and transmitted books of the Indians do indeed speak "of the configuration of the universe in a way that contradicts the truth known to their own astrologers." However, driven by the need to uphold their religious traditions, Indian astrologers pretend to believe in the astrological doctrines of these books even when they are aware of their falsity. With the passage of time, accurate astronomical doctrines were mixed with those advanced in the religious books, which led to the confusion one encounters in Indian astronomy.

Although Biruni recognized that not all Indian religious views contradicted the dictates of the astronomical profession, he still maintained that the conflation of religious and astronomical knowledge undermined Indian astronomy and accounted for its errors and weaknesses. This conflation of scripture and science was contrasted by Biruni with the Islamic astronomical tradition, which in his view suffered from no such shortcomings. In Biruni's view, therefore, the Qur'an and religious dogma did not interfere in the business of science, nor did they infringe on its realm. Evidence from the writings of religious scholars suggests that Biruni's view was in conformity with prevalent views within Islamic discursive culture. This confluence of attitudes between scientists like Biruni and religious scholars further suggests a conceptual separation of science and religion in the mainstream of classical Islamic culture.

GHAZALI ON THE RELATIONSHIP BETWEEN SCIENTIFIC AND RELIGIOUS KNOWLEDGE

One of the most celebrated Muslim religious thinkers, al-Ghazali, is often considered an enemy of science and one of the main causes of its decline.[22] Close examination of Ghazali's views reflects, however, a much more nuanced religious attitude toward the sciences.[23] Ghazali was critical of the metaphysical part of philosophy, which, he argued, may be in conflict with religion. In his *Incoherence of the Philosophers*, he maintained that philosophers cannot claim harmony between their beliefs and the tenets of Islam. Ghazali's attack on philosophers revolves around three main points of contention with the Islamic Aristotelians: their assertion that the world is eternal; their denial of God's knowledge of particulars; and their denial of the resurrection of bodies.[24] Ghazali's objection is to metaphysics, a science whose subject matter overlaps with that of theology. This is why religion is not silent on the implications of metaphysics. Furthermore, according to Ghazali, philosophy as metaphysics fails to satisfy the conditions of demonstrative proof.

In contrast to his criticism of philosophy-cum-metaphysics, Ghazali argued that mathematics is demonstrably true and has no bearing on religious matters. He said that mathematicians ought to be warned against the possible philosophical underpinnings of their craft. However, this potential pitfall does not affect Ghazali's positive evaluation of mathematical knowledge. Indeed, those who claim that religion is opposed to either mathematics or logic would be doing a great disservice to religion by posing it against something that cannot be refuted. In his words: "such matters rest on geometrical and arithmetical demonstrations that leave no room for doubt. Thus when one who studies these demonstrations and ascertains their proofs . . . is told that this is contrary to religion, he will not suspect this science, but only religion."[25]

If mathematical knowledge was valid and undeniable in Ghazali's view, logic was a doctrinally neutral tool. It is not just useful, but essential for all sciences, including theology and jurisprudence. Ghazali's extensive discussion of logic not only legitimized it from a religious point of view but also produced an Islamic discourse on the subject, replacing the technical terms used by earlier philosophers with terms used by jurists. As a result, logic was naturalized and legitimized as an indispensable science for all forms of knowledge. In Ghazali's words, logic is "no more than the study of the methods of proof and standards for reasoning, the conditions of the premises of demonstration and the manner of their ordering, the conditions of correct definition and the manner of its construction. . . . Nothing of this ought to be denied. It is the same kind of thing the theologians and religious speculative thinkers mention in their treatments of proof."[26]

Finally, Ghazali maintained that a part of the natural sciences is demonstrable and certain. He did, however, reject the principle of causation, which is the cornerstone of Aristotelian demonstrative science. Ghazali resolves this apparent contradiction between the possibility of natural knowledge and the denial of causality by distinguishing between God's recurrent creation of the natural order and God's creation in humans of the knowledge of natural patterns. This distinction allows Ghazali to argue that human knowledge of nature involves discerning uniformity in nature while at the same time denying that this uniformity is a natural necessity. In other words, natural causation is not necessary because actions belong to willing agents, and nature is not a willing agent. However, by shifting discussion from the natural order to human knowledge of this order, Ghazali maintained that scientists could study a habitual or customary natural order and at the same time accept the unlikely, and statistically insignificant, possibility of a disruption of this order, if and when the agent creating this order so chose. If there is a final definition of the orthodox position on science, it should be sought in the normative works that incontestably define Islamic orthodoxy and set its norms. Ghazali's works rank high among these. In fact, there is abundant evidence that his message was well received by other Muslims. The famous fourteenth-century historian Ibn Khaldun mentioned that, after Gazhali, all religious scholars studied logic using new sources, not the books of the ancients.[27]

RAZI ON THE EXEGESIS OF QUR'ANIC REFERENCES TO NATURE

Any discussion of the relation between science and religion in Islam must address the Qur'anic attitude toward science. The main source in which Qur'anic paradigms of science are articulated is the genre of Qur'anic exegesis (*tafsir*, plural *tafasir*). Rather than adducing a Qur'anic stand on science by directly reading the Qur'an, as many contemporary Muslims do, exegetical works represent a dynamic interaction between the scripture and the real historical communities that embodied Islamic culture. Even as they insist on grounding themselves in the immutable text of the Qur'an, exegetical works are repositories of larger cultural debates and reflect the prevailing views at their time and place. Traditional Qur'anic exegetical works contain plenty of material of possible scientific import. Collectively, however, these traditional materials do not add up to a scientific interpretation of the Qur'an. Traditional interpreters did not present themselves as engaging in an interpretive exercise. Moreover, there are no instances in which exegetes claim authority in scientific subjects on account of their knowledge of the Qur'an. The following examination of the paradigmatic treatment of scientific subjects in Qur'anic exegesis is based primarily on the exegesis of Fakhr al-Din al-Razi (d. 1210). One of the main representatives of the dominant theological school of Islam, the Ash'ari school, Razi is perhaps the most distinguished memberof this school after Ghazali. Razi wrote on natural philosophy and was fully familiar with the natural-philosophical debates of the time. He also wrote an influential Qur'anic exegesis notable for its discussions of quasi-scientific subjects. In fact, Razi's discussion of such subjects exceeded most other exegetical works of the classical period and was certainly the most influential.[28]

The instances of scientific discourse in the classical Qur'anic commentaries are invariably mixed with other kinds of discourse that have no connection to science. Commentaries often focused not just on the meaning and appropriateness of using certain terms but also the logic of their order of appearance in the Qur'an. For example, Razi explored why the word "heavens" occurs before the word "earth" in most cases where they are mentioned in the Qur'an. Among the virtues of the heavens is that they are ornamented by God with such objects as the stars, sun, and moon, as well as the throne, the pen, and the preserved tablet. God also used complimentary names to refer to the heavens in order to underscore their high status. Their other merits are that they are the abode of angels, where God is never disobeyed, that prayers are directed to them, that hands are raised toward them in supplication, and that they have perfect color and shape. The one advantage of the heavens over the earth that invokes a common scientific view of the time is the notion that the heavenly world influences the sublunar world whereas the earth is acted upon. Razi also listed some of the merits of the earth according to those who prefer it to the heavens, including the fact that prophets are sent in it and mosques for the worship of God are built in it (Razi, Al-Tafsir al-Kabir, 1–2:106–7). The noticeable absence in this comparison is of any discussion of a natural superiority of heaven over earth, which would be the standard argument of natural philosophy with which Razi was fully familiar. Rather than using the Qur'an to elucidate science, or using science to extract the proper meaning of the Qur'anic text, these quasi-scientific discussions often aimed at explaining the order of words and at demonstrating the linguistic, rhetorical miracles of the Qur'an. Indeed, it is not just the creation of a perfect and wondrous world that is underscored in the commentaries, but also the fact that God refers to this creation with words that cannot be emulated by the most eloquent humans (Razi, 1–2:105).

The marvel of creation is a recurrent theme of Qur'anic commentaries. These marvels are viewed as signs of God and proofs that God exists, is all-powerful and all-knowing, the willing creator of all being. A commonly cited verse urging contemplation of the signs of the heavens and the earth is Qur'an 3:190–91: "In the creation of the heavens and the earth, the alternation of night and day, are signs for the wise. Those who remember [pray for] God, standing or sitting or lying on their sides, who reflect and contemplate on the creation of the heavens and the earth, [and say]: Not in vain have You made them. All praise be to you, O Lord preserve us from the torment of Hell." In his commentary on this verse, Razi contended that the human mind is incapable of fully comprehending the manner in which a small leaf on a tree is created, how it is structured or how it grows; needless to say, the larger task of discovering God's wisdom in the creation of the heavens and the earth is next to impossible. One must therefore concede that the creator is beyond full comprehension. The ultimate purpose of reflection, according to Razi, is to establish the limitations of human knowledge and its inability to comprehend creation, not to establish a scientific fact and demonstrate its correspondence with the Qur'an (Razi, 8–10:137–41). In these commentaries, the contemplation that the Qur'anic text calls for is outside the text, in nature. It does not move back to the text, nor does it follow or correspond to any particular Qur'anic scheme. As such, contemplation does not imply a correlation between science—whether natural philosophy, astronomy, or medicine—and the Qur'an. The latter directs people to reflect on the wisdom of creation, but provides no details on the natural order or of ways of deciphering it. When such details appear in classical Qur'anic commentaries, they are drawn from the prevalent scientific knowledge of the time.

The most striking feature of the discussions of the Qur'anic signs of creation, especially the heavenly ones, is the mixing of information drawn from astronomy and natural philosophy with a wealth of other, nonscientific information. Thus one of the benefits of the rising and setting of the moon is that, while its rising helps night travelers find their way, its setting shelters fugitives trying to escape from their enemies. Additionally, among the signs of the heavens is the fact that shooting stars or meteors serve as missiles that drive devils away, preventing them from spying on the angels (Razi, 1–2:108–9, 15–16:76, 17–18:37). Another common feature of commentaries on the "sign verses" is that, while the complexity and perfection of creation is a sign of the wise creator, the primary proof resides in the benefits to humanity from its organization and arrangement. It is this benefit to humans that ultimately proves the existence of a wise and willing creator.

Classical commentaries often introduced elaborate discussions of scientific subjects to illustrate the idea of God's wise choice of creation as a way of maximizing human benefit. For example, in his commentary on Qur'an 2:22, Razi outlined the prerequisites for making the earth a bed (firash). After asserting that one prerequisite is that the earth not move, Razi proceeded to prove his contention (Razi, 1–2:101ff). If it were to move, the earth's motion would be either linear or circular. If it were linear, it would be falling; yet since heavier objects move faster than slower ones, the earth would fall at a faster speed than people on its surface; as a result, they would be separated from the surface of the earth and hence could not use the earth as a bed. If, on the other hand, the earth's motion is circular, the benefit for humans would not be complete, since a person moving in a direction opposite to its motion would never reach his destination. Razi then surveyed the evidence adduced by various scholars to prove that the earth is stationary. The closest he got to engaging the prevalent scientific view of his time was when he reported, and rejected, the Aristotelian argument that the earth, by nature, seeks the center of the universe. Razi objects that because the earth shares the trait of physicality with all other bodies in the universe, its acquisition of a specialized trait that makes it stationary must be logically contingent. Thus, it is the free volition of the maker, and not any inherent nature, that accounts for the earth's stillness. If anything, Razi added, the nature of the earth is to sink in water, and God reversed its nature so that it does not submerge in water, thereby making it a place on which humans can reside (Razi, 1–2:102–4).

This elaborate, quasi-scientific discourse was evidently not aimed at upholding a particular scientific view of nature. Nor did it aim at making positive contributions to the accepted body of scientific knowledge. Rather, the primary purpose was to argue the contingency of the created order and its ultimate dependence on God. Nowhere in this and other classical commentaries does one encounter the notion that a certain scientific fact or theory is predicted or even favored by the Qur'an. Instead, these commentaries reject explanations of Qur'anic verses that are grounded in the notion of a natural order. The sign verses serve as evidence of the creator not in the particular knowledge that they convey about nature but in the ultimate conclusion in each and every verse that there is a choice in creation, and thus a creator who makes this choice, that the "world is created with perfect management, comprehensive determination, utter wisdom, and infinite omnipotence" (Razi, 1–2:109).

In a move that further clarified his exegetical strategy, Razi noted that most commentators on a verse in which the sun is mentioned agreed that the sky is a plane and has no edges or peaks (Razi, 25–26:75–76). In response, however, he maintained that there is nothing in the text of the Qur'an that suggests with certainty that the sky has to be plane and not spherical. On the contrary, Razi added, sensory evidence indicates that the sky is actually spherical. After giving some of this "sensory" evidence to illustrate his point, he added that such evidence is abundant and that its proper place is in books of astronomy. To Razi, therefore, the authority on this matter is the science of astronomy, and not the Qur'an, however understood. The only reason he entered into this extra-Qur'anic discussion was to undermine the claims of other commentators who wrongly extended the authority of the Qur'an outside its proper realm. In the absence of a clear statement in the Qur'an, one seeks answers to scientific questions in their respective fields. The contrary, however, is not true, since the text is not science. When there is an apparent conflict between a Qur'anic text and a scientific fact, commentators did not present the Qur'anic text as the arbiter; they simply tried to explore the possibility of alternative scientific explanations and thus suggest that scientific knowledge on such points of contention is not categorical.

It follows from the above that religious knowledge and scientific knowledge are each assigned to their own compartments. This would justify the pursuit of science, and even a limited use of scientific discourse in commenting on the Qur'an. If exploring these subjects and reflecting on them were not permissible, God would not have so frequently urged humans to reflect on these signs of his power and wisdom. "The science of astronomy has no other meaning than reflection on how God ordered the [heavens] and created its [different parts]" (Razi, 13–14:121). The purpose of this exercise is not to establish correspondence between scientific verities and the Qur'an, but simply to reflect and hence reinforce belief in the creator of the impeccable universe. The wondrous nature of the world reinforces belief in God, but this is not contingent on the adoption of any particular scientific view. Scientific facts and theories in themselves do not provide evidence of the oneness of the Creator. Rather, it is the very fact that other natural orders are possible that points to a willing maker who chooses one of these possibilities (Razi, 21–22:161–62). According to this logic, everything in nature, however explained, as well as all scientific discoveries and facts, irrespective of their certainty, would serve as proofs for the existence of the maker. This is the fundamental reason why the scientific and unscientific could appear side by side in commentaries on the Qur'an (Razi, 21–22:163).

MODIFICATION OF LATE THEOLOGICAL WORKS
IN LIGHT OF ASTRONOMICAL RESEARCH

One genre where the subjects of science and religion intersect is speculative theology (*kalam*). Several studies have examined cosmological dimensions of early works on *kalam* and significant aspects of the physical theories discussed in these works.[29] In most of these studies, however, the scientific dimensions of *kalam* are deemed subordinate to what are rightly identified as the primary theological concerns of this field. Furthermore, the little attention given to the physical theory of *kalam* usually focuses on early *kalam* atomism and its connections to Greek atomism. The one notable exception, which does focus on the physical theory of *kalam*, ends in the eleventh century and does not explore later developments in *kalam*.[30] These later developments resulted, predictably, from theoretical developments in numerous fields of study. In particular, various cosmological questions were raised in the many works of theoretical astronomy designed to reform Ptolemaic astronomy. One of the most influential works of *kalam* revealing a significant influence of astronomy is *Kitab al-Mawaqif fi 'Ilm al-Kalam* by the fourteenth-century scholar 'Adud al-Din al-Iji (d. 1355).[31] Iji lived most of his life in Ilkhanid Iran and was fully familiar with the intellectual legacies of this period both in the religious and exact sciences. His book on *kalam* is one of the most influential textbooks on theology. It was the subject of numerous commentaries and is taught in many religious schools, including al-Azhar. Although Iji did not write a separate work on astronomy, he made extensive comments on astronomical subjects where these were connected to theological problems.

In his definition of *kalam*, Iji maintained that it is "a science through which it is possible to confirm (*ithbat*) religious dogma either by means of providing proofs or by removing ambiguities" (*Mawaqif*, 4). Iji added that even an adversary with whom he may disagree would still count as a scholar of *kalam*. Clearly, the truth of *kalam*, according to this relativistic view, is not an absolute truth. Iji also maintained that the questions of *kalam* include "every theoretical judgment concerning a knowable thing which is either one of the religious beliefs, or one on which the establishment of a religious belief depends" (*Mawaqif*, 8). To be sure, Iji maintained that *kalam* is the noblest discipline. This, however, is simply on account of the nobility of its subject matter (the divine and related matters), and not because of a privileged status of theological knowledge in fields other than theology. Moreover, according to Iji, although *kalam* does not depend on the evidence of other derived disciplines, its starting point remains transmitted evidence. It sets out to prove religious dogma already established through transmission.

Kalam, as conceived by Iji, was not a complete philosophical system. Its scope of intellectual authority was certainly not comparable to the scope claimed in philosophy proper. Despite all his pronouncements regarding the elevated status of theology, Iji's ultimate purpose was to undermine the comprehensive claims of philosophy as a complete system of knowledge, not to create an alternative comprehensive system. This is what underlies his recurrent assertions that it is possible to imagine explanations of various natural phenomena different from the ones presented by philosophers as definitive.

The *kalam* for which Iji claimed authority in religious matters had no other epistemological claims outside the limited field that *kalam* defined for itself. Thus, a standard format of Iji's expositions of theories in astronomy and natural philosophy was to ask "why is it not possible" to posit an alternative explanation (for example, *Mawaqif*, 200). Such alternatives, however, were never advocated by Iji; rather, he maintained that the orbs and circles posited in astronomical models are all "imaginary things that have no external existence. [Religious] prohibition does not extend to them, and they are neither objects of belief, nor subject to affirmation or negation" (*Mawaqif*, 207). In other words, these matters do not belong to theology, and *kalam* has no say in connection to them. Iji only mentions them to undermine their inclusion, by philosophers, in theological arguments. He also objected to the attribution of various astronomical phenomena to the volition of heavenly objects and reserved final agency to God (*Mawaqif*, 203–4, 213). In his words, "the purpose of reporting these differences is . . . so that a rational and smart person may confirm that they [the philosophers] have no proof for what they claim" (*Mawaqif*, 215). Rather than exerting the hegemony of *kalam* over these other disciplines, Iji simply tried to disengage them and to guard the autonomy and separateness of the specialized fields of knowledge.

By the time of Iji and his successors, astronomy was no longer an extension of philosophy but was definitely the master of its own abode. The tensions echoed in earlier *kalam* works between theological and physical/cosmological explanations of natural phenomena were now and henceforward significantly reduced. This, however, was a result not of the victory of *kalam* as the superior and all-encompassing system of knowledge but of the deliberate tendency to disengage it from other disciplines. The new sciences, therefore, were not interpretations of the old sciences in light of a new theology. Rather, these sciences emerged long before, and were largely responsible for, the production of the compartmentalized *kalam*.

In conclusion, we see a common trend running through the religious formulations, the epistemological constructs, and the works of scientists. Philosophy, the overarching discipline in the Greek classifications, was gradually relegated in the Islamic hierarchy of knowledge to one subdivision among many other sciences. Having isolated philosophy, Muslims could then single it out as a potential source of conflict with religion without jeopardizing the other demonstrable sciences. Thus conceived, the areas in which science and religion overlap are reduced. As a result, one of the consequences of the Islamization of science in medieval Muslim practice was the epistemological separation of science and philosophy and thereby the separation of religion and science.

NOTES

1. The classic formulation of this view is an influential article written by Ignaz Goldziher, "The Attitude of Orthodox Islam Toward the 'Ancient Sciences,'" in *Studies in Islam*, ed. M. Swartz, 185–215 (Oxford: Oxford University Press, 1975). For a systematic critique of Goldziher's views, see Dimitri Gutas, *Greek Thought, Arabic Culture: The Graeco-Arabic Translation Movement in Baghdad and Early 'Abbasid Society (2nd–4th/8th–10th Centuries)* (London: Routledge, 1998), 165–75. However, numerous studies continue to invoke Goldziher's thesis; for example, Pervez Hoodbhoy, *Islam and Science: Religious Orthodoxy and the Battle for Rationality* (London: Zed Books, 1991); and Toby Huff, *The Rise of Modern Science: Islam, China and the West* (New York: Cambridge University Press, 1993).

2. For three contrasting emphases here, see Franz Rosenthal, *The Classical Heritage of Islam* (London: Routledge, 1992); Seyyid Hossein Nasr, *Science and Civilization in Islam* (Cambridge, Mass.: Harvard University Press, 1968); and F. E. Peters, *Allah's Commonwealth: A History of Islam in the Near East, 600–1000 AD* (New York: Simon and Schuster, 1973).

3. Ghazali, *al-Risala al-Laduniyya*, 106; also see Ibn Khaldun (d. 1406), *Al-Muqaddima*, 2:436.

4. For example, the classifications of 'Amiri (d. 992), *al-I'lam bi Manaqib al-Islam*, and Ibn Hazm (d. 1064), *Tasnif al-'Ulum*. 'Amiri argues for the structural similarity of religious and exact sciences, whereas Ibn Hazm underscores the utility of the various sciences.

5. Ghazali, *Ihya' 'Ulum al-Din*, 30, 37.

6. Ghazali, *Al-Munqidh min al-Dalal*, 30.

7. Ibn Khaldun, *Al-Muqaddima*, 3:246ff.

8. More detail on astronomy is given in the next section.

9. Abu Rayhan al-Biruni, *Isti'ab al-Wujuh al-Mumkina fi San'at al-Arturlab* (Comprehending all the possible aspects of the craft/making of the astrolabe), Bodleian Library, Oxford University, Manuscript Marsh 701, 267r.

10. The list of astronomers working within this tradition comprises some of the greatest and most original Muslim scientists, including Mu'ayyad al-Din al-'Urdi (d. 1266), Nasir al-Din al-Tusi (d. 1274), Qutb al-Din al-Shirazi (d. 1311), Sadr al-Shari'a al-Bukhari (d. 1347), Ibn al-Shatir (d. 1375), and 'Ala' al-Din al-Qushji (d. 1474).

11. The names associated with this research tradition include Ibn Baja (d. 1138), Jabir Ibn Aflah (fl. 1120), Ibn Tufayl (d. 1185), Averroes (d. 1198), and Al-Bitruji (fl. 1200).

12. In theoretical astronomy, for example, E. S. Kennedy, George Saliba, F. J. Ragep, and others have documented the highly original contributions of Mu'ayyad al-Din al-'Urdi, Nasir al-Din al-Tusi, Qutb al-Din al-Shirazi, Ibn al-Shatir, Sadr al-Shari'a al-Bukhari, and al-Khafri, in the period between the thirteenth and sixteenth century. The studies of Roshdi Rashed on mathematics also confirm the existence of a wide range of original scientific production way beyond the eleventh century.

Other examples of original scientific research include the contributions of Ibn al-Nafis (d. 1288) in medicine and Kamal al-Din al-Farisi (d. 1319) in optics.

13. Edward Grant, *The Foundations of Modern Science in the Middle Ages: Their Religious, Institutional and Intellectual Contexts* (Cambridge: Cambridge University Press, 1997), 185; and Huff, *Rise of Early Modern Science*. A debate between Huff and his critic George Saliba can be followed in the *Bulletin of the Royal Institute for Inter-Faith Studies (BRIIFS)* 1.2 (1999) and *BRIIFS* 4.2 (2002).

14. George Makdisi, *The Rise of Colleges: Institutions of Learning in Islam and the West* (Edinburgh: Edinburgh University Press, 1981), 77–78.

15. Critiques of Makdisi's thesis include Jonathan Berkey, *The Transmission of Knowledge in Medieval Cairo: A Social History of Islamic Education* (Princeton, N.J.: Princeton University Press, 1992); Michael Chamberlain, *Knowledge and Social Practice in Medieval Damascus, 1190–1350* (Cambridge: Cambridge University Press, 1994); Daphna Ephrat, *A Learned Society in a Period of Transition: The Sunni 'Ulama' of Eleventh-Century Baghdad* (Albany: SUNY Press, 2000). These studies undermine Makdisi's theory about the institutional character of Islamic legal/religious education; but, as far as science is concerned, they only reinforce Makdisi's thesis of informality and marginalization.

16. The discussion in this section is based on Sonja Brentjes, "On the Location of the Ancient or 'Rational' Sciences in Muslim Educational Landscapes (AH 500–1100)," *BRIIFS* 4.1 (2002): 47–71.

17. Nahyan Fancy, "Pulmonary Transit and Bodily Resurrection: The Interaction of Medicine, Philosophy, and Religion in the Works of Ibn al-Nafis (d. 1288)" (Ph.D. diss., University of Notre Dame, 2006).

18. The examples of Sadr al-Shari'a al-Bukhari (d. 1347) and al-Nishaburi (d. 1329) are discussed, respectively, by Ahmad Dallal, *An Islamic Response to Greek Astronomy: The Astronomical Work of Sadr al-Shari'a al-Bukhari* (Leiden: E. J. Brill, 1995), and Robert Morrison, "The Intellectual Development of Nizam al-Din al-Nishaburi" (Ph.D. diss., Columbia University, 1998).

19. David King, *Astronomy in the Service of Islam* (Aldershot, U.K.: Variorum, 1993); and *Islamic Mathematical Astronomy* (London: Variorum, 1986).

20. This interpretation contrasts with that of Huff, *Rise of Modern Science*, 65. For further discussion see Brentjes, "On the Location of the Ancient Sciences," 53.

21. For the following discussion and quotes, see Abu Rayhan al-Biruni, *Tahqiq ma lil-Hind min Maqula Ma'qula fi al-Aql am Mardhula*, 219–21, of which there is an English translation by C. Edward Sachau, *Alberuni's India*, 2 vols. (London: Trubner, 1887–88; repr., 1910).

22. Ghazali's major work, in which he delivered a very effective attack on philosophy, is *Tahafut al Falasifa* (The incoherence of the philosophers), which many scholars consider the Islamic death sentence against science and rational thinking in general. For a typical example, see Max Meyerhof, "Science and Medicine," in *The Legacy of Islam*, 2nd ed., ed. Joseph Schacht and C. E. Bosworth (Oxford: Oxford University Press, 1974).

23. Ghazali addressed the question of the relation between science and religion at great length in many works. These included, in addition to *The Incoherence of the Philosophers*, *Mi'yar al-'Ilm* (The measure of knowledge), *Al-Qustas al-Mustaqim* (The right balance), *Maqasid al-Falasifa* (The intentions of the philosophers), *al-Mustasfa*

min 'Ilm al-Usul (The essence of the science of principles of jurisprudence), and *Ihya' 'Ulum al-Din* (The revival of the sciences of religion). My discussion of Ghazali is based on these and other works.

24. Ghazali, *Tahafut al-Falasifa*, 293–95.

25. Ibid., 66.

26. Ghazali, *Al-Munqidh min al-Dalal*, 24.

27. Ibn Khaldun, *Al-Muqaddima*, 143.

28. Fakhr al-Din al-Razi, *Al-Tafsir al-Kabir* (Cairo: Al-Matba'a al-Bahiyya al-Misriyya, 1934–62).

29. Classic studies of early *kalam* include Shlomo Pines, *Beitrage zur islamischen Atommenlehre* (Berlin: 1936); Harry Wolfson, *The Philosophy of Kalam* (Cambridge, Mass.: Harvard University Press, 1976); and the comprehensive studies of Josef van Eess, *Theologie und Gesellschaft im 2. und 3. Jahrhundert Hidschra: eine Geschichte des religiosen Denkens im fruhen Islam*, 6 vols. (Berlin: Walter De Gruyter, 1991–97).

30. Alnoor Dhanani, *The Physical Theory of Kalam: Atoms, Space, and Void in Basrian Mu'tazili Cosmology* (Leiden: E. J. Brill, 1994). Among other things, Dhanani's study underscores the significance of theology for the study of the history of Islamic science.

31. 'Adud al-Din al-Iji, *Al-Mawaqif fi 'Ilm al-Kalam* (Beirut, Cairo, Damascus, n.d). See also A. I. Sabra, "Configuring the Universe: Aporetic, Problem Solving, and Kinematic Modeling as Themes of Arabic Astronomy," *Perspectives on Science* 6.3 (1998): 288–330.

6

Modern Islam

Ekmeleddin İhsanoğlu

The Ottoman Empire emerged as a small principality at the turn of the four-teenth century, but within three centuries it developed to be the most powerful, prosperous, and advanced state in Islamic history. When the empire was at the zenith of its power, its territories in southeastern and central Europe extended from Slovakia to Morea; its lands included the khanate of Crimea, the Circas-sian lands, and the Caucasus and reached up to Buda. The Ottomans estab-lished their political authority on the northern coast of Africa and in the Indian Ocean through their control over the Persian Gulf and the Red Sea. The empire's front in Asia included Tabriz, Baghdad, Azerbaijan, and Iraq.

Scholarly activities in the Ottoman Empire were carried out in the clas-sical institutions of learning and according to centuries-old traditions and practices. These institutions, with origins in the Abbasid period of Islamic history, gained a new vigor and dynamism during the Ottoman period. Besides these activities, the selective transfer of "European" science began in the seventeenth century in a relatively more conspicuous way than they had earlier. From the end of the eighteenth century to the end of the nine-teenth, a long process of establishing the modern scientific tradition, with new institutions arising alongside the old ones, took place. In this chapter, I examine the development of science in the Ottoman Empire within the framework of these two traditions and explore the relationship between sci-ence and religion and the attitude of Islam toward the important "revolu-tionary" concepts of modern science.[1]

SCIENCE TRANSFER BETWEEN THE HOLDERS OF "FALSE RELIGION" AND "INFIDELS"

Heirs to the illustrious Islamic civilization as well as keepers of the rich Seljuk scientific tradition in Asia Minor, the Ottomans were actively interested in other Arabic and Islamic cultural centers, such as those in Iran, Egypt, Syria, and Turkestan (Central Asia). Hundreds of students were educated in the *medreses* that had been established in the Ottoman lands in a short period and had become centers of a new scholarly environment in the Muslim world. By the end of the sixteenth century, the Ottomans had built 324 *medreses* throughout the empire and expanded their reach to the newly established centers of Islamic culture in southeastern Europe. The sciences taught in the *medreses* were divided into two categories: *ulum-ı âliyye* (ancillary sciences), also known as *cüz'iyyat* (special sciences), and *ulum-'âliye* (high sciences). The first consisted of grammar and syntax *(sarf ve nahiv)*, rhetoric *(belagat)*, logic *(mantık)*, Islamic theology *(kelam)*, arithmetic *(hesab)*, geometry *(hendese)*, astronomy *(heyet)*, and philosophy *(hikmet)*. The second comprised commentary on the Qur'an *(tefsir)*, traditions of the Prophet *(hadis)*, and Muslim canonical jurisprudence *(fiqh)*.

Until the seventeenth century, the classical scientific tradition had produced its finest works in the scholarly milieu that developed around the classic institutions of learning—in addition to *medreses* there were palace institutions (offices of the chief physician and the chief astronomer) and the short-lived Istanbul observatory—but also through master-disciple relationships that transmitted scientific knowledge across generations. This classic tradition preserved the basic features of Islamic science during the gradual modernization period of the eighteenth century, when translations from European languages introduced new elements of learning.

The Ottoman Empire was also a European country and had common borders with other states in Europe, which helped make it the first country outside the Western world where Western science and technology was spread. Proximity provided the Ottomans with an awareness of the new explorations and inventions appearing in Europe, and led to a selective process of transfer, which characterizes the nature of the Ottomans' attitude vis-à-vis Western science and technology. The early adoption of European innovations by the Ottomans differed from those of the Russians and the Japanese. Also, it does not conform to the theoretical categories of "central-peripheral" and "exploiter-exploited" in the spread of Western science outside its initial cultural environment. The position of the Ottomans toward Western science and technology was interpreted as a selective attitude adopted by a powerful empire in response to developments outside its own sphere of influence. The Ottomans started to transfer European technology, especially in the field of firearms, cartography, and mining, in the fifteenth century. Furthermore, they had the opportunity to become acquainted with Renaissance astronomy and medicine through Jewish scholars who had taken refuge in the Ottoman Empire. In spite of this, the

Ottomans considered themselves superior to the Europeans, both spiritually and culturally, while being confident of their economic and military power. Furthermore, their selective attitude in the transfer of science may be attributed to their self-sufficiency in regard to their educational system and economy. Thus, it is obvious that the Ottomans, in their periods of strength, did not feel the need to follow closely the intellectual and scientific activities—such as the "Renaissance" and the "Scientific Revolution"—emerging in the West. The interpretations of some modern historians implying that the Ottomans did not understand that these developments would constitute a danger in the future are anachronistic. Like the peoples of other nations with their own established scientific traditions, the Ottomans became aware of the advancement of the Europeans in science and technology only through the effects of the Industrial Revolution.[2]

The continuous expansion of the early Ottoman Empire, when it seized control of the Mediterranean and led naval campaigns in the Red Sea, Black Sea, and the Indian Ocean, created a need for new geographic knowledge. The works of classical Islamic geography and the contemporary literature in Europe were relied upon for information. Furthermore, Ottoman geographers also produced original works with their own observations.

Ottoman cartography produced its greatest works with the activities of Piri Reis in the sixteenth century. The extant fragment of a map drawn by Piri Reis in 1513, part of a large-scale world map presented to Sultan Selim I in Cairo in 1517, was based on Christopher Columbus's map of America and different European and Islamic maps, as well as on his own experiences. This map includes information about the coastlines of southwestern Europe, northwestern Africa, and southeastern and central America. It is a portolano type of map, which does not have longitude and latitude lines, but it incorporates the coasts and the islands. Piri Reis presented his second world map to Sultan Süleyman I in 1528. This map, of which only a small part has survived, includes the North Atlantic Ocean and newly explored places in northern and central America. Piri Reis wrote a geography book by the name of *Kitab-ı Bahriye* (Book of the sea), which he presented to Süleyman I in 1525. This important book, which made use of Eastern and European sources, includes maps and drawings of the cities in the Mediterranean and Aegean Seas, and gives extensive information on navigation and marine astronomy based on Reis's own observations.

Ottoman admiral Seydi Ali Reis (d. 1562) is one of the outstanding persons on the subject of marine geography during this period. He wrote a very valuable work in Turkish called *el-Muhit* (The ocean) containing astronomic and geographic information needed for long sea voyages and his own observations in the Indian Ocean. Another important contribution in Turkish was

Matrakçı Nasuh's *Beyân-ı Menâzil-i Sefer-i Irakeyn* (Description of the stopping places on the campaign to the two Iraqs), one of the best examples of descriptive geography.

Tarih-i Hind-i Garbî (History of the West Indies, probably written by Muhammed b. Emir el-Suûdî el-Niksarî [1591] in the sixteenth century) is another study that mentions America and new discoveries. This work, based on sources written in Spanish and Italian, was presented to Sultan Murad III in 1573. In its largest section, consisting of two-thirds of the book, the explorations of Columbus, Magellan, Cortez, and Pizarro, from 1492 to 1552, are narrated.

As it will be clear from different examples below, the Ottomans' interest in the scientific knowledge of the Europeans—whom they considered "infidels"—had nothing to do with their religious affiliations as was the case for Europeans. What really did matter was the urge to acquire what was needed from the other side. Likewise, European scholars—who viewed Muslims as "holders of false religion"—were keen to acquire Muslim knowledge, which they deemed superior to their own and which they needed.

The Italian nobleman Comte de Marsigli, who lived among the Ottomans and wrote a book on the military state of the Ottoman Empire (1732), appreciated the Islamic tradition of science despite his critical observations on Islam as religion.

> In their schools, the principles of their "false religion" are taught first; one learns about matters of faith and develops a capacity to judge. Those who wish to make further progress in literature continuously exercise writing prose and poetry, and later write their history with insight and great accuracy, which is even boring, because they care too much for describing every detail and circumstance. They take great interest in logic and other fields of ancient philosophy and especially in medicine.
>
> Alchemy is very pleasant to them. They mix their medicines according to the old prescriptions of Avicenna and Dioscorides, and have a certain knowledge of botanics. They very seriously study geometry, astronomy, geography and ethics; I can give, as evidence, a catalogue of more than eighty-six thousand authors of the last century, which I have in my library in Bologna, compiled for the use of scholars.[3]

It is important to note that at a time when the Ottomans were translating and compiling geography books from European sources, de Marsigli wrote about the need for Europeans to translate Ottoman geographical literature. "As a matter of fact, we will never have perfect maps of the Ottoman, Persian, Tartar and Arab Empires if we do not make use of the translation of these authors' works on geography."

Almost a century later the Italian priest Toderini, who stayed in Istanbul between the years 1781 and 1786, shared the opinion of de Marsigli. His words about Ottoman scholars are noteworthy: "The Ottoman scholars are knowledgeable and reliable since they do not have any uncultivated intellectual activities and they all know Arabic and Persian." Toderini expanded his studies to include all kinds of scientific activities of the Ottomans. His numerous remarks about the *medreses*, which he called "academies," and their curriculum are worthy of attention: "From the viewpoint of scientific autonomy and other aspects they [and the educational institutions, the *vakfs*] are more advanced than their counterparts in Europe."[4]

BETWEEN OLD AND NEW

Although they had a well-established tradition and a rich literature on different theoretical and practical topics of astronomy, the Ottomans were always looking for more updated astronomical tables and corrections for the shortcomings of the tables they were using.[5] The most important among these tables were produced under the royal patronage and scholarly leadership of the Timurid King Uluğ Bey. These tables, which were made after extensive astronomical observations and serious work of the great astronomers and mathematicians of the time—including an Ottoman scholar of the name Kadızâde Rumî (d. ca. 1440)—were universally known as the *Uluğ Bey Zij*. Sultan Murad III's chief astronomer, Takiyeddin al-Rasid (Takiyeddin the Observer), made a series of observations in the short-lived but famous observatory of Istanbul with a group of fifteen scholars. His works constitute the last apex of the science of astronomy in Islam. Indeed, his observations were more precise and closer to the present observations than were those of his European contemporary Tycho Brahe. Nevertheless, in their quest for more updated ephemerides, Ottoman astronomers also followed the works of their European counterparts, particularly the ephemerides based on new observations.[6]

One of the first works to be translated from a European language on the subject of astronomy was an astronomical table by the French astronomer Noel Duret (d. ca. 1650), called *Ephemerides Celestium Richelianae ex Lansbergii Tabulis* and printed in Paris in 1641. The Ottoman astronomer Tezkereci Köse Ibrahim Efendi of Szigetvar translated this work in 1660 as *Secencelü'l-Eflak fî Gayeti'l-Idrak* (Mirror of revolving spheres of heaven on the limits of perception). This translation is at the same time the first book in Ottoman literature mentioning Copernicus and his heliocentric system of the universe. The first reaction to this book reflected the Ottomans' feelings toward Europeans, with whom they were still engaged in fighting: in the words of Mehmed Efendi, the chief astronomer of the period, "such presumptuousness is abundant among the Europeans." However, after learning how to use the table from the translator and after comparing it with the *Uluğ Bey Zij*, Mehmed Efendi appreciated the value of the work and awarded the translator. The initial reaction of the chief astronomer is a typical example of the cautious approach of the Ottomans, who were sure of their own scientific tradition and experiences, and did not immediately accept the scientific superiority of the West.

The eighteenth century witnessed an intensive interest among the Ottomans in modern astronomy. The astronomical tables of Clairot, Cassini, and Lalande were translated into Arabic and Turkish. Moreover, the visit of the Ottoman ambassador Yirmisekiz Mehmed Çelebi to the Paris observatory in 1721 and his lengthy discussion with Jacques Cassini demonstrates the knowledge of an Ottoman diplomat in the science of astronomy as well as the common scientific background that he shared with his European counterpart. This passage from Mehmed Çelebi's travel accounts is very revealing in this regard: "When Cassini (Father Jean Cassini) died before he completed his observations, his son became the director of the observatory and all the treasures were handed over to him. He wrote down the matters which his father considered to be contrary to Uluğ Bey's tables and gave us this. His father's writings have not been printed yet, but his son wishes to print them after he completes the observations."[7]

The translation of Cassini's astronomical tables had important influences on the Ottoman practice of compiling ephemerides. Upon the order of Sultan Selim III (r. 1789–1807), calendars began to be organized according to Cassini's tables, and Uluğ Bey's tables were abandoned in the course of time.[8]

Studying the above-mentioned and similar works translated from European languages did not lead to any questioning of Islamic faith. The issues of the sun being the center of the universe and the earth being in motion, which were the basic components of the Copernican view that created major disputes in Europe, were considered technical details (a change of vector) by the classical Ottoman astronomers, not a subject of polemics. The main reason is that the Ottoman astronomers did not know of any religious dogma opposed to this notion.

Subsequent translations of major texts from European scientific literature display the Muslim scholars' stand toward European science and the relation between science and religion. Kâtip Çelebi (d. 1657) translated the work of Mercator and A. S. Hondio called *Atlas Minor* with the name of *Levamiü'n-Nur fî Zulmeti Atlas Minör* (Flashes of light on the darkness of Atlas Minor) in the seventeeth century. His *Cihannümâ*, which he wrote by making use of Western and Eastern sources, is a valuable work from the point of view of Ottoman geography and cultural history. Kâtip Çelebi enriched the Ottoman and Islamic culture and was a great influence on

Ottoman scholars through other works, in the fields of bibliography and biography and his translations of histories by European authors to Turkish. The Ottoman science of geography, which started with Piri Reis, developed further with *Cihannümâ*, and this movement continued without interruption until the nineteenth century.

Abu Bakr al-Dimashqi's (d. 1691) nine-volume translation of Janszoon Blaeu's work in Latin—briefly known as *Atlas Major* and made by the order of Sultan Mehmed IV (r. 1648–87)—is one of the early examples of a Muslim work including an explanation of the religious implications of European texts. The first volume of the translation of *Atlas Major* kept at the Topkapı Palace Museum Library contains general information on geography and cosmography; volumes two through five are on European countries, volume six on the African continent, volume seven on Italy, volume eight on China, and volume nine on America and the islands. After stating the importance of the science of astronomy and the need for it in his introduction, al-Dimashqi gives some information on the state of the science of astronomy in the Muslim world and on the views of the Europeans concerning this subject. He rejects the claims of European scholars that imply that the science of astronomy had declined among Muslims so much so that nobody knew its name. He takes notice of the fact that there were numerous scholars in Islamic lands well informed in the science of astronomy, and particularly that the teachers with whom he studied were unmatched. He stated that many people studied the rational sciences—particularly astronomy and geometry—but were more occupied with the theoretical aspect of these sciences rather than their application, for in the past someone who knew astronomy would also know geography and astronomical observation. Thus, Abu Bakr al-Dimashqi admits in a critical manner that Islamic science remained on the theoretical level since it had receded gradually from the compilation of geographical and astronomical observations. He stated that Islamic astronomy fell behind the developments in Europe and concluded that, owing to their advancements in astronomy, the "infidels" now predominated the countries of the world and excelled in thwarting the Muslims.

In the chapter titled "The Center of the Universe," al-Dimashqi presents Blaeu's detailed account of the different systems of Ptolemy, Copernicus, and others, as well as Blaeu's judgment that the geocentric system is correct and theories that run contrary to the Bible ("*Sacrae Scripturae*" in the Latin text) are wrong. Al-Dimashqi however, does not relate Blaeu's statement that the theory of Ptolemy has been considered appropriate by everyone for centuries and is still valid. It is clear that al-Dimashqi, while relating the information and arguments on different theories about the universe, had no prejudice against the new astronomy (Copernicanism). In the introduction of the work he presented to the Sultan, he makes explicit statements verifying and stressing the importance of the science of astronomy from different aspects, such as its necessity and its compatibility with the Holy Qur'an.

The Ottoman translators that came after al-Dimashqi showed a preference for the Copernican view, despite the orthodox opinion of the European authors of the texts they translated. One salient example is Osman b. Abdül-mennan's (d. ca. 1779) comments, in his Turkish translation of *Geographia Generalis* (by Bernhardus Veranius, d. 1676), declaring his preference for the heliocentric system on rational bases.[9]

In the eighteenth century, we begin to see for the first time a kind of religious sensitivity in the introduction of modern astronomy to a Muslim audience. The two examples cited below, though related to each other (the first was the source of the second), illustrate the new sensitivity in totally diverse contexts.

Ibrahim Müteferrika (d. 1745), a Hungarian convert to Islam, Ottoman statesman, diplomat, and vanguard of reform policy, made a major contribution to Ottoman cultural and intellectual life by establishing the first Ottoman printing press. Among the books he printed was Kâtip Çelebi's well-known *Cihannümâ*, in 1732. Müteferrika added a chapter containing detailed explanations of the systems of the universe and the new astronomy. During the century following its publication, this supplement was the most extensive text in the Ottoman world dealing with the "new astronomy." After a year, and upon the order of the sultan, with Müteferrika's translation from Latin of the astronomical work titled *Atlas Coelesti*, a separate work dealing with the old and the new astronomy was introduced into the Ottoman scientific literature.

In his supplement to *Cihannümâ*, Müteferrika first stated that all scholars of astronomy agreed that the universe was constructed of concentric spheres, one inside the other, while having different approaches to the structure and the details of the subject. Then he divided the conceptions of the structure of the universe into three groups. He attributed the first point of view to Aristotle and Ptolemy, the second to Pythagoras, Plato, and Copernicus, and the third to Tycho Brahe. He noted that European scholars qualify the first view as "old astronomy" and the second and third views as "new astronomy."

Before explaining these different views, Müteferrika pointed to the relationship between them and matters of religion and belief. In his view, it was a requirement of religion to believe that the universe is the work of the exalted creator. Once this is accepted, approving any one of the views concerning the shape, arrangement, and order of the universe does not depend on religion. Thus Müteferrika clearly stated that the stance of Islamic religion on this subject would be impartial; whichever of these views one

subscribes to, the religious aspect of the matter is merely related to the existence of the creator of the universe. On the other hand, he assumed a hesi-
tant and extremely cautious attitude by saying that "the first view is held
acceptable and superior by everyone, while the second and third views are
not held in respect and are rejected." Nevertheless, he stated that the explanation of these three views will be beneficial and deemed it appropriate to
affix this supplement to such an important work as *Cihannümâ*. He
explained all three views because he considered it necessary for those who
wish to know and hear that which everyone in the world already knows and
sees, as well as for those who pursue knowledge. He also added illustrations
to the book to facilitate the "pictorial representation of the state of the universe and the conception of the sphere of the world."[10]

The most remarkable feature of Müteferrika's supplement to the *Cihannümâ* was his cautious explanation of the heliocentric system. He assumed
this attitude because he anticipated a reaction in the Muslim world similar
to the strong and violent opposition against the Copernican system that
arose in the Christian world. Müteferrika was well aware of this reaction in
Christendom since he had once been a priest and then converted to Islam.
In his introduction of the heliocentric system, where he referred to Aristotle's view and qualified it as appropriate and sound, he repeated that the
acceptance of this new view had no connection with religious belief, and he
called upon bold scholars to criticize this new view and support Aristotle's
view. Without giving any examples or details, he claimed that even Muslim
scholars opposed the heliocentric view. Although this new view may be
"null and void," he said, it attracted supporters in every period since it was
the view of the predecessors and many works had been written on it. Nevertheless, he fell short of stating his opinion but instead used dubious and
contradictory statements. This cautious attitude of Müteferrika on the heliocentric system was to change to a great extent, however, when he translated
the *Atlas Coelestis* from Latin (printed in 1709) shortly after the publication
of the *Cihannümâ*.

Müteferrika began this translation upon the order of Sultan Ahmed III,
in the year 1733, and he titled it *Macmu'at el-Hey'et el-kadîme ve'l-cedîde* (The
Compendium of old and new astronomy). It is significant that he was
ordered by the sultan the very next year to translate into Turkish a work
devoted exactly to the appendices he added.[11] One of the remarkable points
in Müteferrika's new translation is his manner, now less prudent than his
very cautious approach in the *Cihannümâ*. A possible reason for this change
may be that, contrary to his fears, the publication of *Cihannümâ* met with no
opposition similar to the attacks on heliocentrism made by European men
of religion and statesmen. Although Müteferrika mentioned the connection
of the subject with religion in his new book, using his previous words and

passages, he did not repeat them as frequently, and he was more assured in presenting his views.

The second important illustration of the relation between science and religion in Islam at this time is the book called *Marifetname* by Ibrahim Hakkı of Erzurum (d. 1780), a versatile scholar, widely read author, and a renowned mystic. *Marifetname* circulated in many handwritten and printed versions that present quite interesting and rather different images of the cosmos. In his introduction to the book, Hakkı described what he called "Islamic astronomy," which he represented as a kind of folk cosmology.

This information, which is presented as the words of the commentators on the Qur'an *(mufassir)* and the traditionists of the Prophet *(muhaddith)*, is related neither to the Holy Qur'an and the sound traditions of the Prophet—the two basic sources of Islamic religion—nor to the science of astronomy that developed in the golden age of Islamic civilization and was based on theory and observation. Written in a lyrical style and ornamented with metaphorical expressions mixed with legend, having no connection with religion and science, the introduction appealed to the taste of the uneducated masses. It appears that this material was drawn from what the *muhaddith* classified as fictitious *(mawdu')* traditions.

Ibrahim Hakkı's "Islamic folk astronomy" was based on an influential book by al-Suyuti (d. 1505), one of the most prolific writers of the Mamluk period. Al-Suyuti's work, titled *al-Hay'at al-saniyya fi'l-hay'at al-sunniyya*, was reorganized with some additions by Ibrahim ibn Abdurrahman el-Karamanî el-Âmidî (fl. 1654) under the title of *Risala fi'l-hay'a 'ala tariq ahl al-sunna wa'l-jama'a*. Nazmizâde Hüseyin Murtaza b. Ali el-Bağdadî (d. 1722) later translated Karamanî's work into Turkish.

Ibrahim Hakkı's second presentation on astronomy is in the first of three parts of his book. Here, he presented the concepts of the new science of astronomy.[12] He explained that when the scholars advanced the heliocentric theory, uneducated people first reacted negatively but that the new astronomy gained currency as a result of improved observations over time. Moreover, he stated that it is irrelevant to religion to consider whether the center of the universe is the earth or the sun. In principle, he argued, one should believe that the universe is the work of the exalted creator, but the different beliefs concerning the shape of the universe do not concern religious matters. Hakkı's discussion of the planets revolving in their orbits around the sun at the center, the period of their orbital movements, and their satellites had a completely scientific nature.

Ibrahim Hakkı favored the heliocentric system even though he was not a professional astronomer involved technically with mathematics and astronomy. He expressed his view clearly and more boldly than his predecessors had without deeming it necessary to act cautiously, as Müteferrika, who was his main source, did. In his words, "it is much easier, more proper and reasonable for this spherical Earth, which is more suitable for movement owing to its small mass, to revolve around the great Sun once a year."

Hakkı's ideas concerning the compatibility of modern science with religion drew on the authority of the twelfth-century scholar Abu Hamid Muhammed al-Ghazali (d. 1111). An outstanding theologian, jurist, and religious reformer, al-Ghazali argued, in his well-known book *Tahafut al-Falasifa*, that studying astronomy is not against religious law. The findings of astronomers, whatever they are, should not be construed as opposing religion as long as they acknowledge that the world, irrespective of its shape, is created by God. Referring to al-Ghazali's argument, Ibrahim Hakkı criticized those who would use religion to attack science and he refuted their claims by saying: "A wise enemy is better than a foolish friend."

One reason for the contradictory statements in *Marifetname* may be Hakkı's fear of the reaction of some narrow-minded *ulama* (religious scholars) against him. Since Ibrahim Hakkı had been informed that the *mufti* Kadızâde Muhammed Ârif b. Muhammed el-Erzurumî (d. 1760) planned to interrogate him, he may have added the section on "Islamic astronomy" to avoid trouble. The organization and contents of *Marifetname* indicate that this section was added to the work later. Indeed, contrary to the folk cosmological explanation in this part of his work, Ibrahim Hakkı explained natural events in a completely scientific way in the rest of his work.

Detailed examination of the adaptation, translation, and compilation of modern scientific books and tables (in the case of astronomy) during the seventeenth and eighteenth century, and of the travelogues and reports of Ottoman ambassadors to Europe, shows clearly that the Ottomans went through two different stages in acquiring the new science. In the first stage of awareness and familiarity, they were capable of following the developments in Europe closely. However, being conscious of their own rich experience and great scientific tradition, of which they were representative, they did not accept the superiority of the newly emerging tradition right away. They accepted it only after observing its compatibility with their own scientific tradition. In the following stage, in the second half of the eighteenth century, the proven validity of European science led to its widespread use and application.

Although no conflict was observed between science and religion in this period, one notices that the common people showed sensitivity to the new view owing to folk religious beliefs. However, this kind of sensitivity did not have any significant role.

Our research indicates that in these two stages, the principal European sources and theoretical works that brought about fundamental changes in astronomy were not preferred candidates for translation; the Ottomans felt content with their own literature and were in greater need of the practical aspects of modern science.

In the first half of the nineteenth century modern astronomy was accepted to the extent that Muslim scholars remained in favor of it from the religious point of view. A good example is a book called *Asrar al-Malakut*, written by the Azeri scholar Kudsî of Baku (d. 1848) and translated and presented to the Ottoman Sultan Abdülmecid in 1846. Kudsî, after presenting a short history of astronomy, maintained that the Copernican theory was the most successful and correct one for solving the current astronomical problems:

> Whether one prefers the Ptolemaic or the Copernican system, no inconvenience would ensue from the viewpoint of our religion because these matters are related to reason, not religion. Since imitation *(taqlid)* would not be lawful in matters pertaining to the intellect, we accept what the intellect prefers. Some Muslim scholars of new astronomy, who compared the Copernican view with the rules of reason and observation, defended its correctness on the basis of the Qur'anic verses and the traditions of the Prophet. They were surprised to see how the Ptolemaic view, which did not conform to the principles of science and observation, continued to be well known for such a long time. I realized that the Copernican view conforms to the clear and definite proofs deduced from geometry and moreover, to the Qur'anic verses and the traditions of the Prophet; as for the Ptolemaic view, it is the opposite.

Kudsî concluded that the new conception of the universe was supported by the Qur'anic verses and the traditions of the Prophet. Here, the author endeavored to reach an agreement between religion and science to an extent we have not seen in any of the works mentioned above.[13]

A quarter of a century after the wide acceptance of the new astronomy and the assertion of its compatibility with Islam in Istanbul, the capital of the Islamic caliphate, a debate started in the newly emerging city of Beirut, which was a part of the Ottoman province of Syria. Beirut witnessed the influx of missionaries of different denominations from the West. They established schools and institutions of higher education. Among these institutions, the Syrian Protestant College and the Jesuit St. Joseph College were prominent. The graduates of these schools started to publish a journal, partly as a means of disseminating their ideas to the broader Arabic reading public. The graduates of the Syrian Protestant College dedicated a journal titled *al-Muqtataf* to the promotion of modern science and technology. The graduates of St. Joseph's did the same by producing *al-Bashir*, then the Maronite community of Beirut started to produce their own journal, *al-Jinan*.

The debate began among Christian Arabs through an article, published in 1876 in *al-Jinan*, defending the old astronomy with its fixed earth. The debate between the followers of the three denominations in their respective journals was joined by the representative of the Greek Orthodox Patriarch, who listed verses from the Old Testament, including the famous miracle of Joshua ordering the sun to stand still.

An interesting turn of events happened when two Christian writers argued about the pros and cons of what they understood to be the Copernican theory. *Al-Muqtataf* received a letter from the Egyptian Muslim intellectual and deputy minister of education Abdullah Fikri Pasha, who lent his support to Copernican astronomy by affirming that the notion of the mobility of the earth was in no way a novel idea and that one could find it in earlier Muslim writings. Meanwhile, he provided the Islamic point of view in support of this by referring to al-Ghazali,—as Ottoman scholars had done in Istanbul at least one and a half centuries ago. Fikri used the statements of al-Ghazalî to support a position that would allow astronomical doctrines that had been demonstrated to be true to take precedence over the outward statements of revelation, and according to which revelation ought to be interpreted.[14]

In sum, the debate over modern astronomy conducted by Christian writers affiliated with missionary schools was not strictly formulated along denominational lines. In the case of Darwinism, as will be elaborated below, the sides were more clearly drawn. Jesuits tended to side against Darwin, whereas the graduates of the Syrian Protestant College supported him. A famous commencement lecture in which he advocated Darwinism, given in 1882 by Edwin Lewis (1839–1907), a Harvard graduate and professor of chemistry at the college, stirred up a controversy between these supporters and college professors taking the adversary position. For example, the dean of the School of Theology charged that Darwin was an atheist who did not believe in Jesus Christ. In turn, Lewis submitted his resignation, which was immediately approved by the college's Board of Trustees in New York.

THE LONG NINETEENTH CENTURY AND THE EMERGENCE OF CHALLENGE

Two distinct phases are observed in the relationship between science and religion in the nineteenth century. The first phase is characterized by a harmonious relationship; the second is marked by disputes and conflicts, as was the case in the Western world. This conflict was observed more intensely in the first decades of the twentieth century. The main reasons behind this categoric change could be summarized as the establishment of modern educational institutions where training in foreign (European) languages enabled Muslim intellectuals to form clear contacts with Western philosophy.

Upon the crushing defeat of the Ottoman navy against the Russians in 1770, important changes occurred in the Ottoman administrators' attitude toward Western science and technology. Among these changes, a small number of technicians, who embraced Islam, were brought from Europe. This was not sufficient, however, and the Ottomans felt the need to establish new military educational institutions. The new process of training young officers in modern sciences and technology started in the imperial shipyard *(Tersâne-i Âmire)* in Istanbul, where three educational projects—in shipbuilding, engineering training, and medical training—developed through time to become the Imperial Military Engineering School, the Imperial Naval Engineering School, and the Imperial Medical School. These schools went through different stages and their curricula updated. Remarkably, at the very beginning of their establishment and until the middle of the nineteenth century no conflict of faith and science was observed. The opening ceremonies of all these institutions were attended by top-ranking *ulama*, who led the prayers. Moreover, the students of these institutions were taught religion and oriental languages. Besides, the first teachers of mathematics and medicine, the major subjects of these institutions, had been educated according to the classical tradition.

At the Imperial Naval Engineering School mathematics was taught by the famous mathematician and *müderris* (professor) Gelenbevî İsmail Efendi (1730–91), who later became a *kadı* (judge). Gelenbevî had been educated under the traditional system, and he wrote books not only on arithmetic, geometry, logarithm, and trigonometry but also on literature, *fiqh* (jurisprudence), theology, logic, philosophy, and other classical subjects of *medrese* scholarship, most of which were published.[15]

Two Ottoman scholars who figured most prominently in the introduction of modern medical science in the first quarter of the nineteenth century were the historian and physician Şanizade Ataullah Efendi (1796–1826) and the chief physician to the Sultan, Hekimbaşı Mustafa Behcet Efendi (1774–1843), both of whom had received a *medrese* education. Their translations and adaptations of European medical books made available the new medical knowledge developing in the West. They exerted great efforts to introduce modern medicine, and their published works pioneered in this field. Behcet Efendi also played a major role in the establishment of the Imperial Medical School in 1839, the institution responsible for establishing modern medical education in the Ottoman Empire. His brother, Abdülhak Molla, who contributed to the establishment of this school, was also a physician educated at the *medrese*.

A careful study of the biographies of the forerunners of systematic modern scientific education reveals that most of the original teaching staff were graduates of the *medreses*. Yet, they did not hesitate to take up posts in these newly founded institutions. This shows that the *ulama* were not opposed to the new educational institutions. Nevertheless, it is undeniable that a divergence of attitude later emerged between the intellectuals who graduated from these new educational institutions and those who were graduates of the *medreses*. This divergence undoubtedly resulted in the situation described by many researchers as "dualism" in Ottoman thought. An important question here is whether this dualism, or conflict between the modern and traditional, was actually a conceptual conflict or a social one. In other words, was it a result of a conflict between the concept of science based on Islam and Islamic scientific heritage upheld by the *ulama* and represented by the *medrese* teachers and the concept that was based on European knowledge and upheld by the new-style intellectuals trained in contemporary science?[16]

The students of the medical school, which was reorganized in 1839, illustrated both the social and conceptual roots of this conflict. Among the attempts to modernize the curriculum and the teaching staff, the most important one was adopting French as the language of teaching. Young Ottoman candidates for medical careers came in direct contact with French culture for the first time as they became acquainted with the works of the philosophers who led the way to the French Revolution and materialistic philosophical trends. An American traveler, Mac Farlane, who visited this school in 1847 noted that young Turkish students read *Système de la nature* by Baron d'Holbach and *Jacques le fataliste* by Diderot. He also mentioned that particularly the last edition of d'Holbach's book, which was published in Paris, was widely read, as many passages in the book had been underlined.[17]

In the second half of the nineteenth century, various trends of Western thought and disputes on the relation between religion and science were introduced to the world of Islam for the first time. Later, in the last quarter of the nineteenth century, these discussions were carried on among the Arabic-speaking intellectuals in Beirut, which was part of the province of Syria.

In the 1860s the first journal with the aim of introducing modern science to great masses of people was published in the Muslim world, in Istanbul. *Mecmua-i Fünun* (Journal of Science) appeared (1862–67) under the leadership of Münif Pasha (1830–1910), one of the reformist intellectuals of the Tanzimat (Ottoman reform movement), who was minister of education for a certain period. Many articles of Münif Pasha and other intellectuals of the time, particularly on modern science, appeared in this journal.[18] An examination of these writings indicates that the Ottoman intellectuals did not consider themselves the heirs of a tradition different from that of Europe in regard to science or civilization. In their view the issue was not one of harmonizing two different civilizations. None of the articles in the journal mentioned a conflict between "Islamic civilization" and "European civilization." This attitude probably stemmed from the fact that ancient Greek legacy constituted a common background between the two traditions and that the Ottomans were still untouched by the influences of the civilizing mission of Europe.

Münif Pasha introduced the idea of biological evolution to Turkish-reading intellectuals for the first time with his articles titled "Introduction to the science of geology" and "Ethnological evolution of the monkey called orang-outang" a decade later. Another member of the *ulama*, Hoca Tahsin Efendi (1813–81), who was at one time the director of the Ottoman University, wrote a "History of the Genesis and Creation." In this work he stated that the universe was created through various stages over billions of years and that it is necessary to have knowledge of different scientific disciplines to be able to understand these stages. Moreover, it appears that he was greatly influenced by the French edition of Ludwig Büchner's book *Kraft und Stoff* (Force and matter). It is interesting that Hoca Tahsin Efendi preferred to present the theory of evolution as the "law of evolution" that rules over the universe and its beings.

One of the most salient characteristics of the relations between science and religion in this stage is the fact that members of the old *ulama* class had an accommodative approach and a harmonious attitude in presenting new philosophical and scientific theories to a wide range of readers. Modern intellectuals, who had been educated in modern institutions of learning, began to oppose religion. In the early stage, however, this elitist attitude was limited to their circle and did not reach the larger public.

A watershed event for the position of science in Islam occurred in Paris, in 1883, at a Sorbonne conference. The French scholar Ernest Renan stated that Muslim societies had their previous successes in the fields of science and philosophy not *because* of Islamic religion but *despite* Islam. Moreover, he asserted that the Arab people, by virtue of being Semitic and their social structure, were not suitable for metaphysical thought or philosophy. He added that it was the ascetics, the atheists, and the non-Arab and Aryan people that gained successes for Islam in these fields. Renan claimed that "as European science spread, Islam would perish." Jamal al-Din Afghani (1839–97), the famous reformer who was in Paris at the time, responded to these accusations, as did Namık Kemal (1840–88), the renowned Ottoman intellectual, poet, and writer, and the Russian Muslim intellectual Ataullah Bayezid. Their writings on this subject led to the emergence of discussions on the relations between science and religion in the Islamic world.[19]

Afghani's point of view was that these criticisms do not apply to Islam; on the contrary, Islam was in harmony with the the principles discovered by scientific reason and was indeed the religion demanded by reason. Afghani in a different context maintained the opinion that reason should be used fully in interpreting the Qur'an. If the Qur'an seems to be in contradiction with what is known, it should be interpreted symbolically.[20] The debate also led to a new topic of discussion. This was the issue of whether Islam is conducive or obstructive toward progress and science. This discussion later turned into an intellectual polemic about factors leading to the progress or regression of society. In this polemic, it was not sociological or economic reasons but religion, mentality, culture, and civilization that were seen as directly responsible for the progress or regression of a society or empire.

The impact of Darwin's evolutionary theory on the Ottoman intellectuals gained new dimensions by the end of 1880s. Until then, only Lamarck's name was mentioned in relation to the theory of evolution, but Darwin's name would replace it. This was due to several reasons. First, the theory of evolution that had influenced the Ottoman intellectuals came by way of France. Until the 1890s the French evolutionary intellectuals brought Lamarck to the forefront and neglected Darwin's work. Darwin's fame in France spread mainly after the 1880s. Thus, in parallel to the developments in France, Darwin's name began appearing in the Ottoman literature along with Lamarck's at the same time. Second, Büchner, who had most influenced the Ottoman intellectuals with his materialist views expressed in *Kraft und Stoff* (1855), took Darwinism seriously and referenced it extensively in his analyses. Third, and probably most important, we should mention the influence on Ottoman intellectuals of Hüseyinzade Ali (1864–1942), who had graduated from Petersburg University (1889), where almost all of the pro-Darwinist philosophers were concentrated, and brought the new theories with him to the military medical school.[21]

The discussions related to Darwinism that took place in Istanbul differed from those in Europe particularly in one respect. Contrary to the discussions in Europe, those in Istanbul began with evolutionary and social Darwinist thought instead of biological Darwinism. Ottoman intellectuals came into closer contact with biological Darwinism from 1908 on, after they were introduced to German (Büchner, Haeckel) and French (Le Bon, Domolins) thought and after putting these ideas into practice in the service of their political struggle.

One can gain a better understanding of this situation by looking at the Ottoman intellectuals' stand toward the "fate" of their empire during its last century. As the philosophical trends that initiated in the West took religion as their target, a parallel situation occurred among the Ottoman intellectuals who not only studied the modern sciences in the newly established schools but also knew European languages. The book by John William

Draper on the *Conflict between Religion and Science*, published in 1874 in the United States and in French in 1875, also had a great impact. The Ottoman encyclopedist and prolific writer Ahmet Midhat published the Turkish translation, with a long supplement, as a work of two thousand pages in four volumes (1895, 1897, 1900).

Ahmet Midhat (1844–1912) believed that although the subject of Draper's work was Catholicism, some young Muslims might think that his criticisms apply to all religions. He therefore wrote the long supplement to his translation with the purpose of presenting the particular attitude of Islam toward science. Midhat pointed out that the attitude that arose among the Ottoman youth toward religion lacked any basis and that Draper's arguments concerning Catholicism did not hold true for Islam. He added that Islam encourages scientific endeavors and that Muslims throughout history had made important contributions to science. In fact, if the young Muslims wished to be adorned with wisdom, they should not stray from Islam. On the contrary, if they fully understood the new philosophy and science and complemented their knowledge with belief in Islam, they would become wise *(hakîm)* in the true sense of the word and realize that Draper's accusations concerning religion were not valid for Islam. However, if they were to study in detail the various topics discussed by Draper, they might attain the truth. Imitation is not preferable to investigation, neither according to the method of religion nor according to the method of philosophy.[22]

In the late 1800s, discussions on various aspects of Darwinism began to take place in another corner of the Ottoman Empire, namely in Beirut. As was true for the introduction of Copernican astronomy to Islamic learning, journals were particularly influential in spreading ideas that flourished in Beirut's missionary schools. These journals are important in that they show the diverse effects of these discussions and the extent to which the religious views of the authors were prevailing. A bitter controversy over Darwinism started in 1882 at the Syrian Protestant College, involving teachers, students, missionary members, and intellectuals, and ended with the resignation of its Harvard-educated teacher Edwin Lewis, as explained earlier. The editors of the journal *al-Muqtataf*, Ya'qup Sarraf and Farris Nimr, found themselves involved in conflicts with their own American Protestant patrons as well as various Catholic and Orthodox critics. In 1885 they moved to Cairo, where they started to issue *al-Muqtataf*, having learned their lesson that discussions of science should be kept separate from issues of faith. The discussions initiated by *al-Muqtataf* in Egypt tended to deal more with social Darwinian ideas and with Herbert Spencer in particular. One of the best-known medical materialists—Shibli Shumayyil (ca. 1850–1917), a physician by training—showed distress with religious conflicts as well as his hope that progress and world peace would follow the dissemination of the theory of evolution and the development of technology and the natural sciences.

In contrast to the radical evolutionism and unabashed materialism of Shibli Shumayyil, most late-nineteenth-century Arabic discussions of the natural world (as in Europe) preferred a "natural theological" approach—an approach that typically emphasized God's providential control over nature and argued that natural phenomena revealed evidence of divine purpose, wisdom, and design. These discussions cut across geographic and religious divides.

The coming of Darwin, of course, complicated the reconciliation of science to faith. The implications of natural selection had to be assimilated by classical arguments of design. With the emergence of materialist views of creation, moreover, some writers, like Shumayyil, began to argue for a separation—if not an explicit antagonism—between science and faith. Against such views, a highly acclaimed treatise in defense of faith—"in harmony with the laws and sciences of nature"—was published in Tripoli in 1888. It came not from the Syrian missionary societies but from a reform-minded Muslim cleric and Sufi leader of a certain renown, Husayn al-Jisr al-Tarablusi. An educational reformer and loyalist whose ambitious projects for the reform of Islam took him from Tripoli to Beirut and Istanbul, al-Jisr was one of the first Muslim notables of Syria to address thoroughly the challenges to faith presented by evolutionary naturalists and materialists alike.[23]

Husayn al-Jisr's work "A Hamidian treatise on the truth of Islam and Muslim law" (*Risala hamidiyya fi haqiqat al-diyana al-islamiyya wa haqiqat al-shari'a al-muhamidiyya*) was, essentially, a Muslim view of natural theology: it emphasized divine providence, wisdom, and design in nature and even included a discussion of Darwin's theory of natural selection—which al-Jisr claimed could be seen as compatible with a Muslim cosmology and faith in the created world. This formula proved instantly popular. Afghani, who much admired the work, called the author the new "Ash'ari of his time" in homage to his attempts to bring together religion and philosophy.[24] More than four hundred pages long, among its various themes the treatise included a thorough refutation of materialism in the form of a dialogue between a Muslim and an evolutionary materialist. It made reference, time and again, to God's work and wisdom in nature, thereby reconciling naturalist views to faith.[25]

Al-Jisr's work was dedicated to Sultan 'Abd al-Hamid II. It proved quickly popular and underwent several editions by the turn of the century. It was translated into Turkish and other languages, and some 20,000 issues were published in Istanbul alone. Sultan 'Abd al-Hamid awarded it a Sultan's Prize in 1891, for which al-Jisr received an annual income of 50 liras for his contribution to Ottoman letters. He was also invited by the Sultan to spend time in his Imperial court, and he stayed there for just under a year. During his stay, al-Jisr was also invited by the Sultan to write a rationalist defense of Islam, which he drafted in 1892 under the title *Al-husun al-hamidiyya lil-muhafaza 'ala-al-'aqaid al-islamiyya* (A Hamidian fortress for the protection of Muslim faith). "This book," al-Jisr wrote in the introduction, "corresponds to the will of the Sultan, who desired a short treatise be composed on Islam and replete with rational proofs. This was to be a defense against doubters and unbelievers who formed dangerous errors of opinion based on modern philosophy and science."[26]

Another interesting and remarkable example of the Ottoman official stance toward Darwinism is a textbook for schools written by Dr. Bishare Zalzal under the title *Tanwir al-Adhhan* (*The Enlightenment of Minds*), printed as early as 1880 in Alexandria with the permission of the Ottoman Ministry of Education in Istanbul and dedicated to Sultan Abdulhamid II. This well-documented textbook covers natural history, zoology, animal classification, anthropology and human biology, religion, sociology, and civilization. The sections on biology represent a state-of-the-art exposition of the knowledge available at that time. It includes comparative anatomy and physiology, cytology, histology and embryology. The part devoted to animal taxonomy starts with chapters on Lamarckism, Darwinism, evidence of evolution, natural selection, zoogeography, and a discussion of Darwinism.[27]

That this book was published before the above-mentioned discussions occurred and that the Ministry of Education authorized its publication is significant. It is an interesting example indicating that the relations between religion and science would not lead to controversies if they were kept separate from political struggles and if the religious beliefs of the masses were not denounced.

THE TWENTIETH CENTURY: BACK TO ACCORD

The Muslim world during the twentieth century witnessed a systematic introduction of modern science through the expansion of education and particularly the establishment of the first faculties of science (1900 in Istanbul, 1925 in Cairo universities). The discord between science and Islam observed among some graduates of institutions of higher learning in the previous century was no longer the case. The discord was, however, between Islam and modern philosophical currents like positivism, naturalism, and social Darwinism, which challenged religion and the belief in God (or at least attempted to take their place). On the contrary, a new trend of scholarship started to emerge that aimed to prove the existence of a powerful compatibility and harmony between science and religion. This effort was farther-reaching than the attempt by Kudsî of Baku in the mid-nineteenth century to accord the new astronomy with religious implications. The first important example of this new course was the work of the Ottoman grand vizier, commander, and astronomer Gazi Ahmed Muhtar Pasha (1839–1919). His work, titled *Serâir al-Kur'an* (Secrets of the Qur'an [1918]), was the precursor of a new trend in the Islamic world. An authority on astronomy, calendar making, and timekeeping, Muhtar Pasha made an attempt to explain the related verses of the Qur'an with the findings, discoveries, and theories of modern science: in the first part he dealt with the creation of the universe and the beginning of life; in the second part, with doomsday and the end of the world; and the third, with resurrection after death.

The main argument in this book and subsequent similar works maintained that the verses on cosmic events (later called "cosmic verses") in the Holy Qur'an, which is revealed by God, should be congruent with the truth attained by modern science. Although these verses reflect the language of the period in which they were revealed, they have eternal value; hence they should be both in agreement and concordant with the findings of modern science. According to the author, when there is a conflict between the scientific truth and the expressions in the holy verses, the latter need to be interpreted. This book, which was translated from Turkish to Arabic, attracted great attention of the Arab world, and many other books were subsequently inspired by it.

The tradition of relating traditional Islamic thought with the findings of modern science entered a new phase with Bediuzzaman Said Nursi (1877–1960). As a scholar trained in traditional *medreses*, Said Nursi was well aware of the consequences of turning a blind eye to the challenge of modern scientific worldviews. In their more ideological forms, Darwinism and scientific materialism had questioned the very foundations of the medieval worldview, including that of Islam. Some traditionalist *ulama* refused to have any interaction with modern science; they considered it simply to be outside the purview of Islamic religion. Said Nursi, on the other hand, confronted the issue head-on and provided a number of very interesting responses to the materialistic and antireligious claims of the scientistic worldview. Like many of his contemporaries, he firmly believed that modern science in and of itself was not against religious belief in general and the Islamic faith in particular, because Islam had already produced one of the most enduring traditions of science. What seemed to bring religion and science to a collision was the misinterpretation of modern scientific findings to discredit religion.

In developing his view of modern science, Said Nursi studied modern science and cosmology closely. His works, collected under the title *Risale-i*

Nur, have numerous references to new scientific findings—something we do not see in other works of the period. In his extensive commentaries, Said Nursi sought to reconcile modern science with traditional Islamic cosmology, and drew parallels between the rational-mechanistic depictions of the Newtonian universe and the traditional arguments from design *(nizam).* In this sense, he became one of the champions of what is now called "scientific commentary" *(al-tafsir al-'ilmi).* His followers today continue to interpret modern science in light of traditional Islamic beliefs.[28]

The followers of Muhtar Pasha's example furthermore maintained that the "miracles" of the Qur'an were addressed not only to the Muslims but also, upon scrutiny, merited praise from Christians and Jews. It was because of the compatibility between the Qur'an and science that the people of different religions should recognize the Qur'an's genuineness and grandeur. This kind of scholarship became fashionable in the second half of the twentieth century.[29]

In recent years, the standard reference work propagating this type of approach to science and Islam is *The Bible, the Qur'an, and Science,* by Maurice Bucaille, a French surgeon. After a thorough and detailed analysis of the "holy scriptures in the light of modern knowledge," Bucaille, whose book has been translated into most Muslim languages and enjoys a huge following in Muslim intellectual circles, concludes that

> The Qur'an most definitely did not contain a single proportion at variance with the most firmly established modern knowledge, nor did it contain any of the ideas current at the time of the subjects it describes. Furthermore, however, a large number of facts are mentioned in the Qur'an which were not discovered until modern times. So many in fact, that on November 9, 1976, the present author was able to read before the French Academy of Medicine a paper on the "Physiological and Embryological Data in the Qur'an." The data—like many others on differing subjects—constituted a veritable challenge to human explanation—in view of what we know about the history of the various sciences through the ages. Modern man's findings concerning the absence of scientific error are therefore in complete agreement with the "Muslim exegetes" conception of the *Qur'an as a Book of Revelation.* It is a consideration which implies that God could not express an erroneous idea.[30]

This trend reached a more advanced stage in the last decades of the twentieth century. Scholars and writers who were interested in the harmonious relation between religion and science began to conceive of the Holy Qur'an as a miraculous text not only because of its highly literary style and inimitable expression *(al-i'jaz al-bayani)* but also of its miraculous scientific nature *(al-i'jaz al-'ilmî).* They maintain that the holy text revealed fourteen centuries ago consisted of implicit references to cosmic phenomena that could be interpreted only by modern science. This trend, which followed in the footsteps of Gazi Ahmed Muhtar Pasha, developed into a civil society movement promoting "societies of scientific inimitability *(i'jaz)* in the Holy Qur'an." The movement was established in Cairo, with many branches all over the country, particularly among faculty members and students of science departments in different provincial universities. Similar societies were formed in other Arab countries, especially in Yemen. This movement, which is another manifestation of religious revival in Arab countries, turned out to be a social solidarity movement as well.

A new phase in discussing the relation of science and religion in the Muslim world started under the influence of Karl Popper and Thomas Kuhn and other critics' works. Although the belief in the objective and neutral nature of science is paramount, the awareness of the fact that scientific knowledge is socially constructed began to be discussed in many Muslim academic and intellectual circles. The interest in discovering a contemporary style of doing science that fully incorporates the ethical dictates of Islam and is an embodiment of Islamic culture and tradition became particularly strong among the young scientists and intellectuals. Some of these scholars, despite preserving the belief in neutrality and universality of science, argue that when science is pursued within an Islamic polity, its functions are modified to serve Islamic ideals and Muslim society.

A major debate on the relation between science and religion has recently been started by Seyyed Hossein Nasr, who argues that there is an Islamic alternative to Western science. Nasr maintains that while science is legitimate in itself, the role and functions of Western science and its applications have become illegitimate and highly dangerous because they are completely divorced from a higher form of knowledge. The alternative is to pursue science in a clearly defined framework of values. Islam provides both a system of enlightened, coherent values, and through its history of science and technology in Islamic civilization, it provides an example of how science can be pursued within the confines of values. Nasr explains that Islamic science in history was deeply immersed in the worldview of Islam and that it was able to synthesize and transform any idea coming from outside, such as the Greek scientific knowledge, and bring it in line with its own worldview.[31]

Nasr, who dismissed evolution "as an ideology and not as a scientific theory which has been proven," appealed largely to Muslim intellectuals. Aiming at a more popular level was the Science Research Foundation, founded in 1990 by the Turkish interior designer-turned-philosopher Adnan Oktar (b. 1956). At times imprisoned or confined to a psychiatric hospital, he nevertheless managed to produce a stream of anti-evolution books under the pen name Harun Yahya. In his widely distributed book, *The Evolution Deceit: The Collapse of Darwinism and Its Ideological Background* (1997), which circulated in the millions in more than twenty languages, he attacked evolution for being atheistic, materialistic, and immoral. Although not committed by the Qur'an to a recent creation, he at times collaborated with American "young-earth" creationists.[32]

Despite this clear stand on religion and science being in concordance since the emergence of Islam, and despite the receptive approach of the Muslim scholars toward new knowledge and modern science since the sixteenth century, it must be noted that the followers of a school of thought established by Ibn Hanbal (d. 855), which gives precedence to dogma over reason, form rather a stray minority in today's world. Some advocate the rejection of modern science as one of "the sciences of the heretics"—those who reject the idea of the existence of a creator and do not recognize the revelation. One of the best illustrations of this strand is the claim that the earth is "static and motionless." The followers of this view represent no more than a marginal school of thought that is in no way popularly accepted today, as it used to be in the time of the main proponent of this trend, Ibn Taymiyya (d. 1328).[33]

GLIMPSE OF THE FUTURE

With the advent of the twenty-first century, the position of Islam toward science has developed more in the direction of achieving advanced knowledge and know-how in a rather pragmatic way. The importance of scientific enterprise became more prominent and the need for excellence in research is felt in more advanced Muslim nations.

A new vision to meet the challenges of the twenty-first century was forged in 2005 at the Extraordinary Summit of the Organization of Islamic Conference. The summit highlighted the need to reform higher education and underlined that priority should be given to science and technology while emphasizing the tolerant and moderate understanding of the religion of Islam. It also urged the member states to strive for quality education that promotes creativity and innovation and to increase their expenditure on research and development.[34] Debates about Islam and science in the future will be mainly about achieving these broad goals. The nineteenth-century conflict, which was of Western descent, could not have deep roots in the Muslim world.

Notes

1. For science during the Ottoman period (1299–1923), see Ekmeleddin İhsanoğlu, "Ottoman Educational and Scholarly-Scientific Institutions," in *History of the Ottoman State, Society and Civilisation*, vol. 2, ed. İhsanoğlu, 357–515 (İstanbul: Research Centre for Islamic History, Art and Culture, 2002); and İhsanoğlu,

"The Ottoman Scientific-Scholarly Literature," in *History of the Ottoman State*, 517–603. For a brief introduction, see İhsanoğlu, "Ottoman Science," in *Encyclopaedia of the History of Science, Technology, and Medicine in Non-Western Cultures*, ed. Helaine Selin, 799–805 (Dordrecht: Kluwer, 1997). See also İhsanoğlu, "Science in the Ottoman Empire," in *Ottoman Civilization*, ed. Halil İnalcık and Günsel Renda (Ankara: Ministry of Culture, 2003), 1:318–43; and İhsanoğlu, "Ottoman Educational Institutions," in ibid., 1:344–85. Hereafter the Research Centre for Islamic History, Art and Culture is abbreviated as IRCICA.

2. İhsanoğlu, "Science in the Ottoman Empire," 331.

3. Ekmeleddin İhsanoğlu, "Some Remarks on Ottoman Science and Its Relation with European Science and Technology up to the End of the Eighteenth Century," in *Science, Technology and Learning in the Ottoman Empire: Western Influence, Local Institutions, and the Transfer of Knowledge* (Aldershot, U.K.: Ashgate, 2004), chap. 1, 47.

4. Ibid., 48–49.

5. For the astronomical literature during the Ottoman period, see *Osmanlı Astronomi Literatürü Tarihi* (History of Astronomy Literature during the Ottoman period), ed. Ekmeleddin İhsanoğlu (İstanbul: IRCICA, 1997), 2 vols.; hereafter abbreviated as *OALT*.

6. See Sevim Tekeli, "Taqi al-Din," in *Encyclopaedia of the History of Science, Technology, and Medicine in Non-Western Cultures*, 934–35. For a Turkish version, see *OALT*, 1:199–217.

7. Ekmeleddin İhsanoğlu, "The Introduction of Western Science to the Ottoman World: A Case Study of Modern Astronomy (1660–1860)," in İhsanoğlu, *Science, Technology and Learning in the Ottoman Empire: Western Influence, Local Institutions, and the Transfer of Knowledge* (Aldershot, U.K.: Ashgate, 2004), chap. II, 31.

8. Ibid., 31.

9. For Ottoman geographical literature, see Ekmeleddin İhsanoğlu and Ramazan Şeşen, "Introduction to History of Geographical Literature in the Ottoman Period," in *Osmanlı Coğrafya Literatürü Tarihi* (History of Geographical Literature during the Ottoman Period) ed. İhsanoğlu, XXXI–LXXXIV (İstanbul: IRCICA, 2000); hereafter abbreviated as *OCLT*.

10. İhsanoğlu, "Introduction of Western Science," 15–16.

11. Ibid., 19.

12. Ibid., 24.

13. Ibid., 38.

14. For this debate, see George Saliba, "Copernican Astronomy in the Arab East: Theories of the Earth's Motion in the Nineteenth Century," in *Transfer of Modern Science and Technology to the Muslim World*, ed. Ekmeleddin İhsanoğlu, 145–55 (İstanbul: IRCICA, 1992).

15. Ekmeleddin İhsanoğlu, "Some Critical Notes on the Introduction of Modern Sciences to the Ottoman State and the Relation between Science and Religion up to the End of the Nineteenth Century," in İhsanoğlu, *Science, Technology and Learning in the Ottoman Empire*, chap. 5, 243.

16. Ibid., 244.

17. Charles MacFarlane, *Turkey and Its Destiny* (Philadelphia, 1850), 2:181–84, quoted in Niyazi Berkes, *The Development of Secularism in Turkey* (Montreal: McGill University Press, 1964), 117–18.

18. For the content analysis of *Mecmua-i Fünun*, see Cemil Aydın, "Mecmua-i Fünun ve Mecmua-i Ulum Dergilerinin Medeniyet ve Bilim Anlayışı" (master's thesis, University of İstanbul, 1995).

19. For the English translation of this letter, which was published in the issue of *Journal des Debats* dated 18 May 1883, see "Answer of Jamal ad-Din to Renan," trans. Nikki R. Keddie and Hamid Algar, in Nikki R. Keddie, *An Islamic Response to Imperialism: Political and Religious Writings of Sayyid Jamal ad-Din al-Afghani* (Berkeley: University of California Press, 1968), 181–87. For discussions on this subject, see Cemil Aydın, "Mecmua-i Fünun." For a comprehensive bibliography on the polemic created by Renan on the relationship between science and Islam, see Dücane Cündioğlu, "Ernest Renan ve 'reddiyeler' bağlamında İslam-bilim tartışmalarına bibliyografik bir katkı," *Dîvân* 2 (1996): 1–94.

20. Albert Hourani, *Arabic Thought in the Liberal Age, 1798–1939* (Oxford: Oxford University Press, 1962), 120–29.

21. Atila Doğan, *Osmanlı Aydınları ve Sosyal Darwinizim* (Istanbul: Istanbul Bilgi University Publications, 2006), 169.

22. Orhan Okay, *Batı Medeniyeti Karşısında Ahmet Midhat Efendi* (Ankara: Millî Eğitim, Gençlik ve Spor Bakanlığı Yay., 1989), 40, 236, 263.

23. Marwa Elshakry, "Darwin's Legacy in the Arab East: Science, Religion and Politics, 1870–1914" (Ph.D. diss., Princeton University, 2003), 179. See also Elshakry, *Reading Darwin in the Middle East* (Chicago: University of Chicago Press, forthcoming).

24. Afghani was referring to Abu'l-Hasan 'Ali b. Isma'il al-Ash'ari, the tenth-century theologian and founder of the school of orthodox theology bearing his name. See W. Montgomery Watt, "Al-Ash'ari, Abu'l-Hasan, 'Ali b. Isma'il," in *The Encyclopaedia of Islam*, new ed., vol. 3, ed. B. Lewis et al., 694–95 (Leiden: Brill, 1979).

25. Elshakry, "Darwin's Legacy," 180–81.

26. Ibid., 208–9.

27. A. H. Helmy Mohammad, "Notes on the Reception of Darwinism in Some Islamic Countries," in *Science in Islamic Civilisation: Proceedings of the International Symposia "Science Institutions in Islamic Civilisation" and "Science and Technology in the Turkish and Islamic World,"* ed. Ekmeleddin İhsanoğlu and Feza Günergun, 247 (İstanbul: IRCICA, 2000),.

28. For an evaluation of Said Nursi's view of science, see Ibrahim Kalın, "Three Views of Science in the Islamic World," in *God, Life, and the Cosmos: Christian and Islamic Perspectives*, ed. Ted Peters, Muzaffar Iqbal, and Syed Nomanul Haq, 43–75 (Aldershot, U.K.: Ashgate, 2002).

29. Abdullah Omar A. Al-Omar, "The Reception of Darwinism in the Arab World" (Ph.D. diss., Harvard University, 1982).

30. Quoted in Ziyauddin Sardar, *Islamic Futures: The Shape of Ideas to Come* (London: Mansell, 1985).

31. For a brilliant discussion on science and Islam, see ibid. See also Ziyauddin Sardar, *Explorations in Islamic Science* (London: Mansell, 1989); and Sardar, *The Touch of Midas* (Manchester: Manchester University Press, 1984).

32. See Ronald L. Numbers, *The Creationists: From Scientific Creationism to Intelligent Design*, expanded ed. (Cambridge, Mass.: Harvard University Press, 2006),

421–27; and Salman Hameed, "Bracing for Islamic Creationism," *Science* 322 (2008): 1637–38, which quotes Nasr.

33. A typical illustration of this school of thought is Abdul Karim Salah Al Humeid's book *Hidayeat Al Hayran Fi Mas'alati Dawaran* (A Guide for the Perplexed on the Issue of the Earth's Revolving Motion), 3rd ed. (Burayda, Saudi Arabia, 2003).

34. Ekmeleddin İhsanoğlu, *The Islamic World in the New Century: The Organisation of the Islamic Conference*, 1969–2009 (London: Hurst & Co., 2010).

7

Early Chinese Religions

Mark Csikszentmihalyi

In the nineteenth and twentieth centuries, Chinese governments repeatedly launched campaigns to modernize China and improve its technological infrastructure. At the same time, these campaigns were greeted with the worry that adapting foreign methods might lead to an undue "Westernization" of values. In the reform movements of the late Qing Dynasty, the May Fourth movement of 1919, the 1959 "Great Leap Forward," and the "Four Modernizations" of the 1980s, anticipation of the economic and technological advantages of scientific development was tempered by a sense that science was not unconnected to religions and values, and that foreign cultural or ideological values had to be resisted.

Slogans like the nineteenth century Self Strengthening (*ziqiang* 自強) movement's "Chinese learning for essential principles and Western learning for practical applications" (*Zhongxue wei ti, Xixue wei yong* 中學為體 西學為用) point to an assumed linkage between beliefs about the spiritual and natural worlds. Given the tremendous sophistication of scientific thinking in certain periods of traditional China, it is worth probing the thinking behind this assumption. Are there different kinds of science, each indexed to the particular culture in which it developed? If so, it is possible to distill these cultural productions into a universal (and portable) science? Is it possible to describe the way that Chinese religions encouraged or suppressed the development of a universal science? The answers to these sorts of questions get to the core issue of the relation between religion and science. The same questions have been asked quite often about the relationship between the "Scientific Revolution" and Christianity in Europe, but other cultures may provide their own answers.

The history of natural philosophy and the early history of Chinese religions are just as intertwined as they are in ancient cultures throughout the world, which is to say that there was no formal division between the two. During the formative period prior to the self-conscious division into the "three teachings" (*sanjiao* 三教) of Confucianism, Daoism, and Buddhism, religious expression in China had dual centers: one focused on social and ritual practices oriented to maintaining order and harmony with the ancestors and the unruly spirits, the other on personal cultivation practices geared to forming a self that was spiritually or physically perfected.

A rich record of clan-based sacrifice and ceremony predates the start of the Zhou period in the twelfth century BCE, but the most important early community that had an independent social organization was the one associated with the ritual teacher and itinerant political advisor Confucius (Kongzi 孔子, trad. 551–479 BCE). Using recitation of the *Classic of Poetry* (*Shijing* 詩經) as the cornerstone of his curriculum, Confucius distilled Zhou Dynasty cultural norms into a personal cultivation regimen geared to developing behavioral traits that would make practitioners into compassionate, pious, and incorrupt rulers and officials. Much of what made a person into an ideal Confucian was mastery of cultural forms and imitation of the culture heroes of the past, like the sage kings of old. Yet many of those culture heroes, like Hou Ji 后稷, a Zhou progenitor celebrated in the *Classic of Poetry* song "Giving birth to the people" (*Sheng min* 生民), became culture heroes because of their mastery of the natural world. In Hou Ji's case, this mastery led to his invention of agriculture. Section 17.9 of the *Analects* (*Lunyu* 論語), the record of Confucius's conversations with rulers and his disciples, explains that one of the goals of the *Classic of Poetry* is "acquiring wide knowledge of the names of birds, beasts, plants and trees." The concept that united nature and culture was that of the "heavens" (*tian* 天), a term usually translated as "Heaven." However, in the usage of early Confucian works like *Master Xun* (*Xunzi* 荀子), from the third century BCE, the term means something closer to "cosmos" or "nature." The Confucian ideal is someone who is able to recognize and exploit the similarity between the patterns of human society and the patterns that govern the heavens.

In imperial times, Confucianism became institutionalized in a way that drastically changed its social role. By the second century BCE, the classics associated with Confucius became the basis of the imperial examination system. The social and political emphasis on harmony—which was part of ancient clan-based religious practice and which had been integrated into Confucius's social teachings—became central to the state-sponsored version of the religion. Over the two thousand years of China's imperial period, then, the positive value of knowledge of the natural world was something that many traditional Confucian scholars took to heart, but the ossification of its social vision and the exploitation of ritually based hierarchies by the imperial clan must have also retarded the dissemination of new learning.

Along with Confucianism, China's other major indigenous tradition is Daoism. In the first centuries CE, the long-standing contrast between the social teachings of the Confucian scholars, newly integrated into the system of the empire, and a set of teachings associated with alternative centers of power was elevated to the status of a religious distinction: Confucianism and Daoism began to be conceived of as distinct traditions. The catalyst for this change was likely the arrival of Buddhist monks and sutras (discourses of the Buddha) in China from points west, bringing with them a new set of challenges in the form of a religious system with a fundamentally different cosmology and epistemology. Looking for a viable alternative to the Confucianism allied with the state, Han practitioners of Daoism wove together disparate strands of shamanistic healing methods that required mastery of spiritual techniques, immortality techniques associated with the legendary ruler the Yellow Emperor (Huangdi 黃帝) and his advisor, the sage Laozi 老子, and new conventions and practices in part modeled on the ones the Buddhists brought with them. These were integrated through a concept of *dao* 道, an overarching "way" that functioned in the newly unified empire as a metaphysical substratum of truth capable of synthesizing different regional and cultural explanatory systems. In some ways similar to the use of the word *tian* in the Confucian text *Master Xun*, Dao was elevated to the level of a cosmic truth that underlay the efficacy of the various methods and techniques in which the Han practitioners claimed expertise. During this period, alchemical and herbal methods to attain immortality were the subject of intensive research, since the natural world was considered just as clear an expression of the workings of the Dao as any other realm of inquiry. By contrast with the more diffuse Confucian institutions, Daoism developed its own clerical and, later, monastic structures that gave it a separate and at times antagonistic relationship to the state.

At the end of the fourth century CE, the first of a series of revelations changed the attitude of many Daoists toward the proper sources of religious knowledge. In 364 CE, Yang Xi received a set of texts from the Highest Clarity (*Shangqing* 上清) Heaven that became the basis of the Highest Clarity sect of Daoism. Other important revelations in 397 and 415 CE led to the formation of competing sects, each of which had its own corpus of texts and practices. These revelations became the center of the elite practice of Daoism, while at the popular level Daoism competed and mixed with popular religious practices. Over the next several centuries and in the Tang (619–907 CE) Dynasty, Daoism periodically enjoyed imperial patronage. The compilation of the various revelations into a canon began at this time; eventually, this textual canon took on a conservative character.

The third of the "three teachings," Buddhism came to China from India and Tibet, with the first exposure taking place during the first two centuries

CE. Initial reports of Buddhism reflect the degree to which it was seen as a foreign version of indigenous traditions, especially similar to Daoism. Indeed, some Daoist works falsely argue that Buddhism was begun by Laozi when he went to India. In the fourth and fifth centuries, as the renunciation involved in monastic life became perceived as a threat to the family values (especially filial piety) of Confucianism, and as its ontological claims (that is, those having to do with the nature of being) began to be more fully understood, Buddhism became more controversial and at times was the object of official persecution. Perhaps in part due to the social chaos of the Six Dynasties Period (222–589 CE), Buddhism as a religion of personal salvation began to enjoy widespread popularity as it adapted itself to Chinese culture. The most influential sects in China were Mahayana, those promoting the bodhisattva ideal of universal salvation. Both the sixth-century Heavenly Terrace (*Tiantai* 天台) sect and the eighth-century Flower Garland (*Huayan* 華嚴) sect of Fazang are less intellectualist than earlier forms of Buddhism, emphasizing universal salvation through the intercession of bodhisattvas like Guanyin 觀音 (in Sanskrit, Avalokitesvara) and developing the idea of "expediencies" (*fangbian* 方便, in Sanskrit, *upaya*). The last idea, that the Buddha had different ways of explaining the "cosmic law" (*fa* 法, in Sanskrit, *dharma*) to different beings, allows for the relatively harmonious coexistence of many different sects, despite the fact that they emphasize different, even contradictory teachings. Chan 禪 (in Japanese, Zen) Buddhism developed as a monastic school in China during the seventh and eighth centuries. Chan followers were devoted to the secret transmission of a method of seeking enlightenment based in large part on meditation. As with the Daoist practices mentioned earlier, Buddhist meditation emphasized turning inward rather than outward to find true knowledge.

The relationship between Buddhism and science is discussed in chapter 9 of this volume, but in its early stages in India there was little conflict between the study of natural philosophy and the teachings of the Buddha. By the time Buddhism came to China, however, it was already developing an orthodox canon in the same way that post-Han Confucianism and post-Tang Daoism did. While it is difficult to generalize about the nature of the relationship between science and the "three teachings" of Chinese religion, the closure of each of their canons did have the important effect of partially sealing off an important source of religious knowledge from new understandings of the natural world. It is important to note that the production of commentaries and their important role in Chinese religions did allow for even closed canons to admit of modification of a kind. For example, the famous translator Yan Fu's 嚴復 (1854–1921) commentaries on early Daoist works take pains to point out where they anticipate the work of Thomas

Henry Huxley (1825–95), the British biologist and champion of Darwinian evolution whose *Evolution and Ethics* Yan Fu rendered into Chinese.

It is important to note that throughout much of Chinese history, the "three teachings" have not been as exclusive as many non-Asian traditions are. Late imperial times saw many instances of syncretism (that is, the combination of different systems of belief). For example, the Complete Perfection (*Quanzhen* 全真) sect of Daoism, founded in 1163 CE, incorporates a monastic order and meditation practices very similar to those of Chan Buddhism. The Buddhist idea of accumulating merit for one's ancestors was incorporated into many types of Song (960–1127 CE) Daoism, and adopting basic precepts of Confucian morality became a precondition of imperial toleration of both Buddhism and Daoism during the Qing (1644–1911 CE) Dynasty.

The rest of this chapter examines three episodes from the history of science and religion in China. These are not intended to be exhaustive but rather to sketch representative acts in the drama of that interaction. The episodes were chosen to contrast both different areas of knowledge about the natural world and different stages in the development of the Chinese polity. The first episode, from the pre-imperial period (that is, prior to the unification of the Warring States by the Qin in 221 BCE), concerns the way that acoustics was in part a response to the ritual requirement of completeness in musical instruments, which played an important part in ritual and political order. The second episode takes place in the early imperial period, beginning in the third century BCE and leading into the encounter with the Jesuits in the sixteenth century. This period included Buddhism's arrival in China in the first century CE, and it was the early empire that laid many of the political and cultural cornerstones of the Chinese state and society. This episode illustrates the way that medical knowledge was organized according to different natural cycles, like *yin* and *yang*, and the interplay between Confucian-influenced government bureaus and independent Daoists in creating knowledge about the natural world. Finally, the third section turns to the early-modern period, a period when Chinese dynasties alternated with those controlled by other ethnic groups, like the Mongols and Manchus, when knowledge and technologies were exchanged much more freely between East and West. This episode describes the development of hybrid astronomies in the wake of Jesuit and Islamic influence in the state scientific bureaucracy and how the use of the metaphor of Heavenly "patterns" aided this accommodation.

Rather than retelling the history of natural philosophy in China, this chapter charts approaches to the production of knowledge about the natural world in three distinct social locations in Chinese history, and it illustrates how both religious worldviews and the understanding of natural laws associated with them differ as a result. These three locations do not paint a comprehensive picture of Chinese natural philosophy as much as provide a cross-section of three distinct kinds of Chinese science and their relationships with key elements of Chinese religions and culture. Just as the different optical theories of Newton and Boyle, or the different cosmologies of Gassendi and Descartes, resulted in multiple systems for the creation of knowledge based on different conceptions of science in Europe, so too the regions under imperial Chinese control enjoyed a similar diversity.[1] It should not be surprising that over China's millennia of social ferment, also, there evolved multiple knowledge-making legacies.

NATURAL SETS AND RITUAL BELLS: ACOUSTICS AND ARTISANS

In the period before the advent of the unified empire in 256 BCE, the area of what is now called China was divided into kingdoms ruled by hereditary nobles bound by the common cultural influence of the previously dominant kingdom of Zhou 周. Much of what we know about this period comes from artifacts preserved because they were buried in the tombs of this nobility, most often valuable objects scrupulously appropriate to the rank of the deceased according to the Zhou ritual rules. One such set of ritual bells—cast by the Marquis Yi of Zeng 曾侯乙 in 433 BCE—has been called one of the most significant archeological finds of the twentieth century.[2] The metallurgical skill behind the construction of these massive bells relies on technology to fashion bronze alloy vessels that dates back in part to the eighteenth century BCE, when bronzes excavated at Erlitou 二里頭 in Henan Province were first cast.[3] The intact nature of the set provides insights into the state of early Chinese acoustical knowledge that made the casting of the bells possible and into the way that the religious role of sumptuary ritual vessels provided an incentive to apply knowledge of the natural laws that governed the production of sound.

Archeologists discovered this complete set of sixty-four bronze bells in the tomb of the Marquis of Zeng in modern Hubei Province in 1978. The set was likely once central to ritual musical performances at the court of the Marquis. An inscription on the set indicates that the bells were cast in 433 BCE in the state of Zeng. Chinese bells at this time did not have clappers but were designed to be struck at two places, along the center of the flatter face of the bell or at a point along the side. The two pitches produced were separated by a minor or a major third. Chen Cheng-Yih describes the technology in this way:

> The fact that the two notes in each bell can be separately produced without appreciable beats suggests strongly that the bell-makers were rather successful

in superimposing the antinodal lines of one mode on the nodal lines of the other. Thus, the front strike point locates the position at which an antinode of the lower vibrational mode is superimposed on a node of higher vibrational mode. The side strike point located the position of the reverse. This remarkable achievement attests to not only the bell-makers' mastery in campanology but also their advanced knowledge of acoustics.[4]

The creation of the pentatonic scales that the bells describe was based on a knowledge of acoustics that may not have survived the end of the state of Zeng—future bell sets did not match this fifth-century BCE achievement.

The social circumstances of the production of the bells reveal a world in which politics and religion were two sides of the same coin. Since the Shang period (ca. 1600–1050 BCE), at the edge of Chinese written history, bronze making was the province of a number of local hereditary artisans.[5] As the bell set was a funeral object, it probably had a religious function related to afterlife beliefs of the time in addition to its musical function. Tombs of the period had plates of different sorts of food, clothing, and sumptuary objects, suggesting a concept of postmortem immortality. Bells and other musical instruments may have been placed in the tomb because of the connection, found in many early texts, between music and the moral authority of the ruler.

In both the Marquis of Zeng's tomb and the tombs of later officials, a similar type of musical technology is found: the pitch pipe. In addition to being funeral objects, pitch pipes were vital in geomancy (often grouped with astronomy in later times) and had both predictive and calendrical applications. Astronomers used the pitch pipe for measuring the flow of pneumas (qi 氣) via the practice of "watching the pneumas" (houqi 侯氣), which in later periods involved putting full sets of pipes in the ground and filling them with ash that was blown out by the rising pneumas of the earth.[6] These instruments were used for predicting future events because it was assumed that the movement of pneumas was often a harbinger or cause of other changes in the physical world. Each musical pitch was associated with a type of earthly and heavenly pneuma. In the "Tones and Pitches" (Yinlu 音律) chapter of the 239 BCE Springs and Autumns of Master Lü (Lüshi chunqiu 呂氏春秋), each month is associated with a pitch and so also with a particular movement of natural pneumas. For example, in the month associated with the third of the twelve pitches, the first month of the new lunar year, "Great Budding" (taicu 太蔟), "Yang pneumas start to be created, and plants and trees proliferate and grow." As a result, the ruler is supposed to "order farmers to open up the earth, else the moment be lost."[7] Mastery of the phases of the annual cycles of the pneumas made a ruler a good one, and so acoustical knowledge was as political as it was scientific.

This overlap is characteristic of what sociologists like C. K. Yang call diffused religions, and China's early history provides a textbook example.[8] A diffused religion has institutions that are not separate from the social structure. In the Shang period, the earliest known religious expression in China was a reflection of the clan-based social structure, in which the "priest" was the clan leader and the "gods" were the ancestors; the Shang ruling clan was concerned with one deity that played the role of a more abstract highest ancestor called Shangdi. Sacrifice to ancestors continued through the Zhou period and into the period of the Chinese empire, but the Zhou also elevated the "heavens" (*tian*) to become their highest deity, one that intervened in history to support virtuous rulers. The clan-based system of ancestral sacrifice was then translated into a state cult that preserved many of the same practices. The writings of Confucius were based on the revival of these Zhou practices but argued not as much for their political role as their effectiveness in catalyzing individual moral transformation. Toward the end of the period, the natural order was described as the "Way of the Heavens" (*tiandao* 天道), and both state sacrifice and popular religion were organized around the idea that the principles behind the workings of the Way of the Heavens were applicable to politics and other areas of life.

It was against the background of just such politically charged cosmology that the early Zeng artisans produced musical instruments for their patrons, allowing the latter to demonstrate their moral qualities, signs that might then accompany them into the afterlife. For this reason, the most desirable characteristic for both the pitch pipes and the bell sets was their *completeness*. In representing all the tones of the scale (or several scales) they were comprehensive, and comprehensiveness confirmed the scope of their owner's moral-political authority. Completeness was a facet of many things that artisans created for the ruler; that quality was meant to reflect on the ruler's universal authority. The earliest literary form of the early empire in China was the rhapsody (*fu* 賦), a prose poem that often resembled a comprehensive list of the flora and fauna of the entire domain under the emperor's control. At the same time, imperial rituals included sacrifices to the spirits of Heaven, Earth, and many of the stars in the night sky, as well as imperial tours to each of the regions of the empire.

A metaphor for these natural sets that dates to the early period of Chinese civilization could be seen as the prototype for these musical natural sets. The sixty-four hexagrams (*gua* 卦) of the *Classic of Changes* (*Yijing* 易經) were natural signs that determined the potential of the moment of divination. The milfoil stalks used to cast the hexagrams were like the ash in the complete set of pitch pipes in the sense of being a medium from the natural world that was assigned a value in a "natural" symbol system. The symbolic system of the *Classic of Changes* was considered complete in the sense that it corresponded to all the possible kinds of change that might occur at a given moment. It was this completeness that gave both the divinatory framework and the ritual objects their power. These were precisely the elements that have been associated with bronze-work artisans since the Shang, according to the noted historian of early China, David Keightley:

> It was the king who made fruitful harvest and victories possible by the sacrifices he offered, the rituals he performed, and the divinations he made. If, as seems likely, the divinations involved some degree of magic making, of spell casting, the king's ability to actually create a good harvest or a victory by divining about it rendered him still more potent politically.[9]

The "natural sets" of the hexagrams and also of the bells and pitch pipes were then tied to the moral and political authority of their possessors.

Acoustics was by no means the only field in which patterns of nature were systematically investigated in pre-imperial times. Agriculture and astronomy were also of tremendous importance. Legendary agricultural deities like Hou Ji were credited with agricultural inventions like the alternating-field crop-rotation system and the ox-drawn plow. The Zhou period, beginning in the twelfth century BCE, saw the development of large-scale irrigation systems, culminating in major projects like the Dujiangyan 都江堰 dam system north of the city of Chengdu, designed in the third century BCE. Astronomy played an important role in agriculture, and maintaining an accurate calendar was one of the earliest roles of government, along with predicting anomalies like eclipses. As in the above quotation of *Springs and Autumns of Master Lü*, understanding natural patterns like the phases of the seasons was seen to translate into knowledge of good government.

Ritual rules like the ones that regulated the production of the Marquis of Zeng's bells became an important part of the teachings of Confucius, and ritual propriety a trait that Confucians promoted. Still, the bells were cast just a few decades after Confucius's death, and it would be wrong to call this a facet of the relation between science and Confucianism. In fact, the fashioning of such sets of bells, like sets of Daoist guardian statuary or images of Buddhist arhats, grew out of the same sense of completeness as an expression of universal scope or vision. Music and acoustics in pre-imperial times were closely associated with ritual performance and political authority, and the production of complete natural sets of ritual objects was associated with moral perfection and hence political authority. The institutionalization of these practices under the imperial state, beginning in the fourth and third centuries BCE in dynastic China, changed the role of artisans—it made them employees of the unitary imperial state. This changed the priorities and nature of their practice, and as a result new models for explaining the operation of the natural world began to thrive.

NATURAL CYCLES AND HOMOLOGIES: PERSUASIONS ABOUT MEDICINE

It has been observed that the social situation of the itinerant persuaders of the Warring States period changed at the beginning of the early empire in the third century BCE. The political and institutional standardization under a single central government in 221 BCE had important consequences for the creation and transfer of knowledge:

> The aftermath of the [Qin] unification transformed scholarship. . . . From then on, many [scholars] saw a primary object of education to be ensuring that the classics of their tradition were not lost. That made memorization of the exact text and meticulous copying of manuscripts all the more important.[10]

The description here is of the advent of differing traditions and the creation of canons that fixed these traditions. Across the entire Chinese empire, early-imperial technical arts (*shushu* 數術, literally, "procedures and techniques") included a wide variety of local practices that were gradually integrated into the centralized culture of the unified empire. In many areas of life, the standardization enforced by the empire necessitated the creation of a higher-level entity under which diverse practices could be integrated— just as the position of the emperor was created above that of "king" (*wang*) of the previously autonomous states.

The Han universe was filled with different kinds of correspondences, natural cycles governed by the overarching monad of the "Way" (*dao* 道 or "tao"). Among these natural cycles were the binary alternation of *yin* 陰 and *yang* 陽, the succession of the five phases (*wuxing* 五行), and the sexagenary cycles of sixty compounds, each made of one of ten stem (*gan* 干) terms and another of twelve branch (*zhi* 支) terms that formed the basis of the calendar. Describing the universe in terms of these cycles, identifying each phenomenon as the result of a change of one phase to another, implies the existence of regular patterns of change and alternation.

Over the last century, there has been much talk about the development of natural cycles theory as "proto-scientific" or as compatible with scientific thinking. They are seen by many as part of what the noted historian of Chinese philosophy A. C. Graham called a "correlative cosmology" that lacked a commitment to empirical verification to be fully scientific. Since the time of Durkheim and Mauss's *Primitive Classification*, some anthropologists have grouped similar correspondence schemes as "prescientific" or magical thinking, and differences between the schemes themselves have been downplayed. In fact, the various cyclical schemes in early-imperial China implied slightly different relationships between their elements and were related to direct observation and verification in different ways. For example, an early use of the terms *yin* and *yang* was to compare the sunny and shady sides of valleys in a way that reflected the characteristic differences between their flora, while the popular books of "lucky days" (*rishu* 日書) appear to assign daily activities to the ten stems of the calendar in what appears to be an arbitrary, if possibly socially useful, way. The integration of these different schemes effectively abstracted what had been categories for describing nature that had been applied in separate realms. In the Han they were all seen as equally valid aspects of the Way of the Heavens.

An example of an integrative system that relied on the correlation of different schemes of natural cycles is Han Dynasty medicine. The early medical classic *Basic Questions of the Yellow Emperor's Inner Classic* (*Huangdi neijing suwen* 黃帝內經素問), a second- or third-century CE text, applies all of the cycles mentioned above to the body. Historians generally believe the word "inner" in its title means it may have had an esoteric transmission, and its association with the Yellow Emperor, known for his apotheosis on the back of a dragon, testifies to its efficacy for extending one's lifespan. In its twenty-second chapter, "A discussion of how pneumas of the five organs model on the seasons" (*Zangqi fashi lun* 藏氣法時論), the phases of wood (*mu* 木), fire (*huo* 火), earth (*tu* 土) metal (*jin* 金), and water (*shui* 水) correspond to other sets of fives, including the five organs in the body (*wuzang* 五臟: liver, heart, spleen, lungs, and kidneys) and the five tastes (*wuwei* 五味: sour, bitter, sweet, spicy, and salty). The compilers of such medical treatises in the newly centralized empire took the plural medical canons inherited from regional traditions of the Warring States period and integrated them into a single universal scheme.

The social context of the delivery of medical knowledge involved a professional class of physicians whose expertise was passed down through private networks. "A discussion of how pneumas of the five organs model on the seasons" is written in the form of a dialogue between the Yellow Emperor and his advisor, Qi Bo 岐伯. Formally, the text describes the position of the experts responsible for integrating and systematizing relative to the new imperial order. The Emperor asks: "In the method of adapting the human form so that it models on the four seasons and five phases, I would like to understand the principles of how one knows if one is following or resisting them, and what are the advantages and disadvantages of doing so?" In his answer, Qi Bo outlines what the Emperor should eat to deal with deficiencies in each of his five organs. In the case of the liver, he says:

> The liver rules spring. The Foot "Faint Yin" (*jueyin* 厥陰) [a pneuma conduit] and "Minor Yang" (*shaoyang* 少陽) [conduits] rule its treatment. Its days are those [in the sexagenery cycle] that begin with [terms] *jia* 甲 and *yi* 乙. The liver afflicts with rapidity, and so one should quickly ingest something sweet to slow things down.[11]

Combining five different schemes into a single correspondence theory, Qi Bo is able to connect several different categories: two of the calendar's "ten stems," one of the five phases, one of the five organs, one of the five tastes, one of the four seasons, and two of the ten conduits through which pneumas flow in the body. Each organ is associated with a phase in the cycle of the five phases, and so a problem in a certain organ indicates a problem with the circulation of pneuma to that organ. The pneuma travels a particular conduit that connects the organs affected by surplus or deficiency of that pneuma. By ingesting a taste corresponding to the successor phase in the cycle, the Emperor will be able to cure the affected organ.

This understanding of organ systems has interesting parallels with some non-Asian systems descended from Greek humoral traditions. J. B. Van Helmont's theory of disease is an example: "Acharacteristic *archeus*—a kind of overseer—was postulated in each organ, responsible for organizing its chemical and metabolic activity."[12] In the *Basic Questions of the Yellow Emperor's Inner Classic*, the ruling relation is between two sets of natural cycles. Later Daoists from the Shangqing sect postulated an anthropomorphic overseer for each organ, however, and made these overseers central aspects of their meditation techniques.[13] As Nakayama Shigeru has rightly emphasized, not all Chinese medicine is a matter of natural cycles, and in fact the *materia medica* traditions have a strong empirical component.[14] But in the case of foundational works like the *Basic Questions of the Yellow Emperor's Inner Classic*, the dominant model for nature is a set of interrelated natural cycles.

Early imperial religion continued to develop similar schemes for organizing the universe, even as it went through dramatic changes and evolved institutions independent of the state. The most important changes were ushered in by the arrival of Buddhist institutions over the Silk Road and other routes. Fairly quickly, both Confucians and Daoists adapted aspects of Buddhist organization and practice and for the first time developed institutional frameworks that lasted throughout Chinese imperial history. The early empire, then, was really when the "three teachings" of Confucianism, Daoism, and Buddhism began to take on many of the characteristics of religions.

In the imperial period, the roles of each of these religions with respect to the development of natural science differed. The integration of Confucian temples and sacrifices to Confucius into the imperial state cult began in the first two centuries CE, and as a result the religious aspect of Confucianism continued to straddle the boundary between diffused and institutional religions. To the extent that Confucianism served as a kind of "state ideology" during the imperial period, Han officials like the Grand Minister of Works (in charge of city walls, canals, and dikes), the Prefect Grand Astrologer (who drew up the annual calendar), and the Grand Minister of Agriculture (who oversaw taxation, storage of imperial grain, and state monopolies on salt and iron) were "Confucians."[15] Yet while scientific advances were made by the occupants of such offices, scriptural tradition competed with efficacy as a justification for the methods they used. Geoffrey Lloyd has also argued that China had an academic milieu that emphasized patronage in a way that decreased debate.[16] As a result of both these tendencies, the development of knowledge of the natural world was both more a function of the official world and less amenable to reform based on empirical disproof.

Buddhism, by contrast, brought Indian and Tibetan traditions to China. Illness was understood to be a function of the mind, and so Buddhist meditation was efficacious in both moral and medical senses. Zhi Yi 智顗 (538–597 CE), the founder of the Tiantai Buddhist sect, identified three possible causes of illness in his *Dharma Essentials of Meditation and Sitting Practice* (Xiuxi zhiguan zuochan fayao 修習止觀坐禪法要). First, the "four elements and five organs" combined the five organs of Chinese traditional medicine with the Buddhist four elements (in Pali, *catudhatu*) of earth, water, fire, and air. The second possible cause was demons and spirits. The third was as a result of negative karma. As Li Shen 李申 has pointed out, Zhi Yi's translation of Indian Buddhism into Chinese involved internalizing cardinal principles of Chinese medicine into the Buddhist system.[17] Indeed, Zhi Yi's typology combined both organ system and supernatural etiologies of traditional Chinese medicine with karmic and other explanations deriving from traditional Indian frameworks of thinking about the mind.

It was Daoism's independent institutions and reliance on medical and alchemical knowledge that made it play a larger role in the history of Chinese science. Institutional Daoism, as reflected in the second century CE Way of the Celestial Masters (Tianshi dao 天師顗) movement, combined a variety of healing practices with a crowded and inclusive pantheon. The movement created, in what is now Sichuan province, its own semi-autonomous government, organized into twenty-four administrative districts that were governed by religious leaders. One area of particular importance to the heirs of this prototypical Daoist institution was the chemical transformation of gold, mercury, and cinnabar into alchemical elixirs that would benefit the Daoist adept's quest for riches and immortality. By the Tang dynasty, some five or six emperors died of ingesting such concoctions. Perhaps in part because of this, alchemy increasingly became a metaphor for "inner alchemy" (*neidan*), the transformation of interior states through Daoist breathing and meditation techniques.

Perhaps the most celebrated claim about Chinese religion and science is Joseph Needham's that Daoist speculation and insight into nature is "at the basis of all Chinese science."[18] Later work has called into question some of the historical assumptions behind this statement. In addition, in the decades since Needham wrote, the idea that intellectual factors such as "insight into nature" determine the production of scientific knowledge has increasingly come into question. Still, the Daoist quest for immortality did foster the development of knowledge about the interaction of certain chemical reagents. Proof of the latter claim is Needham's example of gunpowder's discovery deriving from Daoist alchemical practice. The Daoists who did this work utilized the same systems of correspondence, notably *yin* and *yang*, seen in the earlier *Basic Questions of the Yellow Emperor's Inner Classic*.

In the early imperial period, such correspondence-based knowledge was characterized by the view that the universe was organized according to a set of homologies, and that knowledge of these homologies was associated with a group of experts that enjoyed patronage at least in part based on the lineage of their methods. While many of the sciences were the purview of scripturally bound court officials, medicine and chemistry played an important role in the institutionally independent religions of Buddhism and Daoism. "Science" conceived of as the set of disciplines that we associate today with the sciences, such as chemistry or physics, was so deeply integrated into the ritual and religious life of China that it was not seen as an independent entity until interaction with the West introduced the term.

NATURAL PATTERNS IN THE HEAVENS: TECHNOLOGIES AT THE IMPERIAL OBSERVATORY

The 1442 Astronomical Observatory (guanxiangtai 觀象台) at the southeast corner of the city walls of Bejing houses a collection of Qing Dynasty astronomical instruments. Among them is a 1673 Ecliptic Armilla (Huangdao jingwei yi 黃道經緯儀) designed by Ferdinand Verbiest (1623–88). Perched on the backs of two dragons, the rings that circumscribe nested globes used to measure the ecliptic longitude difference and the latitude of celestial bodies are inscribed with the twenty-four "solar terms" (jieqi 節氣). These solar terms, such as *xiaoman* 小滿 ("[grains] begin to fill in," starting around May 22), defined the traditional agricultural calendar and date to well before Verbeist or any other Jesuit scientist had reached China. As with the Buddhist example, the arrival of Abrahamic religions in China led to an integration of Western and indigenous scientific knowledge. Today, the Astronomical Observatory is situated just off the busy Beijing Central Railway Station, and the Armilla embodies the way that indigenous categories for describing the natural world were blended into hybrid systems that adapted European scientific knowledge.

Although both were described using the same rubric of imperial dynasties, the organization of government and learning in the early-modern period was different in significant ways from their organization in the early empire. After a period of chaos and political fragmentation, from the late sixth through the early tenth centuries, the Sui and Tang dynasties reunited the Chinese empire and ushered in an artistic renaissance. After the Chinese-ruled Tang and Song (960–1279) dynasties, the later imperial period was characterized by periods of foreign rule, most notably the Mongol Yuan dynasty (1271–1368) and the Manchu Qing dynasty (1644–1911). It was in the late imperial period that the "three teachings" developed fixed canons and otherwise took on many of the conservative characteristics of mature traditions. At the same time, Christianity and Islam were introduced as early as the Tang dynasty, and these traditions eventually brought with them missionaries and foreign scientific traditions. As a result, the late imperial period was characterized by the beginning of an imperial program of scientific exchange that was catalyzed by military and economic ambitions, as well as new kinds of hybrid scientific knowledge. An emphasis on the consolidation of political control and periodic attempts at modernizing military and other technology-related areas of the government affected the criteria for judging the utility both of knowledge regimens (the efficacy of religions being evaluated on their ability to foster social stability) and of scientific endeavors in terms of their benefit to the security of the state.

Serious Sino-European scientific contact began in the Tang and Song dynasties. While some have raised doubts about Marco Polo's 1275–92 service at the imperial court, records of visits to China by others, such as a Franciscan friar, Arnold of Cologne, are documented from the early fourteenth century. The Spanish friar Francisco Xavier (1506–52) arrived in Macao in 1541, spearheading a Jesuit presence that was continued by his successor Matteo Ricci (1552–1610). Soon afterward, Jesuits like Johann Adam Schall von Bell (1591–1669), also from Cologne, served in official positions in the Chinese government. Schall served as Director of the Astronomical Bureau beginning in 1637, and in 1644 the calendar system he developed was adopted by Emperor Shunzhi (1638–61). At the same time, the publication in Europe of works like Gottfried Leibniz's 1697 *Novissima Sinica* introduced Chinese methods to Europe while simultaneously arguing for increased cultural exchange.

Accommodations to the traditional Chinese calendar by the Jesuits, who were in charge of the Astronomical Observatory during the late Ming (1368–1644) and early Qing dynasties, characterize the way in which Western religions adapted to China. But as a metaphor for Sino-Jesuit accommodation, the Ecliptic Armilla introduced above is incomplete in that it fails to express the conflicts between astronomers of different backgrounds and cosmological commitments. In the year 1267 of the late Yuan dynasty, for instance, astronomical instruments were exported east across the Mongol Empire by Islamic astronomers such as Jamal al-Din al-Bukhari (Zhamaluding 札馬魯丁), who worked on calendars for the Yuan emperors in the imperial astronomy bureau. The first emperor Khubilai Khan established an Islamic astronomy bureau (Huihui sitianjian 回回司天監) in 1271 in Beijing, which competed with the Jesuit bureau for influence at court.[19] This influence continued in the Ming, when several major astronomical works were translated from Persian.

The conflict between the indigenous approaches and these two competing, albeit related, foreign astronomical systems came into clear relief in the seventeenth century. A group of Chinese astronomers grew increasingly critical of Jesuit influence in the areas of both science and religion. This criticism came to a head in 1644, when Verbiest was imprisoned and condemned to death on charges of plotting rebellion and spreading heterodox beliefs. According to Benjamin Elman's exhaustive *On Their Own Terms: Science in China, 1550–1900*, Verbiest's chief critic, Yang Guangxian 楊光先 (1597–1669), attacked the Jesuits for their inattention to methods that derived from earlier kinds of indigenous natural knowledge. Specifically, Yang criticized Verbiest's inattention to pitch pipes and his selection of an inauspicious date for the burial of a prince because he had used the wrong version of the "five phases."[20] Yang was faulting Verbiest for not integrating the traditional methods of astronomy into his universal explanations, and for not understanding that calendars and the pitch pipes (similar to the ones buried in the tomb of the Marquis of Zeng's tomb 2,000 years earlier) were intimately related and could not be treated in isolation. The universal science of the Jesuits was accused of being not universal enough to include China's classical methods. These conflicts, however, gave way to a hybrid approach symbolized by the integration of the traditional solar terms on the Ecliptic Armilla (designed by Verbiest three decades after he was released from prison).

The template for the combination of Chinese and Western scientific approaches was in some ways the same one that allowed for the integration of distinct regional traditions at the start of the imperial period. The concept of *tian* 天 (the heavens) remained a central integrative metaphor for the integration of diverse schemata into a single unified theory. The term itself retained the multiple meanings of "cosmos," "the heavens," "Nature," or "the sky," and, as a result, it was seen as both the subject of astrology and astronomy but also as the ordering principle behind the efficacy of observing the heavens to understand events in the natural world. From the time of the Warring States period, the phrase "natural procedures" (tianshu 天數) was used in the context of applying the motions of the heavens and the hierarchy between the heavens and the earth to human society. The term for astronomy (tianwen 天文) itself refers not to the study or observation of the heavens but, literally, to "patterns of the heavens." In other words, the universality of the heavens was a given; different cultures just noticed different patterns in it. This metaphor facilitated the hybrid astronomical schemes that the government bureaus developed. As Li Shen has pointed out, the "resonance between the heavens and the human" (tianren ganying 天人感應) was a major aspect of the imperial Chinese worldview, and the term "patterns of the heavens" exemplified this resonance. In these ways, the ability to combine different systems became a long-standing characteristic of Chinese astronomy.

Yang Guangxian's rear-guard insistence on the older paradigm of completeness aside, the Qing astronomical bureau had generally adapted to the different political imperatives of the early-modern period. The major change in method that separates the attitude of the early imperial and later imperial astronomer was that accurate prediction had become the dominant criterion in the later period for adapting new systems; the pedigree of the system itself was of less importance. By the later imperial period, the use of empirical data allowed for success in astronomy to be measured along a single metric: ability to find patterns that resulted in a working calendar. As a consequence, there was nothing strange about employing Islamic and Catholic astronomers: the important thing was the quality of their predictions about heavenly motion.

CONCLUSION

These three case studies attempt to describe some differences between the models for the natural world used at different places and times over Chinese history. The choice to focus on different explanatory models was a deliberate one. Unlike some of the comprehensive religious systems of the non-Asian world, the plural systems of China were rarely so insulated from the surrounding culture (certain types of Buddhism being an exception) that they could sustain and preserve a fixed attitude to the natural world. In other words, the story this chapter tries to tell is not how the doctrines of the "three teachings" of Confucianism, Daoism, and Buddhism each dictated a certain approach to natural philosophy; rather, it illustrates some of the ways in which the wider religious-cultural matrix of which they were a part did so.

Instead of a single attitude or underlying metaphor for the natural world being dominant in China, it is apparent that a variety of conditions and conceptions governed the creation of scientific knowledge. The casting of a

complete set of acoustically sophisticated bells by artisans in the pre
imperial state of Zeng was governed by the sumptuary requirements of the
ritual-political order; the endeavor privileged completeness. The elaborate
schemes of the early-imperial medical corpus associated with the Yellow
Emperor give pride of place to an underlying system of natural cycles, key to
a view of the universe that emphasized homologies. Finally, the Chinese/
Jesuit hybrid Armilla was the product of a synthesis of Western and Chinese
techniques, a product of a politicized state-run system that effectively compared the efficacy of different astronomical patterns against one another.

Rather than recounting the history of natural philosophy in China, this
chapter charts approaches to the production of knowledge about the natural
world in three distinct social locations in Chinese history; it also illustrates
how both religious world views and the understanding of natural laws associated with them differ as a result.

The differences between the central metaphors in these three examples
are significant. The dual pitches of bells do not cycle, and later imperial
astronomical bureaus would not accept a natural cycles theory that failed to
predict astronomical phenomena. The reason these metaphors differed had
much to do with specific historical contexts. The engine that drove development of acoustic technology had much to do with the need to demonstrate
the moral and political authority of the bells' possessors. The synthetic correspondence theory that was key to the mapping of the body, and later
became the basis for key elements of the Daoist religion, was an outgrowth
of the synthetic tendencies of the newly united empire. Finally, the new
global realities of the early-modern period resulted in the employment of
Islamic and Christian scholars in state positions, allowing China's cosmopolitan capital to catalyze the development of a new hybrid astronomy. Thus,
the interactions between science and religion in China are plural and varied;
those two terms themselves were not introduced until the nineteenth century, through the recently coined Japanese translations *kagaku* 科学 (science, literally "fields of specialized learning") and *shûkyô* 宗教 (religion,
literally, "teachings of a clan").

This is worth emphasizing because it modifies a key observation that
has been very influential in the history of Chinese science. The most important figure in that field is without doubt Joseph Needham, creator of the
monumental collection *Science and Civilization in China*. Needham's
position was that, generally speaking, Chinese religions did not support the
discovery of natural laws, and as a result modern science failed to develop
in China. He credited the tradition of Daoism with inspiring most of
pre-modern China's proto-scientific discoveries, because of its relatively
more conducive attitude to nature. In the mid-twentieth century, taking
European history as normative—as Needham did—was common. The

dominant view was that science prospered in the West in the sixteenth and seventeenth centuries because people were willing to entertain the idea that a sovereign deity had designed the natural world and that the design could be discovered through a process of mathematical modeling and abstraction.

The present approach to relating science to religion is one way of revising the view that scientific progress is the unveiling of existing "natural laws," a perspective that characterized Joseph Needham's monumental history of Chinese science. By focusing on three different analogies animating scientific discoveries in China—none of which are, strictly speaking, "natural laws"—this chapter emphasizes the heuristic role of analogies in the development of thinking about nature. Reworking Needham's insistence on a concept of "natural law" linked to a notion of a designing, law-making deity, we may instead talk about alternative analogies in different periods of Chinese history, such as "natural sets," "natural cycles," and "natural patterns," respectively. These moments are not reducible to cosmologies associated with particular religious traditions, but they do correlate very well with the dynamics of the religious world views of the social groups responsible for the production of knowledge about the natural world or technology based on that knowledge.

Today, China's attitude to natural philosophy is in many ways an extension of the hybrid approach of the late-imperial period. What this overview suggests, however, is that there is no consistent Chinese approach to science, and that religions in China are part of a broader set of social and cultural concerns that determine the way that approach may change.

NOTES

1. See Stephen Shapin, *The Scientific Revolution* (Chicago: University of Chicago Press, 1990), 109–17; and Margaret J. Osler, *Divine Will and the Mechanical Philosophy: Gassendi and Descartes on Contingency and Necessity in the Created World* (Cambridge: Cambridge University Press, 1994).

2. See Robert Bagley, "Percussion," in *Music in the Age of Confucius*, ed. Jennry F. So, 34–63 (Washington, D.C.: Smithsonian, 2000).

3. Tsun Ko, "The Development of Metal Technology in Ancient China," *Science and Technology in Chinese Civilization*, ed. Chen Cheng-Yih, 225–43, 226 (Singapore: World Scientific, 1987).

4. Chen Cheng-Yih, "The Generation of Chromatic Scales in the Chinese Bronze Set-bells of the–5th century," in *Science and Technology in Chinese Civilization*, 155–98, 160.

5. Anthony Barbieri-Low, *Artisans in Early Imperial China* (Seattle: University of Washington Press, 2007).

6. Benjamin A. Elman, *On Their Own Terms: Science in China, 1550–1900* (Cambridge: Harvard University Press, 2005), 137.

7. Chen Qiyou 陳奇猷, *Lüshi chunqiu xin jiaoshi* 呂氏春秋新校釋 (Shanghai: Shanghai guji, 2002), 328–329. John Knoblock and Jeffrey Riegel have translated the *Springs and Autumns of Master Lü* as *The Annals of Lü Buwei* (Stanford, Calif.: Stanford University Press, 2000), compare 158.

8. C. K. Yang, *Religion in Chinese Society: A Study of Contemporary Social Functions of Religion and Some of Their Historical Factors* (Berkeley: University of California Press, 1961). See also Wenfang Tang and Burkart Holzner, eds., *Social Change in Contemporary China: C. K. Yang and the Concept of Institutional Diffusion* (Pittsburgh: University of Pittsburgh Press, 2006).

9. David N. Keightley, "The Religious Commitment: Shang Theology and the Genesis of Chinese Political Culture," *History of Religions* 17 (1978): 211–25, on 202.

10. Geoffrey Lloyd and Nathan Sivin, *The Way and the Word: Science and Medicine in Early China and Greece* (New Haven, Conn.: Yale University Press, 2002), 46.

11. Mark Csikszentmihalyi, *Readings in Han Chinese Thought* (Indianapolis, Ind.: Hackett Publishing, 2006), 182.

12. John H. Brooke, *Science and Religion: Some Historical Perspectives* (Cambridge: Cambridge University Press, 1991), 72.

13. On Shangqing Daoism, see Isabelle Robinet, *Taoist Meditation: The Mao-shan Tradition of Great Purity.* (Albany: State University of New York Press, 1993).

14. Nakayama Shigeru, *Rekishi toshite no gakumon* 歴史としての学問, published in 1974 and translated as *Academic and Scientific Traditions in China, Japan, and the West* (Cambridge, Mass.: MIT Press, 1984).

15. Two excellent sources for descriptions of these offices are Hans Bielenstein, *The Bureaucracy of Han Times* (Cambridge: Cambridge University Press, 1980), and Charles O. Hucker, *A Dictionary of Official Titles in Imperial China.* (Stanford, Calif.: Stanford University Press, 1985).

16. Most recently in Lloyd and Sivin, *The Way and the Word.*

17. Li Shen, *Zhongguo gudai zhexue yu ziran kexue* 中国古代哲学和自然科学 [literally, Philosophy and natural science in ancient China] (Shanghai: Shanghai renmin, 2002), 618.

18. Joseph Needham, *Science and Civilization in China* (Cambridge: Cambridge University Press, 1956), 2:1.

19. Ho Peng Yoke, *Li, Qi and Shu: An Introduction to Science and Civilization in China* (Hong Kong: Hong Kong University Press, 1985), 164–69.

20. Elman, *On Their Own Terms*, 138–40.

8

Indic Religions

B. V. Subbarayappa

There are three major Indic religions: Hinduism, Jainism, and Buddhism. According to the *Census of India* (2001), Hinduism claims the great majority of adherents in India (about 800 million or 80 percent of the population), with additional millions scattered from Nepal and Sri Lanka to Malaysia, Singapore, and Thailand. Buddhism and Jainism have about eight and five million Indian followers, respectively. Although each of these religions possesses a distinctive approach to the phenomenal world of matter and motion, space and time, they share the ultimate goal of attaining liberation from suffering in this life. None of the three is a monolith; each has its subdivisions, sects, and cults, ranging from the sublime to the bizarre.

The Indic religions differ significantly from the three monotheistic religions: Judaism, Christianity, and Islam. Though Hindus generally accept God as Creator, and some embrace a personal God, most believe that the Creator is immanent in the created world. They advocate the doctrine of unity or monism, and teach that the self or the embodied consciousness is synonymous with Universal Self or Universal Consciousness called *Brahman*.[1] Thus Hinduism typically goes beyond the idea of personal God and posits that the underlying principle of the universe as a whole is the same as that which constitutes the innermost essence of man; the ultimate reality is spiritual.

Jainism, which dates back to Parshvanatha (eighth century BCE) and Vardhamana (sixth century BCE), rejects the idea of a Supreme God. It teaches that the inanimate and animate world is eternal and uncreated, and regards all life as sacred, not to be slain. Because reality is multiple in character, human knowledge of it is relative. However, Jainism visualizes perfect knowledge, free from doubt, as supersensory, comprehending "all things and all phases of them."[2] The history of Buddhism is addressed in chapter 9. As we shall see, the origins of traditional Indian "sciences"—astronomy, mathematics, medicine and related biological ideas—developed initially as part of these early religious systems.

THE RELIGIOUS MATRIX OF EARLY INDIC SCIENCE

Although Hinduism refers to a diverse range of beliefs and practices—and the English term "Hindooism" was not coined until 1829—its roots can be found in the Vedic period from ca. 1600 to 700 BCE.[3] The Vedic period owes its sustenance to the ideas and rituals articulated in the four Vedas (*Veda* literally means "to know" or "knowledge")—the *Rigveda, Yajurveda, Samaveda*, and *Atharvaveda*, their associated liturgical texts (*Brahmanas*), and several metaphysical treatises (*Upanishads*). The Vedas are believed to be of divine origin, revealed to ancient sages who, through their rigorous asceticism and meditation, were supposed to be the recipients.

The religious world of the Vedas encompassed a host of celestial, atmospheric, and terrestrial gods. The sun, moon, air, clouds and rain, lightning, fire, and other natural phenomena were extolled as divinities. Nevertheless, Vedic gods, worshipped in hymnal prayers, had no physical forms. Gradually over time the idea of a single god in the pantheon emerged, which eventually led to the concept of ONE, a primal unitary principle believed to be the quintessence of all celestial and terrestrial manifestations.[4]

The Vedic sages intuitively recognized that the universe is ordered and not capricious. They believed that Vedic natural laws, called *Rita*, governed the entire spectrum of the observable phenomena—the cyclic events of day and night, the changes of seasons, the flow of rivers, and all forms of life. Even the Vedic gods were enjoined to follow these laws as a moral obligation. The Vedic sages regarded natural laws as being embedded in their primal religious kernel, called *Yajña*, the performance of sacrifices involving the worship of fire with extensive chantings. The sacrificial altar or the sacrifice itself was considered to be the abode of natural law, the navel of the world, a pathway of experiencing the consonance of microcosm and macrocosm.[5]

The study of astronomy was essential for determining the timing of rituals and sacrifices, which involved three activities: the construction of several forms of sacrificial altars, precise chantings, and the determination of celestial events such as solstices, when sacrifices had to be performed. The first activity gave rise to Vedic geometry (ca. 600 BCE); the second, concerned with the metrical (long and short sounds) aspects of chants, initiated the methods of permutations and combinations; the third related to the study of the motion of the moon and the sun along with some star-groups.

Thus religious necessity provided the impetus for the early practice of mathematics and astronomy.[6]

Vedic astronomers generally belonged to a priestly class; by prolonged observation of recognizable star-groups (now called constellations) these students of the stars were able to provide a frame of twenty-seven of them as the lunar zodiac. The interrelated trinity of the sun, the moon, and the twenty-seven star-groups constituted the core of this pioneering observational astronomy. Each of the asterisms was associated with a presiding deity and was used to determine auspicious and inauspicious times for consecrating the sacred fire of the sacrificial altars.[7] Vedic astrology based on the twenty-seven star-groups remained dominant until about the sixth century CE, when Hellenistic planetary astrology, particularly Ptolemy's *Tetrabiblios*, was assimilated into Vedic asterism-based astrology. Conspicuously absent (until the early centuries of the current era) were any planetary observations.

RELIGION AND SCIENCE IN THE PRE-COLONIAL PERIOD

Vedic religion and its associated philosophies rejected the worship of *forms* in any manner, including physical symbols and images of gods and goddesses. This non-anthropomorphic tradition continued until the early centuries of the current era, when new techniques—yogic, meditational, and mystic—began to appear. Such practices, known as *tantricism*, were adopted to a great extent from the Buddhists and Jainas, but the followers of Hinduism took tantricism even further. By this time Hindu mythology had acquired a plethora of gods and goddesses, represented in stone carvings and bronze castings, to whom they appealed for boons or blessings. Over time devotees constructed numerous temples, built according to strict architectural guidelines. These developments spurred an ardent devotional movement associated with the goal of *god-realization*.[8]

Despite this burst of religiosity, some Indian mathematicians, astronomers, and medical men continued to pursue scientific investigations. For example, by the fourth century CE Indian mathematicians had developed the (now universally used) system of decimal place-value numeration, using nine digits and zero—misleadingly called Arabic numerals after the Islamic mathematicians who adopted them. During the following centuries Hindu mathematicians contributed significantly to trigonometry and algebra as well. The first mathematics-based astronomical text, the *Aryabhatiyam* of Āryabhaṭa (b. 476 CE), states that the science of astronomy is a revelation from the creator Brahma, but apart from this passing allusion, there are no further references to religion. Astronomy, however, served religious

purposes inasmuch as it accurately determined the positions of the planets
and the rising and setting of the sun and moon, information necessary for
religious performances, marriages, and festivals. The prediction of dreaded
eclipses, both solar and lunar, attracted special attention. During these
frightening events the devout performed propitiatory rites, such as donating
land and other gifts to the priests, to ward off the anticipated evil effects.
There are hundreds of inscriptions dating from the fifth to the eighteenth
centuries that refer to such gift-giving. One epigraph tells of an astronomer's successful prediction of an eclipse on November 8, 1128, and records
the gifts he subsequently received.[9]

During the Vedic period priests also functioned as healers, appeasing the
wrath of gods, exorcising disease-causing demons, sprinkling special water
on the sick, and applying botanical amulets believed to have supernatural
healing power. These practices began to decline (though far from disappear)
about the sixth century BCE, when the northern part of India experienced
expanding urbanization, which in turn promoted the standardization of
the art of healing. This produced the systematization of medicine in the
Ayurveda (literally knowledge of healthy life), a blend of religious and rational medicine, applicable to plants and animals as well as to humans. The
Ayurveda recommends three therapeutic procedures: divine therapy (associated with incantations and the worship of some divinities), rational therapy
(based on such practices as checking the pulse and examining the urine),
and a form of psychotherapy. In the two classics of *Ayurveda*, the *Charaka
Samhitā* (redacted in the second century CE) and the *Sushruta Samhitā*
(fourth century CE), the former deals by and large with internal medicine,
while the latter also describes surgery. Although these texts begin with references to the divine origin of the *Ayurveda*, virtually nowhere else in the
texts does one finds any religious ideas, not even the word "Hindu."[10]

On occasion Ayurvedic practitioners dissected dead bodies in order to
learn about human anatomy. The *Sushruta Samhitā* gave the following
instructions:

> A dead body chosen for the observation should not lack any of its organs; it
> should not be of a person who has lived up to a hundred years (i.e., a ripe old
> age); nor of one who had died of a protracted disease or poison. . . . The body
> should be placed in slow flowing water . . . and after seven days the body would
> be thoroughly decomposed when the observer should slowly scrape off the
> decomposed skin and other layers with a brush made of grass . . . and carefully
> observe with his own eyes all the organs.[11]

Ayurvedic medicine appealed to all sections of society, including the followers of Buddhism and Jainism. It even became popular in the Islamic
world, where Muslim rulers occasionally invited Hindu physicians to

practice in the hospitals and dispensaries of Baghdad and sponsored the translation of Ayurvedic classics into Arabic.[12] When Greco-Arabic medicine (called *Unani* by Indians) came to India with the Muslim rulers who established hospitals, the Muslim and Hindu physicians worked side by side in these hospitals, transcending their religious differences.

From the eighth to the eleventh centuries Baghdad emerged not only as the capital of the Islamic empire but also as an international scientific center. Hindu scholars invited by the Caliphate collaborated with Muslims in translating important scientific works, especially in astronomy, from Sanskrit into Arabic. Later, information also flowed from Arabic into Sanskrit. Early in the eighteenth century the Hindu Maharaja of Jaipur, inspired by two Islamic observatories—one in Persia, another in Samarkand (Central Asia)—built five huge masonry observatories in Benaras, Mathura, Ujjain, Delhi, and Jaipur.[13]

WESTERN SCIENCE AND INDIC RELIGION DURING THE COLONIAL PERIOD

During the long period of British colonial rule (1757–1947), a practically illiterate (as well as multireligious and multilingual) India came face to face with Western science and other forms of modernity. English became the medium of instruction in elite schools. This encounter triggered new religious and social reform movements as well as a dramatic rise of nationalism, including scientific nationalism. One result was a revival of traditional Indian science—sometimes called "Hindu science"— in which European scholars as well as educated Indians played an active role.

The early glimpses of Western science were those of the scientific surveys—botanical, zoological, geological, meteorological, and geographical— launched by European naturalists, engineers, and medical men who were employed in the colonial administration. Many of them worked for the East India Company, chartered by the English crown in 1600 to exploit the riches of the subcontinent. The European investigators brought with them a commitment to experimentation, observation, and rational thinking. Their superior methodologies highlighted the inherent weakness of traditional knowledge. Initially the colonial masters placed little emphasis on educating the natives, but by the late eighteenth century they were encouraging the establishment of an Islamic *Madrasa* in Calcutta (1781) and a Sanskrit college in the religious town of Benaras (1792). When the British government in London renewed the charter of the East India Company in 1813, it set aside a paltry sum of about one *lakh* (1,00,000 rupees) for the "revival and improvement of literature, and introduction and promotion of knowledge of *sciences* among the natives."[14]

Although the great majority of Indians paid little or no attention to Western science, several Indian thinkers actively cultivated it. In 1816–17 a few liberal-minded Hindu and European gentlemen of Calcutta, including the social reformer Raja Rammohun Roy (1774–1833) and Sir Hyde East (1764–1847), the chief justice of the supreme court, founded a seminary for the instruction of students in European and Asiatic languages and in the sciences. The scientific subjects, offered in the collegiate section, included astronomy, chemistry, and natural philosophy. The first institution of its kind outside of Europe and the Americas, it later became the Hindu College and the nucleus of the Presidency College of Calcutta. According to a statement by an agency of the colonial government, "a command of English language and a familiarity with its literature and science had been acquired . . . to an excellence rarely equaled by any school in Europe." When the government began planning a new Sanskrit school in Calcutta in the early 1820s, Rammohun Roy appealed to the governor-general to include subjects such as mathematics, natural philosophy, chemistry, and anatomy in the curriculum and not to "load the minds of the youth with grammatical niceties and metaphysical distinctions of little or no practical value to the possessors or to the society." In 1835 another governor-general decreed that funds be employed for imparting to the native population a knowledge of English literature and science, stipulating that no portion of it should be expended on the publications of oriental literature.

In 1857 the government established the first three Indian universities, in Calcutta, Bombay, and Madras. (Two more universities, in Lahore and in Allahabad, were opened in the 1880s, and by Independence in 1947 there were sixteen, including the Aligarh Muslim University and the Benaras Hindu University.) The limited spread of scientific and technical education had no perceptible impact on religious beliefs and practices. Despite their exposure to scientific subjects and their rational methods, most students did not cast off their religious garments. Being religiously orthodox at home while engaged in scientific studies in college did not appear to them as a dichotomy—an attitude that persists down to the present.[15]

In 1869 a medical man from Calcutta, Mahendralal Sirkar (1833–1904), described Hindu culture as "a chaotic mass of crude and undigested and unfounded opinions on all subjects, enunciated and enforced in the most dogmatic way imaginable." He exhorted Indians to cultivate science on their own and imbibe its rationality:

> We want an institution which shall be for the instruction of masses, where lectures on scientific subjects will be systematically delivered, and not only

illustrative experiments performed by the lecturers but the audience should be invited to perform by themselves. And we wish that this institution be entirely under native management and control. The kind of knowledge which is best calculated to remove prejudices, and the spirit of tolerance in the mind is what one passes by the name of physical sciences.

To counter fears that this rational approach to nature and life would undermine religion, he proclaimed in a public lecture that "science leads to a firm belief in the Deity and a devout attitude of mind before the great First Cause."[16]

For some of the Indian scientists who first achieved international recognition, it is difficult to determine the relationship, if any, between their scientific and religious beliefs. They articulated their commitment to science and its role in national development in several ways. For example, India's first Nobel laureate in physics (1930), C. V. Raman (1888–1970) exhorted: "There is only one solution for India's economic problems and that is science and more science." But he was neither an atheist nor a supporter of religion. M. N. Saha (1893–1955) earned widespread acclaim for explaining the ordered sequence of the spectra of stars. He stressed the need for the institutionalization of science as part of national development but largely ignored religion. A classmate, the brilliant theoretical physicist S. N. Bose (1894–1974), developed a statistical law governing the behavior of photons, which, after being extended by Albert Einstein, came to be known as Bose-Einstein statistics. (The particles that obey Bose-Einstein statistics are called "bosons" in honor of Bose.) Bose believed in the dissemination of scientific knowledge in local languages of the people and established a science association, but he rarely addressed religious questions.[17] In general Indian scientists, such as Bose, preferred to maintain silence on issues of religion.

In contrast to Raman, Saha, and Bose, the mathematical prodigy Srinivasa Ramanujan (1887–1920), a contemporary, openly attempted to conflate his religious and scientific worlds. Initially self-taught, the young clerk in Madras eventually won a scholarship to Cambridge, where he remained five years, impressing his English mentors with his genius. When asked about his ability to solve difficult problems, he professed to have received assistance from the Hindu goddess Namgiri. He once claimed that "an equation for me has no meaning unless it expresses a thought of God." To his way of thinking, the quantity 2n-1 represented "the primordial God and several divinities." His brilliance, though not his methods, impressed all who knew him. He died at age thirty-three, but his influence on mathematics continues to this day.[18]

J. C. Bose (1858–1937), a distinguished experimental physicist and physiologist who in the 1890s pioneered in the transmission and reception of radio waves, also linked his science and religion. Claiming to detect the

Hindu idea of unity in his investigations of nature, he emphasized the harmony between traditional Indian culture and modern science, even giving his instruments Sanskrit names and investigating the consciousness of plants. In 1917, when he established a scientific institute in Calcutta (now known as Bose Institute), he revealed his intensely divine feeling by declaring: "This is not a laboratory, but a temple."[19]

"HINDU SCIENCE" AND "WESTERN SCIENCE"

In 1828 Raja Rammohun Roy, who was erudite not only in the monotheism of the Hindu scriptures but also in the Qu'ran and the Bible, joined with like-minded friends in Calcutta in establishing an association called *Brahmo Samaj* (the One God Society), dedicated to worshipping one god without any name or form and without any distinction of caste or sect. Despite subsequent schisms, the *Brahmo Samaj* devoted itself to reforming society; it heralded the dawn of a new way of thinking, strongly influenced by Western science and a commitment to a liberal education in English.[20]

Another movement, Arya Samaj (Noble Society), was founded in 1875 by Swami Dayananda Saraswati (1824–83). For years Dayananda had agonized over the grotesque worship of idols, the widespread faith in mythological gods and goddesses, and child marriage. His solution was to return to the Vedas, a source of infallible revealed knowledge that recognized no idolatry and taught the existence of one Supreme Being. Dayananda's "back to the Vedas" initiative did not embrace opposition to the teaching of English or science. In fact, in the years after his death his followers opened in Lahore (now in Pakistan) an institution called the Dayanand Anglo-Vedic School, which combined Vedic learning, an English education, and Western science. While acknowledging the superiority of Western scientific ideas in many ways, Dayananda's society insisted that the Vedas too were repositories of scientific knowledge, often anticipating modern science. Some members even translated some Vedic hymns into Western scientific terms.[21]

Swami Vivekananda (1863–1902), a Bengali who played a pivotal role in the revival of Hinduism in nineteenth-century India and in popularizing it among Westerners, accorded the highest place to the doctrine of one Supreme Being and described the Hindu *Vedanta* (the end of knowledge and spiritual experience) as the goal of science and religion alike. Vivekananda recognized the strength of Western science and technology as well as of Indian spirituality. "We are to give as well as take from others," he exhorted. "We should give our ancient spirituality and culture and get in return Western science, technology, methods of raising the standards of life, business integrity and technique of collective effort."[22]

Christian missionaries, who became especially active in the nineteenth century, as well as other Europeans observed that a wide variety of religious rites, periodical festivals, and marriages were being performed according to the Hindu calendar, prepared annually using traditional astronomical texts. Even the colonial administration depended on Hindu calendars for declaring religious festival-holidays. These observations led to a renewal of interest in "Hindu astronomy" and its associated mathematics. Such interest in the past did not, however, dampen enthusiasm for modern astronomical pursuits. While *Asiatick Researches* in Calcutta was publishing articles on Hindu astronomy (from 1790 on), the East India Company was establishing the Madras Observatory (1792) with a telescope and other instruments. Throughout the nineteenth century astronomers at this observatory, including at least one orthodox Hindu, engaged in cutting-edge observations. Princely endowments led to the creation of two additional observatories, in Trivandrum (1836) and Poona (1890). For decades traditional almanacs, based on Sanskrit astronomical texts, appeared side by side with ones based on the latest science—a practice that still continues.[23]

The appreciation of foreign scholars for traditional science and medicine inspired some Indian scholars to take up the study of "Hindu science" in the closing decades of the nineteenth century and into the twentieth century. Among the foremost of these was P. C. Ray (1861–1944), who had obtained his doctorate in chemistry from the University of Edinburgh. In the first decade of the twentieth century he produced a two-volume *History of Hindu Chemistry*, in which he wrote: "It is generally taken for granted that the Hindus have always been a dreamy, metaphysical people, prone to meditation and contemplation. . . . In ancient India, however, physical science found votaries. India was the cradle of mathematical and chemical Sciences." With the help of traditional scholars he studied the early Sanskrit sources of Ayurvedic medicine and Indian alchemy. Ever the nationalist, he tried on occasion to show the superiority of some Hindu chemical practices to those of other ancient cultures. At times he struggled to balance his interest in the past with his commitment to the present. He recalled that once he had had to put aside completing his history of Hindu chemistry so that he could "catch up and be in current with modern chemical literature." Despite his strong nationalism and his enthusiasm for ancient Indian science, on occasion he complained that Indian soil had been "rendered morally unfit for the birth of a Boyle, a Descartes or a Newton and her very name was all but expunged from the map of the scientific world."[24]

Compared to the impact of evolutionary biology on Western cultures, Darwinism, in the words of the historian Deepak Kumar, "did not cause a ripple in India." However, this does not mean that all Indians ignored the religious implications of evolution. As C. Mackenzie Brown has observed, "Hindu responses to Darwinism, like Christian, have run the gamut from outright rejection to fairly robust but limited accommodations of the Darwinian perspective." The earliest Hindu responses began appearing in the mid-1870s. One of the first to discuss the issue was Keshab Chandra Sen (1838–84). Although more interested in spiritual than in physical evolution, he found no problems with the evolution of humans from animals. Writing in 1877, he described "evolution" as "the great idea of the day." Nevertheless, he declined

> to discuss the details of the philosophy of evolution. Your protoplasm, your natural selection, I leave to be discussed by men like [Thomas] Huxley and [Charles] Darwin. The question perhaps is not so serious after all, whether men have descended from inferior animals. But whether there is a progressive evolution going on in the individual life of man is a question in which we are all interested.[25]

Other Hindu evolutionists, including the influential Swami Vivekananda, not only embraced biological evolution (supplemented by spiritual processes) but traced it back to ancient Vedic texts. At times he sounded more Lamarckian than Darwinian, as when he wrote about the fish-bird transition:

> The little fish wants to fly from its enemies in the water. How does it do so? By evolving wings and becoming a bird. The fish did not change the water or the air; the change was in itself. . . . All through evolution you find that the conquest of nature comes by change in the subject.[26]

Drawing on the Hindu concept of One becoming Many, Vedic protagonists traced all species back to a primordial "Supreme Being" from which everything had devolved. Thus some conservative Hindu writers rejected the transmutation of species, which they dismissed as "just a theory." One of these was Aurobindo Ghose (1872–1950), an English-educated Bengali nationalist and philosopher, who repudiated the materialism of Darwinian evolution for the "involution" of divine consciousness. Hindu creationists, however, never insisted on a young earth. Indeed, they embraced cosmic evolution and the great antiquity of life. Among the early Hindu anti-evolutionists was the previously mentioned Dayananda Saraswati, who dated the origin of species (including humans) to 1.96 billion years ago. In a public lecture in 1878 he reportedly refuted "the Darwinian theory that man was descended from a monkey," arguing that "the copulation of an animal of one species with that of another did not result in off-spring." Dayananda's continuing influence can be seen in the Hare Krishna movement, founded in the United States in 1966 by A. C. Bhaktivedanta Swami

Prabhupada (1896–1977), who denounced Darwin as his followers as "rascals."[27] Despite such demurrers, most Indian scientists accepted biological evolution and taught it in Indian universities.

AFTER INDEPENDENCE

In 1885 Indian nationalists founded the Indian National Congress, which spearheaded the subsequent movement for freedom from British rule. During the early twentieth century Mohandas Karamchand Gandhi (1869–1948), or Mahatma Gandhi as he was respectfully known, emerged as the leader of this movement. Gandhi had studied law in London and practiced in South Africa for over twenty years before returning permanently to India in 1915. While in South Africa he had protested against apartheid, and on returning home he joined the growing freedom movement, energizing it with a commitment to nonviolence and truth. A religious Hindu, Gandhi recognized the universality of God and saw in religion the potential for fostering moral strength in both individuals and society as a whole. His political successor, Jawaharlal Nehru (1889–1964), described him as the "greatest Indian of the day and the greatest Hindu of the Age . . . a man of God." But despite his religiosity, Gandhi did not oppose science, which he viewed as the rational study of nature. However, he hated "the craze for machinery." He feared that industrial civilization would quash the human spirit, and with it moral principles and humanism. His vision of Indian nationhood centered on an ensemble of village communities living harmoniously in an atmosphere of religious tolerance, supported economically by small cottage industries rather than large corporations based on science and technology.[28]

Nehru himself viewed science differently. As a young man he had studied the natural sciences at Trinity College, Cambridge, graduating in 1910. He left Cambridge convinced of the rationality of science and of the paramount role of technology in the elevation of the material standards of life of all people. While pondering the future of India during his imprisonment by the colonial rulers from August 1942 to September 1944, he reflected on the role of science, religion, and philosophy. A nominal Hindu, he wrote:

> Religions have helped greatly in the development of humanity. They have laid down values and standards, and pointed out principles for the guidance of human life. But with all the good they have done, they have also tried to imprison truth in set forms and dogmas, and encouraged ceremonies and practices which soon loose all their meanings, and become mere routine. Instead of encouraging curiosity and thought, religions have preached submission to nature, to established churches, to the prevailing social order.

The belief in a supernatural agency which ordains everything has taken the place of reasoned thought and inquiry.[29]

Nehru was fully aware that science, too, had its limitations. For example, it "ignored the ultimate purpose of life, and looked at facts alone." Yet, he emphasized, "It is the scientific approach, the adventures and the critical temper of science, its search for truth and new knowledge, its refusal to accept anything without testing . . . its reliance on facts and not pre-conceived notions, all of these are necessary not merely for the applications of science but for life itself and the solution of its many problems."[30]

While delivering a convocation address at Allahabad University in 1946, Nehru expressed his conviction in these words: "It is Science and Science alone that could solve the problems of hunger and poverty, of insanitation and illiteracy, of superstition and deadening custom and tradition, of vast resources running to waste, of a rich country inhabited by starving people."[31] During his seventeen-year stewardship as independent India's first prime minister, Nehru laid a solid foundation for the multilevel growth of science and technology. In 1958 he, in collaboration with leading scientists, proposed to the Indian Parliament a Scientific Policy Resolution—perhaps the first of its type in the world—which extolled the role of science and scientists in national development.

India since Independence has made rapid progress in various scientific fields, from agriculture and nuclear energy to space and information technology. At the same time various forms of religion, both sublime and profane, have expanded. New temples have sprung up across the land, and esoteric religious rites have proliferated. The faith of the people in science and technology has grown in tandem with their faith in traditional gods and practices, such as *yoga* (to achieve higher states of consciousness). Throughout India "Hindu astronomy" and "Hindu medicine" exist alongside modern astronomical observatories and sophisticated hospitals. Scientific attitudes and secularism—with equal respect for all religions—are among the guiding principles of the *Constitution of the Republic of India* (adopted soon after Independence) in recognition of the complementarity of science and religion for meaningful lives.

Notes

1. Paul Deussen, *The Philosophy of the Upanishads*, trans. from German by A. S. Geden (New York: Dover Publications, 1966), 85–87.

2. M. Hiriyanna, *The Essentials of Indian Philosophy* (London: George Allen and Unwin, 1949), 63.

3. On the construction of the various world religions, see, e.g., Jonathan Z. Smith, "Religion, Religions, Religious," in *Critical Terms for Religious Studies*, ed. Mark C. Tayler, 269–84 (Chicago: University of Chicago Press, 1998).

4. Ralph T. H. Griffith, *The Hymns of the Rigveda* (Benares: E. J. Lazarus and Co., 1891; repr. 1963), Book 10, 129.

5. Ibid., Book 1:23.5, 144.2, 147.1, 163.5–6, 164. 35; Book 4:7.7.

6. S. N. Sen, "Mathematics," in *A Concise History of Science in India*, ed. D. M. Bose, S. N. Sen, and B. V. Subbarayappa, 145–50; 156–57 (New Delhi: Indian National Science Academy, 1971; repr. 1991); Zaheer Baber, *The Science of Empire: Scientific Knowledge, Civilization, and Colonial Rule in India* (Albany: State University of New York Press, 1996), 28–32.

7. William Dwight Whitney, *Atharva-veda Samhitā*, 2 vols. (Cambridge, Mass.: Harvard University Press, 1905; repr. 1984), 19.7.1–5; T. S. Kuppanna Sastry, *Vedanga Jyotisha of Lagadha* (New Delhi: Indian National Science Academy, 1985), Rigvedic recension, vv. 25–28.

8. T. A. Gopinatha Rao, *Elements of Hindu Iconography*, 2 vols. (Madras: Law Printing House, 1914–1916; repr. 1972).

9. George Sarton, *Appreciation of Ancient and Medieval Science during the Renaissance: 1450–1600* (Philadelphia: University of Pennsylvania Press, 1955), 151 (numerals); B. Datta and A. N. Singh, *History of Hindu Mathematics*, 2 vols. (Lahore: Motilal Banarsidas, 1935–38); David Pingree, "History of Mathematical Astronomy in India" in *Dictionary of Scientific Biography*, 15, supplement, ed. Charles C. Gillespie, 630 (New York: Scribners, 1978); Ebenezer Burgess, *Translation of the Surya-Siddhanta: A Text-Book of Hindu Astronomy* (New Haven, Conn.: American Oriental Society, 1860; repr. 1989), 9–13; K. S. Shukla and K. V. Sarma, *Aryabhatiya of Aryabhata* (New Delhi: Indian National Science Academy, 1976), "Gola," v. 50; *Epigraphia Indica* 22 (1933–34): 161.

10. Mira Roy, "Vedic Medicine: Some Aspects," in *Medicine and Life Sciences in India*, ed. B. V. Subbarayappa, 49–50 (New Delhi: Centre for Studies in Civilizations, 2002); R, H. Singh, "Kayacikitsa (Internal Medicine)," ibid., 128–33. See also David M. Knipe, "Hinduism and the Tradition of Ayurveda," in *Healing and Restoring: Health and Medicine in the World's Religious Traditions*, ed. Lawrence E. Sullivan, 89–109 (New York: Macmillan, 1989); and Kenneth G. Zysk, *Religious Healing in the Veda*, American Philosophical Society, *Transactions*, new ser., vol. 75 (1985), pt. 7.

11. Kaviraj Kunjalal Bhishagratna, *An English Translation of the Sushruta Samhita*, 3 vols. (Calcutta: Self-published by the author, 1907–16; repr. 1963), 3:5.61–63. See also G. D. Singhal and T. J. S. Patterson, *Diagnostic Considerations in Ancient Indian Surgery* (Varanasi: Singhal Publications, 1972–82).

12. Rangesh Paramesh, "The Spread of Ayurveda outside India," in *Medicine and Life Sciences in India*, 517–29.

13. Pingree, "History of Mathematical Astronomy in India" 626; G. R. Kaye, *A Guide to the Old Observatories at Delhi, Jaipur, Ujjain, and Banaras* (Calcutta: Archaeological Survey of India, 1920).

14. Clements R. Markham, *A Memoir on the Indian Surveys*, 2nd ed. (London: Kegan Paul, 1878); H[enry] Sharp, *Selections from Educational Records*, vol. 1 (Calcutta: Government of India, 1920), 19–22.

15. B. V. Subbarayappa, "Western Science in India up to the End of the Nine-teenth Century," in *A Concise History of Science in India*, 543–44; Kapil Raj, *Relocating Modern Science: Circulation and the Construction of Scientific Knowledge in South Asia and Europe, Seventeenth to Nineteenth Centuries* (Delhi: Permanent Black, 2006), 159–64; Sharp, *Selections from Educational Records*, 1:90, 116; S. N. Mukherji, *History of Education in India: Modern Period* (Baroda: Acharya Book Depot, 1955).

16. M. L. Sirkar, "On the Desirability of a National Institute for the Cultivation of the Sciences by the Natives of India," *Calcutta Journal of Medicine* 2 (1869): 286–306. See also S. N. Sen, *A Century for the Cultivation of Science: Early Period* (Calcutta: Indian Association for the Cultivation of Science, 1976).

17. G. Venkataraman, "The Spirit of a Giant," *Current Science* 75 (1998): 1085–94; Robert S. Anderson, *Building Scientific Institutions in India: Saha and Bhabha* (Montreal: McGill University Press, 1975); S. D. Chatterji, "S. N. Bose" in *Biographical Memoirs of the Fellows of the Indian National Science Academy*, 7:1983.

18. S. R. Ranganathan, *Ramanujan: The Man and the Mathematician* (Bombay: Asia Publishing House, 1967); Baber, *Science of Empire*, 234–35.

19. S. K. Mukerji and B. V. Subbarayappa, *Science in India: A Changing Profile* (New Delhi: Indian National Science Academy, 1984), 37–41; Subrata Dasgupta, *Jagadis Chandra Bose and the Indian Response to Western Science* (Delhi: Oxford University Press, 1999). See also P. N. Tandon and H. Y. Mohan Ram, eds., *Pursuit and Promotion of Science: Indian Experience* (New Delhi: Indian National Science Academy, 2001), 28–30.

20. Sivanath Sastri, *History of the Brahmo Samaj*, 2 vols. (Calcutta: R. Chatterji, 1911–12); R. C. Majumdar, *History and Culture of Indian People*, vol. 10, pt. 2: *British Paramountcy and Indian Renaissance* (Bombay: Bharatiya Vidya Bhavan, 1959), 101–5.

21. Dayananda Saraswati's *Satyarth Prakash* was first published in Banaras by the Star Press in 1875; English translations began appearing as early as 1906. See also Mazumdar, *History and Culture of Indian People*, vol. 10, pt. 2, 112–13.

22. *The Complete Works of Vivekananda*, 9 vols. (Calcutta: Advaita Ashrama, 1970–73), 4:5; Majumdar, *History and Culture of Indian People*, vol. 10, pt. 2, 128.

23. S. M. R. Ansari, "Introduction of Modern Western Astronomy in India during 18–19 Centuries" in *History of Astronomy in India*, ed. S. N. Sen and K. S. Shukla, 2nd ed., 395–454 (New Delhi: Indian National Science Academy, 2000). See also *Astronomical and Astrophysical Observatories in India* (New Delhi: Government of India, 1976); and M. K. V. Bappu, *Indian Institute of Astrophysics: A Brief History* (Kodaikanal: Government of India, 1974).

24. P. C. Ray, "Progress of Chemistry in Ancient India," *Science and Culture* 2 (1937): 497; Pratik Chakrabarty, *Western Science in Modern India* (Delhi: Permanent Black, 2004), 219–51. See also P. C. Ray, *A History of Hindu Chemistry*, 2 vols. (Calcutta: Self-published by the author, 1902–1908); P. C. Ray, *Life and Experience of a Bengali Chemist* (Calcutta: Chukervertty, Chatterjee and Co., 1932), 598; and Deepak Kumar, *Science and the Raj: A Study of British India*, 2nd ed. (New Delhi: Oxford University Press, 1997), 212, 214, 220–21.

25. Quoted in C. Mackenzie Brown, "Hindu Responses to Darwinism: Assimilation and Rejection in a Colonial and Post-Colonial Context," *Science and Education* 19 (2010): 705–38.

26. Ibid.

27. Ibid. On the concept of One becoming Many, see the *Rigveda*, Book 10.90 and related hymns in Book 10.

28. *Independence and After: A Collection of Important Speeches of Jawaharlal Nehru* (New Delhi: Government of India Publication, 1949), 20–23 (man of God); M. K. Gandhi, *Collected Works of Mahatma Gandhi*, 90 vols. (New Delhi: Publications Division, Government of India, 1958–84), 25:118ff.

29. Jawaharlal Nehru, *The Discovery of India*, centenary ed. (Delhi: Oxford University Press, 1985), 511.

30. Ibid., 512–14.

31. Quoted in P. N. Tandan and H. Y. Mohan Ram, eds. *Pursuit and Promotion of Science: The Indian Experience* (New Delhi: Indian National Science Academy, 2001), 69.

9

Buddhism

Donald S. Lopez Jr.

It has often been claimed over the past two centuries that among the religions of the world, Buddhism is most compatible with modern science. The nature of this compatibility has fallen across a wide spectrum, with some suggesting that the essential teachings of Buddhism (variously identified) are in no way contradicted by the findings of science (variously enumerated), while others suggest that the Buddha anticipated many of the key discoveries of science, that the Buddha knew more than two millennia in the past what scientists would only discover in modern times. In this essay, I examine the origins of such claims, identify their present manifestations, and consider what is at stake in the conjunction of Buddhism and science. Before doing so, however, it is perhaps useful to provide a very brief description of Buddhism.

A SKETCH OF BUDDHISM

Buddhism traces its origins to the teachings of an itinerant mendicant who lived in northern India during the fifth century BCE. His clan name was Gautama, and his personal name was Siddhārtha. According to traditional accounts, he was born a prince in a small kingdom in what is today southern Nepal. Shielded from the tribulations of life by his father the king, Siddhārtha, at the age of twenty-nine, eventually ventured forth from the royal palace, where on separate excursions he encountered a sick man, an old man, a corpse, and a meditating ascetic. Confronted with the realities of sickness, aging, and death—and with the recognition that there are those who seek to escape them—he departed from the palace, leaving behind his wife and newborn son, in search of a state beyond suffering. After six years of various forms of spiritual exercises, including extreme asceticism, he sat down under a tree and meditated all night. By dawn, he had become enlightened (*buddha*, literally, "awakened") and from that point was known as the Buddha, the awakened one, for he had awakened from the sleep of ignorance.

He decided to teach others what he had learned, seeking out his five former fellow ascetics, to whom he delivered his first sermon. He set forth what are known as the four noble truths: suffering, origin, cessation, and path. The first truth is that existence is qualified by suffering. Like many other Indian teachers of the day, the Buddha believed in rebirth, that beings are reborn in various states throughout the universe. In Buddhism, these states are generally enumerated as six: gods, demigods, humans, animals, ghosts, and hell beings. Although the sufferings undergone in the hot and cold hells are greater than those experienced in the heavens of the gods, each abode is ultimately unsatisfactory in one way or another, and all are unsatisfactory in the sense that even the happiest experiences eventually come to an end and one is reborn elsewhere.

The second truth, the truth of origin, explains why this is the case. The Buddha asserted that suffering is caused by *karma*, a Sanskrit term meaning "action." He denied the existence of an eternal God who is creator and judge, holding instead that experiences of pleasure and pain, and indeed the environments in which they occur, are the result of past deeds. Virtuous deeds done in the past result in feelings of pleasure in the future (a future that can occur in the lifetime in which the deed is done or in any future lifetime). Nonvirtuous deeds done in the past result in feelings of pain in the future. Virtue and nonvirtue are generally defined as helping and harming others, respectively, but are also enumerated. Thus, killing, stealing, and sexual misconduct are physical nonvirtues; lying, divisive speech, harsh speech, and senseless speech are verbal nonvirtues; and covetousness, harmful intent, and wrong view are mental nonvirtues. These negative deeds are in turn motivated by a variety of negative mental states, the most important of which are desire, hatred, and ignorance, sometimes referred to as the three poisons. Among these, ignorance is identified as the root cause of all suffering. Although the nature of this ignorance is among the most extensively examined questions in Buddhist thought, it is generally defined as the belief in self: that among the physical and mental constituents of the person, there is a permanent, partless, autonomous self that is the owner of mind and body and that moves from one lifetime to the next.

The third truth, the truth of cessation, postulates the existence of a state in which suffering is destroyed. The existence of such a state may be inferred from the process by which suffering is produced. That is, suffering is caused by negative deeds; negative deeds are motivated by desire or hatred; desire and hatred result from ignorance. Thus, if ignorance can be destroyed, there can be no desire and hatred; without desire and hatred, there can be no negative deeds; without negative deeds there can be no suffering. The Buddha called the state of the cessation of all suffering and rebirth *nirvana*, a Sanskrit term that might be translated as "extinction."

The fourth and final truth is the truth of the path, the path to that cessation. The path is described in many ways in Buddhist literature; one of the more succinct is the three trainings: in ethics, in meditation, and in wisdom. Ethical deeds, defined as the control of body and speech, result in states of happiness within the cycle of rebirth. However, such deeds cannot, of themselves, bring about liberation from rebirth. Meditation in this context refers to practices that focus the mind to overcome the ordinary state of mental distraction and produce a state of one-pointed concentration on a given object. Such concentration results in states of mental bliss, both in this lifetime and future lifetimes, but does not, in itself, bring about liberation from rebirth. For liberation, wisdom is required, defined in this case as insight into the nature of reality, not simply intellectually but at a level of deep concentration. The precise content of this wisdom is a topic of detailed discourse in Buddhism, but it is generally described as the understanding that there is no self to be found among the constituents of mind and body.

Upon hearing the Buddha's first sermon, the five ascetics all became liberated from rebirth. The Buddha continued to teach over a long career, traveling through northern India, where he received the patronage of kings and merchants. He established an order of monks and nuns that continues until the present day. Forty-five years after his enlightenment, he died or, in the language of the tradition, passed into nirvana, never to be reborn again.

The Buddha wrote nothing during his lifetime. In keeping with the ancient Indian tradition, his teachings were preserved orally; they did not begin to be committed to writing until some four centuries after his death. Around the beginning of the Common Era (CE), new texts, referred to as the Mahāyāna sūtras, began to appear, claiming to be the word of the Buddha. There is thus a vast corpus of scripture attributed to the Buddha; how much of it can be traced directly to the Buddha himself has long been a point of contention among Buddhists and scholars of Buddhism.

In the centuries after his death, the Buddha's teachings (and those attributed to him) were spread by monks throughout Asia, from Afghanistan in the west to Japan in the east, from Mongolia in the north to Indonesia in the south. Monasteries were founded and texts were translated. The tradition grew and changed in significant ways, so much so that some scholars prefer to speak of several "Buddhisms" rather than a single "Buddhism."

THE COLONIAL ENCOUNTER

Prior to the nineteenth century, European scholars divided the peoples of the world into four nations: Christians, Jews, Mahometans, and Idolators (or Pagans). The Buddhists encountered across Asia by European explorers, travelers, and Roman Catholic missionaries were placed in the last category, and statues of the Buddha were regarded as idols. It was only in the nineteenth century that the Buddha was identified with certainty as a historical figure of Indian origin, no longer a stone idol but the founder of a great religion.

European travelers encountered Buddhism all over Asia but not in India, the land of the Buddha's birth. By the fourteenth century Buddhism had all but disappeared from India. The reasons for its disappearance were complex (the invasion of northern India by Muslim armies was one of many causes), but its consequences were profound. For by the nineteenth century, when European scholars trained in South Asian languages began a sustained study of the culture and history of India, what they would come to call "Buddhism" (a term which, according to the *OED*, first appeared in English, spelled "Boudhism," in 1801) was an artifact. There were no Buddhists in India, although there were Buddhists almost everywhere else in Asia. Instead, India had monuments (often in ruins), cave temples (overgrown by jungle), and statues (often broken). There were stone inscriptions to be deciphered, and there were Sanskrit manuscripts preserved in Nepal to the north of India and Pali manuscripts in Sri Lanka to the south of India. These were the materials from which European philologists would build their Buddhism.

The nineteenth century thus saw the birth of what the Jesuit historian Henri de Lubac has called the "scientific discovery" of Buddhism, that is, the study of Buddhism by scholars who could read Buddhist texts in the original. This was made possible by significant advances in the science of philology, with the discovery of language families and ancient connections between the classical Indian language of Sanskrit and the classical European languages of Greek and Latin, as well as modern German, French, and English. These were called the Indo-European or Aryan languages; *āryan*, a Sanskrit term meaning "noble" or "superior," was the name that ancient peoples of northern India used to refer to themselves. Through a complicated process, theories of language groups eventually gave rise to theories of racial groups. The kinship between the people of ancient India and the people of ancient Greece and hence (through a certain leap of faith) the peoples of modern Europe became not simply a matter of verb roots but of bloodlines.

Because there were no Buddhists living in India during the colonial period, the Buddhism of India—that is, the first Buddhism—became the domain of European and, later, American and then Japanese scholars. In 1844, the French Sanskritist Eugène Burnouf (1801–52) argued convincingly that Buddhism is an Indian religion and that it must be understood first through texts in Indian languages. For the remainder of the nineteenth century, India became the primary focus of Buddhist Studies in Europe, and Sanskrit (together with Pali) became the lingua franca of the academic field. Much of the early scholarship focused on the life of the Buddha and on the early history of Buddhism in India, prior to its demise there, referred to by such terms as "original Buddhism," "primitive Buddhism," sometimes "pure Buddhism." This austere system of ethics and philosophy stood in sharp contrast to what was perceived as the spiritual and sensuous exoticism of colonial India, where Buddhism was long dead. This ancient Buddhism, derived from the textual studies of scholars in the libraries of Europe, could be regarded as the authentic form of this great religion, against which the various Buddhisms of nineteenth-century Asia could be measured—and were generally found to be both derivative and adulterated. Buddhism thus came to be regarded as a tradition that resided most authentically in its texts, such that it could be effectively studied from the libraries of Europe; many of the most important scholars of the nineteenth century never traveled to Asia. They created a Buddha and a Buddhism that was unknown at the time in Asia and that may never have existed there before the late nineteenth century. Just as there was a quest for the historical Jesus, there was a quest for the historical Buddha, and European Orientalists felt that they had found him.

As a result, the Buddha was not so foreign. He was in fact, racially, an Aryan, unique among the founders of the world religions; Moses, Jesus, and Muhammad were all Semites. But the nobility of the prince who had renounced his kingdom was not only of the hereditary kind. The Buddha had famously rejected the idea of the inherited nobility of the Indian caste system, claiming that nobility derived instead from wisdom. He thus called his first teaching, the four truths for the noble (āryan), the term usually translated as "four noble truths." Indeed, this Buddha was doubly noble. He was noble by birth, by blood, and by language, yet he was also noble because he renounced his royal birth to achieve a spiritual nobility. He was portrayed as a great reformer, described by some as "the Luther of Asia" who condemned the vapid priestcraft of the Brahmins and the caste system they controlled. In a Europe obsessed with questions of race and questions of humanity, the Buddha was both racially superior and a savior for all humanity, an ancient kinsman, a modern hero. Furthermore, his ancient teachings, as represented by Victorian scholars, seemed most modern.

THE BUDDHA OF SCIENCE

Buddhism, then, could be hailed as a religion whose founder was neither a god nor a prophet of God, but a man. This man, through his own efforts and his own investigations, discovered the nature of the universe and then compassionately taught it to others. This Buddha described a universe that was not created by God but that functioned according to laws of cause and effect. These laws were not limited to the material world but extended also to the moral realm, where virtue leads eventually to happiness and sin to suffering, not through the whims of a capricious God but through the natural law of karma.

This Buddha understood the mechanisms of the mind in precise detail. He explained how desire, hatred, and ignorance motivate actions that eventually result in all manner of physical and mental pain, and he set forth techniques for bringing the chattering mind and the unruly emotions under control in order to reach a state of serenity. Beyond this, he analyzed the myriad constituents that together are called the person, finding among them nothing that lasts longer than an instant. Thus, he discovered, through his analysis, that there is no self, that there is no soul, that what we call the person is but a psychophysical process, and that the realization of this fundamental truth results in a certain liberation.

This Buddha then extended this analysis to the phenomena of the universe, declaring the universal truth of *pratītyasamutpāda*, dependent origination, according to which everything is interrelated, each entity connected to something, nothing standing alone; effects depend on their causes, wholes depend on their parts, and everything depends on the consciousness that perceives it, appearing differently depending upon one's perspective. Yet whether wave or particle, there is no uncertainty about the ultimate nature of reality, which the Buddha calls *śūnyatā* or emptiness. Emptiness is not nothingness; it is the absence of what is called *svabhāva*, self-nature, a false quality projected upon the objects of our experience by ignorance; that ignorance is destroyed by wisdom.

This Buddha's discoveries were not limited to psychological truths and philosophical insights. He described multiple universes, each with its own sun, universes that arose out of nothingness and returned to nothingness over the course of vast cosmic phases of creation, abiding, and disintegration, measured in massive units of time called "countless eons." And he explained how countless beings are born in these universes across these eons, each moving, through a process of spiritual evolution, to a state of perfect wisdom.

This Buddha discovered these truths not through revelation but through investigation and reasoned analysis, testing hypotheses in the laboratory of his mind to arrive at conclusions. He articulated these truths in his teachings, truths that derive not from faith but from the Buddha's own experience. And when he died, he did not ascend into heaven. He lay down between two trees and said to his monks, "All conditioned things are subject to decay. Strive on with diligence." Then he passed away, like a flame going out.

For Europeans and Americans seeking an alternative to theistic religions—seeking to preserve religion, or at least a religion, in the light of science—this was a Buddha to whom all manner of scientific insights could be ascribed, from the mechanisms of the universe to the structure of the atom, from a natural law of morality to the deepest workings of the mind. His was a religion, if it was a religion at all, that required no dogma, no faith, no divinely inspired scriptures, no ritual, no worship of images, no God. This Buddha enjoyed particular popularity among the more anticlerical of the European scholars. Thomas Henry Huxley (1825–95), "Darwin's Bulldog" himself, described Buddhism in 1894 in these terms:

> A system which knows no God in the western sense; which denies a soul to man; which counts the belief in immortality a blunder and the hope of it a sin; which refuses any efficacy to prayer and sacrifice; which bids men look to nothing but their own efforts for salvation; which, in its original purity, knew nothing of vows of obedience, abhorred intolerance, and never sought the aid of the secular arm; yet spread over a considerable moiety of the Old World with marvellous rapidity, and is still, with whatever base admixture of foreign superstitions, the dominant creed of a large fraction of mankind.[1]

For Huxley and other Victorians, Buddhism was a tradition that saw the universe as being subject to natural laws without the need for any form of divine intervention. This led many European enthusiasts to declare Buddhism as the religion most suited to serious dialogue with science, because both postulated the existence of immutable laws that governed the universe.

This Buddha was rather different from the Buddha whose words were recited and whose image was venerated across Asia. Despite the chronological and geographical range of the tradition, he was portrayed with great consistency in Asia. He was believed to have perfected himself over the course of millions of lifetimes as a bodhisattva, performing the virtuous deeds called perfections (*pāramitā*). He was believed to have taken rebirth in heaven in his penultimate life, where he perused the world to select the city of his final birth, his caste, his clan, and his parents. He was believed to have achieved enlightenment at the age of thirty-five, sitting under a tree along the banks of a river. With this enlightenment, he was believed to possess all manner of supernormal powers, including full knowledge of each of his own past lives and those of other beings, the ability to know others' thoughts, the ability to create doubles of himself, the ability to rise into the air and simultaneously shoot fire and water from his body. It was said to be an extraordinary body, endowed with the thirty-two marks of a superman (*mahāpuruṣa*), including forty teeth, webbed fingers, the sign of wheels on the soles of his feet, and a crown protrusion (*uṣṇīṣa*) on his head. Although he passed into nirvana at the age of eighty-one, he could have lived "for an eon or until the end of the eon" if only he had been asked to do so.

Rather than narrating the events of his final lifetime, the traditional biographies of the Buddha, which did not begin to appear until some four centuries after his death, seemed more intent on describing his previous lives and the previous buddhas he encountered along the way. They were less concerned with portraying the Buddha's individuality and his humanity than with exploring his identity with other buddhas, those said to have come in the distant past and those who were prophesied to come in the future. He was but one of many buddhas; each taught the same truth, the same path to liberation from suffering. There were indeed elaborate descriptions of the Buddha's final birth, but they appeared centuries after his death, and even in these texts it was his continuity with the buddhas of epochs past, rather than his unique character, that provided the foundation of his authority. Indeed, all buddhas are said to be remarkably similar in word and deed; they differ from each other in just a few ways, one of which is the circumference of their auras.

THE BUDDHA RETURNS TO ASIA

The Buddha who had been created in Europe did not remain there. By the latter half of the nineteenth century, much of Buddhist Asia had come under European control. Ceylon and Burma were British colonies, Indochina was a French colony. Although China, Korea, Japan, and Tibet did not come under direct European or American control, they each had varying levels of contact with Europe, including the establishment of Christian missions; the most extensive contact occurred in China, the least in Tibet. As in the classical economic model of colonialism, raw materials, in this case Buddhist texts in Sanskrit and Pali, were extracted from the colony and shipped to Europe, where they were refined to produce a new Buddha, one that had not existed before. To complete the circuit, that Buddha was then exported back to Asia and sold to Asian Buddhists, who sent him into battle against the Christians.

Christian missionaries to Asia continued to regard Buddhists as heathens and sought to demonstrate the errors of Buddhism, sometimes condemning it as superstition, sometimes as idolatry. To counter these claims, Buddhist elites claimed that Buddhism was in fact superior to Christianity, in part because it was more compatible with science. At a lecture delivered

at the Town Hall in New York in 1925, the Sinhalese activist Anagārika
Dharmapāla (1864–1933) declared:

> The Message of the Buddha that I have to bring to you is free from theology,
> priestcraft, rituals, ceremonies, dogmas, heavens, hells and other theological
> shibboleths. The Buddha taught to the civilized Aryans of India 25 centuries
> ago a scientific religion containing the highest individualistic altruistic ethics,
> a philosophy of life built on psychological mysticism and a cosmogony which
> is in harmony with geology, astronomy, radioactivity and relativity. No creator
> god can create an ever-changing, ever-existing cosmos. Countless billions
> of aeons ago the earth was existing but undergoing change, and there are
> billions of solar systems that had existed and exist and shall exist.[2]

In China, the challenge came not only from Christian missionaries but
from a growing community of Chinese intellectuals who saw Buddhism as
one of several forms of primitive superstition preventing China's entry into
the modern world; for them, Buddhist practice was fraught with ghosts and
demons, and Buddhist doctrine was "life denying." As a religion imported
from India long ago, Buddhism had periodically been regarded with suspicion by the state over the course of Chinese history and had been subjected
to imperial persecution on four occasions (in 564, 567, 845, and 955 CE).
Criticism of Buddhism intensified in the early decades of the twentieth century (especially after the Republican revolution of 1911), when Buddhism
was denounced both by Christian missionaries and by Chinese students
who returned from studying abroad, among whom the works of John Dewey
and Karl Marx were particularly popular. Again, the new Buddha was sent
into battle. In a lecture published in 1928, the Chinese monk Taixu (1890–
1947) described Buddhism not only as compatible with modern science but
superior to it:

> Scientific discoveries have brought about a certain doubt as to religious evi-
> dence. The old gods and religions seem to have been shaken in the wind of
> science, and religious doctrines have no longer any defence, and the world at
> large seems to be handed over to the tyranny of the machine and all those
> monstrous powers to which Science has given birth.
>
> Buddhism takes quite a different view, and holds that Science does not go
> far enough into the mysteries of Nature, and that if she went further the Bud-
> dhist doctrine would be even more evident. The truths contained in the Bud-
> dhist doctrine concerning the real nature of the Universe would greatly help
> Science and tend to bring about a union between Science and Buddhism.
>
> By the use of such scientific methods the Buddhist scholar is aided in his
> research. When we go beyond these methods we find that Science is unable to
> grasp the reality of the Buddhist doctrine. The reality of the Buddhist doctrine
> is only to be grasped by those who are in the sphere of supreme and universal
> perception, in which they can behold the true nature of the Universe, but for

this they must have attained the wisdom of Buddha himself, and it is not by the use of science or logic that we can expect to acquire such wisdom. Science therefore is only a stepping stone in such matters.[3]

We see here one of the more strident views of the relation of Buddhism and science, a view that would be repeated in the future: that science can confirm the insights of the Buddha but is incapable of gaining those insights through its own means. Science—identified here, as is often the case in discourses on Buddhism and science, with a somewhat bewildering and frightening technology—can be of benefit in investigating the world, but its scope is limited. In order to penetrate beyond appearances to the true nature of reality, science is inadequate. In order to understand the nature of reality, one must achieve buddhahood.

In the last decades of the nineteenth century, Buddhism was also under attack in Japan. In an effort to demonstrate the relevance of Buddhism to the larger interests of the Japanese nation, Buddhist leaders sought to promote a New Buddhism that would play an active role in Japan's attempts to modernize and expand. In the early years of the Meiji period (1868–1912), Buddhism was portrayed as a foreign and anachronistic institution, riddled with corruption, a parasite on society, and a purveyor of superstition, impeding Japan from taking its rightful place among the great nations of the modern world. The New Buddhism that was espoused in response to such charges was represented as both purely Japanese and purely Buddhist, more Buddhist, in fact, than the other Buddhisms of Asia, especially those of China and Korea, which many Buddhist leaders conceded were corrupt. The New Buddhism was also committed to social welfare and urged the foundation of public education, hospitals, and charities. It supported the military expansion of the Japanese empire. And it was fully consistent with modern science. The "spirit" of the New Buddhism, as well as its close ties to the expansionist policies of the Meiji government, is expressed in the concluding paragraphs of an address titled "History of Buddhism and Its Sects in Japan," delivered by the Shingon priest Toki Hōryū (1854–1923) on September 14, 1893, to the World's Parliament of Religions in Chicago:

The present Japanese Buddhism has passed several hundred years since the last change. The past experience points out to us that it is time to remodel the Japanese Buddhism—that is, the happy herald is at our gates informing us that the Buddhism of the perfected intellect and emotion, synthesizing the ancient and modern sects, is now coming.

The Japanese Buddhists have many aspirations, and at the same time great happiness, and we can not but feel rejoiced when we think of the probable result of this new change by which the Buddhism of great Japan will rise and spread its wings under all heaven as the grand Buddhism of the whole world.[4]

The consistency of Buddhism with modern science was claimed by many Japanese Buddhist thinkers of the period, including D. T. Suzuki (1870–1966), who would later become renowned in the West for his books on Zen Buddhism. But in his first major work, *Outlines of Mahayana Buddhism*, published in 1907, Suzuki was concerned not with Zen but with Buddhism as a universal religion, and he set forth its correspondence to science. Indeed, as others had argued in the past and would argue in the future, Suzuki announced that the discoveries of science had been anticipated by the Buddha:

> It is wonderful that Buddhism clearly anticipated the outcome of modern psychological researches at the time when all other religious and philosophical systems were eagerly cherishing dogmatic superstitions concerning the nature of the ego. The refusal of modern psychology to have soul mean anything more than the sum-total of all mental experiences, such as sensations, ideas, feelings, decisions, etc., is precisely a rehearsal of the Buddhist doctrine of non-âtman [no self].[5]

Although these and other authors each offered a somewhat different view from the other, together they regard Buddhism as that religion most compatible with science, although they also hold that Buddhism offers access to states of wisdom that science alone can never attain. Some even went so far as to declare that Buddhism was not a religion at all but was itself a science of the mind. The implications of such a claim become clear in light of theories of social evolution of the day, which saw an inevitable advance of humanity from the state of primitive superstition to religion to science. Once declared to be a science, Buddhism—condemned as a primitive superstition both by European missionaries and by Asian modernists—jumped from the bottom of the evolutionary scale to the top, bypassing the troublesome category of religion altogether.

BUDDHISM AND SCIENCE IN THE CONTEMPORARY PERIOD

The discourse of Buddhism and science remained relatively dormant during the 1940s and 1950s, with the exception of parallels drawn by some between psychoanalysis and Zen, inspired largely by the works of D. T. Suzuki.[6] Also relevant in the postwar period, especially in Japan, was the question, raised by Buddhists and others, of the use and misuse of science in the wake of the bombings of Hiroshima and Nagasaki. The Buddhist writing on this topic, much of which has yet to be translated into English, is an important element of discussions of Buddhism and science in the 1950s and 1960s.[7] Claims of compatibility continued to be made by monks of the Theravāda tradition of Sri Lanka and Southeast

Asia. For example, the Burmese Buddhist monk, U Thittila, playing on the multivalence of the word *dharma* (Pali: *dhamma*), declared:

> All the teachings of the Buddha can be summed up in one word: Dhamma . . . Dhamma, this law of righteousness, exists not only in a man's heart and mind, it exists in the universe also. All the universe is an embodiment and revelation of Dhamma. When the moon rises and sets, the rains come, the crops grow, the seasons change, it is because of Dhamma, for Dhamma is the law residing in the universe which makes matter act in the ways revealed by the studies of modern science in physics, chemistry, zoology, botany, and astronomy. Dhamma is the true nature of every existing thing, animate and inanimate.[8]

The discourse of Buddhism and science reemerged in the late 1960s with the efflorescence of interest in Asian religions and Eastern wisdom. The signal publication during this period was an improbable bestseller, *The Tao of Physics*, first published in 1975. The work went on to become a classic of the New Age, selling more than one million copies. Its author, Fritjof Capra (1939–) was a physicist rather than a student of Buddhism and thus relied on secondary sources for his portrayal of Buddhist thought. As was the case with a number of works of this period, Capra spoke as often of "Eastern mysticism" as of a specific tradition. This mysticism included, then, insights from Hinduism, Buddhism, and Taoism:

> When I refer to "Eastern mysticism," I mean the religious philosophies of Hinduism, Buddhism, and Taoism. Although these comprise a vast number of subtly interwoven spiritual disciplines and philosophical systems, the basic features of their world view are the same. The view is not limited to the East, but can be found to some degree in all mystically oriented philosophies. The argument of this book could therefore be phrased more generally, by saying that modern physics leads us to a view of the world which is very similar to the views held by mystics of all ages and traditions. Mystical traditions are present in all religions, and mystical elements can be found in many schools of Western philosophy. The parallels to modern physics appear not only in the *Vedas* of Hinduism, in the *I Ching*, or in the Buddhist *sutras*, but also in the fragments of Heraclitus, in the Sufism of Ibn Arabi, or in the teachings of the Yaqui sorcerer Don Juan.[9]

In the late nineteenth and early twentieth century, the Theosophical Society—founded in New York in 1875 by the Russian medium Helena Petrovna Blavatsky (1831–91) and the American Civil War veteran Colonel Henry Steel Olcott (1832–1907)—declared that all mystical traditions arose from the same deep foundation. A century later, Capra discerned a similar core, one which both anticipates and is confirmed by what he calls "the New Physics." Both mysticism and modern physics derive their insights from empirical methods, yet those insights cannot be expressed in words. They thus remain beyond the comprehension of those who are neither mystics nor physicists. As he writes, "A page from a journal of modern experimental physics will be as mysterious to the uninitiated as a Tibetan mandala. Both are enquiries into the nature of the universe."[10] For the mystic, the result of his inquiry is "a direct non-intellectual experience of reality."

Since the 1980s, the fourteenth Dalai Lama of Tibet has been the most visible and influential Buddhist teacher to embrace the discourse of Buddhism and science. The figures of the late nineteenth and early twentieth centuries—such as the Sinhalese Buddhist activist Anagārika Dharmapāla, the Chinese Buddhist monk Taixu, and D. T. Suzuki—had complicated (and in some cases strained) relations with the Buddhist institutions of their homelands, and none had either the authority or the stature of the Dalai Lama. Born in 1935 in a distant corner of the Tibetan cultural domain, he was identified as a young child as the fourteenth incarnation of the Dalai Lama, a lineage of Buddhist teachers that extends back to the fifteenth century; since 1642, the Dalai Lamas were also the temporal rulers of Tibet. He displayed an interest in mechanical things from the time of his tutelage in the Potala Palace in Lhasa, where he discovered various European gadgets given as gifts to his predecessor. The People's Liberation Army invaded Tibet in 1950, and the Dalai Lama assumed the position of head of state, traveling in 1954 to China, where he was impressed by Chinese feats of engineering. During a failed Tibetan uprising against the occupying army in March 1959, he escaped to India, where he has lived since.

The Dalai Lama made his first trip to the United States in 1979 and has traveled extensively since then, often meeting with scientists and researchers to discuss a wide range of topics, from cosmology to neurology. Owing in part to his interests, over the past twenty years the effects of Buddhist meditation have begun to be measured by neurologists, whose work has added a new dimension to Buddhism and science.[11] Rather than pointing to affinities between particular Buddhist doctrines and particular scientific theories, research on meditation has sought to calculate the physiological and neurological effects of Buddhist meditation. Such research would seem to introduce a welcome empirical element to the Buddhism and science discourse.

The assertions being made in this domain are qualitatively different from the assertion that the Buddha understood the theory of relativity. The claim here is that Buddhist meditation works. In order to understand the laboratory findings, however, one must first identify what is "Buddhist" about this meditation, describe what the term "meditation" encompasses in this case, and explain what "works" means, especially in the context of the exalted goals that have traditionally been ascribed to Buddhist practice.[12] Although these goals are numerous and are variously articulated across the tradition, it can be said that their ultimate goal is not self-help but a radical reorientation toward the world—and in many articulations, a liberation from it—either for oneself or for all beings.

CONSEQUENCES

Through these various peregrinations, the discourse of Buddhism and science has survived from the nineteenth, through the twentieth, and now into the twenty-first century. It began in the arena of polemics, with Buddhists seeking to defend their religion against the attacks of Christian missionaries. By the time that the first claims of affinity between Buddhism and science began to be made in Asia in the late nineteenth century, science had come to carry connotations of authority, validation, and truth separate from and, in some cases, in conflict with, those of the Christian church. It is therefore perhaps unsurprising that Buddhist leaders in Asia would point to what they identified as the scientific aspects of Buddhism in an effort to trump the charges of idolatry and superstition leveled at them by Christian missionaries across the Buddhist world. They argued that the Buddha knew long ago what the science of the Christian West was only now discovering, whether it be the mechanisms of causation that rely on no god, the analysis of experiences into their component parts, the subtle disintegration of matter called impermanence, or the existence of multiple universes.

In this first stage, "Buddhism" was the philosophy of the Buddha, as European Orientalists understood him, an aristocratic teacher who rebelled against the corrupt priestcraft of his day to teach an ethical system that required no god and opened the path to freedom from suffering to all men. Asian Buddhists and European enthusiasts could thus claim Buddhism as the most modern of the world religions, able to uphold morality without the need for an angry creator God, and as the most scientific, fully in accord with the science of the day and its model of a mechanistic universe of cause and effect.

In the period after the Second World War, this science was displaced by Einstein's theories and "original Buddhism" was displaced by Zen, especially as set forth by D. T. Suzuki. The focus turned from cause and effect to relativity and from the law of karma to "interdependence," through creative readings of Nāgārjuna's statements on *pratītyasamutpāda*, "dependent origination." In more recent years, expositions of emptiness and quantum physics have continued (although now drawing on Tibetan interpretations of Indian Buddhist doctrine) with a new element added: the relation of Buddhism to cognitive science, especially through laboratory investigations of the effects of Buddhist meditation on the brain. Thus, in each of its periods of conjunction with science, a different form of Buddhism has been called upon to play its part.

Over the century and a half of its association with Buddhism, *science* has also meant many things. At times, it has designated a method of sober and rational investigation, and has been compared with the Buddha's use of such a method to arrive at knowledge of deep truths about inner and outer worlds. At other times, science has referred to a specific theory—the mechanistic universe, the theory of evolution, the theory of relativity, the Big Bang—whose antecedents are to be found in Buddhist doctrine. At yet other times, science has signified a specific technology—the microscope, the telescope, the spectrometer—that has been used to discover what the Buddha knew without the aid of such instruments; as more precise instruments have been developed over the past century, the claims of the Buddha's knowledge have remained constant. And at still other times, science has meant the manipulation of matter, with dire consequences for humanity unless paired with the compassionate vision of the Buddha.

The referent of "Buddhism" and the referent of "science" have thus changed radically over the course of more than a century, yet the claim for the compatibility of Buddhism and science has continued to be made with a remarkable consistency of rhetoric. And in each case, in order for the claim to be made, each term must be radically restricted. "Buddhism" becomes a single tradition, and within that tradition an isolated set of elite doctrines and practices. The term "science" is often restricted to such an extent that it becomes like a mantra, a potent sound with no semantic value.

From the traditional perspective, the Buddhist truth is timeless; the Buddha understood the nature of reality fully at the moment of his enlightenment, and nothing beyond that reality has been discovered since. From this perspective, then, the purpose of all Buddhist doctrine and practice that have developed over two and a half millennia is to make manifest the content of the Buddha's enlightenment. From the historical perspective, the content of the Buddha's enlightenment is irretrievable, and what is called "Buddhism" has developed in myriad forms across centuries and continents, with these forms linked by their retrospective gaze to the solitary sage seated beneath a tree. From either perspective, if this "Buddhism" is to be made compatible with "science," Buddhism must be severely restricted by eliminating much of what has been deemed essential, whatever that might be, to the exalted monks and ordinary laypeople who have gone for refuge to the Buddha over the course of more than two thousand years.

Buddhists first encountered science, perhaps ironically, in the guise of Christianity; it was a superior knowledge, a knowledge that Christianity possessed and Buddhism did not. By providing yet further proof of the superiority of Christianity, it was a tool of the missionary and a reason for conversion. Later, science would be portrayed as the product of a more generalized "European civilization," something that this civilization would take around the world; the vehicle for that journey was colonialism. The modern Buddhists of the late nineteenth and early twentieth centuries thus had good reason to try to claim science for themselves. Whether to counter the missionary's charge that Buddhism was superstition and idolatry, or to counter the colonialist's claim that the Asian was prone to fanciful flights of the mind and meaningless rituals of the body, science proved the ideal weapon. It was Buddhism, in fact, that was the scientific religion, the religion best suited for modernity, throughout the world. It was an Asian, the Buddha, who knew millennia ago what the European was just beginning to discover. This latter point was made possible only through the strange international network that invented the Buddha as we know him.

A century later, the missionaries have not gone away, but their inroads into Buddhist societies are largely confined to specific times and places of the past: Japan in the sixteenth century, Sri Lanka in the early nineteenth century, Korea in the late nineteenth century. And European colonialism, in its classical form, has died out. Yet the discourse of Buddhism and science persists, unchanged in so many ways. The enemy is slain; the weapon continues to be wielded.

The Buddhist figures mentioned above are a disparate group, coming from different Buddhist cultures, regarding different forms of Buddhism as the most authentic. If we consider them from a different perspective, however, they have something in common. Dharmapāla was a patriot in the struggle for Sri Lankan independence, Taixu sought to prove the relevance of Buddhism to the new Republic of China, Suzuki argued for an essential role for Buddhism in the expanding empire of Japan. As Gyan Prakash has noted, "To be a nation was to be endowed with science."[13] The inevitable links between nation and science help to explain why today the most famous proponent for the links between Buddhism and science is none other than the Dalai Lama, who has struggled for a half-century for the independence of Tibet and is perhaps still seeking to demonstrate that Tibetan Buddhism is not the primitive superstition that the European Orientalists saw in the nineteenth century and that the Chinese Communist Party saw in the twentieth. Rather, Tibetan Buddhism is presented as a worthy interlocutor of science and hence an appropriate ideology of a modern nation that might one day exist.

The argument for the modernity of Buddhism may explain the motivations of the Dalai Lama and the other Buddhist leaders who have invoked science over the decades. But this alone is not enough to sustain the discourse into the twenty-first century.

The Dalai Lama recently said, "I have great respect for science. But scientists, on their own, cannot prove nirvana. Science shows us that there are practices that can make a difference between a happy life and a miserable life. A real understanding of the true nature of the mind can only be gained through meditation."[14] His comments provide a possible model for the relationship of Buddhism and science: Buddhism and science occupy two different domains, "non-overlapping magisteria" in Stephen Jay Gould's memorable phrase. The Buddha taught the ultimate truth: the nature of liberation from rebirth and the path to nirvana. Science is concerned with the conventional truth, investigates the mundane nature of the world, and offers much insight into its operation. Yet each tradition, one called "Buddhism" and one called "science," has produced important tomes on both the conventional and the ultimate, the outer and the inner, the vast and the minute, the mundane and the profound.

There is another difference between Buddhism and science. In the scientific method, at least in its idealized form, reality or truth (whatever those terms might mean in a given case) has not yet been discovered; hypothesis and experiment are employed to arrive at a truth that is at the time unknown, or at least unverified. That truth can change, and has changed many times over the history of science; a new truth sometimes refines an old truth, and sometimes the new completely replaces the old. The image is one of augmentation and revision, moving toward an ever-receding horizon of omniscience, a Theory of Everything.

Over the long and varied development of the Buddhist traditions, there remains the shared belief that the nature of reality was discovered long ago by the Buddha; before him, it was discovered by the buddhas of the distant past, and that same reality was understood by all buddhas in its entirety and its fullness. This reality is represented not as a discovery by the Buddha but as a rediscovery. In a famous metaphor, the Buddha describes a traveler coming across an ancient city at the end of an ancient path through a great forest. A once-great city, it is now deserted and in ruins. The traveler informs the king, who restores the city to its former glory. The Buddha is that traveler, discovering the same path to enlightenment that the buddhas of the past had found. Thus, in Buddhism, the truth is found, and then lost, and then found again. This is why it is said that the next buddha does not appear in the world until the teachings of the previous buddha have been completely forgotten. As long as the path to the city of reality remains passable and the city itself remains prosperous, there is no reason for repair. But when the city falls into ruins and the path is overgrown with oblivion, then the path must be cleared again and the city restored. This is what the buddhas do, again and again, over the eons.

In a sense, then, Buddhism is profoundly retrospective—it looks to the past to understand the present in order to secure a haven safe from a hazardous future. There is a comfort in the knowledge that the course to that haven has already been clearly charted. There is comfort in the knowledge that that course has already been safely navigated. There is comfort in the knowledge that the other shore has already been reached. Science, in a popular representation, offers a different appeal, an appeal to the quest for what has never been known by anyone, yet is somehow there, waiting to be discovered, if we just knew how to find it. In the meantime, we must live in doubt of our deepest knowledge. Perhaps this is why we yearn for the teachings of an itinerant mendicant in Iron Age India, albeit one of profound insight, to somehow anticipate the formulae of Einstein.

Notes

This essay is derived from Donald S. Lopez Jr., *Buddhism and Science: A Guide for the Perplexed* (Chicago: University of Chicago Press, 2008), and is reprinted with the kind permission of the publisher.

1. Thomas H. Huxley, *Evolution and Ethics and Other Essays* (London: Macmillan, 1894), 68–69.

2. Anagārika Dharmapāla, "Message of the Buddha," in *Return to Righteousness: A Collection of Speeches, Essays and Letters of Anagārika Dharmapāla*, ed. Ananda Guruge, 27 (Ceylon: The Government Press, 1965).

3. His Eminence Tai Hsu [Taixu], *Lectures in Buddhism* (Paris, 1928), 43, 47–48. A somewhat similar view, apparently uninfluenced by Taixu, was expressed sixty years later by the prominent Sinhalese monk Walpola Rahula in an address at the University of Kelaniya in Sri Lanka. He cautioned against seeking to make religions modern and accessible by validating religious truths with science, and notes that "We have almost become creatures or slaves of science and technology. Soon we shall be worshipping it. Early symptoms of it are that we tend to seek support from science to prove the validity or our religions, to justify them and to make them up-to-date, respectable and acceptable. It is not surprising, therefore, that some well-intentioned Buddhist monks as well as some Buddhist laymen are making an ill-advised effort to prove that Buddhism is a scientific religion." Rahula did not dispute for a moment that the Buddha clearly and precisely taught the latest scientific worldview, but he held that "to put on the same footing, the Buddha and a philosopher or a scientist, however celebrated he may be, is a gross disrespect to the Great Teacher." See Ven. Dr. Walpola Rahula, "Religion and Science," *Dharma Vijaya: Triannual Publication of Dharma Vijaya Buddhist Vihara Los Angeles* 2.1 (May 1989): 10, 14. I am grateful to Martin J. Verhoeven for providing me with a copy of this article. See also Martin J. Verhoeven, "Buddhism and Science: Probing the Boundaries of Faith and Reason," *Religion East and West: Journal of the Institute for World Religions* 1 (June 2001): 77–97.

4. See Horin Toki [Toki Hōryū], "History of Buddhism and Its Sects in Japan," in *Neely's History of the Parliament of Religions and Religious Congresses at the World's Columbian Exposition*, 4th ed., ed. Walter R. Houghton, 226 (Chicago: F. Tennyson Neely, 1894). On Meiji policies regarding Buddhism and Buddhist responses, see James Edward Ketelaar, *Of Heretics and Martyrs in Meiji Japan* (Princeton, N.J.: Princeton University Press, 1990); Richard Jaffe, *Neither Monk nor Layman: Clerical Marriage in Modern Japanese Buddhism* (Princeton, N.J.: Princeton University Press, 2001); and Brian Victoria, *Zen at War* (New York: Weatherhill, 1997).

5. Daisetz Teitaro Suzuki, *Outlines of Mahayana Buddhism* (Chicago: Open Court, 1908), 40.

6. See, e.g., Daisetz Teitaro Suzuki, Erich Fromm, and Richard De Martino, *Zen Buddhism and Psychoanalysis* (New York: Harper, 1960); and Alan Watts, *Psychotherapy, East and West* (New York: Pantheon Books, 1961).

7. The writings of D. T. Suzuki on science, composed in Japanese and English over the course of more than half a century, merit their own study. The complicity of Japanese Buddhists (including Suzuki) in the Pacific War has been a source of both repentance and recrimination. See, for example, Brian Daizen Victoria, *Zen at War*, 2nd ed. (Lanham, Md.: Rowman and Littlefield, 2006); James W. Heisig and John C. Maraldo, eds., *Rude Awakenings: Zen, the Kyoto School, and the Question of Nationalism* (Honolulu: University of Hawaii Press, 1995); and Jamie Hubbard and Paul L. Swanson, eds., *Pruning the Bodhi Tree: The Storm over Critical Buddhism* (Honolulu: University of Hawaii Press, 1997).

8. U Thittila, "The Fundamental Principles of Theravada Buddhism" in *The Path of the Buddha: Buddhism Interpreted by Buddhists*, ed. Kenneth W. Morgan, 67 (New York: Ronald Press, 1957).

9. Fritjof Capra, *The Tao of Physics: An Exploration of the Parallels between Modern Physics and Eastern Mysticism*, 3rd ed. (Boston: Shambhala, 1991), 19. The reference to Don Juan is probably significant, since Capra notes in the preface, "In the beginning, I was helped on my way by 'power plants' which showed me how the mind could flow freely; how spiritual insights come on their own, without any effort, emerging from the depth of consciousness" (12).

10. Ibid., 36.

11. For an insightful account of the recent role of Asian religions, including Buddhism, in neurological research, see Anne Harrington, *The Cure Within: A History of Mind-Body Medicine* (New York: W. W. Norton, 2008), 205–42.

12. For a useful survey and analysis of recent scientific research on the effects of meditation, see Maria B. Ospina et al., *Meditation Practices for Health: State of the Research*, Evidence Report/Technology Assessment No. 155, AHQR Publication No. 07-E010 (Rockville, Md.: Agency for Healthcare Research and Quality, June 2007).

13. Gyan Prakash, *Another Reason: Science and the Imagination of Modern India* (Princeton, N.J.: Princeton University Press, 1999), 7.

14. Quoted in Dian J. Land, "Scientists Meet with Dalai Lama to Study Meditation," *Research News and Opportunities in Science and Theology* 1 (July/August 2001): 2.

10

African Religions

Steven Feierman and John M. Janzen

The inherited language of healing in eastern and central Africa presents an immediate paradox to those who would study the zone of interaction between science and religion. In many of the societies where Bantu languages are spoken (all across the center and the south of the continent), people have long made a distinction between illnesses of God and illnesses brought by other agents—often by humans, who are seen as having complex, ambiguous, and sometimes negative motives. The surprise here is that the term "illness of God" is used to refer to illnesses that happen without any moral cause—that just happen. People with university educations, whether in Africa or in the north, would say that these happen "naturally." So, illnesses of God happen naturally, without a moral cause, while "illnesses of man," or "of person," or illnesses brought by the ancestors or other agents are seen as being defined, in a deep and powerful way, by moral relations. Illnesses brought by anger, by aggression, or by violations of the proper order by which human bodies, plants, animals, the wind, the rain, lightning, and all the other material elements interact—these are deeply moral and therefore the antithesis of illnesses of God.[1]

The focus on health as an illustration of the larger field of knowledge, the cosmos, and the moral order—or science and religion—may be justified for several reasons. The debates of scholars over whether science, as we know it in the modern West, is even a part of historic African civilizations reflects widely diverging opinions, ranging from those who argue that "science," as a form of knowledge production that originated in the West, does not map neatly onto distinctively African ways of producing knowledge—e.g., Paulin Hountondji, V. Y. Mudimbe, Kwame Gyekye[2]—to those who seek to reclaim bodies of technology and theory destroyed by colonialism, or to reconstruct ethnoscience or ethnophilosophy—e.g., Cheikh Anta Diop, Placide Tempels.[3] These debates are complex beyond the scope of this essay. Many scholars, however, recognize the sophisticated knowledge and practices found in many African civilizations. Medicine and healing are usually at the forefront of those discussions, as suggested recently by Kai Kresse, a scholar of Swahili thought: "healing is a good example of a wide-ranging systematic field of knowledge-oriented practices that are performed in everyday life but also derive from coherent epistemologies, which in turn are linked to regional cosmologies and religions."[4] Medicine is the research focus of the present co-authors, and so we focus on this realm to explore the contours of practical knowledge in central and eastern African societies in general. Other fields could as easily be examined.

The therapeutic practices of this region have changed drastically, as we will see, and are changing with increasing velocity. The twentieth century saw the slow and fitful introduction of European-style medicine by government hospitals and dispensaries (thus expanding the therapeutic possibilities for illnesses of God). Christian missionary physicians and nurses added another set of possibilities, sometimes aimed at undermining what they saw as the enchanted (or, in their language, superstitious) therapeutic world of ancestors and other spiritual agents—an attempt to secularize their patients before resacralizing their world in a Christian key. Other missionaries combined healing with Christian prayer from the start. In many places, Africans founded churches based on their own principles. Sometimes these churches reintegrated moral causes of illness, in the sense of the inherited categories, along with a modified Christian theology. Other syncretic churches prohibited any kind of therapeutic action outside the church—whether in government hospitals or by traditional healers. In these cases only religion in its purest form has had the capacity to heal. Still other religious movements introduced new varieties of therapy through dance accompanied by symbolic action—building in new ways on inherited forms—with the intention of reconfiguring relationships among people, and between people and spiritual forces, all with the goal of healing the sick.

All of these initiatives, whether by missionaries, by practitioners of *ngoma* (healing) dance therapy (see p. 238), or by the bishops of new churches—all of them had to come to terms, in some way, with the ideas embedded in inherited practice: that chronic and serious illness is both natural and moral at the same time. Such illness exists in both the world of material substances (in the body of the sick person and the efficacy of herbs) and in the world of relations among people or between people and spirit-agents. In most difficult illnesses (that is, in cases that were *not* illnesses of God), the practitioner needed to intervene simultaneously and in intertwined (perhaps integrally melded) ways with both sick bodies and moral relations, with herbs and with spirits, with symptoms and with personal quarrels. So, we have treatment of the body and its symptoms in a way that is inseparable from a set of actions that, in the United States, would be some combination of three elements: treatment in an internist's office, family therapy, and religious ritual.

Our discussion will be limited to the societies of eastern, central, and southern Africa where Bantu languages are genealogically related; the discussion is limited also to interactions that involve both the region's older, inherited religions and Christianity. Defining our subject in this way may seem unnecessarily restrictive, but in fact the subject matter is audaciously broad. It takes in regularities underlying societies where five or six hundred separate languages are spoken, and where several hundred million people occupy a land area as large as Europe and China combined. A synthesis over this huge area is possible because the languages are closely related to one another—as closely related as the Romance languages—and because the very fact that the languages are both so numerous and so deeply similar in vocabulary and syntax gives the specialized methodologies of historical linguistics great power. It is possible to study widely distributed cognate words that are inherited from common ancestral languages in order to identify classical verbal concepts. These, then, when elucidated with the help of comparative ethnography, suggest well-developed ancient structures of knowledge and society. For example, the root *-ganga*, for doctor or specialist, is pervasive across the Bantu-speaking world that extends from Cameroon to Tanzania and down to South Africa. Related to the verb *-vanga*, to make or do, it applies to all manner of specialists, both in the healing arts and beyond. Thus, in Western Bantu, *nganga mbuki* is a "doctor of medicine," *nganga nkisi*, a doctor of consecrated medicines (see p. 235), *nganga lufu*, a "doctor of the forge," or blacksmith, master of a highly revered specialty in the knowledge of iron smelting and forging. Catholic priests are called *Banganga Nzambi*, "doctors of God." The head of a Mungano guild of snake handlers would be called an *mganga Mungano*, doctor of Mungano. Throughout the wider region it is possible to trace verbal concepts and related nouns at the basis of cultural practices, social institutions, and technical inventions and their distribution.

As we have suggested, and as the further illustrations will detail, the notion that African knowledge in the pre-colonial centuries blended empirical discovery with moral legitimation (ancestors, spirits, priests) is pervasive. Sharp opposition of science and religion as we know it in the organization of these fields in the modern university is a reflection of post-Enlightenment assumptions that thoroughly secularize specialized scientific knowledge. Sub-Saharan African history of knowledge should prove very instructive in grasping the character of a way of apprehending the world that while it fosters knowledge for a variety of practical ends, is open to the continuous interaction between visible and invisible, worldly and sacralized realms.[5]

We sketch several examples from pre-colonial, colonial, and post-colonial African history to demonstrate this. The pre-colonial period ended early in small parts of southern Africa but continued in most of tropical Africa up to the 1880s, when Europeans formally partitioned the continent into colonial spheres, which began as markings on a map, to be occupied over several decades. The colonial era ended in the early 1960s, when most colonies gained independence, although some remained under white control or were engulfed in wars of independence for several decades more. "Post-colonial" is both a time period, following colonialism, and a set of political and cultural conditions among independent nation-states, which to varying degrees continue to experience (and struggle to change) colonial administrative and economic structures, along with languages, and attitudes that shape all aspects of life.

RITUALIZED IRON SMELTING IN UFIPA AND THE GREAT LAKES REGION

The integration of science and the spirits, the idea of technical actions that have a powerful symbolic valence, is an ancient one in the region of the Bantu languages. Historical archeologists have found the same kind of integration in their work on iron smelting in the regions near Lakes Victoria and Nyasa. The process of refining iron was one of great technical complexity, since it involved combining ore with charcoal under conditions that carefully controlled the flow of oxygen in order to reduce the ore by chemical action. Near Lake Victoria, the particular tree used in making the charcoal was rich in calcium and potassium, thus serving as a minor flux (a substance mixed with a metal to facilitate its fusion). Carefully chosen grasses were added to the furnace, and the grass char served to remove oxygen from the iron oxides, promoting the formation of an iron bloom through both chemical and mechanical processes. Similar grasses were found in very old furnaces near Lake Nyasa, showing (along with much other evidence) that the process is not a new one. These technical elements were integrated with symbolic-social ones, in a way that is similar to the therapeutic process. The efficacy of technical acts depended on the moral context in which they were performed. The furnace itself was shaped like the womb of a pregnant woman; air flow was controlled by its passage through phallic tuyeres (earthen nozzles entering the bottom of the furnace). The grasses and the species of charcoal tree had great symbolic significance. And the production process only worked if the men who worked at the furnace abstained from sex. In other words, the womb-furnace would produce its iron only if placed in the correct symbolic-moral-spiritual context.

The medical domain was similar. Healers were serious in their treatment of the technical side of healing the sick—they were careful, for example, in their choice and preparation of herbs. But herbal medicines in the wrong social and moral context stood as much chance of healing the sick person as the furnace did of producing iron when the smiths had violated the rule of abstinence.[6]

CENTRAL AFRICAN SHRINES AND RITUALLY DIRECTED ECOSYSTEMS

A similar emphasis on moral and symbolic ways of constituting technical acts can be found in many of the shrines of central Africa. Father Matthew Schoffeleers, a Catholic priest and distinguished anthropologist, has spoken of a "ritually-directed eco-system."[7] Shrine authorities, whose role might superficially be seen simply as arranging ritual forms of mediation between spiritual agents and those who attended the shrine, also sometimes had the job of regulating land use: of deciding when a field ought to be left fallow, when a stream ought to be closed to fishing, or when a particular agricultural practice was harmful to the fertility of the land. At the Bunda shrine, in central Malawi, the agents of the shrine had control over the process of burning old and dried-out vegetation, which was central to the preparation of the soil for a new farming season. The process of burning was technically complex. Colonial agricultural researchers took decades before they fully understood its significance. In Zambia, where a form of burning called *citemene* was practiced, agricultural officers found that "the fertilizing effects of ash were clearly important, but other things were happening when a citemene field was burned . . . the phosphate and potash status of the soil were enhanced by burning, and . . . freshly burnt soil also contained a high concentration of calcium that improved its physical condition. . . . Furthermore, burning appeared to have increased soil acidity, which meant that the added phosphates could be more easily maintained."[8] In Mozambique, a British naturalist found that control of disease-bearing insect pests depended on the timing and intensity of burning—something that could be achieved, in a coordinated way, only by either shrine authorities or political leaders. Once again, as with the healing of individual bodies (which also took place at some of the same shrines), we have a seamless integration of technical, moral, social, and symbolic acts. Not all of technical knowledge was integrated into such a domain. Just as people suffered from illnesses of God—illnesses that just happened, to be treated by herbs that just worked, with no shrine mediator or traditional healer—so farmers knew many techniques that just worked, in a pure (and rich) domain of practical knowledge.

Given these forms of social action, it is difficult to isolate a set of relations or beliefs that map, in some easy, predictable, and legible way, onto the domain of religion. Historians of religion tend to look for beliefs, and yet the healing practices and shrine practices, the ways of healing by reordering relations between the living and the ancestors, or the forms of therapeutic dance that brought people into a relationship with spirits, or the words spoken over chemically active grasses when they were put into an iron furnace—none of these actions came with explicit articles of faith. Words spoken to the grasses, songs sung at shrines, the gestures a healer makes when treating a patient, all can be read by scholarly analysts as implying certain relationships between humans and spirits, implying that the spirit world, approached in this way, has certain regularities. But the person doing the reading is the scholarly analyst. It is not a credo recited by a believer, nor is it a catechism to instruct, and measure the faithful obedience of, adherents.

Looking for beliefs in this context is problematic and vexed for a different reason. Rodney Needham, the British anthropologist, wrote a book addressed to the question of whether belief is an experience.[9] His exploration of the complexities and ambiguities of the word "belief" make it clear that the act of interpreting non-European practices in terms of belief is a profoundly problematic strategy—one that short-circuits more nuanced explorations of the ideas and assumptions embedded in ritual practice and the associated discourse, whether in African or European contexts.

The world of medicine, and more generally of knowledge for technical ends, presents an additional set of problems for anyone who wishes to isolate a domain of religion, or a set of generally accepted spiritual ideas, in the varied settings of the world where Bantu languages were spoken. It is that many varieties of knowledge are socially constituted. In societies with either no literacy, or very limited literacy, but with great quantities of technical, social, and aesthetic knowledge, complex bodies of knowledge were preserved, reproduced, and put into use by being divided among many holders. In many cases, the people who held knowledge were also interested participants in a process of political or social negotiation. For example, in the precolonial period in what is now Malawi, people resorted to the shrine of the Mbona spirit to deal with problems of epidemic, drought, and large-scale threats to survival and reproduction. The shrine house was itself a medicine-object, and it needed to be rebuilt at moments of great public crisis. But it could only be rebuilt through a process of political collaboration. Every major holder of political authority or influence in the region around the shrine needed to participate in the process of construction. Without this political collaboration, the parts would never fit together, and the shrine would lack efficacy.[10] In the Lower Congo region near the Atlantic Ocean, the objects known as *min'kisi*, used for healing illness (among other things), were seen as lacking in life until endowed with power through a complex process of social composition. In the most complex of these, a major ritual needed to be performed if the object was to be endowed with power. This involved many different holders of knowledge and many different performers of ritual and practical action. People could not endow the objects with power without the spirits, but these could never be addressed except through the correct social process, which was also one in which specialized participants assembled knowledge that was otherwise divided and fragmented.[11]

This process of composing a medicine was a social negotiation, a way of addressing the spirits, a technical act, and an aesthetic performance, all at the same time. To insist on defining a distinct and bounded domain of religion, and another one of science, is under these circumstances counterproductive.

TREATING BODY PAINS IN WESTERN BANTU

In Western Bantu languages spoken along the western equatorial coast (from Cameroon to Angola), and inland from there, technosocial knowledge and problem solving crystallized, historically, around *min'kisi* (singular, *nkisi*). A range of historical evidence indicates that *min'kisi* have been part of this region's therapeutic landscape for at least a millennium, perhaps two. One of the present authors, Janzen, has at times defined the *nkisi* as a consecrated medicine, but this definition (like all simple definitions of this complex phenomenon) is inadequate. The concept needs to be unpacked piece by piece if it is to be understood.

Not all medicines are called *min'kisi*. An *nkisi* is the product of an interaction between the relevant substances or objects on the one hand and, on the other, a specialist with therapeutic or transformative capacities—that is, by an *nganga*. A simple plant that has not been treated, or invoked, or composed by an *nganga* is not an *nkisi*. Plants, whether treated or not, are called *minti* (trees or bushes) or *makaya* (leaves). A more general term for medicine is *bilongo*—natural ingredients that have been combined or treated in some way, though not necessarily by an *nganga*. The term *bilongo* includes combinations of plants compounded together, bottles of ointments, pills, injections, and other hospital medicines. What differentiates the *nkisi* from other medicines is not the ingredients but the relationship to the *nganga* and to the moment when the *nkisi*'s efficacy was brought into being.

Each *nkisi* has a remembered moment of origin, a charter that is necessary in signifying its efficacy and the nature of its powers. Each *nkisi*, each consecrated medicine, originated at some time in the past in an individual vision or in a relationship between an individual and a spiritual entity. The *nkisi*'s defining elements were fixed at that original moment of creation. These elements include recipes of ingredients (*bilongo*), techniques of composition and use, the songs, dances, and words without which its power would not exist, and the prohibitions that define proper and improper behavior for the person who operates the *nkisi* and the one who is treated with it. Generally, an *nkisi*'s ingredients were held in a container of some kind: a bag, a gourd, a sculpture, or a basket.

An *nkisi* is too "hot" to be handled by laymen. At the moment of origin it was properly handled by the ancestor who had invented it, and then by the *nganga* to whom it came through a chain of transmission, and who then taught it to an apprentice. If the *nganga* is to use it properly, he or she must be inaugurated in a relationship with the *nkisi*. Without this inauguration, without the proper relationship, the *nkisi* is dangerous and could cause madness.

It we look back at the history of *min'kisi*, we see that some appeared at moments of general societal crisis, moments when people felt that core social values were threatened. They were also used (and still are) for treating individual physical illness, like a stomach ache, or for an emotional, social, and spiritual crisis in an individual's life.

Min'kisi must be "composed" if they are to be effective—if they are to be living *min'kisi* and not simply inert objects. The act of composition may be modest, as when an individual *nganga* combines herbal medicines and invokes their power, or they can be enormously complex, involving a great many people. Massive ritual organizations—large-scale associations that played a practical role in regulating markets and organizing politics—could also have as their central purpose the composition of an *nkisi*. One such large association was Lemba, an association that existed in western equatorial Africa from the seventeenth century on. The characteristic way to join such an association was to become ill: one needed to be initiated in order to be healed. People's careers as individuals suffering from affliction, and as healers, progressed in a seamlessly unified way. Each act of initiation into a more responsible level in the association was also a therapeutic act meant to treat an illness. The large-scale rituals in which people came together, with drumming and dancing, were also, at the same time, the actual act of composing an *nkisi* and giving it efficacy. In the case of Lemba, which thrived at the time of the trade in slaves, in copper, and in ivory, the healing association also provided some elements of public security. Senior *banganga* kept peace at marketplaces, even in locations where no centralized political authority was able to guarantee security. People whose kinship groups were weak, or who were cut off from relatives altogether, could have a "mother" or "father" in Lemba.

Min'kisi are, thus, not one simple kind of object, but a whole rich world of objects that can act effectively on individual bodies and on social situations, the only irreducible requirements being that they must be composed (*handa*) and that each one needs to have some kind of relationship to an *nganga*. The history of the past 450 years is thus a complex story of a great many different *min'kisi* and of many different varieties of *banganga*. Different kinds of specialists have come into fashion, and gone out of it, over the years. Lemba, for example, no longer exists today. Over centuries, the main gatekeepers to the diverse universe of *banganga* were the diviners called *banganga Ngombo*. These days their role has diminished, and prophet-seers play a more central gatekeeping role. Some *banganga* have been narrowly specialized, like cupping-horn users, who appear to have been a constant over centuries, or the *nganga lunga*, who deals with conditions of the bones, the *nganga mpu*, who inaugurates a chief, the *nganga mukoko*, who cures women's infertility, the *nganga mpansu*, who deals with mental illness, and so forth. Others are generalists; the *nganga nkisi* is supposed to know about all medicines. The inventory, over those 450 years of recorded history, is stunningly rich.

Any one variety of *nkisi* might also change over time. *Nkisi Makongo*, for example, appears in documentation over three centuries as a main treatment for *lubanzi*, literally "side," or "stitch-in-the-side."[12] The condition appears not just in the side but in the neck and shoulder area. It corresponds to what we might call tension in the back, shoulder, or neck, or to headache. *Nkisi Makongo* has not been exactly the same thing over the three centuries for which we have records. In the 1960s and 1970s, when Janzen was doing field research, patients and their caregivers sometimes explained it in terms of organic symptoms ("pneumonia," "crossing of the ribs," "bad blood") and sometimes in terms of interpersonal aggression or tension (and in this case not to be treated in hospitals or clinics). In the early twentieth century (and also earlier), *Nkisi Makongo* was represented by a statue of a human. Today, *Makongo* figures are found in museums, with wedges and nails driven into the shoulders, sides, and neck, each one for a case that was treated by the *nganga* who owned the *Makongo* statue. Each iron wedge is thus a vivid memento of pain, aggression, and treatment.

By the 1960s, *Makongo* statues no longer played any role in the treatment of *lubanzi*. At that time, discussions of *lubanzi* between *banganga* and Janzen revealed a subtle logic of diagnosis and treatment, of a kind that may have existed earlier but is difficult to perceive by simply looking at the statues and reading the sources. *Banganga* saw the process of treatment and diagnosis as unfolding over time. They began by treating the physical symptoms, through massage and tranquilizing medicines to remove the pain or the stitch. If these treatments worked, it was confirmed that the case was merely physiological. Sometimes even a hospital treatment worked for the disease, if it did not involve some form of human aggression. If treatments of the symptoms did not work, the failure led to the conclusion that some sort of human conflict was involved. The stages of treatment echoed the progression of the disease. *Lubanzi* was seen as progressing from superficial causes (involving muscles and joints), which might be addressed directly, to internal ones, affecting the heart as a moral-emotional center, and the very being of the individual. If *lubanzi* was not treated early—if its progression was not arrested—then the illness might go on to be destructive of the heart, taken as the self, and might lead ultimately to madness, perhaps to death.

We have already seen in the case of Lemba that it was possible for people to create an *nkisi* that had an ongoing life as a form of collective action—a life that was more than the sum of individual treatments. *Min'kisi* of this kind were characterized by the people of the region as "drums" (in Kongo, *ngoma*, *nkonko*, or *n'konzi*). In the Kongo way of seeing things, "drums" are a particular form taken by corporate groups, the members of which come together for periodic ceremonies, whereas simpler *min'kisi* are the focus of treatments that draw people together on an ad hoc basis. "Drums" are also a large-scale collective process by which *min'kisi* are composed. "Drums" are multifunctional, whereas a standard *nkisi* has only a single function. Most important of all, the "drum" took on an institutional life of its own. It had a continuing group membership, with its own forms of recruitment, the purpose of which was to achieve individual and collective health.

The name or central characteristic of the "drum" related to a particular mode of affliction, and membership consisted of fellow sufferers with this common affliction who, in drawing together, produced a bond, a social contract. Those afflicted or recruited and cured or stabilized in their relationship to the sickness—be it reproductive disorders, hernias, alienation, twins, entrepreneurial zeal—were considered best suited to become specialized *banganga* of the ailment for which the drum was known. Sickness was often seen as a sacred calling, manifested as possession by a spirit of a former drum member. If the possessing sickness was placated, the disease brought under control, recovery at once purified and energized the individual, placing him in debt to the group, which henceforth expected him to consecrate his newly found gifts as medium in this specialized domain to the service of others. The ingenious quality of the historic, fully incorporated drum is that it reproduced a set of intellectual and performative understandings of disease; it presented those who were afflicted with the support necessary for sustaining treatment and with support in the more general tasks of life.

The healing associations, or "drums," as ongoing institutions based on shared affliction and mutual support, still exist today over wide areas of the Bantu-speaking region, although in many places they now coexist with (or have in some cases been supplanted by) healing churches that have many of the same characteristics: group identity, recruitment through affliction, an emphasis on mutual support, and an ongoing purpose in individual and collective health.

The Kongo (and, more widely, western equatorial African) vision of health that stood behind the continuum of medicines has been expertly formulated by Mahaniah.[13] We have seen that it included (and still includes) individual plants (*nti, makaya*), compounded medicines (*bilongo*), consecrated medicines and actions (*min'kisi*), and, at the largest collective level, corporate therapeutic associations (*ngoma,* or *nkonko*). When sickness occurred, community members were mobilized to find a rapid and effective solution, including above all the reestablishment of the subject's equilibrium. This treatment aimed to purify the community and, with the return of harmony, to guarantee general well-being. These practices, at once religious and medical, were seen as an intervention involving supernatural forces and natural processes, all bound up together. Thus, to treat a sufferer was not only to reestablish his physical normality but also to re-create the order characterized by social and ritual harmony. A harmonious society is one in which there are no social conflicts, no sicknesses, no disasters, epidemics, or premature deaths.

The western equatorial African *nkisi* thus played a substantial social role, sometimes alongside political authority, in centralized kingdoms or chiefdoms. In modern states, it served sometimes as a source of public order in the absence of sovereign centralization, and sometimes (in relation to states) as a place where alternative social visions—a semi-autonomous sphere of critique—have been located. The *nkisi*'s role was, at one and the same time, technical and moral, political and intimately personal; it was related to productive technologies like iron working and forms of environmental control in agriculture and hunting, and was capable of dealing with moral threats, like aggression and infertility, and with broad social change (like the overseas mercantile trade of the seventeenth century). Partly because of its capacity for carving out a partially autonomous political sphere, and partly because its vision of the world mapped partially (and however imperfectly) onto Western conceptions of religion, *min'kisi* came under attack in the colonial period. Colonialism's moral agents (missionaries) and its power brokers (colonial officials), along with the dictates of the head tax and forced labor, overwhelmed this system of knowledge. Anything having to do with *min'kisi* and operated by *banganga* was branded as heathen and superstitious and was attacked, uprooted, defamed. We will see how the

West's categories of religion and science (especially medicine) were imposed upon a more integrated African civilization—one whose functional domains of knowledge differed from European ones.

COLONIAL MISSIONARIES AND "MIDDLE FIGURES"

A separate domain of religion certainly exists in Africa today, but this was, to a very considerable extent, created through an interaction between Africans and missionaries, through complex processes, in many different places and many different ways. At the same time, missionaries struggled to define an appropriate role for medicine, as a secular European science within a Christian tradition of healing. Terence Ranger describes the "medical modernization" undertaken by the Universities' Mission to Central Africa (today Tanzania) as an all-out initiative to provide scientific education for African dispensers and nurses as a means of counteracting indigenous practices.[14] The missionaries were joined in this effort to create new domains of "science" and "religion" by African lay evangelists, teachers, nurses, auxiliary medical workers, and (in some places) even priests. Historians of Africa have come increasingly to appreciate the crucial role played by these people, often defined as "middle figures," in Nancy Hunt's term.[15] People in these positions were fully grounded in their own African societies and had an intuitive understanding of local social practices that Europeans could never achieve, yet they also had an understanding of European goals and ways of doing things. These middle figures were often devoted, in their own right, to the propagation of Western medicine and the Christian religion, but they understood how to advance these goals in ways very different from missionary approaches.

For Africans subjected to proselytization in the early colonial period, conversion did not mean the simple acceptance of one set of religious beliefs or practices in place of another, nor was it only a matter of re-mapping conceptual or functional domains (making religion something distinct from therapeutics). In the central highlands of Kenya, when the Gikuyu came to engage with European missionaries and missionary doctors, they needed first to relate to a network of social relations, spirits, and objects in a new and different way—to disentangle themselves from old relationships, to deal more frequently with objects that needed to be treated as though they were inert. What in Kongo would have been called "dead" *min'kisi*—that is, *min'kisi* that had not been activated by ritual performance, mere objects that did not have the power to transform human bodies, lives, and relationships— these dead things were said by missionaries to have the power to cure. Gikuyu were subjected to a cultural regime in which individuals needed to

become disentangled from the social webs in which knowledge was preserved and selfhood, health, and illness defined. It is for this reason (the
need to disentangle) that the first converts in eastern Africa were usually
people who had been cut off from their families. Missionaries worked to
transform subjectivity through the construction of villages of square-
cornered houses, in rows (in place of round ones in clusters), and through
the introduction of clocks so that the day's work and prayer could be coordinated through the mechanical management of time. "Structuring the mundane in time and space thus helped define the subjective, personal space of
belief."[16]

Meanwhile, the missionaries worked, as they saw it, to unearth (in part,
actually, to invent) a Gikuyu conception of God, so as a to constitute a religion with belief at its center. The historian who has worked to interpret the
words and meaningful gestures of Gikuyu of that period explains that in the
period before conquest Ngai, "God," was neither the cause nor the cure of
most illnesses, which were entangled in relationships at a more intimate
level. Every now and then people sacrificed to Ngai when misfortune struck
on a scale that was too large to be controlled by ordinary methods of reordering relationships among people or between people and ancestors. At the
wider environmental boundary between the dynamic wilderness on the one
hand and land controlled by fluidly interacting social groups on the other,
people were forced to gamble, to take a chance on Ngai. A broad famine or
epidemic proved that ordinary means of control did not work, and so people
were compelled to roll the dice—to make a gesture to Ngai. Missionaries
interpreted these dynamic and contingent gestures to Ngai as a timeless
form of worship—one expressive of belief. One missionary reported a conversation, in 1911, in which people argued that speaking of Ngai would
make them sad, for this was a subject about which people thought when
rains fail or when "people are in sorrow or pain."[17]

Derek Peterson, the historian who has studied this process most closely
among Gikuyu, explains:

> Missionaries sought to turn Gikuyu social praxis toward the atemporal cate-
> gories of ritual and religion. By representing creative, dangerous practices as
> timeless ceremonies, by dividing up human activities with clocks and fences,
> by judging human actions with immutable laws, missionaries worked to
> create a mechanical world, a society governed by rules. . . . The textualization
> of social life, the rendering of process into religious ritual and law, was as
> much a colonization of Gikuyu society as were the great moments of military
> conquest.[18]

Peterson and Paul Landau (in this case writing about people in early colonial Botswana) both argue that missionary medical practices were a part of
this deeper conversion of subjectivity. According to Landau,

Tswana specialists in healing (*dingaka*, a cognate of *banganga*) immersed
themselves in those experiential relationships that, epitomized by the ancestors, *defined and united persons within their community*. In contrast, . . . missionaries' therapeutic practice tended to *disrupt this prior community* and substitute
for it the idea of the individual as enclosing the relevant field of sickness/
wellness.[19]

In Botswana, missionary healers of the early twentieth century learned to
speak of the body in mechanical terms, of digestion as a "manufacturing
plant" and the heart as a "force pump," and this, too, served to locate illness
in the individual body (consisting of quasi-mechanical parts). This strategy
did not, however, constitute a thoroughgoing attempt to secularize medicine, since illness was linked to sin and healing to God's mercy. The result
was, however, a transformation of older African ideas about links between
illness and impropriety or hurtfulness. The key change was that the sinner,
as described by the missionaries, was an individual, extracted from his or
her community, whereas older practices placed the broad web of relationships at the heart of both illness and therapy.[20] We have already seen that
this process of individualization, and of making objects (even parts of the
body) seem inert and mechanical, was also necessary if people were to begin
speaking with missionaries about individual belief as a basis for religion.

Christian medical treatment as extraction from community was, however, only a transitional moment. Both Landau and William Tuesday Kalusa
(writing about Mwinilunga District, in Zambia) describe how converts
worked with great energy to create therapeutic Christian communities
within mission churches. In Botswana *baruti*, African evangelists, introduced group prayer for illness and "dealt with troubled or sick people as
members of the Christian *community*," in a way that had not been a part of
missionary practice.[21] Zambian Christians did much the same thing. All-
night collective prayer vigils for the sick became a part of Christian practice
in both places. Today in Mwinilunga, group prayer has been integrated into
mission hospital practice as an essential ingredient immediately before a
patient is treated. In other words, in Zambia, Botswana, and many other
places, African patients were extracted from their communities but then
later chose to integrate themselves into new kinds of healing communities.
The people who were crucial in this creative process were the middle figures:
the African evangelists, nurses, and teachers who had a rich understanding
of both missionary practice and practice within their own local communities and who therefore had the necessary knowledge for creating novel
social forms.[22]

The process by which missionaries defined a domain of religion, revolving as it did around questions of belief, also had the effect of separating out—placing in a very different category—those aspects of inherited

therapeutics that deal with spiritual beings. We have seen that among the Kongo, as in many parts of the Bantu-speaking region, *min'kisi* are powerful, in part, because of their links to the ancestors who first created them. The centrality of community relations in older forms of healing—the necessity to cure the patient by reordering his or her social relations—was not limited to relationships with the living. The effective community includes also family members who have died. The dead comprise another, more distant, class of elders. In some languages, the word for ancestor is identical to the word for a living elder.[23] We can see, in this case, that a therapeutic intervention that addresses the patient's body, while reordering his or her network of social relations, necessarily involves both the living and the dead.

When European observers, missionaries, and administrators separated out therapeutic relations from social ones, they also, at the same time, created a world of African religion separate from the therapeutic or technological practices that had always been in an integral, undifferentiated relationship with the ancestors and other spiritual beings. The politics of African resistance in the early colonial period guaranteed that this new split between healing and religion would be a sharp one—an enormous gulf separating aspects of what had been either a single phenomenon or perhaps a tightly focused cluster of related phenomena.

European conquerors, during the first two decades of colonial rule, faced enormous rebellions by Africans who saw European rule as a threat to their own reproduction and survival. Europeans, puzzled by the coordination of political and military action on a huge scale, across lines of language and culture, focused on the role of public healers: people who specialized in therapy, in actions to increase fertility and well-being, but who did not limit themselves to individual illnesses, instead treating armies, chiefdoms, and whole territories. The great uprising in 1895–96 that almost drove the British and South Africans from what is now Zimbabwe, the similarly powerful threat posed to German East Africa by the Maji Maji Rebellion of 1905–7, and the uprisings in the name of Nyabingi in western Uganda all provoked similar responses among Europeans. The colonizers emphasized the roles of spirit mediums, shrine priests, and other similar leaders. The region's new rulers characterized these leaders as practitioners of irrational religions (of "witchcraft") and passed laws making everything these people did illegal. In the relevant Tanzanian ordinance, for example, the definition of the punishable offense included "the purported possession of any occult power."[24] What had been integrated practices—for treating bodies and the body politic, for dealing with material-technical substances and with the ancestors— now fragmented, with missionaries and Muslim leaders taking care of the domain of "religion" and local-level traditional healers, along with a few scattered hospitals and dispensaries, representing "medicine." Medicine and religion are therefore, in their current forms, the creations of colonial-period crises and transformations.

POST-COLONIAL INTEGRATED AFRICAN COSMOLOGIES

In this section we consider post-colonial scholars, practitioners, educational administrators, scientists, and therapists who strive to integrate something of the ancestral holistic cosmology with biomedical knowledge and cosmo-politan professionalism. They provide a fascinating commentary within a larger scientific-religious field with many different points of view. Priests in mainline churches, professionals educated to a secondary or university level, and many others often adopt an approach similar to the North American or Western European one: that science and religion are at one level rigorously separate domains, while at another level we all struggle with zones of tension and interpenetration. In the medical fields, most hospitals across the continent enforce policies that rigorously exclude the practice of traditional medicine, while some integrate Christian (or Muslim) prayer into their daily routines. Beyond this, a small minority of Christian churches—a subset of those whose principles and practice have been rein-vented locally—exclude both biomedicine and traditional medicine and rely exclusively on healing through community prayer and through the charisma of church leaders.

A very interesting and important set of intellectuals, scattered across many countries, reflect on this larger scene and respond by attempting to forge an original and characteristically African synthesis of science and religion. The scholars quoted early in this essay have emphasized that any at-tempt to reconnect historic knowledge with modern science in Africa must be part of universal science in order to be credible. The issues at stake in such a reconnecting are ably sketched by the contemporary Ghanaian phi-losopher Kwame Gyekye, who has studied the history of the relationship of thought, technology, and religion in pre-colonial and post-colonial Africa.[25] Gyekye asks, from his post-colonial point of view, how the African sciences can be brought into harmony with Western science. Generally, in his remarks, he notes the extensive and original developments of African agri-culture, medicine, and various technologies, all rooted in empirical innova-tions and adaptations. What has generally been missing in the pre-colonial tradition when seen from the point of view of Western science, in Gyekye's account, is the emergence of scientific theory that builds knowledge for its own sake and allows for the variety of abstract reasoning characteristic of modern science. He points out that the prevalence of secrecy in African traditional knowledge is a hindrance to such scientific development. While acknowledging the rich empirical observations and practical techniques of African arts, Gyekye suggests that the tendency to ascribe knowledge to spiritual agents must be dealt with in order to reconcile this knowledge with the hallmarks of modern science, namely experimentation and sustained investigation.[26] We will review a number of contemporary African scholars, practitioners, and administrators who seek to reconcile universal science with African medicinal traditions.

The late Rwandan scholar and physician Pierre-Claver Rwangabo offers an insight into contemporary African thinking on illness causation. Even though not all aspects of the Rwandan medicine system are amenable to modern science, Rwangabo believes that it is a part of modern reality rather than a fossil.[27] He divides medicine into "physical" and "mystical" causes. Diseases range across a variety of types that may be attributed to either causal category or to both. Rwangabo's medical training is evident in his listing of disease classes that include parasitic diseases, microbial diseases, systemic diseases and bodily accidents, gynecological and obstetrical diseases, and psycho-mental and behavioral diseases. But under the latter group he identifies current psychopathologies that entail abnormal behavior as understood in traditional thought and diseases believed to be caused by broken prohibitions and beliefs about ancestors (*abazimu*) and other spirits (*ibitega, amahembe, nyabingi, amashitani, amajini*) often identified in relation to mental illnesses. "Poisoning," the result of human aggression, is a major aspect of the human source of misfortune. Misfortunes brought on by the breach of social rules also have a mystical though not necessarily mysterious causal character. Rwangabo's insight into the character of traditional medicine lies in the observation that most pathologies may have both a physical and a mystical dimension. This affects the way therapy will be arranged. The decision to seek physical or other therapy has to do with the context in which it occurs, its severity, the suspected human etiology, and response to treatment.

Byamungu lua Lufungula is a Congolese pharmacist with a medicinal factory in Bukavu and pharmacies in Uvira and Goma. He works with healers, and in this region of extensive pastoralism some of these healers are veterinarians. He has adapted African materia medica, making them commercially saleable. In his scholarship he has also studied the healing cults of the region; thus his interests cover a broad therapeutic spectrum, from herbal medicines to spirit possession cults. Does his emulation of the West's secular pharmaceutical approach to healers' medicines compromise the integrated character of this knowledge? His French training in pharmacy gives his pharmaceutical inventions scientific legitimacy, yet his writing and work with healers anchors him in a broader integrated cosmology.

Philip Guma is one of the new South Africa–educated elites who integrates the traditional knowledge of the initiated (*sangoma, igqira*) as well as
Western university education. He teaches at the University of the Western
Cape in Cape Town. His doctoral research explored the relationship of childhood malnutrition and the well-being of the soul of a child in the eyes of
mothers, nurses, and healers in Khayelitsha, South Africa.[28] Guma's study
deals with the social interpretation of childhood diarrhea among the Xhosa-
speaking people of the Western Cape. It highlights how in this area political
consciousness and moralist discourses strongly influence relationships
between different health care systems and the production of continuing
conflicts around problems of health care delivery. It argues that if meaningful relationships can be found between older African social health-seeking
strategies and biomedical classifications of enteric and other diseases of
women and children, they could facilitate the provision of more equitable,
effective, and widely acceptable health care.

Furthermore, Guma's study compares the etiological explanations of
childhood illness signs and symptoms adopted by non-elite mothers and by
health practitioners of two kinds: professional nurses trained in biomedicine, and indigenous African health practitioners (IHPs). The comparison
focuses particularly on the interpretation of stool quality and associated
symptoms. For stool quality the study refers to the color and texture of children's feces that mothers and health practitioners identify and associate
with distinctive conditions of affliction. There is variation, even ambiguity,
in the interpretation of commonly understood illness categories and with
respect to diarrheal illnesses. Knowledge remains contested between
mothers and professional nurses. Moreover, the availability of a wide range
of therapeutic options in Khayelitsha diversifies the mother's causal explanations. It was found this diversity in causality and management of illnesses
is manifested in the quality of children's stools, "green" feces in particular.
Their interpretations draw on senses of value, ideas, social histories, different forms of power, systematic knowledge, and a great variety of other
forms of significance that are embedded in the concrete domains of everyday life. In addition to the notion of *isuntu* (that is, humaneness), the study
more importantly reveals that among Nguni of the Western Cape a tripartite
relationship of *umoya* (vital force), *inyongo* (gallbladder), and *ithongo* (ancestral dream) is the dynamic philosophical component that describes Nguni
experiences of health and illness.

Sidonie Matokot-Mianzenza is a trained psychotherapist in Brazzaville
who has tried to come to terms with the dark side of modern warfare, in
particular the use of sexual violence as a weapon.[29] She worked with many
women and girls who had been raped and impregnated by strangers during
Brazzaville's civil war of the 1990s. She found that the most effective way of

dealing with these traumas was through traditional kin therapy supported by both older women and female peers, with the approval of male elders who had the capacity to legitimize the women's actions. It is clear from historical records concerning kinship therapy all across eastern and central Africa that healers and families have long had effective and carefully structured methods for reintegrating, and embracing, people who are deeply wounded and who, without this therapy, might be treated as morally inferior. Matokot-Mianzenza's book concludes with a discussion of whether the relationship of traditional therapy to Western psychotherapy is "competitive" or "complementary."

One of the most remarkable post-colonial synthesizers was the university founder and scholar Kimpianga Mahaniah, of Luozi, Lower Congo, Democratic Republic of Congo. The Université Libre de Luozi (ULL) is one of several dozen new universities in the DRC that either grew up out of the rubble of the National University or arose as altogether new creations.[30] These new universities are decidedly local efforts, the work of loyal and determined supporters—teachers, landowners, merchants, churches— often with the support of national and foreign nongovernmental organizations. Although Mahaniah lives and works in his home community, his education is solidly cosmopolitan, in Protestant mission schools of Lower Congo and at Temple University in Philadelphia, where he received his Ph.D. in history. The ULL, under Mahaniah's direction, has concentrated on agriculture, commerce, development, and the environment. Outreach has also played an important role in this university through the Centre de Vulgarisation Agricole, which stages short-term conferences and publishes relevant pamphlets and books on the work of the university.[31] Mahaniah's own research on the history of Christianity in the region seeks to integrate the historical place of missions with ancestral religion and practical knowledge.[32] Yet in the early twenty-first century the ULL has a decidedly practical aspect to it, rooted at one and the same time in the sciences, in up-to-date electronic technology, and also in local ecological knowledge about ancestral lands and other assets that must be protected for future generations. One reaches Luozi best by small aircraft—or by the Internet. Once there, one can enjoy the ambiance of an African village or retreat to a forest preserve that features the herbarium of trees and medicinal plants.

These Western-trained African scholars and practitioners, all of whom bridge the science/religion continuum, emphasize the context of the causal attribution that makes all the difference in how sufferers, their therapy managers, diviners, healers, and medical practitioners will treat illness. If the misfortune is considered to be ordinary and predictable, it will be seen as a phenomenon of the material world. If catastrophic forces or circumstances have precipitated it, or if it seems to be the result of the chaos of underlying affairs in the human and mystical realm, it must be handled differently. Thus the same condition may need to be treated with different medicines. The first realm we might term "natural," the second "unnatural." But this very recognizably African way of thinking requires closer examination so that we do not simply read into it the influences of Western thinking.

The African scholarly universe appears to be open to acceptance of religion and science in the same framework, all the while many African scientists adhere to the Western separation of science from religion. It would appear that the moral and humanistic envelope of knowledge that integrates science and religion may well be a genuine contribution of African tradition to the world community.

Notes

1. Feierman's research shows that people in Lushoto District, in northeastern Tanzania, make this distinction in the Shambaa language. See also John Janzen, *Quest for Therapy in Lower Zaire* (Berkeley: University of California Press, 1978), 8; and Wyatt MacGaffey, *Art and Healing of the Bakongo Commented by Themselves* (Bloomington: Indiana University Press, 1991), 9. For the same distinction in Malawi, among Tumbuka, see Steve Friedson, *Dancing Prophets: Musical Experience in Tumbuka Healing* (Chicago: University of Chicago Press, 1996), 40–42.

2. Paulin J. Hountondji, *African Philosophy: Myth and Reality* (Bloomington: Indiana University Press, 1983), 98–100; V. Y.Mudimbe, *The Invention of Africa: Gnosis, Philosophy, and the Order of Knowledge* (Bloomington: Indiana University Press, 1988), xi; Kwame Gyekye, "Philosophy, Culture, and Technology in the Postcolonial," in *Postcolonial African Philosophy: A Critical Review*, ed. Emmanuel Chukwudi Eze, 25–44 (Oxford: Blackwell, 1997).

3. Cheikh Anta Diop, *Towards the African Renaissance: Essays in African Culture and Development, 1946–1960* (London: Karnak House, 1996); Placide Tempels, *Bantu Philosophy* (Paris: Presence Africaine, 1959).

4. Kai Kresse, "Knowledge: An Overview," *New Encyclopedia of Africa*, vol. 3, ed. John Middleton and Joe Miller, 152 (New York: Charles Scribner's Sons, 2008). As if acceding to the view that this African knowledge is not science, the *New Encyclopedia of Africa*, as the latest word among scholars of Africa, carries no entry on science.

5. See, e.g., the Dwight Harrington Terry Foundation's lecture series on Religion in the Light of Science and Philosophy, which recently included Mary Douglas's *Thinking in Circles: An Essay on Ring Composition*, (New Haven, Conn.: Yale University Press, 2007). The invocation reads: " . . . [not the simple] promotion of scientific investigation and discovery, but rather the assimilation and interpretation of that which has been or shall be hereafter discovered, and its application to human welfare, especially by the building of the truths of science and philosophy into the structure of a broadened and purified religion."

6. Bertram Baltasar Mapunda, "An Archaeological View of the History and Variation of Ironworking in Southwestern Tanzania" (Ph.D. diss., University of Florida, 1995); Peter R. Schmidt, *Iron Technology in East Africa* (Bloomington: University of Indiana Press, 1997), 58, 60, 76, 81, 86, 90, 93, 94, 115, 121, 216–21, 225. 227, 228. See also Eugenia W. Herbert, *Iron, Gender, and Power: Ritual Transformation in African Societies* (Bloomington: Indiana University Press, 1993).

7. Matthew Schoffeleers, ed., *Guardians of the Land: Essays on Central African Territorial Cults* (Gwelo: Mambo Press, 1979), Introduction, 3. Feierman does not fully agree with the idea that this was a ritually directed ecosystem, since many of the elements of control came from commonly accepted knowledge and only some were imposed by ritual authorities. But this idea is nevertheless a useful one.

8. On the Bunda shrine, see Schoffeleers, *Guardians*, 3; Matthew Schoffeleers, "The Religious Significance of Bush Fires in Malawi," *Cahiers des religions africaines* 5 (1969), 271–82. See also Henrietta L. Moore and Megan Vaughan, *Cutting Down Trees: Gender, Nutrition, and Agricultural Change in the Northern Province of Zambia, 1890–1990* (Portsmouth, N.H.: Heinemann, 1994), 28–30.

9. Rodney Needham, *Belief, Language, and Experience* (Oxford: Blackwell, 1972).

10. Matthew Schoffeleers, *River of Blood: The Genesis of a Martyr Cult in Southern Malawa, c. A.D. 1600* (Madison: University of Wisconsin Press, 1992), 6ff.; Matthew Schoffeleers, "The Story of a Scapegoat King in Rural Malawi," in *The Quest for Fruition through Ngoma: Political Aspects of Healing in Southern Africa*, ed. Rijk van Dijk, Ria Reis, and Maria Spierenburg, 99–116 (Oxford: James Currey, 2000). For a detailed and explicit example of social composition, see Steven Feierman, "On Socially Composed Knowledge: Reconstructing a Shambaa Royal Ritual," in *In Search of a Nation: Histories of Authority and Dissidence in Tanzania*, ed. Gregory Maddox and James Giblin (London: James Currey, 2005). For an early article on social composition, see Jane Guyer and Samuel M. Eno Belinga, "Wealth in People as Wealth in Knowledge: Accumulation and Composition in Equatorial Africa," *Journal of African History* 36 (1995): 91–120.

11. Wyatt MacGaffey, ed., *Art and Healing of the Bakongo* (Stockholm: Folkens Museum–Etnografiska), 95; John M. Janzen, *Lemba, 1650–1930: A Drum of Affliction in Africa and the New World* (New York: Garland, 1982); Wyatt MacGaffey, *Astonishment and Power* (Washington, D.C.,: National Museum for African Art of the Smithsonian Institution, 1993); John M. Janzen and Wyatt MacGaffey, eds., *An Anthology of Kongo Religion: Primary Texts from Lower Zaire* (Lawrence: University of Kansas Publications in Anthropology, no. 5, 1974).

12. John M. Janzen, "Lubanzi: The History of a Kongo Disease," in *African Health and Healing Systems: Proceedings of a Symposium*, ed. P. Stanley Yoder, 107–19 (Los Angeles: Crossroads Press, 1982).

13. Kimpianga Mahaniah, *La Maladie et la Guerison en Milieu Kongo* (Kinshasa: Centre de Vulgarisation Agricole, 1982), 29.

14. Terence O. Ranger, "Godly Medicine: The Ambiguities of Medical Missions in Southeastern Tanzania, 1900–1945," 274, in *The Social Basis of Health and Healing in Africa*, ed. Steven Feierman and John M. Janzen, 256–82 (Berkeley: University of California Press, 1992).

15. Nancy Hunt, *A Colonial Lexicon: Of Birth Ritual, Medicalization, and Mobility in the Congo* (Durham, N.C.: Duke University Press, 1999).

16. Derek Peterson, "Gambling with God: Rethinking Religion in Colonial Central Kenya," in *The Invention of Religion: Rethinking Belief in Politics and History*, ed. Derek Peterson and Darren Walhof, 42 (New Brunswick, N.J.: Rutgers University Press, 2002). See also Jean Comaroff and John Comaroff, *Of Revelation and Revolution* (Chicago: University of Chicago Press, 1991), vol. 2, on missionaries' material practices as a way of transforming African ways of experiencing the social order and individual subjectivity.

17. Peterson, "Gambling with God," 46.

18. Ibid., 45.

19. Paul S. Landau, "Explaining Surgical Evangelism in Colonial Southern Africa: Teeth, Pain and Faith," *Journal of African History* 37 (1996): 263.

20. Paul S. Landau, *The Realm of the Word: Language, Gender, and Christianity in a Southern African Kingdom* (Portsmouth, N.H.: Heinemann; 1995), chap. 5. On mechanical parts, see 121.

21. Ibid., 127.

22. William Tuesday Kalusa, "Disease and the Making of Missionary Medicine in Colonial Northwestern Zambia: A Case Study of Mwinilunga District, 1902–1964" (Ph.D. diss., Johns Hopkins University, 2003), 207–8, 216; Landau, *Realm of the Word*, 129. The dental image of extraction from community is from Landau's account of Botswana, where early nonmedical missionaries pulled teeth as part of their daily activity; see Landau, "Explaining Surgical Evangelism."

23. Igor Kopytoff, "Ancestors as Elders in Africa," *Africa: Journal of the International African Institute* 41 (1971): 129–42.

24. Tanganyika Territory, "An ordinance to provide for the Punishment of Witchcraft and of Certain Acts connected therewith," Ordinance no. 33 of 1928, vol. 9, no. 61 (December 28, 1928), supplement 1, 157–60. This account is drawn from Steven Feierman, "Colonizers, Scholars, and the Creation of Invisible Histories," in *Beyond the Cultural Turn: New Directions in the Study of Society and Culture*, ed. Lynn Hunt and Victoria Bonnell (Berkeley: University of California Press, 1999). See also Steven Feierman, "Healing as Social Criticism in the Time of Colonial Conquest," *African Studies* (Johannesburg) 54 (1995): 73–88.

25. Gyekye, "Philosophy, Culture, and Technology," 25–44.

26. Ibid., 27.

27. Pierre-Claver Rwangabo, *La médecine traditionnelle au Rwanda* (Paris: Karthala, 1993).

28. Phillip Mthobeli Guma, *The Politics of Umoya: Variation in the Interpretation and Management of Diarrheal Illnesses among Mothers, Professional Nurses, and Indigenous Health Practitioners in Khayelitsha, South Africa* (Ph.D. diss., University of North Carolina at Chapel Hill, 1998).

29. Sidonie Matokot-Mianzenza, *Viol des femmes dans les conflits armés et thérapies familiales: Cas du Congo Brazzaville* (Paris: L'Harmattan, 2003).

30. http://www.nekongo.org/uni_luozi/index.htm

31. Bahelele K. Ndimisina, *Bingana bia Nsi Eto* [Proverbs and sayings of our country] (Kinshasa: Editions Centre de Vulgarisation Agricole, 1989), a re-edition of a popular work on deep tradition by a well-known Protestant pastor; Dianzungu dia Biniakunu, *Nsi Yankatu Ngongo Eto: Tuzolele Nsi Yalubutu, Yantoko ye Yicilumukanga Maza* [We reject the loss of our land: we claim a land that is fruitful, beautiful, and

springs with water] (Kinshasa: Editions Centre de Vulgarisation Agricole, 1987), an ecological consciousness-raising analysis and polemic by a well-known high school teacher and administrator.

32. Kimpianga Mahaniah, *L'Impact du Christianisme au Manianga, 1880–1980* (Kinshasa: Editions Centre de Vulgarisation Agricole, 1988); *La Maladie et la Guérison en Milieu Kongo* (Kinshasa: Editions Centre de Vulgarisation Agricole, 1982).

11

Unbelief

Bernard Lightman

Richard Dawkins, a trained zoologist, has become one of the most celebrated popularizers of science of our time. Dawkins has explored the implications of evolutionary biology for traditional religious beliefs in many of
his works. In a recent book, *The God Delusion* (2006), Dawkins argues that
Darwin's theory of evolution by natural selection is "the ultimate scientific
consciousness-raiser" as it "shatters the illusion of design within the domain
of biology, and teaches us to be suspicious of any kind of design hypothesis
in physics and cosmology as well." According to Dawkins, Darwin showed
that the apparent design in nature was the "end product of a long sequence
of non-random but purely natural causes," of "graded ramps of slowly
increasing complexity."[1] Darwin's significance, then, lies in his demolition
of the design argument, the foundation of natural theology. Unabashedly
atheistic, Dawkins maintains that the proper conclusion to draw from the
current state of scientific knowledge is that unbelief is the most enlightened
position to embrace.

   Whereas Dawkins asserts that atheism lies at the heart of modern science, Sir Isaac Newton, the great hero of the seventeenth-century scientific
revolution, believed that the scientific study of nature revealed the existence
of universal laws of nature that could be grasped mathematically. The existence of natural law led, in turn, to the recognition that a creative deity had
provided an order to nature. The divine order could be found in the systematic arrangement of the heavens as well as in the designed, symmetrical
bodies of living beings. Newton declared that "this most beautiful system of
the sun, planets, and comets could only proceed from the counsel and
dominion of an intelligent and powerful Being." Atheism, however, according to Newton, was inimical to the scientific spirit. Newton wrote, "atheism
is so senseless and odious to mankind that it never had many professors."[2]
Many of Newton's contemporaries and fellow natural philosophers shared
his belief that theism and science were inextricably connected. Juxtaposing

Dawkins and Newton illustrates the dramatic shift that has occurred over the past three centuries in the ways that scientists, intellectuals, and the public perceive the implications of natural knowledge for religious belief. At some point the close link between science and theism in Newtonianism was severed, and science came to be associated with unbelief.

Dawkins's explanation for the change in the relationship between science and (un)belief is far too simplistic. Dawkins sees the construction of a powerful connection between science and unbelief as being due solely to Darwin's attack on the design argument. Although there is some truth to the notion that a critical shift took place in the age of Darwin, this insight holds true only for the British context. The real story is far more complex and must take into account the multiplicity of national contexts in which unbelief developed from the time of Newton. Darwin could not single-handedly undermine the theistic framework of science built upon Newtonianism. Moreover, it would take more than just a new scientific theory to make unbelief acceptable to members of the intellectual elite and the public.

In this essay I focus on the shifting relationship between science and unbelief since the seventeenth century, in particular forms of unbelief such as atheism and agnosticism. I will try to answer the question: When and where did unbelievers manage to instill into science ideas widely considered to be congenial to their attack on traditional religious institutions and beliefs? In other words, I will trace the history of how groups of intellectuals in different national contexts and at different times, forged the link between science and unbelief. Given the power of Newtonian science in the seventeenth century and beyond, this link had to be created in such a way that it seemed intellectually rigorous, philosophically necessary, and even profoundly natural. However, transforming the grounds of unbelief into a legitimate deduction from natural knowledge was not enough as long as individuals could be persecuted, even imprisoned, for adopting heterodox opinions. Unbelief had to become socially respectable. Only then could unbelief become a live option for members of the Western intelligentsia.[3]

The systematic construction of an alliance between science and unbelief was first attempted in the eighteenth century by radical Enlightenment thinkers in France. Their efforts were stymied by the power of Newtonianism. Since Newton had infused his theories with theistic concepts, reinterpretations of Newtonianism by those French Enlightenment thinkers could only go so far in providing intellectual legitimacy for unbelief. Heterodox opinions were also subject to legal sanctions in many countries in eighteenth-century Europe. Unbelievers had to be discreet or they faced imprisonment. Nevertheless, the theory of evolution by natural selection presented by Darwin in his *Origin of Species* (1859) became the Trojan horse within the fortress of science that opened it up to the forces of unbelief. Whereas radical Enlightenment thinkers were restrained by the theistic structure of Newtonianism, Darwin provided British unbelievers of the middle of the nineteenth century with the opportunity to refashion science from the ground up. For Darwin did not begin in the heavens with theistic presuppositions; rather, he and his British allies aimed to secularize nature. By making evolutionary theory the basis of a new science, unbelievers could argue—as Dawkins has—that an empirical examination of nature offers no evidence to support traditional religious beliefs. Moreover, Darwin's allies supplied unbelievers with a means for making their position socially acceptable. They rejected atheism and cultivated a new form of unbelief designed to maintain an aura of respectability. But the construction of a link between science and unbelief in British intellectual life could not be exported immediately to other national contexts. The creation of such a link did not take place in Russia and the United States until the twentieth century.

NEWTONIANISM, VOLTAIRE, AND THE MODERATE ENLIGHTENMENT

A devout Unitarian, Isaac Newton (1642–1727) believed that a cosmic order—a design—lay at the heart of nature. His theology shaped his conception of nature. Newton's mechanical universe, in which passive material was moved by a system of spiritual forces outside of matter, pointed to the existence of a providential creator who regulated and controlled nature. Newton explicitly connected natural philosophy to natural theology in the second edition of his *Opticks* (1717). Here he affirmed that the chief business of natural philosophy was to answer a series of questions, including "How came the Bodies of Animals to be contrived with so much Art, and for what ends were their several Parts? Was the Eye contrived without Skill in Opticks, and the Ear without Knowledge of Sounds?" He declared that the study of "Phænomena" suggested "there is a Being incorporeal, living, intelligent, omnipresent." Fearing that unbelievers were using the theories in his *Philosophiæ Naturalis Principia Mathematica* (Mathematical Principles of Natural Philosophy, 1687) to justify their heterodoxy, he appended a new section, titled the "General Scholium," to the second edition in 1713. Here he spelled out his biblical conception of God as a creative and omnipotent deity, ever active in a natural world. Newton's "General Scholium" positioned him as a vigorous opponent to unbelievers, as well as to deists, who, though acknowledging the existence of a god, conceived of this divine being as indifferent to his creation. Privately, he held some heterodox beliefs of his own. An anti-Trinitarian millennialist, obsessed with alchemy, he kept these views hidden. His contemporaries, and subsequent generations, regarded him as an orthodox Christian whose natural philosophy was a boon to the faithful.[4]

Newton's *Principia* assumed a special place in Protestant England in the aftermath of the Revolution of 1688–89 that brought William of Orange to the English throne. Newton's divinely controlled mechanical universe became the model for the triumph of the new Whig constitution and for the liberal Christians who supported it. The natural, divine order at the core of Newton's system sanctioned a stable social and constitutional order. It provided a means for Christian natural philosophers to prevent atheists from opportunistically hijacking atomism and fitting it into a materialistic system reminiscent of such ancient Greek atomists as Epicurus or Lucretius. Natural theology demonstrated that a chaos of atoms could not possibly produce the order observed in the physical world. Since natural theology dealt with the design of anatomical structures, it was applicable to the realm of natural history, as well as to natural philosophy, and even touched on such fundamental issues as the immortality of the soul and the evidential value of miracles. With Newton's consent his science was used by the early Newtonians, including the clergyman Richard Bentley (1662–1742) and the metaphysician Samuel Clarke (1675–1729), to shore up the newly reconstituted monarchy and the established church as the bulwarks of order and stability.[5] But it was not only the moderate English intellectuals who found Newtonianism useful as a defense of the status quo. Newtonianism came to dominate significant sectors of the conservative Enlightenment in Europe and to claim a general hegemony. Earlier philosophies, such as Cartesianism, could be discarded for Newton's more empirical and mathematically rigorous approach, which restored order and certainty. By the 1740s, Newtonianism had become well established throughout Europe, and the British political model connected to it was widely admired.[6]

Newtonianism seemed particularly effective as a counter to the forms of unbelief that nourished the radical wing of the Enlightenment. The two wings, moderate and radical, were separated by a huge gulf. They were grounded on different principles that entailed very different moral, political, social, and intellectual consequences. Whereas the conservative or moderate Enlightenment thinkers attempted to blend theological and traditional categories with new critical-mathematical rationality, radical Enlightenment figures, such as Denis Diderot (1713–84) and Baron d'Holbach (1723–89), rejected such compromises, pushed to sweep away all existing structures, and relied on reason alone. They were attracted to unbelief, to republicanism, and to a conception of human society based on personal liberty, equality, and freedom of thought and expression. Their heroes were Thomas Hobbes (1588–1679) and especially Benedict Spinoza (1632–77), who, the radicals believed, had abolished the dualism between matter and spirit, and then constructed a single set of rules to govern the whole of reality. Hobbes, Spinoza, and their followers were perceived to be atheists and materialists, though they themselves may have denied it. Few persons, if any, in the first half of the eighteenth century admitted to being atheistic, or one who denied the existence of God, since persecution, even imprisonment, could be the consequence. Atheism existed largely in a covert form in this period. Although the radicals were in the minority up until the middle of the eighteenth century, the more mainstream moderates never entirely overwhelmed them.[7]

The powerful alliance between Newtonian science and religious belief in the first half of the eighteenth century is nowhere more evident than in the career of Francois-Marie Arouet (1694–1778), otherwise known to the world as Voltaire. Notorious for his famous battle cry of *"ecrasez l'infâme,"* which summed up his desire to wipe out the infamy of organized religion, Voltaire is often viewed as one of the most important Enlightenment unbelievers. But Voltaire was a fervent opponent of atheism and radical Enlightenment thought. He was committed to a strongly providential deism based on the argument from design and believed that the stability of the moral and social order was dependent on the acknowledgement of a benign Creator. In this sense, he can be placed with the believers, despite his attacks on the credibility of belief in some Catholic dogmas. Voltaire drew extensively on Newtonian science to undermine forms of unbelief based on Cartesian science and on Spinozism. Indeed, Voltaire was one of the key figures responsible for introducing Newton to the Continent, touching off a wave of Anglomania that swept Europe during the 1730s and 1740s. Suddenly, English ideas, influences, and styles were in fashion. For the first time, English poetry and plays were widely studied. The British constitutional monarchy began to be widely admired, and Newton and the English philosopher John Locke were lionized throughout Europe.[8]

Voltaire experienced the repressive tyranny of the French absolutist monarchy firsthand. Imprisoned from May 1717 until April 1718 for his satirical verses, Voltaire found himself back in the Bastille in 1726. Upon his release he left France for England. While in England from 1726 to 1728, Voltaire met with English Newtonians, among them Samuel Clarke, who influenced his views on God, toleration, philosophy, and science. By 1732 he was an enthusiastic Newtonian. His *Letters Concerning the English Nation* (1733), published a year later in French, was intended to advance the cause of the Lockean-Newtonian Enlightenment. Voltaire's aim was to demonstrate, particularly to his French readers, that Newtonianism curbed materialism and Spinozism far more effectively than Cartesianism. Newton's "sublime theory" of gravitation accounted for the motion and inequalities of the planets, and comets as well. Newton, Voltaire maintained, had discovered "a new property of matter, one of the Creator's secrets," whose effects could be demonstrated and its proportions calculated, although its cause could not be explained.[9]

At first, government officials reacted unfavorably to Voltaire's *Letters Concerning the English Nation*. A *lettre de cachet* was issued for his arrest for publishing without a royal license, and Voltaire quickly left Paris. But Voltaire's book did not provoke any real opposition from the forces of authority or the Catholic Church, in part because he had avoided expressing his disdain for theologians. Through the publication of this book Voltaire was able to forge an alliance between moderate Enlightenment *philosophes* and the French religious and political establishment, based on a shared admiration for English ideas. Voltaire's vision of a moderate Enlightenment appealed even to the liberalizing Jesuits, who saw the potential for placing Newtonianism at the center of a new enlightened Catholic philosophical worldview. By forging a *rapprochement* with the intellectual elite of the French church, Voltaire hoped to establish a position from which he could launch a campaign for more toleration and reduced censorship, in the end curbing ecclesiastical influence in France.[10]

Voltaire's *The Elements of Sir Isaac Newton's Philosophy* (1738) pushed his agenda forward by making Newton's philosophy intelligible to his readers. Whereas in *Letters Concerning the English Nation* Voltaire tended to avoid detailed discussions of Newtonian natural philosophy, in the later book he offered a close analysis of, first, Newton's discoveries about light in the *Opticks* and, second, the theory of gravitation from the *Principia*, presented as if they were part of one coherent system. Accusing Descartes of tending toward pantheism, Voltaire also defended Newton from the charge of atheism. Newton's theories, Voltaire maintained, revealed the divine design in nature. Inspired by Newton's ideas on comets, Voltaire pointed out to the reader that comets are designed to retain heat although they travel far away from the sun. This led him to exclaim how this observation "makes us equally admire, the Wisdom of the Creator." Although Descartes was one of Voltaire's targets, another was the monistic Spinozists, who conceived of matter as self-moving while denying divine providence and human free will. Voltaire realized that the Newtonian vision of a divinely decreed cosmic order, based on the argument from design, collapsed if matter had the power to move itself.[11]

Voltaire's *Elements* strengthened the influence of mainstream moderate Enlightenment thought and was well received within France. The Jesuits were now willing to support not just the general propagation of Newtonianism in their colleges, universities, and academies but also the spread of Voltaire's national influence. As long as Newton and Locke were seen to represent what was most up to date, progressive, and convincing in the worlds of science and philosophy, "enlightened" Christians could assert that materialism, Spinozism, and all atheism were outmoded remnants of ancient paganism. The French establishment by 1745 had become fully

converted to Newtonianism. Since Voltaire veiled the full extent of his hostility to Christianity, he continued to be seen as a semi-establishment figure
and as a proponent of an enlightenment sanctioned by liberal churchmen
across Europe from the publication of the *Elements* to the early 1750s. His
strategy allowed him to dominate the European scene for almost two
decades. But his success made an alliance between science and unbelief
impossible. Rather, Newtonian science became the bulwark of Christianity
against atheism not only in England but, thanks to Voltaire, throughout
much of Europe.[12]

D'HOLBACH AND THE RADICAL ENLIGHTENMENT

By 1745 it had become clear that Voltaire's strategy no longer appealed to the
Parisian *philosophes*. After that point, a powerful contrary movement, dominated by monistic and materialistic unbelievers who rejected Voltaire's
Anglomania, opposed the moderate Enlightenment. Younger *philosophes*,
such as Denis Diderot, broke with Voltaire. Diderot, along with Jean
d'Alembert (1717–83), Claude Adrien Helvétius (1715–71), d'Holbach, and
others, became the leaders of a revitalized radical Enlightenment tradition.
These radicals became increasingly anti-Newtonian in attitude, turning
against physico-theology and adopting atheistic Spinozist doctrines. Lim-
iting their rejection of French Anglicism at first to British philosophy,
religion, and science, they later, in the mid 1750s, also questioned admiration for the British political system, when a wave of Anglophobia swept
France preceding the outbreak of the Seven Years War in 1756. During this
period a new theme arose: Britain's imperial arrogance and aggression. By
the 1770s the British political model was as much out of favor with the
French intellectual *avant-garde* as was Newtonianism. Diderot and his circle
embraced a more radical social and political position, which emphasized the
ideas of toleration, equality, individual freedom, freedom of expression,
sexual liberation, and anti-colonialism. Though small in numbers, this was
a group that became influential in the latter half of the century, and they
were the first group of intellectuals to espouse atheism. Because they shared
little in common with the Newtonian moderates, their attempts to draw on
Newtonianism to forge an alliance between science and unbelief were
highly problematic.[13]

   Diderot and d'Holbach played a key role in the history of unbelief. They
introduced atheism into the intellectual culture of the West with such
strength that its presence was permanently secured. Diderot emerged as the
supreme anti-Newtonian of the High Enlightenment in the late forties. By 1747
he had broken with the world of Voltaire, Newtonianism, physico-theology,

and the entire tradition of the French Enlightenment that had been based on Locke and Newton. Diderot and his allies became modern Spinozists. They sought a consistent naturalism. Diderot collaborated with d'Alembert (1717–83) and more than one hundred authors to produce the *Encyclopédie* (1751–72), emblematic of the radical Enlightenment. Comprising seventeen volumes of text and eleven more of plates, it was intended as an antidote to English cultural and intellectual hegemony. The preface to the first volume claimed that Locke and Newton, in addition to the philosopher Francis Bacon (1561–1626) and the chemist Robert Boyle (1627–91), had inspired the project. But this was purposely misleading. The appeal to English luminaries was meant to reassure churchmen, academics, and royal officials that the project would be in line with the conservative aims of the Newtonian Enlightenment. However, although they invoked the names of Locke and Newton, many of the contributors to the *Encyclopédie* departed radically from their ideas. Under cover of the heroes of the moderate Enlightenment, Diderot and his allies rejected the entire metaphysical apparatus of the past, and urged new research, experiment, and investigation as the route to more and better-grounded knowledge. The articles, which collectively pleaded for freedom of expression, presented the most advanced critical ideas in philosophy, religion, and government.[14]

D'Holbach, a contributor to the *Encyclopédie*, held atheistic and radical opinions broadly in line with Diderot's. From about 1750 to 1780 d'Holbach was at the center of a group of *Parisien* savants that gathered for discussion and dinner on a weekly basis at his salon on the rue Royale. Not all of d'Holbach's guests were atheists, but his salon was distinguished by its uncharacteristic openness. His *System of Nature or Laws of the Moral and Physical World*, published anonymously, burst upon the French reading public in 1768. Its appearance confirmed the worst fears of moderates such as Voltaire, as well as defenders of Christianity. D'Holbach rejected the deism of moderates, grouping it together with theism. The "God of the *deist* is useless," he declared. He unabashedly defended atheism as the logical consequence of a rational inquiry into nature. Instead of dismissing atheists as "absurd or knavish speculators," d'Holbach positively portrayed them as men who destroyed "chimeras prejudicial to the human species, in order to reconduct men back to nature, to experience, and to reason."[15]

D'Holbach's main goal in *The System of Nature* was to erect a system of nature based purely on the notion of self-acting matter. Whereas Newton had conceived of matter as inert and passive, which required the guiding hand of a divine being to set it into motion, d'Holbach contended that there was nothing outside of Nature. He asserted that the universe "presents only matter and motion: the whole offers to our contemplation nothing but an immense, an uninterrupted succession of causes and effects." As he developed the notion that "the essence of matter is to act," D'Holbach cleverly pressed Newton into service as an ally. He co-opted Newton's world system in his efforts to offer another world system in its place, turning the arguments of Newton for the existence of God upside down. "If, indeed, by Nature is meant a heap of dead matter, destitute of properties, purely passive," D'Holbach declared, "we must unquestionably seek out of this Nature the principles of her motion." But if nature were understood to be "endowed with diverse and various properties; which oblige them to act according to these properties . . . which gravitate towards a common center . . . then I say, there is no necessity to have recourse to supernatural powers to account for the formation of things." The operations of nature could be explained fully through Newton's theory of gravity without any need to resort to a divine being. Having established that motion was an inherent characteristic of matter, d'Holbach presented natural philosophy as having its own enclosed world and its own principle, while eliminating the natural theologies of the Christian believer or the Voltairian deist.[16]

In his examination of the proofs of the existence of God presented by Newton, d'Holbach distinguished between Newton the natural philosopher and Newton the religious thinker. "This man," d'Holbach asserted, "whose extensive genius has unraveled nature and its laws has bewildered himself as soon as he lost sight of them." When Newton left "physics and demonstration, to lose himself in the imaginary regions of theology," he was "no more than an infant." Logically inconsistent, Newton was unable—or unwilling—to apply his own scientific discoveries and method to the issue of the existence of God. Nature was not, as Newton and the natural theologians would have it, a work requiring a designing workman. Nature "has always been self-existent," and her works were "the effect of her own energy." D'Holbach's criticisms of Newton and his followers were not restricted to the realm of theology alone. The "God of Newton is a despot," he declared; Newton, like all theologians, pictured God as a being who could behave in a completely arbitrary fashion. This unsavory theological concept served to legitimize the despotism of earthly rulers. The "government" of Newton's God, d'Holbach maintained, "takes for a model that which the kings of the earth sometimes exercise over their subjects." Although d'Holbach may have drawn on Newtonian concepts to construct his system of nature, he drew more heavily on the radical Enlightenment tradition for intellectual sustenance. Besides being influenced by lesser figures in this tradition, he was also indebted to Hobbes, Locke, and the Irish freethinker John Toland (1670–1722).[17]

The famous encounter in 1802 between the physicist Pierre-Simon Laplace (1749–1827) and Napoleon Bonaparte has sometimes been interpreted as indicative of the alliance between science and unbelief at the end of the Enlightenment. Laplace championed the effort within French science in the second half of the nineteenth century to advance the Newtonian research program. In his mathematical physics, he drew on gravitational theory to resolve apparent anomalies in the movements of Jupiter and Saturn, and thereby demonstrated that Newtonian principles were sufficient for an understanding of the functioning of the entire solar system. When they met, Bonaparte asked Laplace where God fit into his scientific system. Laplace is reputed to have replied, "I have no need of that hypothesis." If Laplace is taken as being representative of the radical Enlightenment, this story seems to imply that Newtonianism was a major resource in a concerted effort to construct a powerful new atheistical tradition. But like d'Holbach, Laplace recognized the serious problems inherent in drawing unbelief directly from Newtonianism. Near the end of his life Laplace began to inquire about Newton's private life and he became preoccupied with the question, why did Newton make his unexpected pronouncements on religious matters in the second edition of the *Principia*? Laplace could not accept the notion that a genius like Newton held genuine religious beliefs. He viewed them as inconsistent with the rest of Newton's natural philosophy, and possibly the result of a post-*Principia* mental illness.[18]

HUXLEY AND THE ORIGINS OF AGNOSTICISM

The vigorous opposition of British intellectuals in the second half of the eighteenth century to French atheists of d'Holbach's ilk indicates that their impact was limited to parts of continental Europe. The British chemist and liberal clergyman Joseph Priestley (1733–1804) was repulsed by the professed atheism of the philosophers he met while in Paris. David Hume was amused by the dogmatism of French atheists and by their ridicule of his reluctance to follow them to a more radical position. Horace Walpole (1717–87), fourth earl of Oxford and a man of letters, wrote from Paris in 1765, that "the *philosophes*—are insupportable, superficial, overbearing, and fanatic: they preach incessantly, and their avowed doctrine is atheism; you would not believe how openly—Don't wonder, therefore, if I should return a Jesuit." The historian Edward Gibbon (1737–94) criticized the hypocritical position of the French atheists. The "friends of d'Holbach and Helvétius . . . preached the tenets of skepticism with the bigotry of dogmatists, and rashly pronounced that every man must be either an Atheist or a fool."[19]

The attempt of radical Enlightenment figures to link unbelief with Newtonian science was not widely persuasive. In his *Natural Theology* (1802), the Anglican clergyman William Paley (1743–1805) updated Newton's views on divine design in nature. He defended natural theology against the criticisms put forward in David Hume's *Dialogues Concerning Natural Religion* (1776). Whereas Hume drew on the Epicurean tradition to undermine the design argument, Paley argued that human reason was powerful enough to detect empirical evidence for the existence of a powerful, wise, and benevolent God.[20] Paley's book exerted a strong influence on British scientific thinking during the first half of the nineteenth century. It reinforced support for an alliance between natural science and religious belief during a period when British intellectuals were blaming the destructive views of the radical philosophes for the French Revolution. The entomologist William Kirby (1759–1850), author of one of the *Bridgewater Treatises*, a series of eight books published in the 1830s that placed science into a natural theology framework, attacked the French evolutionist Jean-Baptiste Lamarck (1744–1829) and Laplace in his introductory essay. By portraying nature as the product of blind and random self-regulation, Kirby declared, they had revived Epicureanism. An alternative to design since the time of Newton, the tradition of pagan atomism was always in the background as a threat to the supporters of natural theology. But not only was atheism depicted as being dangerous philosophically, it was also presented as a threat to the established social and political order.[21]

Although schools of unbelief arose in Europe in the early nineteenth century that were linked to science, such as radical British Lamarckianism or German scientific materialism, their opposition to the status quo ensured their marginal status. However, to understand how a new, more powerful alliance between science and unbelief was constructed in the second half of the nineteenth century, we must return to Britain, where Newtonianism had been created and nurtured. Only after the troubled social and political unrest of the 1830s and 1840s had passed in Britain and prosperity returned could evolutionary agnosticism be born.[22] Already, before the evolutionary agnostics appeared on the scene, there were signs that religious faith had begun to decline in Britain. The rapid growth of Methodism and evangelicalism at the start of the nineteenth century had given way to a gradual drop in the rate of church attendance, which fell to 50 percent of the population by mid-century. In the 1860s widespread concern was expressed about the absence of the working classes from church. By the 1880s there were indications that members of the middle class were also beginning to cease regular attendance and to reject the social and moral authority of the church. The corrosive power of new scientific theories was not always the chief cause of the loss of faith. For some British Victorians, the loss of faith was a moral rather than an intellectual matter. They were appalled by the immorality of Christian doctrines and ministers, by the church's support of corrupt ruling groups and reactionary politics, and by the emphasis on morally repugnant doctrines such as eternal punishment and the Atonement. As Susan Budd has argued, the revolution in scientific thinking was at first largely irrelevant for the working-class secularists; it was not until near the end of the century that such unbelievers moved away from Bible-bashing to more scholarly arguments that drew on scientific ideas. Developments in science were more important for the educated middle and upper classes, for whom evolutionary agnosticism provided a new and coherent way of looking at the world once confidence in organized religion had been seriously shaken.[23]

In his *Origin of Species* (1859) Charles Darwin's (1809–82) primary aim was to make a case for common descent, as well as for his theory of evolution by natural selection. He recognized that shocking the religious sensibility of his readers would only interfere with their serious consideration of the relevant scientific issues. Though he offered sound scientific reasons for rejecting the design argument throughout the book, in the closing sections of the conclusion he reassured his readers that their religious beliefs were in no way threatened by evolutionary theory. In the first edition he asserted that "it accords better with what we know of the laws impressed on matter by the Creator, that the production and extinction of the past and present inhabitants of the world should have been due to secondary causes, like those determining the birth and death of the individual." In the second edition he added, "I see no good reason why the views given in this volume should shock the religious feelings of any one."[24] Darwin's critics were hard-pressed to find in the *Origin* an unambiguous statement of a scientifically informed unbelief. Instead of portraying nature like an atheistic materialist—as if it were only a dead mechanism—he filled the *Origin* with expressions of awe and wonder more characteristic of a natural theologian. In the closing paragraph of the *Origin* he asserted that the competitive evolutionary process had produced the higher animals, the most exalted object that could be imagined. Then, in the final sentence, Darwin left the reader with a stirring statement of his profound appreciation of the grandeur of nature. Later, as he was revising the first edition of the *Origin*, he altered the final sentence to link his reverence for an evolving natural world with a divine being. "There is grandeur in this view of life," he wrote, "with its several powers, having been originally breathed by the Creator into a few forms or into one." The phrase "by the Creator" was inserted by Darwin into the second edition (issued in December 1859) and thereafter retained.[25] Darwin's direct role in constructing an explicit link between evolution and unbelief was therefore limited, especially before the publication of his more aggressive *Descent of Man* (1871).

The architects of evolutionary agnosticism were the biologist Thomas Henry Huxley (1825–95), often referred to as "Darwin's bulldog" for his vigorous defense of evolutionary theory, and Herbert Spencer (1820–1903), an influential philosopher who produced a multivolume synthesis of all knowledge based on the idea of evolution. Both came from outside the Anglican dominated world of Oxford and Cambridge. They were able to take advantage of the controversies surrounding the publication of Darwin's *Origin* to create a new form of unbelief that disrupted the alliance between science and religious belief based on Newtonianism. Since it was widely believed that Darwin's theory of evolution had the potential to revolutionize science, they were provided with an unparalleled opportunity: to build unbelief into the foundations of a new evolutionary science, in the same way that Newton had infused his physics with natural theology. Unlike the radical Enlightenment thinkers, they succeeded in forging a powerful link between science and unbelief, and in creating a form of unbelief that was palatable to members of the intellectual elite in Britain. Unlike contemporary unbelievers, such as Dawkins, the evolutionary agnostics rejected atheism and offered a less militant version of unbelief.

Huxley recognized that eighteenth-century efforts to forge a strong bond between science and unbelief had been ineffective.[26] His own contribution to the development of science-based unbelief lay in two areas. First, he was one of the leading proponents of making a rigid distinction between science and religion. By dividing science and religion into two separate spheres, he was able to challenge the close relationship between science and natural theology that existed within Newtonianism. Second, he created a new form of unbelief, agnosticism, which he used in defense of evolutionary naturalism and to challenge the cultural authority of the Anglican clergy. He fought to ensure that agnosticism was not confused with atheism and that it was considered as a respectable position for a member of the intellectual elite to hold. His articles in the *Nineteenth Century* near the end of his life also led to the public acceptance of agnosticism as a form of unbelief that had the backing of an eminent biologist.

Huxley was one of the most forceful advocates in the second half of the nineteenth century of the notion that the spheres of science and religion had to be kept apart from each other. While religion belonged to the realm of feeling, science was a part of the world of intellect. If rightly conceived, Huxley believed, science and religion could never come into conflict because each realm was distinct and without authority outside its proper sphere of interest. Initially, he put a very positive spin on this approach. In an anonymous article in 1859 on "Science and Religion," he argued that the achievements of science were due to the divinely created human mind. "For," Huxley declared, "the winning of every new law by reasoning from ascertained facts; the verification by the event, of every scientific prediction, is, if this world be governed by providential order, the direct testimony of that Providence to the sufficiency of the faculties with which man is endowed." This implied that science and religion were not opposed. Rather, "true science and true religion are twin-sisters." But Huxley's vision of a harmonious relationship between science and religion had a catch. Later, he began to distinguish between religion and theology, the latter operating in the scientific world of intellect because of its claim to embody feelings in concrete facts. Theology was potentially in conflict with science. When theology was confused with religion, then there could appear to be a war between science and religion. Huxley asserted that "the antagonism between science and religion about which we hear so much, appears to me to be purely factitious—fabricated, on the one hand, by short-sighted religious people who confound a certain branch of science, theology, with religion; and, on the other, by equally short-sighted scientific people who forget that science takes for its province only that which is susceptible of clear intellectual comprehension."[27]

In the British cultural context of the second half of the nineteenth century, Huxley's division of science and religion into two separate spheres of authority really amounted to a declaration of independence for scientists operating in a space dominated by the established Anglican Church. Scientific research, Huxley declared, had demonstrated that "the accounts of the Creation and of the Deluge in the Hebrew scriptures are mere legends." Huxley also believed that the scientist was freed from the crippling effects of traditional natural theology, as articulated by Newton and Paley. Darwin, Huxley claimed, had demolished the vain search for divine design in the organic world. "The teleology which supposes that the eye," he affirmed, "such as we see it in man, or one of the higher vertebrata, was made with the precise structure it exhibits, for the purpose of enabling the animal which possesses it to see, has undoubtedly received its death-blow." By dividing science and religion into two spheres, Huxley essentially broke the bonds between them and, for better or for worse, allowed scientists to pursue their investigations of nature guided by principles that they established independently of religious authorities.[28]

Huxley had a catchy name for his new vision of an emancipated, professionalized science: scientific naturalism. He believed that the development of scientific naturalism had been in the making for centuries. "It is important to note," he wrote, "that the principle of the scientific Naturalism of the latter half of the nineteenth century, in which the intellectual movement of the Renascence has culminated, and which was first clearly formulated by Descartes, leads not to the denial of the existence of any Supernature; but simply to the denial of the validity of the evidence adduced in favour of this, or that, extant form of Supernaturalism." Huxley argued that proper science excluded any reference to a divine being—scientists should stick to studying observable causes and effects in nature. Huxley was one of the leaders of a significant group of intellectuals that aggressively pushed for a redefinition of science in the latter half of the nineteenth century. The ranks of scientific naturalists included Darwin, Spencer, the physicist John Tyndall (1820–93), the mathematician William Kingdon Clifford (1845–79), the eugenicist Francis Galton (1822–1911), and a larger group of scientists, physicians, journalists, editors, and writers. Since scientific naturalism had the backing of so many distinguished scientists of the period, the claim of its adherents to speak on behalf of science was far more convincing than that of previous unbelievers. D'Holbach's group of radical Enlightenment thinkers had comprised primarily philosophes rather than scientists.[29]

Huxley drew on the principle of scientific naturalism to defend Darwin from the attacks of those who rejected his theories on religious or theological grounds. Though he never committed himself completely to Darwin's theory of natural selection, Huxley argued that it was scientifically legitimate since it only took naturalistic causes into account. In his "Lectures on Evolution" (1876) he presented evolution as a theory that was imbued with the modern emphasis on the natural order. Scientists now ignored, "even as a possibility," the idea of "any interference with the order of Nature." This included, of course, any supernatural interference. Later in the essay, Huxley identified the theory of evolution as being aligned with the naturalistic concept of the order of nature, noting that "the hypothesis of evolution supposes that in all this vast progression there would be no breach of continuity, no point at which we could say 'This is a natural process,' and 'This is not a natural process.'" Huxley could use scientific naturalism to defend Darwin precisely because he built naturalism into his concept of evolution.[30]

Huxley's second contribution to the formation of a powerful alliance between science and unbelief was his invention of the notion "agnosticism." By distinguishing agnosticism from atheism or materialism, Huxley could more easily present unbelief as an intellectually viable, and eminently respectable, option for intellectuals who were disenchanted with Christianity. Huxley could then draw on his new form of unbelief to attack Christian theologians who violated the rigid demarcation between science and religion. Huxley's agnosticism was therefore closely linked to his scientific naturalism. Huxley coined the term "agnosticism" in 1869 at one of the early meetings of the Metaphysical Society, a remarkable club of major English thinkers that met nine times a year in London from 1869 to 1880 to discuss ultimate philosophical and religious questions. While all of the other members of the society had some label they used to describe their religious position, Huxley had none and thus decided to invent the label "agnosticism." For Huxley, the agnostic could neither affirm nor deny the existence of God due to the limits of human knowledge.[31] By identifying himself as an agnostic, Huxley could distance himself from radical forms of unbelief that were associated with the working class, while maintaining his standing within the respectable intellectual elite. Nevertheless, Huxley, as well as his friends Tyndall, Clifford, and even Darwin, faced numerous accusations of encouraging indecency, atheism, and materialism.[32]

After coining the term "agnosticism," Huxley had a stronger response to his critics. In his 1889 essay "Agnosticism," he refused to accept the label of "infidel" that one Christian bishop had used to describe him. "'Infidel,'" Huxley declared, "is a term of reproach, which Christians and Mahommedans, in their modesty, agree to apply to those who differ from them." Huxley argued that the respectable agnostic was not to be confused with the atheist, materialist, or infidel. But by the 1880s agnostic beliefs were debated openly in fashionable middle-class periodicals (such as the *Nineteenth Century*). Huxley's new coinage contributed significantly to the development of a new openness that allowed unbelievers to express their beliefs in public without fear of serious legal consequences or risk of social ostracism.[33]

Huxley not only opened up a public space for moderate forms of unbelief, he linked agnosticism to science. Agnosticism, he maintained, was not a creed; it was a method that rigorously applied one principle, which was also "the fundamental axiom of modern science." Stated positively, the principle was: "In matters of the intellect, follow your reason as far as it will take you, without regard to any other consideration. And negatively: In matters of the intellect do not pretend that conclusions are certain which are not demonstrated or demonstrable." Agnosticism and science, then, started from exactly the same principle. But for other unbelievers of this period, agnosticism was more directly tied to a specific scientific theory, evolution. In his *Autobiography*, Darwin agonized over the problem of God's existence. In the end he was drawn toward agnosticism as he doubted that the human mind, "developed from a mind as low as that possessed by the lowest animals," could be trusted "when it draws such grand conclusions." A product of the evolutionary process, the human mind was not reliable when it tried to tackle theological issues.[34]

ANTHROPOLOGISTS, SPENCER, AND THE APPLICATION OF EVOLUTIONARY THEORY

Evolution, Huxley believed, was slowly transforming all of the natural sciences as well as the study of society and religion. "Scientific investigation, in all directions," Huxley declared, "is tending" to find a "sufficient foundation for the doctrine of evolution" in astronomy, physics, chemistry, the development of human society, of language, and of religions.[35] Evolutionary theory was applied in at least two different ways in the latter half of the nineteenth century, which proved to be powerfully corrosive of religious faith. First, it was used—particularly by anthropologists—to create a new tradition of secular theorizing about religion without reference to the truth-content of its claims. Scientific explanations for religious belief tended to be subversive. Huxley approved of this first application, but he had serious doubts about the second: the use of evolutionary theory as the key to the construction of a new system of knowledge. It provided intellectuals, such as Spencer and his disciples, with the tools for inventing a new, non-Newtonian groundwork for all knowledge that was not imbued with the spirit of natural theology.

By applying evolutionary theory to the study of human cultures, Edward Burnett Tylor (1832–1917) became a key figure in the establishment of anthropology as a scientific discipline. Whereas tribal societies had been seen previously as fallen, degenerated cultures, Tylor believed that they contained clues to the beginning of human history. His *Primitive Culture* (1871) treated human culture as a part of nature and thus governed by unchanging laws. Tylor conceived of evolution as strongly directional and explicitly progressive. All human cultures began in savagery and moved, at different rates, toward civilization according to the same universal process. European, Asian, and Native American societies had begun at the same primitive level, but Asians had developed more quickly than Native Americans, and Europeans had evolved beyond both of them. But survivals or relics from earlier stages of cultural development could persist in even the most advanced cultures. The implications of Tylor's evolutionary approach to understanding religion as an aspect of human culture were enormous. Religion did not originate in some divine revelation; rather, it arose naturally in primitive cultures when the concept of a soul was extended to animals and objects and then to the idea of spirits and gods. Tylor tied religion to the primitive phase of human development. Civilized societies began to abandon religion when they discovered science. If religion continued to exist in a civilized society, it was merely the persistence of a cultural relic. Since relics were an impediment to progress, he paid particular attention to the primitive survivals embedded within modern Christianity, including baptism, the consecration of the communion bread and wine, and other key Christian rituals.[36] Like Tylor, James George Frazer (1854–1941), an English classicist and anthropologist, applied evolutionary principles to the study of primitive cultures in his *Golden Bough* (1890). In his subsequent works he maintained that there was an evolutionary progression in human cultures from magic to religion to science.[37] Anthropology provides a good example of how the social sciences, often influenced by evolutionary theory, started to be used to understand religion in a way that undermined the authority of Christianity.

Spencer's construction of a new system of nature, reminiscent of d'Holbach's and Voltaire's, included evolutionary anthropology and much,

much more. Whereas Voltaire and d'Holbach drew on Newtonian natural philosophy in the creation of their systems—the former to critique, and the latter to defend, radical Enlightenment unbelief—Spencer's building blocks were made of evolutionary material. After working as a railway engineer from 1837 to 1846, subeditor of the *Economist* from 1848 to 1853, and then a freelance journalist, Spencer suffered a so-called nervous breakdown in 1854, which affected his health for the rest of his life. In 1858, as he was correcting essays for republication, he suddenly recognized that all of his work was tied together by a single grand insight into the workings of the universe: the entire cosmos was subject to evolutionary law. He devoted the next thirty-six years of his life to one project: writing the multivolumed *System of Synthetic Philosophy*. Intended as a synthesis of all knowledge connected through the concept of evolution, he wrote books on biology, psychology, sociology, ethics, and religion. He completed his magnum opus in 1896, after years of hoarding his energy, living in virtual isolation, and sacrificing everything to his work. The first volume of Spencer's *Synthetic Philosophy*, titled *First Principles of a New System of Philosophy*, appeared in 1862. In addition to outlining Spencer's evolutionary synthesis, it contained a lucid, systematic statement of agnosticism. It was actually the first major account of agnosticism. Although Huxley had not yet coined the term when *First Principles* was published, Spencer later accepted it as an appropriate designation for his convictions, and Victorian thinkers regarded the book as the agnostic bible.[38]

In part 1, titled "The Unknowable," Spencer's avowed goal was to find the "basis of a complete reconciliation" between science and religion. He began by dividing science and religion into two separate spheres in a manner similar to Huxley's. After examining both spheres, he concluded that both "Ultimate Religious Ideas," such as atheism, pantheism, and theism, and "Ultimate Scientific Ideas," such as matter, space, time, and force, were all "literally unthinkable," since they posited concepts beyond the limits of the human intellect. But each acknowledged "the consciousness of an Inscrutable Power manifested to us through all phenomena." More theistic than Huxley, Spencer affirmed the consciousness of a God, though he also maintained that nothing could be known of this being. Spencer had a name for this elusive deity, the "Unknowable."[39]

Having placed religion firmly into the sphere of the unknown, Spencer was now free in "The Knowable" to search for truths that would allow him to synthesize scientific knowledge into one system. He quickly deduced that "the universal law of redistribution of matter and motion" is "evolution." Evolution was the process underlying the entire Newtonian universe composed of matter, force, and motion.[40] After deducing that the law of evolution was what he had been seeking as his unifying truth, Spencer then offered empirical proof drawn from astronomy, geology, biology, psychology, and sociology that "the Cosmos, in general and in detail, conforms to this law." He concluded that all phenomena were subject to the evolutionary process. "Alike during the evolution of the Solar System," he declared, "of a planet, of an organism, of a nation, there is progressive aggregation of the entire mass." Having neutralized all religious objections to his grand project, Spencer now had the foundation for his subsequent volumes, which affirmed the existence of the Unknowable as a force that lay behind matter.[41]

During the 1880s Spencer reached the peak of his popularity. In that decade a group of English dissident secularists began to view Spencer as their master and the Unknowable as their deity. His theories in biology, psychology, and sociology were winning him international recognition, particularly in the United States. His philosophy attracted a number of American liberal Protestants, though he had many enemies within conservative Christian circles. Like Huxley, Spencer had a global impact thanks, in part, to the relatively open intellectual environment of the second half of the century as well as to the new publishing conditions. The development of a mass reading public in both Europe and the United States, catered to by publishers who could make use of new printing technologies to produce an ample supply of cheap books and periodicals, ensured that Spencer's ideas circulated internationally. Agnosticism flourished in Britain, Europe, and the United States—especially in the industrialized, modernized, and urbanized societies of the latter half of the nineteenth century. Spencer, along with Huxley and other scientific naturalists, established a public space in Britain for intellectuals to link science to unbelief.[42]

TWENTIETH-CENTURY SCIENCE AND UNBELIEF

The space in Britain created by Huxley, Spencer, and their allies for intellectuals to connect science to unbelief was somewhat unusual. Although Western intellectuals in other national contexts attempted to create a similar space in their countries during the second half of the nineteenth century, they were not as successful as their British counterparts. It was not until the twentieth century that such spaces became more common. In Russia, the Bolsheviks made science central to their campaign to undermine the power of the Orthodox Church and transform Russian society. From the first days of the October Revolution in 1917 science popularization was seen by the young Soviet regime as an important means for forming a new ideology based on scientific principles that would be attractive to the common man. The notion of a struggle between science and religion was emblematic of the Bolshevik cultural revolution in the 1920's and was enthusiastically supported by Vladimir Lenin (1870–1924). At the Twelfth Party Congress of

1923, a special resolution was passed concerning the need to emphasize the role of science and education in the campaign to stamp out religious fervor. The resolution read, "the party must not forget that all our antireligious agitation and propaganda will fail to affect the masses until long-term educational programs stressing natural-scientific knowledge are fully organized in the urban and rural areas."[43] Editors of scientific journals for a popular audience believed that articles on evolution would teach readers to give up religious explanations for those that were based on scientific ones. Evolutionary theory was used to substantiate scientific materialist philosophy and Marxian theories about social change. Though, starting in 1929, scientists were condemned and arrested for not adhering to the party line, well into the Stalinist era the czarist past was portrayed as being scientifically backward while the socialist future was envisioned as being technologically advanced.[44]

In the United States the establishment of a public space for a scientifically based unbelief took much longer. Before the middle of the nineteenth century, atheism and agnosticism seemed absurd to Americans. By the 1880s, however, unbelief was viewed as a viable intellectual option in American culture, in part because Christian theologians themselves had confidently endorsed science as a valid route to knowledge. Christian intellectuals embraced methodological naturalism as the norm of scientific discourse in order to accommodate Darwinism, but this left an opening for the unbelievers. A Republican antislavery lawyer and a masterful public orator, Robert Ingersoll (1833–99) became the leading voice of American free thought in the second half of the nineteenth century. He argued that the U.S. Constitution had been based on secular and rationalist principles by the Founding Fathers, since they had been influenced by Enlightenment ideals. He also integrated Darwinian evolution into his agnostic pronouncements. The press reacted with hostility toward Ingersoll's speeches, and his anti-religious views were so widely disliked that they destroyed any hope he may have had for a political career. The years from 1875 to 1914 proved to be the high-water mark of free thought as an influential movement in American society. Despite the existence of unbelievers like Ingersoll, American public culture remained firmly rooted in Protestantism up to the end of the nineteenth century. The fundamentalist counterattack of the 1920s, characterized by opposition to evolutionism and "atheistic communism," left the free-thought movement severely weakened. The revolutionary event in 1917 that provided the necessary conditions for the establishment of a public space in Russia where the link between science and unbelief could be presented, constrained the creation of such a space in American culture. By the time of the second Red Scare in the fifties, the connection between irreligion and communism was even more widely accepted by the American public than it had been during the anti-Bolshevik zeal after World War I.[45]

Although American public culture slowly moved away from its Protestant basis during the twentieth century and toward religious pluralism, the power of secular perspectives made surprisingly little headway. One reason for the slow pace of secularization in the twentieth century in the United States relative to other industrialized societies in the North Atlantic West (e.g., Great Britain) has to do with the absence of an established church. Ironically, this has "enabled religious affiliation to function, like other voluntary organizations in 'civil society,' as mediators between the individual and the nation."[46] Studies of American religious belief by social scientists have shown that the overwhelming majority of the general population are theists while a small majority of scientists do not believe in the existence of a personal God. However, the percentage of unbelievers among scientists has been fairly constant throughout the twentieth century. In his groundbreaking survey of one thousand randomly selected U.S. scientists in 1914, the American psychologist James H. Leuba (1867–1946) found that 58 percent expressed disbelief or doubt in a personal God who hears and answers prayers (although slightly more than 50 percent professed to believe in human immortality). When Leuba repeated his survey twenty years later, though in a different form, he discovered that the percentage had increased to 67. In 1996 Edward Larson and Larry Witham repeated Leuba's 1914 survey and found little change: 60.7 percent expressed disbelief or doubt.[47] A more recent study by Elaine Howard Ecklund of 1,646 natural and social scientists at twenty-one "elite U.S. research universities" has yielded similar results. She found no appreciable differences in the attitudes of natural and social scientists, but discovered that 51.8 percent of the scientists reported no religious affiliation, compared to only 14.2 percent of the general U.S. population. While nearly 34 percent of academic scientists identified themselves as atheists and 30 percent as agnostics, the general U.S. population figures were 3 percent and 5 percent respectively. Perhaps most surprising, 22 percent of the atheistic scientists and 27 percent of the agnostic scientists described themselves as "spiritual."[48]

Steven Weinberg, the eminent physicist, has confirmed that many scientists today are unbelievers. "As far as I can tell from my own observations," Weinberg has asserted, "most physicists today are not sufficiently interested in religion even to qualify as practicing atheists." In the past, Weinberg himself has been an eloquent spokesman for unbelieving American scientists. In his *Dreams of a Final Theory* (1994) he declared that rather than finding "signs of the workings of an interested God" in nature, scientists had uncovered "a chilling impersonality in the laws of nature." He rejected the idea of identifying the laws of nature with a remote and disinterested God, as had Einstein. "The more we refine our understanding of God to make the concept plausible," Weinberg maintained, "the more it seems pointless."[49]

In comparison to a new group of unbelievers, Weinberg seems almost timid in his criticism of religious belief. The post-9/11 environment has spawned the "New Atheists," an aggressive and militant group far more vocal than Ingersoll or Weinberg. They have produced a series of best-selling books in both England and the United States. Not satisfied with an attack on creationists, intelligent design, and conservative Christianity, they are prepared to take on all religions and all shades of opinion within each religion, liberal as well as orthodox. All of them look to scientific theories to support their unbelief. In his *Breaking the Spell: Religion as a Natural Phenomenon* (2006), Daniel Dennett draws on evolutionary biology to investigate religion as if it were "one natural phenomenon among many." Sam Harris's *Letter to a Christian Nation* (2006) portrays the belief system behind the Bible as "primitive" in comparison to the progressive, scientific system of the twenty-first century. He argues that we see extraordinary complexity in the natural world but not "optimal design." Dawkins maintains in his *The God Delusion* (2006) that evolutionary science logically leads to the atheistic position. In his *God Is Not Great* (2007), Christopher Hitchens judges all attempts to reconcile faith and science to be doomed to failure. Whereas religion is a part of humanity's childhood, science works well enough without assuming a God. Hitchens criticizes those who try to conceive of the evolutionary process as directed by a divine being. They only succeed in making God into a "fumbling fool" who "took eons of time to fashion a few serviceable figures and heaped up a junkyard of scrap and failure meanwhile."[50] As a group, the "New Atheists" are determined to eliminate the stigma attached to atheism, especially in the United States.

Today evolutionary theory provides a rich resource for unbelievers when they seek scientific justification for their views. Huxley and Spencer ensured that, from the start, evolutionary theory provided no endorsement for conventional religious beliefs. Since the idea of evolution has virtually become the basis for our modern worldview, believers have been forced to come to grips with a secularized version of science no longer informed by the spirit of Newtonianism. Those who maintain that traditional religious beliefs can be put in alignment with the key theories of contemporary science have found that the burden of proof has shifted and it is up to them to persuade the public that current science has not, as Dawkins maintains, rendered God a mere delusion.

Notes

The author would like to express his gratitude to those who offered useful suggestions for revising earlier versions of this paper, including John Brooke, Joy Dixon, Frederick Gregory, Ron Numbers, and Margaret Osler.

1. Richard Dawkins, *The God Delusion* (Boston: Houghton Mifflin, 2006), 114, 116–18.

2. H. S. Thayer, ed., *Newton's Philosophy of Nature: Selections from His Writings* (New York: Hafner, 1953), 42, 65.

3. I will concentrate on upper- and middle-class intellectuals and only touch on working-class unbelief.

4. Sir Isaac Newton, *Opticks; or, A Treatise of the Reflections, Refractions, Inflections and Colours or Light*, 2nd ed. (London, 1717), 344; Stephen D. Snobelen, "'God of gods, and Lord of lords': The Theology of Isaac Newton's General Scholium to the *Principia*," *Osiris* 16 (2001): 172–77, 202; and Margaret J. Osler, "The Newtonian Scholarship and the Fate of the Scientific Revolution," in *Newton and Newtonianism: New Studies*, ed. James Force and Sarah Hutton, 8–10 (Dordrecht: Kluwer, 2004).

5. John Brooke and Geoffrey Cantor, *Reconstructing Nature: The Engagement of Science and Religion* (Oxford: Oxford University Press, 1998), 194; Margaret C. Jacob, *The Radical Enlightenment: Pantheists, Freemasons and Republicans* (London: George Allen and Unwin, 1981), 83, 91.

6. Jonathan Israel, *Enlightenment Contested: Philosophy, Modernity, and the Emancipation of Man 1670–1752* (Oxford: Oxford University Press, 2006), 202–4.

7. Ibid., 11–12; David Berman, *A History of Atheism in Britain: From Hobbes to Russell* (London: Croom Helm, 1988), ix, 110; Michael Hunter, "Science and Heterodoxy: An Early Modern Problem Reconsidered," in *Reappraisals of the Scientific Revolution*, ed. David C. Lindberg and Robert S. Westman, 444 (Cambridge: Cambridge University Press, 1990).

8. Israel, *Enlightenment Contested*, 53, 364; Jonathan Israel, *Radical Enlightenment: Philosophy and the Making of Modernity 1650–1750* (Oxford: Oxford University Press, 2001), 515.

9. Israel, *Enlightenment Contested*, 751, 754; Voltaire, *Philosophical Letters*, trans. Ernest Dilworth (Indianapolis, Ind.: Bobbs-Merrill, 1981), 64, 71, 74.

10. Israel, *Enlightenment Contested*, 751, 754–57.

11. P. M. Rattansi, "Voltaire and the Enlightenment Image of Newton," in *History and Imagination: Essays in Honour of H. R. Trevor-Roper*, ed. Hugh Lloyd-Jones, Valeri Pearl, and Blair Worden, 219 (London: Gerald Duckworth, 1981); Voltaire, *The Elements of Sir Isaac Newton's Philosophy*, trans. John Hanna (London: Frank Cass 1967), 76, 78, 102–3, 184, 334; Israel, *Enlightenment Contested*, 765–68.

12. Israel, *Enlightenment Contested*, 758, 760, 764, 772, 781.

13. Ibid., 363, 365, 367–68, 370–71.

14. Michael J. Buckley, *At the Origins of Modern Atheism* (New Haven, Conn.: Yale University Press, 1987), 34, 322; Israel, *Enlightenment Contested*, 222, 367, 780, 791, 793, 808, 818, 842, 845.

15. Israel, *Enlightenment Contested*, 842; Buckely, *Origins of Modern Atheism*, 256–57; Alan Charles Kors, "The Atheism of D'Holbach and Naigeon," in *Atheism from the Reformation to the Enlightenment*, ed. Michael Hunter and David Wootton, 273 (Oxford: Clarendon Press, 1992); Baron d'Holbach, *The System of Nature or Laws of the Moral and Physical World*, 2 vols in one (New York: Burt Franklin, 1970), 2:258–59, 300, 305.

16. D'Holbach, *System of Nature*, 1:11, 15, 18–19, 21; Buckley, *Origins of Modern Atheism*, 253, 282.

17. D'Holbach, *System of Nature*, 2:224, 227, 229, 232; Buckley, *Origins of Modern Atheism*, 320.

18. Roger Hahn, *Pierre Simon Laplace 1749–1827: A Determined Scientist* (Cambridge, Mass.: Harvard University Press, 2005), 172, 201.

19. Joseph Priestly, *Memoires of Dr. Joseph Priestly (written by himself) with a Journal of his Travels, in the Autobiography of Joseph Priestly*, ed. Jack Lindsay, 111 (Bath: Adam and Dart, 1970), as cited in Buckley, *Origins of Modern Atheism*, 255; Horace Walpole, *The Letters of Horace Walpole*, ed. Peter Cunningham, 4:436 (Edinburgh: John Grant, 1906), as cited in Buckley, *Origins of Modern Atheism*, 255; Edward Gibbon, *Autobiography: Memoir C.*, ed. John Murray, 223 (New York: Fred de Fau, 1907), as cited in Buckley, *Origins of Modern Atheism*, 255.

20. Frederick Ferré, "Introduction," *Natural Theology*, by William Paley, ed. Frederick Ferré (Indianapolis, Ind.: Bobbs-Merrill, 1963), xi, xxii–xxv.

21. Brooke and Cantor, *Reconstructing Nature*, 195–96.

22. Adrian Desmond, *The Politics of Evolution: Morphology, Medicine, and Reform in Radical London* (Chicago: University of Chicago Press, 1989); Frederick Gregory, *Scientific Materialism in Nineteenth Century Germany* (Dordrecht: D. Reidel, 1977).

23. Susan Budd, *Varieties of Unbelief: Atheists and Agnostics in English Society 1850–1960* (New York: Holmes and Meier, 1977), 4–5, 107–16, 123–33.

24. Charles Darwin, *The Origin of Species* (London: John Murray, 1859), 488; Charles Darwin, *The Origin of Species*, 2nd ed. (London: John Murray, 1860), 481.

25. Darwin, *Origin of Species*, 2nd ed., 490.

26. T. H. Huxley, *Science and Christian Tradition* (New York: D. Appleton, 1894), 18–20.

27. [T. H. Huxley], "Science and Religion," *Builder* 18 (1859): 35; Thomas H. Huxley, *Science and Hebrew Tradition* (London: Macmillan, 1893), 160–61; Bernard Lightman, *The Origins of Agnosticism: Victorian Unbelief and the Limits of Knowledge* (Baltimore, Md.: Johns Hopkins University Press, 1987), 131–32.

28. Huxley, *Science and Hebrew Tradition*, vi, x; T. H. Huxley, "On the Reception of the 'Origin of Species,'" in *The Life and Letters of Charles Darwin*, ed. Francis Darwin, 2 vols. (New York: D. Appleton, 1887), 1:554.

29. Huxley, *Science and Christian Tradition*, 38; Lightman, *Origins of Agnosticism*, 28–29; Bernard Lightman, "'Fighting Even with Death': Balfour, Scientific Naturalism, and Thomas Henry Huxley's Final Battle," in *Thomas Henry Huxley's Place in Science and Letters: Centenary Essays*, ed. Alan Barr, 323–50 (Athens: University of Georgia Press, 1997); Frank Turner, *Between Science and Religion: The Reaction to Scientific Naturalism in Late Victorian England* (New Haven, Conn.: Yale University Press, 1974), chap. 2.

30. Huxley, *Science and the Hebrew Tradition*, 47, 55.

31. Lightman, *Origins of Agnosticism*, 10–11.

32. Gowan Dawson, *Darwin, Literature, and Victorian Respectability* (Cambridge: Cambridge University Press, 2007), 2–8, 14–28, 41–43.

33. Huxley, *Science and Christian Tradition*, 233; Bernard Lightman, "Huxley and Scientific Agnosticism: The Strange History of a Failed Rhetorical Strategy," *British Journal for the History of Science* 35 (2002): 271–89.

34. Huxley, *Science and Christian Tradition*, 246; Francis Darwin, ed., *Autobiography of Charles Darwin* (rept. New York: Dover Publications, 1958), 66.

35. Huxley, *Science and Christian Tradition*, 43.

36. Hans G. Kippenberg, *Discovering Religious History in the Modern Age*, trans. Barbara Harshav (Princeton, N.J.: Princeton University Press, 2002), 51–64; Robert A. Segal, "Tylor's Anthropomorphic Theory of Religion," *Religion* 25 (1995): 23, 29; Robert A. Segal, "The Place of Religion in Modernity," *History of the Human Sciences* 17 (2004): 137, 143; Bowdoin van Riper, "Tylor, Edward Burnett," *The Dictionary of Nineteenth-Century British Scientists*, ed. Bernard Lightman, 4 vols. (Bristol: Thoemmes Continuum Press, 2004), 4:2049–53.

37. Kippenberg, *Discovering Religious History in the Modern Age*, 87–97.

38. Lightman, *Origins of Agnosticism*, 73–74, 82.

39. Herbert Spencer, *First Principles of a New System of Philosophy*, 4th ed. (New York: D. Appleton, 1882), 21, 35, 46, 65, 68, 108.

40. Ibid., 285.

41. Ibid., 307–11, 327, 556–58.

42. Lightman, *Origins of Agnosticism*, 140–45; Bernard Lightman, "Ideology, Evolution, and Late-Victorian Agnostic Popularizers," in *History, Humanity and Evolution: New Perspectives in the History of Evolutionary Naturalism*, ed. James R. Moore, 285–309 (Cambridge: Cambridge University Press, 1989); James R. Moore, "Herbert Spencer's Henchmen: The Evolution of Protestant Liberals in Late Nineteenth-Century America," in *Darwinism and Divinity*, ed. John Durant, 76–100 (Oxford: Basil Blackwell, 1985).

43. As quoted in James T. Andrews, *Science for the Masses: The Bolshevik State, Public Science, and the Popular Imagination in Soviet Russia, 1917–1934* (College Station: Texas A&M University Press, 2003), 110.

44. Ibid., 62, 68, 95, 110, 107, 124, 127, 172.

45. James Turner, *Without God, Without Creed: The Origins of Unbelief in America* (Baltimore, Md.: Johns Hopkins University Press, 1985), 44, xii, 262, 193; Jon H. Roberts and James Turner, *The Sacred and the Secular University* (Princeton, N.J.: Princeton University Press, 2000), 28–30; Susan Jacoby, *Freethinkers: A History of American Secularism* (New York: Henry Holt, 2004), 184–85, 125, 171–72, 165, 228, 309.

46. David A. Hollinger, "Why is There So Much Christianity in the United States? A Reply to Somerville," *Church History* 71 (2002): 858. Hollinger has asserted that instead of using the term "secularization" historians should utilize the more accurate term "de-Christianization." Although the move toward pluralism seems to indicate that secular perspectives were gaining strength, he argues, the "de-Christianization" of the United States is often mistaken for secularization. For over the course of the twentieth century what was at issue was the decline in the cultural authority of Protestantism, not all religion. See David A. Hollinger, "The 'Secularization' Question and the United States in the Twentieth Century," *Church History* 70 (2001): 136–37.

47. Edward J. Larson and Larry Witham, "Leading Scientists still reject God," *Nature* 394, July 23, 1998, 313. Leuba, Larson, and Witham also studied "greater" scientists and discovered that the percentage of those who expressed disbelief or doubt was even higher. In 1914 and 1934, Leuba gauged it at 70 percent and 85 percent respectively. In 1998, Larson and Witham used the members of the National Academy of Sciences as their group of "greater" scientists and determined that 93 percent of them were disbelievers. See ibid., 313.

48. Elaine Howard Ecklund and Christopher P. Scheitle, "Religion among Academic Scientists: Distinctions, Disciplines and Demographics," *Social Problems* 54 (2007): 290–91, 297–99; Elaine Howard Ecklund, "Religion and Spirituality Among the Scientists?" *Contexts* 7 (2008): 12–15. The completed study appears in Elaine Howard Ecklund, *Science vs. Religion: What Do Scientists Really Think?* (New York: Oxford University Press, 2010). The figures vary slightly from publication to publication.

49. Steven Weinberg, *Dreams of a Final Theory* (New York: Vintage Books, 1994), 257, 245, 256.

50. Daniel C. Dennett, *Breaking the Spell: Religion as a Natural Phenomenon* (New York: Penguin, 2006), 17; Sam Harris, *Letter to a Christian Nation* (New York: Alfred A. Knopf, 2007), 50, 75; Richard Dawkins, *The God Delusion* (Boston: Houghton Mifflin, 2006), 114; Christopher Hitchens, *God Is Not Great: How Religion Poisons Everything* (Toronto: McClelland and Stewart, 2007), 64, 66, 70, 85.

12

Which Science? Whose Religion?

David N. Livingstone

Steven Shapin's revisionist account of the scientific revolution of the seventeenth century opens with a provocation: "There was no such thing as the Scientific Revolution, and this is a book about it."[1] This collection of essays could appropriately end on a similar note. There is no such thing as the relationship between science and religion, and this is a book about it. It is for this reason that I have taken as my cue, in seeking an appropriate rubric under which to compose these concluding remarks, the title of Alasdair MacIntyre's *Whose Justice? Which Rationality?* In part, MacIntyre's argument is that there is no rationality that is not the rationality of some particular tradition, and that in every instance when an effort is made to provide rational justification for a course of moral action we need to figure out which is the rationality and whose is the justice in question. It is much the same with thinking about science and religion. In every case we need to ascertain which scientific enterprise and whose religious tradition is under consideration. Indeed, I argue in what follows that the story of encounters between particular scientific ventures and specific religious movements needs to be complicated in yet further ways if we are to do justice to the complexities of the historical record rather than succumb to the allure of comfortable typecasting. As Thomas Dixon recently put it in a popular introduction to the whole subject, "There has certainly not been a single and unchanging relationship between two entities called 'science' and 'religion.'"[2]

Further complicating the story of the relations between scientific enterprises and religious traditions is thus my goal in the pages that follow. And it builds on the widespread recognition among historians of science that the old conflict model, presuming inherent antagonism between science and religion, is now moribund. This view, however, is far from universally shared. The recent resignation of Professor Michael Reiss, an evolutionary biologist, from the post of director of education for the Royal Society over some comments he made on creationism is illustrative. On September 13, 2008, the Nobel Prize–winner Sir Richard Roberts of the New England Bio-labs in Ipswich, Massachusetts, supported by several other laureates, wrote to Sir Martin Rees, president of the Royal Society, demanding "that Professor Reiss step down, or be asked to step down, as soon as possible." "We gather Professor Reiss is a clergyman, which in itself is very worrisome," the letter went on. "Who on earth thought that he would be an appropriate Director of Education, who could be expected to answer questions about the differences between science and religion in a scientific, reasoned way?"[3] Enshrined in this communiqué is the presumption that science and religion are inescap-ably at odds, such that inceptive suspicion is necessarily thrown on the scientific integrity of individuals with religious convictions. Commenting on the whole episode in the *New Scientist*, Sir Harold Kroto, recipient of the 1996 Nobel Prize for Chemistry, observed: "There is no way that an ordained minister—for whom unverified dogma must represent a major, if not the major, pillar in their lives can present free-thinking, doubt-based scientific philosophy honestly or disinterestedly."[4] For all the sterling efforts of histo-rians to dispel the myth of inevitable and persistent internecine warfare between science and religion, it seems, the idea of inexorable conflict—like a resilient virus—is proving exceptionally hard to eradicate. Nevertheless, this volume constitutes a collective contribution toward that project.

"What is the relationship between science and religion?" is a question in need of questioning. In different ways, the essays in this collection conspire to trouble the seeming simplicity of the assumption that the task is to map encounters between two realms respectively labeled "science" and "religion." The global reach of the preceding chapters, for example, forces on us the thought that this whole way of proceeding may be a local Western perspective that is imperiously imposed on the rest of the world. This suspicion manifests itself, perhaps with greatest clarity, in the analysis of science, religion, and medicine in sub-Saharan Africa provided by Steven Feierman and John M. Janzen (see chap. 10). Several things are particularly notable about their inter-vention. First, their account proceeds with the understanding that the vocab-ulary of "science" and "religion" as entities whose relationship is at the heart of this inquiry constitutes, in the African case, the imposition of categories of interpretation that do not track well indigenous understandings. As their analysis shows in different ways, whether dealing with iron-smelting practices, eco-sensitive land-use regulation, or the complex relationships between med-ical "objects" and socio-spiritual structures, the idea of a relationship, or boundary line, or dialogue, between "science and religion" misconstrues the issue. Portraying these performances in the language of "science and religion," as though they can be tidily segregated, is to import Western cate-gories and inflict them on non-Western cultures. Imperialism, we should note in passing, can also be of a temporal variety—namely, imposing contemporary categories on historical episodes or engaging in the Whiggish form of inquiry that reconstructs the past only in presentist terms. The danger here is that a manufactured past is constructed by historians who zealously dig out scattered "scientific" hints from sacred texts and thereby create, rather than uncover, some presumed "tradition" or "stance" on "science and religion."

Second, this is the chapter where anthropological apparatus is most clearly brought to bear on the whole subject. This raises the intriguing question why science and religion as belief systems in the Westernized world are not brought so conspicuously within the arc of anthropological scrutiny. Breaking down presumed boundaries between practice and belief, object and meaning, Feierman and Janzen's analysis challenges students of science and religion in other settings to elucidate how various activities, whether dubbed scientific or religious, function in the society in which they are domesticated.

Other insights throughout this collection also disturb the presumption of a singular relationship between science and religion. In different settings, different traditions approach the "problematic" differently, and hence solve—or resolve—it in different ways. In some cases there is a fusion of what in other situations would be disaggregated; in others it is a matter of harmonizing dissonant claims to achieve coherence; in yet others the strategy is to allocate science and religion to different spheres and thereby to prevent the development of any relationship, whether hostile or cordial. In Mark Csikszentmihalyi's chapter on early China (chap. 7), for example, it becomes clear that the ideas of natural cycles and homologies are both religious and scientific conceptions at the same time. In this case the idea of "harmonizing" science and religion is misconceived, as these convictions inherently fuse what elsewhere might be disaggregated into the scientific and the religious. In a comparable way, as Geoffrey Cantor notes in his treatment of modern Judaism (chap. 2), some positive assessments of evolutionary transformation by nineteenth-century rabbis were at least as much to do with their use of Kabbalistic understandings of change as with anything specifically derived from Darwinian biology. Indeed, one rabbi, Abraham Isaac HaKohen Kook, far from setting out to "reconcile" Judaism and modern science, claimed that in adopting Darwin's theory of evolutionary change, naturalists were only coming to recognize a negligible part of a much larger cosmic picture that traditional Judaism had long cherished.

Early Islamic science, it seems, stands in marked contrast to these forms of synaptic blending. According to Ahmad Dallal (chap. 5), the way in which knowledge was classified in early Islam meant that religion and natural science occupied separate spheres of knowledge. For Abu Rayhan al-Biruni (973–1048 CE), Qur'anic teaching and scientific endeavors did not impinge on each other—a perspective reinforced by the Qur'anic exegete Fakhr al-Din al-Razi in the twelfth century. For Dallal, these represent a segregationist perspective that allocates cognitive authority to different domains by assigning religious and scientific knowledges to their own compartments. This partitionist strategy, of course, is not solely the prerogative of religious believers. The Englishman Thomas Henry Huxley was an advocate of the two-spheres model, and he used it to challenge the elision of science and natural theology in the Newtonian world picture. At the same time, as Bernard Lightman (chap. 11) points out, he considered that true science and true religion were "twin-sisters"—a sentiment remarkably similar to that of John William Draper, author of the polemical *History of the Conflict between Religion and Science* (1874), who considered that "modern Science is the legitimate sister—indeed, it is the twin-sister—of the Reformation."[5]

In our own time, the two-spheres tactic has had committed defenders, such as Stephen Jay Gould, whose *Rocks of Ages: Science and Religion in the Fullness of Life* (1999) further popularized the idea of science and religion as two Non-Overlapping Magisteria (NOMA). A couple of years earlier he had put forward this concordat as "the principled resolution of supposed 'conflict' or 'warfare' between science and religion. No such conflict should exist because each subject has a legitimate magisterium, or domain of teaching authority—and these magisteria do not overlap (the principle that I would like to designate as NOMA, or 'nonoverlapping magisteria')."[6] In his review of this proposal, though, Michael Ruse detected that such a stratagem might not be as irenic or benign as it at first appears; Ruse suspected that Gould's territorial cartography drew its boundary line too far on the side of science and not sufficiently toward the middle ground.[7] As noted above, partition is not even an option in some settings. Feierman and Janzen's investigation of sub-Saharan Africa reveals that in this context the very idea of there being two spheres that interact—science and religion—misconceives the issue. Even today, they can itemize a range of scientific-medical practitioners of one sort or another bridging what they refer to as "the science/religion continuum" by integrating pharmaceutical and traditional traditions of health care management.

The essays in this collection, then, advertise complexity in science-religion discourses at different points in time and in different locations. The presumption that the issue is simply how to manage the relationship between two realms is as problematic as the grand narrative that assumes that science is an inescapably secularizing force. As B. V. Subbarayappa notes (chap. 8), to take just one example, the expansion of India's scientific-technological infrastructure has gone hand in hand with the construction of new temples and novel forms of religious observance. Such eventualities alert us to the multifarious ways in which science-religion dialogues have been conducted. In places where science and religion are fused into an indivisible entity, or indeed where speaking of "science and religion" at all is a misconception, the conversation will differ markedly from contexts where epistemic apartheid operates to keep science and religion in isolation from each other. Where the aim is to harmonize the claims of faith with the findings of science, a different dynamic will be in operation, one that sharply contrasts with situations where religious dogma imperiously stifles scientific inquiry or where scientific enterprises ride roughshod over spiritual sensibilities.

COMPLICATIONS

Woven into the fabric of this volume are numerous threads that further complicate our thinking about science and religion. Here I want to offer four recommendations that might appropriately be mobilized to interrogate particular episodes in the history of science and religion. For convenience, we might consider these as a set of hypothetical imperatives: pluralize, localize, hybridize, politicize. This does not mean that all are appropriate tactics for making sense of every encounter; what I mean, rather, is that it is never mistaken to ask if, say, local circumstances are critically important to understanding the dynamic of some particular dispute, or if there are political currents running through the claims of interlocutors.

First, the need to *pluralize*. The singularity that ordinarily attends public discussion of the subject needs to be replaced by a recognition that it is more helpful to think in terms of the encounter between sciences and religious traditions. This realization surfaces in many of the essays in this volume. Dallal's account of science and early Islam, for example, identifies a sequence of different scientific enterprises—astronomy, optics, medicine, and so on—to which Muslims contributed. Similarly, Donald Lopez's scrutiny of Buddhism (chap. 9) carries the warning that a number of scholars insist on the need to speak of several "Buddhisms" rather than a single "Buddhism." He also notes that key Buddhist figures engaging with European sciences during the nineteenth and twentieth centuries came from different Buddhist cultures and held contrasting views on which form of Buddhism they considered to be the most authentic. At the same time he reminds us that the label "science" carries insufficient semantic precision to cover everything from the Big Bang and evolutionary theory to the development of instruments like the microscope and spectrometer. Neither Buddhism nor science is a unified tradition. B. V. Subbarayappa makes a comparable point. Even within the three Indic religious traditions that his chapter encompasses, he insists that none is a monolith.

This pluralizing imperative can be readily extended. Noah Efron begins his analysis (chap. 1) of science and early Judaism with the reminder that "there has been no single, enduring Jewish attitude toward nature and its study." And Geoffrey Cantor confirms this impulse when he contrasts the differences between Sephardi and Ashkenazi Jewry, and notes the marked divergences between Reform and ultra-Orthodox schools. John Hedley Brooke points out (chap. 4) that even within the same Christian tradition attitudes toward particular scientific theories may vary: the doctrine of creation, for example, has been mobilized for very different purposes by Christians—sometimes to support scientific stances, sometimes to oppose them. The collective import of these delineations is to make us suspicious of the familiar "isms" to which we all too readily resort. Buddhism, evangelicalism, Judaism, Calvinism, and so on name faith communities that are, at best, related by family resemblance. Agnosticism and atheism might well be appended to the list. Trading in such intellectual shorthand risks both stereotyping genuine diversity and substituting bloodless abstraction for the messiness of real history. In different locations, for example, Calvinists with seriously similar theological convictions could react very differently to Darwin's theory of evolution depending on a host of other contingent factors.[8] Indeed, the fact that Darwinism itself was differently constructed in different settings and made to mean different things further complicates attempts to sort out religious, cultural, political, and other responses to evolutionary theory.[9]

If pluralizing both science and religion in efforts to construct a map of the historical terrain is desirable, so too is the range of enterprises that could usefully be incorporated within the arc of relevant sciences. Neither the social sciences, notably anthropology and sociology, nor what might be called the historical-cultural sciences, such as philology or textual criticism, ordinarily feature in standard treatments of "science and religion." Here and there throughout the present collection, significant intersections along these lines occur. Donald Lopez, for instance, tellingly reminds us that it was as a result of critical developments in the science of philology that key Buddhist texts could be studied in the original by Buddhist scholars. The development of Sanskrit studies in Europe facilitated the opening up of the early history of Buddhism in new ways. Indeed, there is a sense in which, as part of the intellectual circuitry of colonial networks and imperial imagining, the European interrogation of recovered Buddhist texts conspired to "produce a new Buddha" (see chap. 9). According to Subbarayappa, it also facilitated Europe's encounter with Indian scientific knowledge in medical and alchemical treatises, notably in the work of P. C. Ray.

The need to pluralize goes hand in hand with a second *desideratum*: the value of *localizing* science-religion encounters and placing them in their geographical setting. Indeed, the salience of geography to the entire enterprise of rethinking global science and religion tellingly manifests itself in the titles of various preceding chapters.[10] Mark Csikszentmihalyi, for example, organizes his contribution by region—China—and discusses a range of religious traditions—Confucianism, Buddhism, Daoism—within that geographical space (chap. 7). The different relationships these different religions sustained with natural science, and indeed with the imperial state, highlights something of the geopolitics of the whole subject. Again, Feierman and Janzen bound their study of sub-Saharan Africa by linguistic geography—namely, by dwelling on those areas of eastern, central, and southern Africa speaking variants of Bantu. More generally, the number of geographical modifiers that are attached to religious nouns are considerable: French rabbis, American Jews, Egyptian Muslims, Ottoman medreses, Indian spirituality, Irish monasteries, Scottish Calvinists, British evangelicals, English Anglicans, Japanese Buddhists, and so on. These characterizations alert us to the role of geographical location in the constitution of local traditions. Thus Geoffrey Cantor reminds us that the lineaments of any particular Jewish engagement with scientific knowledge depend "greatly on local factors, such as the level of discrimination against Jews" (see chap. 2). As for early Islamic science, Dallal emphasizes that Arabic astronomy developed differently in different settings, with conspicuous divergences between an eastern Maragha school and developments in North Africa. The same is also true of the evolution of modern atheism. If there are geographies of belief, so too are there spaces of unbelief. As Lightman observes, the fate of atheism has differed from national context to national context. In part, of course, this is because there is a social, as well as intellectual, history of unbelief. Over the years atheists, and proponents of heterodoxy more generally, have had to negotiate their way around legal sanction of one sort or another, and their fortunes have been contingent on the degree to which they could become socially acceptable. Considered seditious and subversive in Newton's time, atheists were later paraded by Enlightenment radicals in France as clear-thinking rational figures battling against the dark forces of superstition and prejudice. In recent times, the pattern of atheist commitment has differed between, say, Russia and the United States in response to contrasting ideologies and the differential role accorded to the idea of a state church. The geography of religion, obviously, goes hand in hand with the geography of secularization.

What is also clear from the foregoing analyses are the different spatial scales at which the location of science and religion may be analyzed. At one scale of operations, Ekmeleddin İhsanoğlu (chap. 6) considers recent Islamic encounters with science within the context of the Ottoman Empire. At another he makes it clear that science, oriental languages, and religion were collectively taught in Islamic medreses and imperial naval and medical schools. In the early Middle Ages, as Peter Harrison and David Lindberg's chapter registers (chap. 3), very specific sites (like the monastery) served as venues for the cultivation of mathematical arts, medicine, and calendrical practices. In the same period, the University of Paris was a vital center of learning and the site of controversy with the banning of Aristotle's writings on natural philosophy at various points in time during the thirteenth century. Addressing the question of location, moreover, directly connects to matters of locution. In different venues different things may be said, and heard, by speakers and auditors alike. Elsewhere I have explored the signif- icance of place in controversial cases where interlocutors paid the price for saying the wrong thing in the wrong place.[11] The geologist Alexander Winchell, who was dismissed from his position at Vanderbilt University in 1878, did not succeed in his self-imposed effort to refrain from "the utter- ance of opinions which I supposed were disapproved of by the officers of the University."[12] His views on human origins rubbed the local Methodist fraternity the wrong way. In this volume, Lightman reminds us that in cer- tain places eighteenth-century atheists and materialists feared persecution if they spoke openly. Such circumstances redraw attention to the impor- tance of locating encounters between science and religion in specific places at particular times.

If localizing the relationships between religious traditions and scientific enterprises allows the disorderliness of history to triumph over theoretical prescription, it also brings into focus the significance of what might appro- priately be called *hybridization*. Many of the stories told in this collection draw attention to cross-cultural syntheses of one sort or another. Chinese science, Csikszentmihalyi tells us, developed what he calls hybrid astron- omies; during the fifteenth century, the Qing dynasty's astronomical instru- ments in Bejing included an ecliptic armilla that had been designed by the Flemish Jewish missionary Père Ferdinand Verbiest. Buddhism brought Indian and Tibetan traditions into China, and the arrival of the Abrahamic religions heralded the integration of indigenous and Western systems of science. Again, early Jewish science changed in response to the different host environments within which it was cultivated and to shifting Islamic or Christian influences. Later, as Cantor notes, Jewish science was shaped by the relations local Jewish communities sustained with the host culture. İhsanoğlu's chapter shows how Islamic astronomy and medicine were influenced by the presence of Jewish scholars taking refuge in the Ottoman Empire. It also includes the intriguing suggestion that the idea of a conflict between science and religion was introduced into Islam from the Christian West through such events as the publication of a Turkish translation of Draper's *History of the Conflict between Religion and Science*, which called forth critical commentary from Ahmed Midhat, and the controversy surrounding the pro-Darwin statements advanced by Edwin Lewis at the Syrian Protestant College in Beirut.[13]

In India, the Hellenistic astronomy of figures like Ptolemy was synthesized with Vedic astrology to facilitate zodiac readings necessary for the proper performance of rituals and festivals. Similarly, the eleventh-century Islamic scholar, al-Biruni, incorporated Hindu astronomy into his writings, while in the thirteen and fourteenth centuries, according to Subbarayappa, Greek Hippocratic medicine was synthesized with Hindu medical knowledge. During the European Renaissance, as Harrison and Lindberg remind us, Christian thinkers debated the value of Aristotelianism for their approach to the natural world. Christian missionaries in sub-Saharan Africa played the intriguing role of disenchanting African "folk" medical customs by castigating them as pagan, first, and then re-enchanting medical practices through the integration of prayer and other spiritual exercises into hospital treatment. As Feierman and Janzen tellingly note, this was a project in the secularization of health care as a prelude to resacralizing it in a Christian key. In missionary contexts, Brooke makes clear, the advancement of scientific knowledge often depended on creative relationships with indigenous knowledge systems. As he points out, several Baptist missionaries in India sought to foster dialogue between European and local ways of knowing by teaching Sanskrit science side by side with European science. Similar patterns are discernible elsewhere too, not least in Africa, where Swiss missionaries working in entomology and botany engaged in a process of mutual knowledge exchange with indigenous Africans. Focusing on the work of Henri-Alexandre Junod, who arrived in Mozambique in 1889, Patrick Harries has shown something of how he "recognized both the different ways indigenous people comprehended and gave meaning to nature and the ways in which they contributed to his knowledge," even though he remained convinced of the superiority of Western knowledge regimes.[14]

As with the natural world, of course, intellectual hybridism has not always been considered fertile. Missionary endeavors are a case in point: in such contexts synthesis has frequently been branded syncretism. But this only serves to underscore the productive role of religious heterodoxy in scientific history.[15] The Unitarianism of Isaac Newton and Joseph Priestley is illustrative. As Brooke points out, it was their concern to cultivate a rationalized Christianity that fostered both social radicalism and a strongly proscientific outlook. Not only do such maneuvers defy the easy bipolarity of doctrinal orthodoxy or unbelieving skepticism, but they underscore the contingency of theological labeling: convictions dubbed heterodox in one place and time may acquire the benediction of conservative orthodoxy—or vice versa—in others. Harrison and Lindberg, for example, compellingly show how atomism, at one point deemed to display atheistic tendencies, could later be staged as a friend, not a foe, of Christianity and certainly more hospitable than Aristotelian matter theory.

Hybridism, of course, steals into intellectual circulation in other ways too, for example, through acts of translation. For translation is never simply transmission; it is transformation. As Marwa Elshakry has pointed out, modern science translations into Arabic have been freighted with cultural politics. The fact that there was no specific Arabic term for the word "species" made translation of Darwin's *Origin* anything but straightforward; the lack of a precise Arabic equivalent for the term "evolution" only compounded the problem. Choosing whether to refashion older terms or to make up new ones had hybridizing implications for intellectual exchange.[16] In the present collection, Ahmad Dallal points out that by translating Greek works into Arabic, Islamic scholars "did more than simply preserve the Greek scientific legacy"—they brought about a significant Islamization of science (see chap. 5). During the colonial period in India, European scientific ideas and practices were not introduced into India through a smooth process of diffusion. Rather, they were domesticated to local needs, not least in the work of Raja Rammohun Roy, who remained Hindu to the core of his being even while championing the introduction of various European-style natural sciences into the curriculum.[17] All of this challenges the assumption that modern European science simply diffused across the globe. Instead, as Kapil Raj has shown, intercultural encounters were of crucial significance for the growth of knowledge about botany, cartography, terrestrial surveying, and linguistics.[18]

Other instances of the hybrid intertwining of different scientific and religious traditions could readily be elaborated. The point is that the collective import of cultivating a sensitivity toward the hybrid, the amalgamated, and the synthetic is that it subverts the idea of science or religion as "pure" enterprises. Their "impurity," moreover, alerts us to the wider context of "science" and "religion," and thus to the ways in which they may be mobilized in the interests of cultural *politics*. Lopez notes how certain versions of Buddhism were adopted by some people in search of a scientific religion as an alternative to traditional theism. In early-modern Europe, as Harrison and Lindberg show, Newtonian science and religion were deployed as resources in the service of monarchy and moderatism against republicanism and radicalism. "Newton's divinely controlled mechanical universe," Lightman writes, "became the model for the triumph of the new Whig constitution and for the liberal Christians who supported it" (see chap. 11). And Brooke points out that Joseph Priestley thought certain Christian doctrines were indispensable for social control. All this serves to remind us that "science and religion" are always embedded in wider socio-political networks and their relationship is conditioned by the prevailing cultural arrangements.

Precisely the same is no less true of "agnosticism." Coined by Thomas Henry Huxley, this term enabled him to place himself somewhere between traditional faith and extremist forms of unbelief that circulated among disreputable working-class radicals.

Science and religion have served as cultural resources in other ways too. Their role in the maintenance of cultural identity, for example, is not insignificant. A critical distinction can be drawn between confessional believers and those resorting to religion simply as a marker of ethnic belonging. Geoffrey Cantor's chapter is illustrative for its treatment of atheistic Jews who align themselves culturally with the Jewish community but possess no specifically religious convictions. Complications of this stripe crucially inflect our understanding of the role of Judaism in scientific enterprises. Such circumstances point to the role of the iconic in elucidating encounters between science and religion. Some episodes achieve symbolic significance and are staged as emblematic of wider intellectual currents. The Wilberforce-Huxley confrontation in Oxford in 1860, the Tyndall furor at the 1874 British Association meeting in Belfast, the Scopes trial in Dayton, Tennessee, in 1925, even the name of Charles Darwin have come to symbolize conservatism, skepticism, intransigence, far-sightedness, or atheism—depending on how they are represented. Here historical fact concedes to cultural politics. Attending to the place of symbolism modulates the interpretation of science and religion in critical ways. In China, for example, Csikszentmihalyi reminds us that the project of adapting indigenous belief to scientific demands ran the risk of being seen as capitulating to the Westernization of values. In a comparable way, as Noah Efron makes clear, natural knowledge was sometimes seen by Jews as embodying foreign wisdom, a view that could breed an attitude of suspicion about science and make it "unseemly." Greater sensitivity to the symbolic significance of pronouncements and performances would enrich our understanding of the long history of science and religion in far-reaching ways.

FLASH POINTS AND TRADING ZONES

If this collection of essays complicates received wisdom about "science and religion" by challenging monochrome portrayals of the relationship as inherently pugilistic or irenic, it also identifies what I want to call flash points and trading zones. By the former I mean those matters—different from tradition to tradition, from place and place, from time to time—that have been seen to matter in religion's encounter with science. Identifying some of these shows how variegated the intellectual landscape has been. By trading zones I refer to those arenas of engagement where the interface between science and religion has facilitated fruitful intellectual exchange. The term "trading zone" has been used in anthropological studies to describe something of the processes by which different cultures have been able to exchange commodities despite their differences in language, social relations, and so on. It has been deployed in studies of science and technology to explain how trading can take place even when the partners, as Peter Galison puts it, "ascribe utterly different significance to the objects being exchanged."[19]

So far as flash points are concerned, the list of potential candidates is a lengthy one, and a few examples must suffice. In Britain and the United States, a persistent though not universal source of contention has centered on questions of design, teleology, and natural theology. As Lightman's chapter shows, Richard Dawkins's recent *The God Delusion*, for example, largely rotates around the conviction that Darwin's theory of evolution shattered "the illusion of design" by showing that apparent purpose is nothing more than the product of humdrum, natural causes (see chap. 11). This, of course, is only the last in a long sequence of scientific assaults on teleology. French advocates of a more radical enlightenment in the eighteenth century, like Diderot and d'Holbach, attacked the Newtonian moderates and pushed for an all-embracing naturalism. Their stance stood in marked contrast to Newton's Unitarian defense of a purposive cosmic order and Voltaire's commitment to providential deism. Later, as Brooke notes, nineteenth-century figures like William Whewell were of the opinion that scientific analysis could not proceed without invoking final causes. Design was also an issue for Islamic encounters with scientific claims. Because traditional Kalam arguments from design remained important, as İhsanoğlu points out, what he calls the "more ideological forms" of Darwinism and materialism, alongside philosophical positivism and social Darwinism, brought discord. By contrast, arguments from design are only conspicuous in Jewish works by their relative absence. At the same time, different stances could be adopted *within* traditions. The flourishing of natural theology in seventeenth-century England represented one Christian response to what were perceived to be the dangers of a mechanistic atomism; by contrast, later writers as diverse as Thomas Chalmers and John Henry Newman did not hesitate to identify theological reservations about the teleological argument. Newman never cared for the design argument because he was never able to see its logical force; Chalmers thought it could never lead to Christian theism.[20]

Other flash points could readily be elaborated. In certain religious traditions the question of origins has loomed large; in others this has not been the case. In contrast to Christian and Islamic anxieties over the implications of evolution, not least for understanding the nature of the image of God and the dignity of the human species, Hindus generally displayed much less distress about Darwinism, because their immanentist philosophy avoided the dualism between creator and creation (as noted in chap. 8). The links between natural philosophy and the tradition of natural magic were more troublesome for some traditions than others. For Jews, Efron reminds us, Talmudic bans on magic were critically important, and later Maimonides sought to undermine astrology. In traditions united by a canonical text, the development of the science of textual criticism could create major difficulties for orthodox believers. In other times, places, and settings, different issues dominated the science-religion skyline. Among these we might refer to the questioning of divine miracle by the idea of omnipresent natural law; the subversion of free will in deterministic projects that conflated mind and brain; the challenges that new theories of matter posed to some understandings of the Eucharist; the materialistic ethos of certain strands of scientific reductionism; the use of scientific research to support various forms of eugenics. All these—and doubtless many more—have been flash points for certain groups in certain places at certain times in science's dialogue with religion. This realization forces us to acknowledge the complexities of science-religion narratives and should curb any inclination to universalize particulars. Because Copernicanism was problematic in parts of Christian Europe, for example, is no reason to presume that it was universally troublesome for religious communities. According to İhsanoğlu, heliocentrism caused no comparable stir among Ottoman scholars when it was reported in Arabic translation.

Flash points in one mode, of course, may surface as trading zones in another. If their commitment to teleology made some religious believers resistant to certain forms of scientific explanation, natural theology in different settings could act as a stimulus to scientific inquiry. The idea of a divinely designed natural world was foundational to the work on natural history conducted by the seventeenth- and eighteenth-century writers John Ray and William Derham. For them, the belief that living things were divinely adapted to their natural environments fostered their inquiries into plant and animal life. The treatises produced by figures like these were thus both theological and scientific at the same time. The doctrine of humanity's fall from grace and the theology of original sin could likewise serve as a trading ground for scientific and theological exchange. Advocates of the new experimental philosophy of the sixteenth and seventeenth centuries frequently took with great seriousness the adverse implications of these particular Judeo-Christian doctrines for human rationality—what Harrison and Lindberg judiciously call "the wounding of reason." Recognition of this fallen condition kindled a sense that mechanisms needed to be put in place to overcome the epistemic consequences of original corruption and its legacy of human depravity.[21] New observational instruments, measuring devices, experimental apparatus, and warranting procedures were all espoused in hopes of introducing greater rigor into knowledge-acquiring enterprises. In this trading zone, productive exchanges could take place between theological thinking about the epistemic implications of fallen humanity and technological developments in scientific instrumentation.

The belief of the monotheistic religions that all humankind have descended from Adam has also fostered intellectual traffic between theological conviction and scientific inquiry. The search for Adam's language, efforts to elucidate human racial differentiation, whether the human race is of monogenetic or polygenetic origin, the relationship between the world chronologies of different regional cultures, how emerging archeological artifacts should be interpreted—stances on all of these subjects were hammered out on the terrain of humankind's Adamic ancestry.[22] The character of reading practices has also been a ground on which science and religion have traded wares. According to Harrison and Lindberg, shifts in how the book of scripture was read had a critical effect on ways of reading the book of nature during the early-modern development of science. The demise of allegorical approaches to Bible reading, they suggest, had subsidiary consequences for the tradition of interpreting the natural order through emblems and symbols. In this case literalism, which in a later era could disrupt science's relationship with theology, had a positive impact on the development of scientific theory.[23]

Such zones of exchange, of course, are not restricted to Judeo-Christian traditions. The eliding of certain strands in Buddhism with various forms of psychoanalysis (in the wake of the contributions by Daisetz Teitaro Suzuki on Zen) and with aspects of modern physics (such as Fritjof Capra's *The Tao of Physics*) are cases in point, as Lopez's chapter illustrates. Indeed it has been claimed that Buddhist philosophy exemplifies the operation of scientific method in the realm of psychological self-scrutiny. The Dalai Lama, for example, has warmly embraced scientific achievements, thereby legitimizing a transfer space between religion and modern science. Zonal trafficking is also part of the story of science and religion in the Vedic traditions. Metaphysics and mathematics, for example, engaged in cross-border trading with the concept of zero serving as tender while, as Subbarayappa shows, the study of eclipses facilitated the development of astronomical techniques for Vedic astrological purposes. More recently, in his pioneering work in physics and physiology, J. C. Bose believed he could see manifestations of the Hindu idea of unity. Commerce in such zones, of course, may not always have dealt in the currency of explanation, but they certainly have made space available for empirical advancements.

Despite widespread reports of secularization in the West, a number of new contact zones have been opened up in the wake of a series of scientific-metaphysical developments during the twentieth century. Brooke advertises several of these in the closing pages of his chapter. The principle of indeterminacy (arising from quantum mechanics), the Big Bang cosmology, and the exceptionally constricted range of conditions necessary for carbon-based life have all been used as resources to underwrite an anti-deterministic defense of free will, the reassertion of the doctrine of creation, and the revisiting of teleology through the idea of cosmic fine-tuning. And the list could be further extended. Pierre Teilhard de Chardin, the Jesuit paleontologist, controversially extended the principle of evolutionary trans-formation into the spiritual realm with his conception of the noosphere as a kind of phenomenological layer of human collective consciousness that evolved after the geosphere and biosphere, and his claim that the Omega Point is the ultimate goal toward which all creation is moving.[24] Wolfhart Pannenberg and others, such as T. F. Torrance, have—no less contentiously—fastened upon the idea of fields of force in modern physics as a resource for thinking about the nature of God.[25] In these proposals and the ensuing debates, modern field theory serves as the territory on which modern the-ology seeks to engage contemporary natural science.

TENSIONS AND POLARITIES

Science and Religion around the World delightfully complicates popular narratives of "the relationship between science and religion." It pluralizes the entire enterprise, identifies cross-cutting themes, highlights the role of cultural politics, and attends to difference and divergence from time to time and place to place. It also discloses the wide range of issues that have been the focal point of contention between religious believers and scientific prac-titioners, as well as zones of contact that have opened up new channels of communication and intellectual commerce. But this does not mean that there is no further work to be done. A sequence of tensions and polarities remain that should form agenda items for future investigation.

In my view, a tension between the particular and the general still persists in accounts of the historical relations between science and religion. When grand narratives are deconstructed by tradition, period, and place, there remains the problem of ascertaining how very specific case studies of indi-viduals or communities relate to broader currents of thought and action. Just how to use a biography or local study without underclaiming or overclaiming remains a difficulty. Figuring out the way in which Belfast Presbyterians responded to the challenge of Darwin in the 1870s—to take one example—tells us something both about Belfast and about Presbyte-rians. It tells us something about two scales of inquiry—local and global.

Exactly *what* it tells about each is no less easy to discern than ascertaining how these different scales of operation relate to one another. How to handle the differences between intellectual leaders and popular audiences also remains a difficulty. As Brooke makes clear, it is important to distinguish between "opinions formulated by an intellectual elite and by relatively unsophisticated members of the public."[26] And at the same time, critical differences may be discernible between different kinds of elites. Jewish understandings of science are not restricted to the commentaries of rabbis; the stances adopted by practicing Jewish scientists also constitute a critical part of the story. These are differences that make a difference, for they disturb any presumption that it is possible to identify *the* Jewish, or Christian, or Hindu, or Muslim reaction to, say, Darwinian evolution, or Freudian psychoanalysis, or Einsteinian relativity.

A careful reading of these essays will also serve to underscore the fact that science and religion may converge on the ground of practice as much as theory. There is much said in the different chapters about ideas, theories, ideologies, and theologies. But from time to time, the critical importance of performance and practice also shines through. Think of how metallurgical skills in China were crucial to the construction of ancient bells used for religious purposes. In China, too, musical technology was mobilized to produce instruments that were integral to the practices of geomancy and other ritual performances. In early Judaism, knowledge about animals was a combination of observation and ritual practice. In sub-Saharan Africa certain "practices, at once religious and medical, were seen as an intervention involving supernatural forces and natural processes" (see chap. 10). Among the Indic religions, the performance of sacrifice required precise determination of timing, which, in turn, stimulated astronomical inquiry, while the construction of sacrificial altars was intimately bound up with developments in Vedic geometry. The production of astronomical devices for determining the sacred direction in Islam, the cultivation of science as itself a godly pursuit in early-modern England, and the use of mathematics for the calendrical calculation of holy dates are just a few additional spheres of practice in which science and religion have come together. Collectively they alert us to the performative dimensions of both science and religion—an association that is too often forgotten.

Finally, understanding the dynamic of science and religion runs the spectrum from what I would call religious science to the science of religion. In spaces where religion tends to dominate the conversation, adjectival science surfaces: Torah science, Hindu medicine, Islamic astronomy, creation science, Catholic psychology. Where science governs the discourse, religion tends to be explained by science: the anthropology of religion, the search for the God gene, the evolution of spirituality, the economics of communal faith, the neurochemistry of religious experience.[27] And yet it would be easy to make unwarranted assumptions at either end of the spectrum, as two concluding cases will illustrate.

The development of a self-conscious Calvinist science at the Free University of Amsterdam during the 1930s, in the wake of Abraham Kuper's vision, constituted a concerted attempt to conduct scientific research on Calvinist principles. But this did not mean confrontation with the conventional science of the time. Ironically, the Calvinist worldview of key members of the faculty permitted a certain freedom of scientific inquiry that facilitated the "acceptance of mainstream science in Dutch Calvinist circles."[28] Through their work on such subjects as radioactivity and the age of the earth, the philosophy of physics and causality, quantum mechanics and the nature of reality, they sought to keep science and religion in tandem.

At the opposite end of the continuum, it was when anthropologically inclined scholars brought religion within the sphere of scientific explanation and treated it as a dependent variable that conflicts arose—as in Ernest Renan's portrayal of Islam as inherently unsuited to the cultivation of science. Among British anthropologists during the latter part of the nineteenth century, the anthropology of religion could be recruited to bolster what Lightman calls "a new tradition of secular theorizing about religion without reference to the truth-content of its claims" (see chap. 12). And yet this was not universally the case. William Robertson Smith's historical anthropology of sacrifice, totemism, and exogamy, despite the assault to which he was subjected by his fellow churchmen, only served to reinforce his belief that through his excavations into the archeology of primitive religion he was unearthing the "first germs" of "eternal" theological "truths."[29]

Counterintuitive stances like these usefully stand as emblematic of the argument that I have sought to marshal in this epilogue. They subvert expectations, they localize encounters, they resist stereotype, and they inspire the conviction that the misplaced certainties of presumption are not to be preferred to the messy contingencies of history.

Notes

1. Steven Shapin, *The Scientific Revolution* (Chicago: University of Chicago Press, 1996), 1.

2. Thomas Dixon, *Science and Religion: A Very Short Introduction* (Oxford: Oxford University Press, 2008), 3.

3. Priya Shetty and Andy Coghlan, "Royal Society Fellows Turn on Director over Creationism" *New Scientist*, September 16, 2008. Available online at: www.newscientist.com/article/dn14744-royal-society-fellows-turn-on-director-over-creationism.

html. The full text of the letter appears on Richard Dawkins's website: http://richarddawkins.net/articles/3119.

4. Quoted in Shetty and Coghlan, "Royal Society Fellows Turn on Director."

5. John William Draper, *History of the Conflict between Religion and Science* (London: Henry King, 1875), 353.

6. Stephen Jay Gould, "Nonoverlapping Magisteria," *Natural History* 106 (March 1997): 16–22.

7. Michael Ruse, "Review of Stephen Jay Gould's 'Rocks of Ages,'" *Global Spiral* (July 1999), available online at: www.metanexus.net/magazine/ArticleDetail/tabid/68/id/3044/Default.aspx.

8. I have discussed this in "Darwinism and Calvinism: The Belfast-Princeton Connection," *Isis* 83 (1992): 408–28, and "Science, Region, and Religion: The Reception of Darwinism in Princeton, Belfast, and Edinburgh," in *Disseminating Darwinism: The Role of Place, Race, Religion, and Gender*, ed. Ronald L. Numbers and John Stenhouse, 7–38 (Cambridge: Cambridge University Press, 1999).

9. See David N. Livingstone, "Science, Text and Space: Thoughts on the Geography of Reading," *Transactions of the Institute of British Geographers* 35 (2005): 391–401.

10. My thoughts on the subject of the historical geographies of science are developed in David N. Livingstone, *Putting Science in Its Place: Geographies of Scientific Knowledge* (Chicago: University of Chicago Press, 2003).

11. David N. Livingstone, "Science, Site, and Speech: Scientific Knowledge and the Spaces of Rhetoric," *History of the Human Sciences* 20 (2007): 71–98. See also Diarmid A. Finnegan, "Exeter-Hall Science and Evangelical Rhetoric in mid-Victorian London," *Journal of Victorian Culture* 16 (2011): in press.

12. Quoted in Leonard Alberstadt, "Alexander Winchell's Preadamites—A Case for Dismissal from the Vanderbilt University," *Earth Sciences History* 13 (1994): 97–112.

13. See also Marwa Elshakry, "The Gospel of Science and American Evangelicalism in Late Ottoman Beirut," *Past and Present* 197 (August 2007): 173–214.

14. Patrick Harries, *Butterflies and Barbarians: Swiss Missionaries and Systems of Knowledge in South-East Africa* (Oxford: James Currey, 2007), 5.

15. See John Hedley Brooke and Ian Maclean, eds., *Heterodoxy in Early Modern Science and Religion* (Oxford: Oxford University Press, 2005).

16. Marwa S. Elshakry, "Knowledge in Motion: The Cultural Politics of Modern Science Translations in Arabic," *Isis* 99 (2008): 701–30.

17. See also Deepak Kumar, *Science and the Raj, 1857–1905* (Delhi: Oxford University Press, 1995).

18. Kapil Raj, *Relocating Modern Science: Circulation and the Construction of Knowledge in South Asia and Europe, 1650–1900* (London: Palgrave, 2007).

19. Peter Galison, *Image and Logic: A Material Culture of Microphysics* (Chicago: University of Chicago Press, 1997), 783.

20. See the discussions in Michael Ruse, *Darwin and Design: Does Evolution Have a Purpose?* (Cambridge, Mass.: Harvard University Press, 2004).

21. Peter Harrison, *The Fall of Man and the Foundations of Science* (Cambridge: Cambridge University Press, 2008).

22. I have discussed this in *Adam's Ancestors: Race, Religion and the Politics of Human Origins* (Baltimore, Md.: Johns Hopkins University Press, 2008).

23. See also Peter Harrison, *The Bible, Protestantism, and the Rise of Natural Science* (Cambridge: Cambridge University Press, 2001).

24. For a discussion of this and comparable evolutionary eschatologies, see Ernst Benz, *Evolution and Christian Hope: Man's Concept of the Future from the Early Fathers to Teilhard de Chardin* (New York: Doubleday, 1966).

25. See Max Jammer, *Einstein and Physics: Physics and Theology* (Princeton, N.J.: Princeton University Press, 1999).

26. For a history of popular responses to science and religion, see Ronald L. Numbers, "Science and Christianity among the People: A Vulgar History," in *Science and Christianity in Pulpit and Pew* (New York: Oxford University Press, 2007), 11–38.

27. A useful brief overview of such contemporary projects is "Where Angels No Longer Fear to Tread: Scientists Try to Explain Religion," *Economist*, March 22, 2008.

28. Abraham C. Flipse, "Against the Science-Religion Conflict: The Genesis of a Calvinist Science Faculty in the Netherlands in the Early Twentieth Century," *Annals of Science* 65 (2008): 363–91, on 363.

29. William Robertson Smith, "Sacrifice," *Encyclopaedia Britannica*, 9th ed., 24 vols. (Edinburgh, 1875–1889), 9:138.

Science and Religion around the World

EDITED BY
John Hedley Brooke and
Ronald L. Numbers

UNIVERSITY PRESS

2011

A Guide to Further Reading

GENERAL

Brooke, John Hedley. *Science and Religion: Some Historical Perspectives*. Cambridge: Cambridge University Press, 1991. The now-standard introduction to the history of science and religion, which stresses the richness and diversity of the relations between science and religion from the medieval period to the present.

Brooke, John Hedley, and Geoffrey Cantor. *Reconstructing Nature: The Engagement of Science and Religion*. Edinburgh: T and T Clark, 1998. Argues for a variety of historical approaches to the study of science and religion.

Brooke, John Hedley, Margaret J. Osler, and Jitse Van der Meer, eds. *Science in Theistic Contexts: Cognitive Dimensions*. *Osiris* 16 (2001). Case studies that explore the roles of religious and anti-religious beliefs in shaping the content of scientific theories.

Dixon, Thomas. *Science and Religion: A Very Short Introduction*. Oxford: Oxford University Press, 2008. The title says it all.

Dixon, Thomas, Geoffrey Cantor, and Stephen Pumfrey, eds. *Science and Religion: New Historical Perspectives*. Cambridge: Cambridge University Press, 2010. Explores the "complexity thesis" and other issues.

Ecklund, Elaine Howard. *Science vs. Religion: What Do Scientists Really Think?* New York: Oxford University Press, 2010. The most up-to-date sociological survey.

Ferngren, Gary B., ed. *The History of Science and Religion in the Western Tradition: An Encyclopedia*. New York: Garland, 2000. A useful anthology of essays exploring key themes in the historical relations between Christianity and science.

Harrison, Peter. "'Science' and 'Religion': Constructing the Boundaries," *Journal of Religion* 86 (2006): 81–106. Puts the categories into historical context.

Numbers, Ronald L., ed. *Galileo Goes to Jail and Other Myths in Science and Religion* Cambridge, Mass.: Harvard University Press, 2009. An antidote to the many myths that circulate in the press and in the popular mind.

Numbers, Ronald L., and Darrel W. Amundsen, eds. *Caring and Curing: Health and Medicine in the Western Religious Traditions*. New York: Macmillan, 1986. Historical essays on the various faith traditions.

Olson, Richard. *Science Deified and Science Defied: The Historical Significance of Science in Western Culture*. 2 vols. Berkeley: University of California Press, 1982, 1990.

Looks at episodes of interaction between science and other aspects of Western culture, including religion, from the Bronze Age to the early nineteenth century.

Nicolaas A. Rupke, ed. *Eminent Lives in Twentieth-Century Science and Religion*. Revised and expanded ed. Frankfurt am Main: Peter Lang, 2009. Biographical studies.

JUDAISM

Cantor, Geoffrey, and Marc Swetlitz, eds. *Jewish Tradition and the Challenge of Darwinism*. Chicago: University of Chicago Press, 2006. A collection of ten papers that addresses a wide range of Jewish responses to Darwin's theory of evolution.

Charpa, Ulrich, and Ute Deichmann, eds. *Jews and Sciences in German Contexts: Case Studies from the 19th and 20th Centuries*. Tübingen: Mohr Siebeck, 2007. Focusing on a number of German-Jewish scientists, contributors to this volume explore the relationship between their scientific activities and the culture, religion, and social situation of German Jews.

Efron, Noah. *Judaism and Science: A Historical Introduction*. Westport, Conn,: Greenwood Press, 2007. An excellent introduction that provides an accessible and wide-ranging overview of the Jewish engagement with science ranging from biblical reflections on nature to Israel's present-day commitment to scientific and technological innovation.

Fisch, Menachem. *Rational Rabbis: Science and Talmudic Culture*. Bloomington: Indiana University Press, 1997. This demanding and illuminating book argues that there is a deep similarity between modern scientific inquiry and traditional Rabbinic inquiry, with both sorts of discourse being highly critical endeavors.

Freudenthal, Gad. *Science in the Medieval Hebrew and Arabic Traditions*. Aldershot, U.K.: Ashgate, 2004. The sixteen essays in this book describe the circumstances in which medieval Jews in Southern France accepted or rejected contemporary physical theories.

Hollinger, David A. *Science, Jews, and Secular Culture: Studies in Mid-Twentieth-Century American Intellectual History*. Princeton, N.J.: Princeton University Press, 1996. Shows how significant numbers of Jews gained entry to American universities in the period from the 1930s to 1960s and the influence they exerted on academia, especially on the physical and social sciences.

Jammer, Max. *Einstein and Religion: Physics and Theology*. Princeton, N.J.: Princeton University Press, 1999. Offers a thoughtful analysis of Einstein's views on religion, ranging from his reflections on religion in general and Judaism in particular, as well as their relation to his physics.

Langermann, Y. Tzvi. *The Jews and the Sciences in the Middle Ages*. Aldershot, U.K.: Ashgate, 1999. These learned essays present a rich composite portrait of the Hebrew and Arabic natural philosophy texts produced by medieval, renaissance, and early modern Jews.

Preuss, Julius, and Fred Rosner. *Biblical and Talmudic Medicine*. Northvale, N.J.: J. Aronson, 1993. This English translation and update of Preuss' classic, massive 1911 *Biblisch-Talmudische Medizin* advances no sustained argument but contains almost every biblical and Talmudic reference to medicine (and, as a matter of course, allied sciences).

Rabkin, Yakov, and Ira Robinson, eds. *The Interaction of Scientific and Jewish Cultures in Modern Times*. Lewiston, N.Y.: Edwin Mellen Press, 1995. This collection of

papers, covering the eighteenth to twentieth centuries, examines the impact
of science on traditional Jewish cultures and also the entry of Jews into the
sciences.

Ruderman, David B. *Jewish Thought and Scientific Discovery in Early Modern Europe.*
New Haven, Conn.: Yale University Press, 1995. Covers the period from the late
sixteenth to the late eighteenth century, demonstrating that Jewish physicians
and other intellectuals creatively combined innovations in science with traditional Jewish modes of thought.

Samuelson, Norbert M. *Jewish Faith and Modern Science: On the Death and Rebirth of
Jewish Philosophy.* Lanham, Md.: Rowman and Littlefield, 2008. Offers a challenging
vision of how Jewish thought could be revitalized in light of crucial developments
in the sciences.

Shatzmiller, Joseph. *Jews, Medicine, and Medieval Society.* Berkeley: University of
California Press, 1994. A social history of medieval Jewish doctors, which describes
the complicated relationships they forged with their Christian patients and patrons
in France, Spain, and Italy.

Tirosh-Samuelson, Hava, ed. *Judaism and Ecology: Created World and Revealed Word.*
Cambridge, Mass.: Center for the Study of World Religions, 2003. Explores
conceptions of nature in Jewish literature.

CHRISTIANITY

Amundsen, Darrel W. *Medicine, Society, and Faith in the Ancient and Medieval Worlds.*
Baltimore: Johns Hopkins University Press, 1996. A collection of essays on
medicine and Christianity before about 1500.

Artigas, Mariano, Thomas F. Glick, and Rafael A. Martínez. *Negotiating Darwin: The
Vatican Confronts Evolution, 1877–1902.* Baltimore: Johns Hopkins University
Press, 2006. Draws on recently unsealed Vatican documents to reconstruct the
Catholic church's response to Darwinism.

Bowler, Peter J. *Reconciling Science and Religion: The Debate in Early-Twentieth-Century
Britain.* Chicago: University of Chicago Press, 2001. Science and religion in Britain
from the late nineteenth century to World War II.

I. Bernard Cohen, ed. *Puritanism and the Rise of Modern Science: The Merton Thesis.* New Brunswick, N.J.: Rutgers University Press, 1990. A useful collection that
discusses one of the classic accounts of the role of religion in the rise of science.

Fantoli, Annibale. *Galileo: For Copernicanism and for the Church.* Translated by George
V. Coyne. 2nd ed. Vatican City: Vatican Observatory, 1996. The best account of the
"Galileo affair."

Ferngren, Gary B. *Medicine and Health Care in Early Christianity.* Baltimore: Johns
Hopkins University Press, 2009. A scholarly, if somewhat biased, survey.

Finocchiaro, Maurice A. *The Galileo Affair: A Documentary History.* Berkeley: University
of California Press, 1989. A valuable collection of primary documents.

Grant, Edward. *God and Reason in the Middle Ages.* Cambridge: Cambridge University
Press, 2001. Traces the rise of reason (and natural philosophy) in the late medieval Christian universities.

Peter Harrison, *The Bible, Protestantism, and the Rise of Natural Science.* Cambridge:
Cambridge University Press, 1998. Explains the role of the Bible, and of new
approaches to its interpretation, in influencing the development of science.

————. *The Fall of Man and the Foundations of Science*. Cambridge: Cambridge University Press, 2007. Shows how the biblical narrative of the Fall and the idea of original sin informed early-modern discussions about knowledge and shaped the methods of the new sciences.

Heilbron, J. L. *The Sun in the Church: Cathedrals as a Solar Observatories*. Cambridge, Mass.: Harvard University Press, 1999. Argues that Catholic churches "were the best solar observatories in the world" and that the "Roman Catholic Church gave more financial and social support to the study of astronomy for over six centuries . . . than any other, and probably all, other institutions."

Lindberg, David C. *The Beginnings of Western Science: The European Scientific Tradition in Philosophical, Religious, and Institutional Context, Prehistory to A.D. 1450*. 2nd edition. Chicago: University of Chicago Press, 2007. The standard account.

Lindberg, David C., and Ronald L. Numbers, eds., *God and Nature: Historical Essays on the Encounter between Christianity and Science*. Berkeley: University of California Press, 1986. A classic collection of scholarly essays that was instrumental in introducing greater sophistication into the discussion of science and religion.

————. *When Science and Christianity Meet*. Chicago: University of Chicago Press, 2003. An introductory text designed to be accessible to readers new to the subject.

Livingstone, David N. *Adam's Ancestors: Race, Religion, and the Politics of Human Origins*. Baltimore: Johns Hopkins University Press, 2008. Traces the history of the idea of non-Adamic human ancestry.

Livingstone, David N., D. G. Hart, and Mark A. Noll, eds. *Evangelicals and Science in Historical Perspective*. New York: Oxford University Press, 1999. In breadth and depth, this provides one of the best accounts of the changing place of science within evangelical Christianity.

McCluskey, Stephen C. *Astronomies and Cultures in Early Medieval Europe*. Cambridge: Cambridge University Press, 1998. A study of astronomy in the monastic culture of the early Middle Ages.

Numbers, Ronald L. *The Creationists: From Scientific Creationism to Intelligent Design*. Expanded ed. Cambridge, Mass.: Harvard University Press, 2006. Traces the growth of antievolutionist movements around the globe.

————. *Science and Christianity in Pulpit and Pew*. New York: Oxford University Press, 2007. Includes a "vulgar history" of science and religion among the people.

O'Leary, Don. *Roman Catholicism and Modern Science: A History*. New York: Continuum, 2006. From Pope Urban VIII (Galileo's nemesis) to Pope John Paul II.

Roberts, Jon H. *Darwinism and the Divine in America: Protestant Intellectuals and Organic Evolution, 1859–1900*. Madison: University of Wisconsin Press, 1988. The most thorough investigation of the reaction of American Protestants to evolutionary theory, emphasizing the biblical concerns of the participants.

ISLAM

Al-Hasan, Ahmad Y., and Donald Hill. *Islamic Technology: An Illustrated History*. Cambridge: Cambridge University Press, 1986. A history of technology and the fine arts in Islam.

Berggren, Lennart. *Episodes in the Mathematics of Medieval Islam.* New York: Springer, 2003. A short but comprehensive review of the major contributions of mathematicians in the Islamic world.

Dallal, Ahmad. *Islam, Science, and the Challenge of History.* New Haven, Conn.: Yale University Press, 2010. A masterful study, originally presented as part of Yale's distinguished Terry Lecture Series.

Elshakry, Marwa. *Reading Darwin in the Middle East.* Chicago: University of Chicago Press, 2011. The best study of the introduction of Darwin's theory in Islamic societies.

Gutas, Dimitri. *Greek Thought, Arabic Culture: The Graeco-Arabic Translation Movement in Baghdad and Early 'Abbasid Society (2nd–4th/8th–10th centuries).* London: Routledge, 1998. An excellent account of the translation movement in Islam.

Haq, Syed Nomanul. "Myth 4: That Medieval Islamic Culture Was Inhospitable to Science." In *Galileo Goes to Jail and Other Myths about Science and Religion,* edited by Ronald L. Numbers, 35–42. Cambridge, Mass.: Harvard University Press, 2009. A brief introduction.

Hogendijk, Jan P., and Abdelhamid I. Sabra, eds. *The Enterprise of Science in Islam: New Perspectives.* Cambridge, Mass.: MIT Press, 2003. Articles on various aspects of science in Islam.

İhsanoğlu, Ekmeleddin, ed. *Cultural Contacts in Building a Universal Civilization: Islamic Contributions.* Istanbul: Research Centre for Islamic History, Art and Culture, 2005. Focuses on the interaction between Islam and the West.

———. *Science, Technology and Learning in the Ottoman Empire: Western Influence, Local Institutions, and the Transfer of Knowledge.* Aldershot, U.K.: Ashgate, 2004. Includes several essays on Islam and science during the Ottoman Empire (1299–1923).

Keller, Richard C. *Colonial Madness: Psychiatry in French North Africa.* Chicago: University of Chicago Press, 2007. Western psychiatry constructs Muslim madness.

Kennedy, Edward S. *Astronomy and Astrology in the Medieval Islamic World.* Aldershot, U.K.: Ashgate, 1998. Essays dealing with technical aspects of astronomy and astrology in Islam.

King, David. *Astronomy in the Service of Islam.* Aldershot, U.K.: Ashgate, 1993. Explores the influence of Islamic rituals on the practice of astronomy in Islam.

Nasr, Seyyed Hossein. *Science and Civilization in Islam.* Cambridge, Mass.: Harvard University Press, 1968. A survey focusing on the influence of Islam on development of science in Muslim states.

Pormann, Peter, and Emilie Savage-Smith. *Medieval Islamic Medicine.* Washington, D.C.: Georgetown University Press, 2007. A recent survey of Islamic medicine that rejects the stereotypical idea that Islamic medicine was merely a translation of Greek writings.

Sabra, A. I. "The Appropriation and Subsequent Naturalization of Greek Science in Medieval Islam: A Preliminary Statement." *History of Science* 25 (1987): 223–43. A classic article about the gradual assimilation and transformation of Greek sciences in Islamic societies.

Saliba, George. *Islamic Science and the Making of the European Renaissance*. Cambridge, Mass.: MIT Press, 2007. Focuses on the transfer of Islamic science to pre-modern Europe.

Sayili, Aydin. *The Observatory in Islam: And Its Place in the General History of the Observatory*. Ankara: Turk Tarih Kurumu Basimevi, 1960. Written by the first trained historian of science in the Islamic world.

Shefer-Mossensohn, Miri. *Ottoman Medicine: Healing and Medical Institutions, 1500–1700*. Albany: State University of New York Press, 2009. An up-to-date study that includes coverage of the relationship between medicine and religion.

Ullman, Manfred. *Islamic Medicine*. Edinburgh: Edinburgh University Press, 1978. A readable introduction to the history of medicine in Islam.

ASIAN RELIGIONS

Arnold, David. *Science, Technology and Medicine in Colonial India*. Cambridge: Cambridge University Press, 2000. Includes illuminating discussions of Hindu science and medicine.

Barbieri-Low, Anthony. *Artisans in Early Imperial China*. Seattle: University of Washington Press, 2007. Provides insight into how the visual and material cultural remains of early imperial China were made and thus illuminates the workshops and socio-economic context of cultural productions.

Brown, C. Mackenzie. "Hindu Responses to Darwinism: Assimilation and Rejection in a Colonial and Post-Colonial Context." *Science and Education* 19 (2010): 705–38. By far the best account.

———. "The Western Roots of Avataric Evolutionism in Colonial India." *Zygon* 42 (2007): 423–47; "Colonial and Post-Colonial Elaborations of Avataric Evolutionism," ibid., 715–47. Explores claims that ancient Hindu myths of Vishnu's ten incarnations foreshadowed Darwinian evolution.

Capra, Fritjof. *The Tao of Physics: An Exploration of the Parallels Between Modern Physics and Eastern Mysticism*. 3rd ed. Boston: Shambhala, 1991. First published in 1975, this bestselling work finds deep parallels between modern physics and several Asian religions, including Buddhism.

Csikszentmihalyi, Mark, ed. and trans. *Readings in Han Chinese Thought*. Indianapolis, Ind.: Hackett, 2006. Includes sections on the natural world and on medicine.

Dalai Lama. *The Universe in a Single Atom: The Convergence of Science and Spirituality*. New York: Morgan Road Books, 2005. The most sustained discussion of science by the leading Buddhist figure of the early twenty-first century, the fourteenth Dalai Lama of Tibet.

Dash, Bhagwan. *Fundamentals of Ayurvedic Medicine*. 7th ed. Delhi: Konark, 1999. A practitioner of Ayurvedic medicine describes its foundational ideas and practices.

Dikshit, S. B. *Bharatiya Jyotish Sastra*. Translated into English by R. V. Vaidya as *History of Indian Astronomy*. 2 vols. New Delhi: Publications Division, Government of India, 1969, 1981. A detailed history of Indian astronomy based on Sanskrit sources, which sheds light on the main characteristics of Hindu astronomy and astronomers.

Eitel, Ernest J. *Buddhism: Its Historical, Theoretical and Popular Aspects in Three Lectures.* 2nd ed. London: Trubner, 1873. Lectures delivered in Hong Kong by a distinguished British missionary and scholar, one of the first works to identify points of similarity between Buddhism and science.

Elman, Benjamin A. *On Their Own: Science in China, 1550–1900.* Cambridge, Mass.: Harvard University Press, 2005. The most detailed look at the social and historical context of the pivotal exchanges and scientific developments of the late imperial period.

Gosling, David L. *Science and Religion in India.* Madras: Christian Literature Society, 1976. A dated but still useful brief introduction.

Gyatso, Janet. "The Authority of Empiricism and the Empiricism of Authority: Tibetan Medicine and Religion on the Eve of Modernity." *Comparative Studies of South Asia, Africa, and the Middle East* 24 (2004): 83–96. An early study related to a book in progress on the intellectual history of Tibetan medicine and its interaction with Buddhism.

Ho Peng Yoke. *Li, Qi and Shu: An Introduction to Science and Civilization in China.* Hong Kong: Hong Kong University Press, 1985. Early Chinese mathematics, astronomy, and alchemy.

Kirthisinghe, Buddhadasa P., ed. *Buddhism and Science.* Delhi: Motilal Banarsidass, 1984. A collection of essays by a variety of authors, most connected with the Theravada Buddhist tradition of Sri Lanka and Southeast Asia, arguing for the compatibility of Buddhism and science.

Keightley, David N. *The Ancestral Landscape: Time, Space, and Community in Late Shang China (ca. 1200–1045 B.C.)* China Research Monograph 53. Berkeley: Institute of East Asian Studies, University of California at Berkeley, 2000. A survey of early Chinese society based on the earliest available records, those of the so-called "oracle bones."

Kumar, Deepak. *Science and the Raj.* 2nd ed. New Delhi: Oxford University Press, 2006). The best introduction to the history of science in British India, with occasional references to religion.

Lloyd, Geoffrey, and Nathan Sivin. *The Way and the Word: Science and Medicine in Early China and Greece.* New Haven, Conn.: Yale University Press, 2002. Offers a framework for a new history of science that pays attention to the social factors that defined the particular way that early Chinese society produced knowledge of the natural world between 400 BCE and 200 CE.

Lopez, Donald S. Jr. *Buddhism and Science: A Guide for the Perplexed.* Chicago: University of Chicago Press, 2008. A history and analysis of claims made over the past one hundred and fifty years for the compatibility of Buddhism and science.

Nakayama, Shigeru. *Academic and Scientific Traditions in China, Japan, and the West* (Cambridge, Mass.: MIT Press, 1984. Explores the social context of the production of scientific knowledge in China, emphasizing the role of the recorders of astronomical regularities and anomalies in maintaining bureaucratic dominance.

Nanda, Meera. *Prophets Facing Backward: Postmodern Critiques of Science and Hindu Nationalism in India.* New Brunswick, N.J.: Rutgers University Press, 2003. A critical discussion of Vedic science.

Needham, Joseph. *Science and Civilization in China.* Cambridge: Cambridge University Press, 1954–. A monumental project of which twenty-seven volumes have appeared to date.

Prakash, Gyan. *Another Reason: Science and the Imagination of Modern India.* Princeton, N.J.: Princeton University Press, 1999. Includes insightful discussions of Hindu science.

Raina, Dhruv, and S. Irfan Habib. *Domesticating Modern Science: A Social History of Science and Culture in Colonial India.* New Delhi: Tulika Books, 2004. Discusses the "tightrope" Indian intellectuals walked in reconciling science and religion.

Robinet, Isabelle. *Taoist Meditation: The Mao-shan Tradition of Great Purity.* Albany: State University of New York Press, 1993. On Shangquing Daoism.

Rochberg, Francesca. *The Heavenly Writing: Divination, Horoscopy, and Astronomy in Mesopotamian Culture.* Cambridge: Cambridge University Press, 2004. Religion and the "celestial sciences" in ancient Babylonia.

Sharma, Chandradhara. *A Critical Survey of Indian Philosophy.* Benaras: Nand Kishore and Bros, 1952. A comprehensive introduction to Indian philosophical systems.

Sivin, Nathan. *Medicine, Philosophy, and Religion in Ancient China: Researches and Reflections.* Aldershot, U.K.: Ashgate, 1995. Especially valuable for its understanding of science, medicine, and the Taoist religion.

Subbarayappa, B. V., ed. *Science in India: Past and Present.* Mumbai: Nehru Centre, 2006. Essays on astronomy, mathematics, medicine, and metallurgy in ancient India and on modern science since Independence.

Wallace, B. Alan, ed. *Buddhism and Science: Breaking New Ground.* New York: Columbia University Press, 2003. A collection of essays on connections between Buddhism and the cognitive and physical sciences.

Watanabe, Masao. *The Japanese and Western Science.* Translated by Otto Theodor Benfey. Philadelphia: University of Pennsylvania Press, 1976. Includes discussions of Buddhism and science and of responses to Darwinism.

Yang, C. K. *Religion in Chinese Society: A Study of Contemporary Social Functions of Religion and Some of Their Historical Factors.* Berkeley: University of California Press, 1961. A classic examination of the sociology of Chinese religions from a Durkheimian viewpoint.

Young, R. F., and G. P. V. Somaratna. *Vain Debates: The Buddhist-Christian Controversies of Nineteenth-Century Ceylon.* Vienna: Publications of the de Nobili Research Library, 1996. A history of the debates between Christian missionaries and Buddhist monks in Sri Lanka, several of which touched on the question of Buddhism and science.

Zysk, Kenneth G. *Asceticism and Healing in Ancient India: Medicine in the Buddhist Monastery.* New York: Oxford University Press, 1991. Highlights the contributions of Buddhist monks to medical care.

———. *Religious Healing in the Veda: With Translations and Annotations of Medical Hymns from the Rgveda and the Atharvaveda and Renderings from the Corresponding Ritual Texts.* Philadelphia: American Philosophical Society, 1985. A valuable collection of documents.

AFRICAN RELIGIONS

Dopamu, P. Ade, ed. *African Culture, Modern Science, and Religious Thought*. Ilorin, Nigeria: African Centre for Religions and the Sciences, 2003. A pioneering anthology.

Fairhead, James, and Melissa Leach. *Misreading the African Landscape: Society and Ecology in a Forest-Savanna Mosaic*. Cambridge: Cambridge University Press, 1996. Two cultural anthropologists explore views of the African landscape, including the role of land spirits (*gina*).

Feierman, Steven, and John M. Janzen, eds. *The Social Basis of Health and Healing in Africa*. Berkeley: University of California Press, 1992. A collection of essays that focuses on African population trends and the historical transformations of therapeutic traditions; it includes Terence O. Ranger, "Godly Medicine: The Ambiguities of Medical Missions in Southeastern Tanzania, 1900–1945."

Ford, John. *The Role of Trypanosomiases in African Ecology: A Study of the Tsetse Fly Problem*. Oxford: Clarendon Press, 1971. A critical study of Western efforts to control trypanosomiasis.

Gyekye, Kwame. "Philosophy, Culture, and Technology in the Postcolonial." In *Postcolonial African Philosophy: A Critical Review*, edited by Emmanuel Chukwudi Eze, 25–44. Oxford: Blackwell, 1997. A prominent West African philosopher identifies the roots and continuing branches of distinctive African technical, philosophical, and cultural practices that could form the basis of an authentic modern science and philosophy.

Horton, Robin. *Patterns of Thought in Africa and the West: Essays on Magic, Religion and Science*. Cambridge: Cambridge University Press, 1993. An influential collection of essays, including "African Traditional Thought and Western Science."

Hunt, Nancy. *A Colonial Lexicon: Of Birth Ritual, Medicalization, and Mobility in the Congo*. Durham, N.C.: Duke University Press, 1999. A rich account of the medicalization of childbirth in the former Belgian Congo.

Janzen, John. *Ngoma: Discourses of Healing in Central and Southern Africa*. Berkeley: University of California Press, 1992. A study of Ngoma in the Western Congo, the Swahili coast, Swaziland, and the Western Cape.

———. *Quest for Therapy in Lower Zaire*. Berkeley: University of California Press, 1978. The first close-up ethnographic study of interaction of African healing and biomedicine.

Mudimbe, V. Y. *The Invention of Africa: Gnosis, Philosophy, and the Order of Knowledge*. Bloomington: Indiana University Press, 1988. A major study by a leading African philosopher of the history of Western political and academic constructions of African society, thought, and cultures, and the internalization of such constructs by African academics, practitioners, theologians, and writers.

Rwangabo, Pierre-Claver. *La médecine traditionnelle au Rwanda*. Paris: Karthala, 1993. Although not available in English, this volume by a Rwandan anthropologist and pharmacist is one of the best formulations of African medicine and how it integrates material, social, and metaphysical realms in the diagnosis of disease and the articulation of treatments.

Schmidt, Peter. *Iron Technology in East Africa: Symbolism, Science, and Archaeology*. Bloomington: Indiana University Press, 1997. Includes discussions of spirit huts and spirit mediums.

Tilley, Helen. *Africa as a Living Laboratory: Empire, Development, and the Problem of Scientific Knowledge*. Chicago: University of Chicago Press, 2011. Examines the mutual influence of science and imperialism in British Africa between 1890 and 1960.

Van Dijk, Rijk, Ria Reis, and Marja Spierenburg, eds. *The Quest for Fruition through Ngoma: Political Aspects of Healing in Southern Africa*. Oxford: James Currey, 2000. Dutch anthropologists compare their own research on the political dimension of *ngoma* ritual knowledge and performance in Southern and Eastern Africa with Janzen's *Ngoma*.

UNBELIEF

Andrews, James T. *Science for the Masses: The Bolshevik State, Public Science, and the Popular Imagination in Soviet Russia, 1917–1934*. College Station: Texas A&M University Press, 2003. On the use of popular science by Soviet authorities to undermine religion.

Berman, David. *A History of Atheism in Britain: From Hobbes to Russell*. London: Croom Helm, 1988. A study of the history of atheism that tries to account for the late emergence of atheism at the end of the eighteenth century.

Buckley, Michael J. *At the Origins of Modern Atheism*. New Haven, Conn.: Yale University Press, 1987. Argues that modern atheism emerged in the eighteenth century in the ideas of Diderot and d'Holbach as they contested overstated arguments from nature to God.

Budd, Susan. *Varieties of Unbelief: Atheists and Agnostics in English Society 1850–1960*. New York: Holmes and Meier, 1977. An intellectual study of secularism and rationalism that emphasizes the moral dimension of the loss of faith and plays down the role of science.

Israel, Jonathan. *Enlightenment Contested: Philosophy, Modernity, and the Emancipation of Man, 1670–1752*. Oxford: Oxford University Press, 2006. A sequel to *Radical Enlightenment* that highlights the struggle between radical and moderate schools of thought.

———. *Radical Enlightenment: Philosophy and the Making of Modernity, 1650–1750*. Oxford: Oxford University Press, 2001. A massive study of the Enlightenment that emphasizes the centrality of radical thought.

Jacob, Margaret. *The Radical Enlightenment: Pantheists, Freemasons and Republicans*. London: George Allen and Unwin, 1982. A still useful study of the political, social, and religious beliefs of radical Enlightenment figures.

Jacoby, Susan. *Freethinkers: A History of American Secularism*. New York: Henry Holt and Company, 2004. Argues that the period between 1875 and 1914 was the high-water mark of freethought as an influential movement in the United States.

Lightman, Bernard. *The Origins of Agnosticism: Victorian Unbelief and The Limits of Knowledge*. Baltimore: Johns Hopkins University Press, 1987. Deals with the first generation of agnostics, including Huxley, Tyndall, Clifford, Spencer, and Leslie Stephen.

Numbers, Ronald L. "Science without God: Natural laws and Christian Beliefs." In *When Science and Christianity Meet*. Edited by David C. Lindberg and Ronald L. Numbers. Chicago: University of Chicago Press, 2003, 265–85. Surveys the rise of methodological naturalism.

Rattansi, P. M. "Voltaire and the Enlightenment Image of Newton." In *History and Imagination: Essays in Honour of H. R. Trevor-Roper*. Edited by Hugh Lloyd-Jones, Valerie Pearl, and Blair Worden. London: Gerald Duckworth, 1981, 218–31. Discussion of how Voltaire dethroned Descartes and installed Newton as a pioneer of the Enlightenment.

Roberts, Jon H., and James Turner. *The Sacred and the Secular University*. Princeton, N.J.: Princeton University Press, 2000. Shows how American institutions of higher education became secularized between 1870 and 1920.

Taylor, Charles. *A Secular Age*. Cambridge, Mass.: Harvard University Press, 2007. A magisterial analysis of the cultural forces that have given rise to modern secular humanism. The primacy of science in the process is heavily qualified.

Turner, Frank Miller. *Between Science and Religion: The Reaction to Scientific Naturalism in Late Victorian England*. New Haven, Conn.: Yale University Press, 1974. Includes a chapter on the principal ideas and proponents of scientific naturalism.

———. *Contesting Cultural Authority: Essays in Victorian Intellectual Life*. Cambridge: Cambridge University Press, 1993. A series of important essays on the fight between scientific naturalists and the Anglican clergy for cultural authority.

Turner, James. *Without God, Without Creed: The Origins of Unbelief in America*. Baltimore: Johns Hopkins University Press, 1985. Argues that religion, not science, caused unbelief.

Index

Abdülmennan, Osman b., 155
African cultures, 5–6, 279–80, 286; healing as example of knowledge produced in, 229–30; and "middle figures" between traditional and Western ways, 240; post-colonial syntheses of local and Western knowledge in, 244–48; pre- and post-colonial, 231–32, 240; resistance to Western conquest by, 243. *See also* Bantu knowledge systems
Agassiz, Louis, 109, 110
agnosticism. *See* unbelief
Albertus Magnus, 74, 77
d'Alembert, Jean, 258
Ali, Hüseyinzade, 164
el-Âmidî, Ibrahim ibn Abdurrahman el-Karamanî, 157
Aquinas, Thomas, 12, 74–75, 77
Arabic: as language of learning, 27–28, 29, 73, 287; translation and criticism in, 120–21
Aristotle, 32, 33; role in Christian theology, 78, 81; works of, 73–74
Āryabhaṭa, 197
Ashkenaz i culture, 32; early-modern migrations and, 35–36; in modern period, 44
Association of Orthodox Jewish Scientists, 61–62
Ataullah Efendi, Şanizade, 161
atheism. *See* unbelief

atomism, 78, 79, 83
Augustine, Saint, 2, 12, 69, 70, 84, 113
Averroës [Ibn Rushd], 33
Avicenna [Ibn Sina], 33. *See also* Ibn Sina

Babylon, as center of Jewish learning, 27
Bacon, Francis, 13, 84, 85, 95, 259
Bacon, Roger, 77
el-Bağdadî, Nazmizâde Huseyin Murtaza b. Ali, 157
Baghdad, as center of Jewish learning, 27
Bamberger, Louis, 57
Bantu knowledge systems: for healing, 235–40; interaction between science and religion in, 229, 231, 234–35; for iron smelting, 232–33; for land use, 233; post-colonial syntheses of local and Western knowledge in, 244–48; and Western ideas brought by missionaries, 240–42; and Western portrayals of "witchcraft," 243–44
Bar Hiyya, Abraham, 29
Barth, Karl, 111
Behcet Efendi, Hekimbaşı Mustafa, 161
Bell, Johann von, 7
Benedict XIV, Pope, 99
Bentley, Richard, 100, 255